Christin Landgraf, Heiko Pleines (eds.)

Interest Representation and Europeanization of Trade Unions from EU Member States of the Eastern Enlargement

CHANGING EUROPE

Edited by Dr. Sabine Fischer, Dr. Heiko Pleines and
Prof. Dr. Hans-Henning Schröder

ISSN 1863-8716

4 *Sabine Fischer, Heiko Pleines (eds.)*
Crises and Conflicts in Post-Socialist Societies
The Role of Ethnic, Political and Social Identities
ISBN 978-3-89821-855-9

5 *Julia Kusznir, Heiko Pleines (eds.)*
Trade Unions from Post-Socialist Member States in EU Governance
ISBN 978-3-89821-857-3

6 *Sabine Fischer, Heiko Pleines (eds.)*
The EU and Central & Eastern Europe
Successes and Failures of Europeanization in Politics and Society
ISBN 978-3-89821-948-8

7 *Sabine Fischer, Heiko Pleines (eds.)*
Civil Society in Central and Eastern Europe
ISBN 978-3-8382-0041-5

8 *Zdenka Mansfeldová, Heiko Pleines (eds.)*
Informal Relations from Democratic Representation to Corruption
Case Studies from Central and Eastern Europe
ISBN 978-3-8382-0173-3

9 *Leonid Kosals, Heiko Pleines (eds.)*
Governance Failure and Reform Attempts after the
Global Economic Crisis of 2008/09
Case Studies from Central and Eastern Europe
ISBN 978-3-8382-0336-2

10 *Andreas Heinrich, Heiko Pleines (eds.)*
Export Pipelines from the CIS Region
Geopolitics, Securitization, and Political Decision-Making
ISBN 978-3-8382-0539-7

11 *Christin Landgraf, Heiko Pleines (eds.)*
Interest Representation and Europeanization of Trade Unions
from EU Member States of the Eastern Enlargement
ISBN 978-3-8382-0744-5

Christin Landgraf, Heiko Pleines (eds.)

INTEREST REPRESENTATION AND EUROPEANIZATION OF TRADE UNIONS FROM EU MEMBER STATES OF THE EASTERN ENLARGEMENT

ibidem-Verlag
Stuttgart

Die Deutsche Nationalbibliothek lists this publication in the Deutsche Nationalbibliografie; detailed bibliographic data are available in the Internet at http://dnb.d-nb.de.

Bibliografische Information der Deutschen Nationalbibliothek
Die Deutsche Nationalbibliothek verzeichnet diese Publikation in der Deutschen Nationalbibliografie; detaillierte bibliografische Daten sind im Internet über http://dnb.d-nb.de abrufbar.

ISSN: 1863-8716

ISBN-13: 978-3-8382-0744-5

Printed in the United States of America

Contents

List of Figures

List of Tables

List of Abbreviations and Acronyms

ABIEC	Asociația Marilor Consumatori Industriali de Energie [Association of Large Industrial Energy Consumers]
AIAS	Amsterdam Institute for Advanced Labour Studies
ASO ČR	Asociace Samotatných Odborů České Republiky [Association of Independent Trade Unions of the Czech Republic]
ASZSZ	Autonóm Szakszervezetek Szövetsége [Autonomous Trade Union Confederation]
ATLAS Uniunea	Uniunea Federativa Sindicala 'ATLAS' [Trade Union Federation 'ATLAS']
AUTOglobal	Europäische Automobilkonferenz [European Automotive Conference]
AWS	Akcja Wyborcza Solidarność [Electoral Action Solidarity]
BBDSZ	Bankok, Biztositok Dolgozoi Szakszervezeteinek [Finance Sector Union]
BBDSZ SZ	Bankok, Biztositok Dolgozoi Szakszervezeteinek Szovetsege [Federation of Unions of the Finance Sector]
BCR	Banca Comercială Română [Romanian Commercial Bank]
BDSZ	Bánya-, Energia- és Ipari Dolgozók Szakszervezete [Mining and Energy Workers' Union]
BG	Belgium
BMASK	Bundesministerium für Arbeit, Soziales und Konsumentenschutz [Federal Ministry of Labour, Social Affairs and Consumer Protection]
BNS	Blocul National Sindical [National Trade Union Bloc]
BoBa	Bohemia-Bavaria
BPS	Balgarski Profesionalni Sauzi [Bulgarian Trade Unions]
CC	Coordination Council
CCMB	Christelijke Centrale der Metaalbewerkers van België [Belgian Christian Union of Metal Industry Workers]

CCMI	Consultative Commission on Industrial Change
CEC Bank	Casa de Economii şi Consemnaţiuni [Savings and Consignments Bank]
CEE	Central Eastern Europe
CFDT	Confédération française démocratique du travail [French Democratic Confederation of Labour]
CI	Communications International
CIS	Commonwealth of Independent States
CISL	Confederazione Italiana Sindacati Lavoratori [Confederation of Trade Unions in Italy]
CITUB	Confederation of Independent Trade Unions of Bulgaria, see also KNSB
CL Podkrepa	Confederation of Labour Podkrepa
CLCA	company-level collective agreements
CMB	Centrale der Metaalbewerkers van België [Federation of the Belgian Metal Workers]
CMB	Centrale der Metaalindustrie van België [Federation of the Belgian metal industry]
ČMKOS	Českomoravská konfederace odborových svazů [Czech-Moravian Confederation of Trade Unions]
CNSLR Frăţia	Confederaţia Naţională a Sindicatelor Libere din Romania – Frăţia [National Confederation of Free Trade Unions of Romania—Brotherhood]
CO_2	carbon dioxide
Conftex	Federaţia Sindicatelor Textile-Confecţii [Federation of Textiles and Clothing]
CONPIROM	Confederaţia Patronală din Industrie, Agricultură, Construcţii şi Servicii din România [Employers' Confederation of Industry, Agriculture, Construction and Services in Romania]
CS KOVO	Československý Svaz KOVO [Czech Metalworkers´ Federation]
CSDR	Confederaţia Sindicatelor Democratice din România [Democratic Trade Union Confederation of Romania]
CSN	Confederatia Sindicala Nationala [National Trade Union Confederation]
CVT	continuous vocational training
CY	Cyprus

CZ	Czech Republic
DGB	Deutscher Gewerkschaftsbund [German Confederation of Trade Unions]
EBRD	European Bank for Reconstruction and Development
EC	European Commission
EC	European Community
EC	Executive Committee
ECHOZ	Energeticko-Chemický odborový zväz [Energy-Chemical Trade Union]
ECO	Economic and Monetary Union and Economic and Social Cohesion
ECOSOC	Economic and Social Council
ECSC	European Coal and Steel Community
EE	Estonia
EEC	European Economic Community
EESC	European Economic and Social Committee
EFBWW	European Federation of Building and Woodworkers
EFCGWU	European Federation of Chemical and General Workers Unions
EFEDOSZSZ	Építő-, Fa- és Építőanyagipari Dolgozók Szakszervezeteinek Szövetsége [Trade Union of Building Materials workers]
EFFAT	European Federation of Food, Agriculture and Tourism Trade Unions
EFRR	Evropský fond pro regionální rozvoj [European Regional Development Fund]
EFTA-TUC	Trade Union Committee for the European Free Trade Area
EIRO	European Industrial Relations Observatory
EIT	European Integration Team
EMCEF	European Mine, Chemical and Energy Workers' Federation
EMF	European Metalworkers' Federation
ÉŐDSZ	Értékszállítási és Őrzésvédelmi Dolgozók Szakszervezete [Trade Union of Value Transportation and Security Workers]
EP	European Parliament
EPSU	European Federation of Public Service Unions
ESFTU	European Confederation of Free Trade Unions
ÉSZT	Értelmiségi Szakszervezeti Tömörülés [Confederation of Unions of Professionals]
ETF	European Transport Workers' Federation
ETS	Emission Trading System

ETUC	European Trade Union Confederation
ETUC	European Trade Union Congress
ETUC-TCL	European Trade Union Federation-Textiles Clothing and Leather
ETUF	European Trade Union Federations
ETUI	European Trade Union Institute
ETUS	European Trade Union Secretariat
EU	European Union
EUCOB@N	European Collective Bargaining Network
Eurofound	European Foundation for the Improvement of Living and Working Conditions
EVDSZ	Egyesült Villamosenergia-ipari Dolgozók Szakszervezeti Szövetsége [The Trade Union of United Electricity Workers]
EVS	European Value Survey
EWC	European Works Council
FDI	foreign direct investment
Federatia Sindicatelor UNICONF	Federaţia Sindicatelor din Confecţii şi Tricotaje Bucureşti 'Uniconf' [Federation of Trade Unions of Garments and Knitwear Bucharest 'Uniconf']
FES	Friedrich-Ebert-Stiftung [Friedrich Ebert Foundation]
FFSZ	Filmművészek és Filmalkalmazottak Szakszervezete Syndicat [Movie and Film Artists' Union of Employees Syndicate]
FGTB	Fédération Générale du Travail de Belgique [General Federation of Labour of Belgium]
FIET	La Fédération internationale des employés, techniciens et cadres [International Federation of Employees, technicians and managers]
FNME	Federatia Nationala Mine Energie [National Federation of Mining and Energy]
FNS Solidaritatea Metal / FNS SMETAL	Federaţia Naţională Sindicală Solidaritatea Metal [National Federation of Trade Unions Solidarity Metal]
FNSM	Federatsiyata na nezavisimite sindikati na minyorite [Federation of the Independent Syndicates of Miners]
FSAB	Federatia Sindicatelor din Asigurari si Banci [Trade Union Federation of Insurance and Banks]

FSC	Federatia Sindicatelor din Comert [Trade Union Federation of Commerce]
FSCOM	Federatia Sindicatelor din Comunicatii [Trade Union Federation of Communication]
FSN	Frontul Salvarii Nationale [National Salvation Front]
FSPCOM	Federatia Sindicatelor din Posta si Comunicatii [Trade Union Federation of Mail and Communication]
FSRT	Federatia Sindicatelor din Romtelecom [Trade Union Federation of Romanian Telecommunication]
FSS METAROM	Federaţia Sindicală a Siderurgiştilor METAROM [Trade Union Federation of Siderurgiştilor METAROM]
FTT	Financial Transaction Tax
FZZ	Forum Związków Zawodowych [Trade Unions Forum]
FZZ PKIS	Federacja Związków Zawodowych Pracowników Kultury i Sztuki [Federation of Trade Unions of Culture and Arts Workers]
FZZ Przemysłu Chemicznego	Federacja Związków Zawodowych Przemysłu Chemicznego [Federation of the Chemical Trade Unions]
FZZP	Federacja Związków Zawodowych Pracowników [Trade Union Federation of Chemical, Glass and Ceramic Industries]
GDP	gross domestic product
GESIS	Gesellschaft Sozialwissenschaftlicher Infrastruktureinrichtungen [Association of Social Science Infrastructure Facilities, today Leibniz Institute for Social Science]
GMBE	Gewerkschaft Metall-Bergbau-Energie [Trade Union of Metal, Mining and Energy]
GUF	Global Union Federation
HGWU	Hungarian Graphical Workers' Trade Union
HLCA	Higher Level Collective Agreements
HOPWTU	Hungarian Oil- and Gas Workers Trade Union
HU	Hungary
ICFTU	International Confederation of Free Trade Unions
ICT	Information and Communication Technology
ICTWSS	Database on Institutional Characteristics of Trade Unions, Wage Setting, State Intervention and Social Pacts
IG BCE	Industriegewerkschaft Bergbau, Chemie, Energie [Industrial Mining, Chemistry and Energy Union]

IG F	International Graphical Federation
IG Metall / IGM	Industriegewerkschaft Metall [Industrial Union of Metalworkers]
IMF	International Metalworkers' Federation
IMF	International Monetary Fund
INT	Section for the Single Market, Production and Consumption (EESC Section)
IOZ	Integrovaný odborový zväz [Integrated Union]
IR	industrial relations
IRTUC / IRTUCs	Interregional Trade Union Council(s)
ISTC	Iron and Steel Trades Confederation
ISTUR	Institute for Social and Trade Union Research
ITUC	International Trade Union Confederation
ITU-CZ	Independent Trade Union of Czech Television
KASZ	Kereskedelmi Alkalmazottak Szakszerveze [Trade Union of Commercial Employees]
KDOS	Koalice dopravních odborových svazů [Coalition of Transport Trade Unions]
KNDP	Kereszténydemokrata Néppárt [Christian Democratic People´s Party]
KNSB	Konfederatsiyata na nezavisimite sindikati v Balgariya [Confederation of Independent Trade Unions of Bulgaria], see also CITUB
KOK	Křesťanská odborová koalice [Christian Trade Union Coalition]
KOZ SR	Konfederácia odborových zväzov Slovenskej republiky [Confederation of the Trade Unions of the Slovak Republic]
KRZ ZPPP	Zwiazek Zawodow y Pracowników Przemyslu Poligraficznego [Trade Union of Graphical Workers]
KS OS KOVO	krajská sdružení odborový svaz KOVO [Regional Association of Czech Metalworkers´ Federation]
KUK	Konfederace Umění a Kultury [Confederation of Arts and Culture]
LIGA	Független Szakszervezetek Demokratikus Ligája [Democratic League of Independent Trade Unions]
LT	Lithuania
LV	Latvia
MEBO	management and employee buy-out

MEF	Mineworkers European Federation
MEGAk	Mitteleuropäische Gewerkschaftsakademie [Central European Trade Union Academy]
MEI	Media and Entertainment International
METACHIM	Federaţia patronală a producătorilor din chimie [Federation of Manufacturers of Chemistry]
METALURGIA	Federaţia patronală a ramurii metalurgie feroasă şi neferoasă şi produse refractare [Federation of Ferrous and Non-Ferrous Metallurgy Industry and Refractories]
MNC	multinational companies
MOL Bányász Szakszervezet	Magyar Olaj- és Gázipari Bányász Szakszervezet [Trade Union of Hungarian Oil and Gas Production Workers]
MOSZ	Mozdonyvezetők Szakszervezete [Locomotive Drivers' Union]
MP	Member of Parliament
MSZOSZ	Magyar Szakszervezetek Országos Szövetsége [National Confederation of Hungarian Trade Unions]
MSZSZ	Magyar Szakszervezetek Szövetsége [Hungarian Confederation of Trade Unions]
MT	Malta
Munkástanácsok / MOSZ	Munkástanácsok Országos Szövetsége [National Federation of Workers' Councils]
NACE	Nomenclature statistique des activités économiques dans la Communauté européenne [Statistical Classification of Economic Activities in the European Community]
NAT	Agriculture, Rural Development and Environment (EESC Section)
NEPSI	Noyau Européen pour la Silice [European Network for Silica]
NETLEX	ETUC network of trade union legal experts
NFTINI	Natsionalna federatsiya 'tekhnicheska industriya, nauka, informatika' [National Federation 'Technical Industry, Science, Informatics']
NGTT	Nemzeti Gazdasági és Társadalmi Tanács [National Economic and Social Council]
NMS	new member states
NRZP ČR	Národní rada osob se zdravotním postižením České Republiky [Czech National Disability Council]

NSZZ Solidarność	Niezależny Samorządny Związek Zawodowy Solidarność [Independent Self-Governing Trade Union Solidarity]
OECD	Organisation for Economic Co-operation and Development
OEGB / OGB / ÖGB	Österreichischer Gewerkschaftsbund [Austrian Trade Union Federation]
OÉT	Országos Érdekegyeztető Tanács [National Interest Reconciliation Council]
OMC	Open Method of Coordination
OPZZ	Ogólnopolskie Porozumienie Związków Zawodowych [All-Poland Alliance of Trade Unions]
OS ČMS	Odborové sdružení Čech, Moravy a Slezska [Trade Union Association of Bohemia, Moravia and Silesia]
OS ECHO	Odborový svaz Energeticko-chemického, see also ECHOZ [Energy-Chemical Trade Union]
OS KOVO	Odborový svaz KOVO [Czech Metalworkers´ Federation]
OS MEDIA	Celostátni odborovy svaz hromadnych sdelovacich prostredku [National Union of Mass Media]
OS PPP	Odborový svaz pracovníků peněžnictví a pojišťovnictví [Trade Union of Banking and Insurance Employees]
OS SKP	Odborový svaz skla, keramiky a porcelánu [Trade Union of Glass, Ceramics and Porcelain Workers]
OS TOK	Odborový Svaz Prakovníků Textilního, Odévního a Kožedělného Průmyslu Čech a Moravy [Trade Union of Textile, Clothing and Leather Industries of Bohemia and Moravia]
OS ZPTNS	Odborový svaz zaměstnanců poštovních, telekomunikačních a novinových služeb [Trade Union of Workers in Postal, Telecommunication and Newspaper Services]
OSPO	Odborovy svaz pracovniku obchodu [Trade Union of Trade Workers]
OZ KOVO	Odborový zväz kováckých odborech
OZ PAL	Odborového zväzu pôšt a logistiky [Trade Union of Mail and Logistics Services]
OZ POCR	Odborový zväz pracovníkov obchodu a cestovného ruchu [Trade Union of Commerce and Tourism]
OZ PPA P	Odborového zväzu Pracovníkov Peňažníctva a Poisťovníctva [Trade Union of Finance and Insurance]

OZT	Odborového zväzu Telekom [Trade Union of Telecommunication Employees]
OZZGNIG	Ogólnopolski Związek Zawodowy Górnictwa Naftowego i Gazownictwa [Trade Union Federation of Polish Oil and Gas Companies]
PATROMAT	Federația patronală din industria materialelor de construcții din România [Employers' Federation of Construction Materials Industry]
PERC	Pan-European Regional Council
PiS	Prawo i Sprawiedliwość [Law and Justice]
PL	Poland
ProAlt	Iniciativa pro kritiku reforem a na podporu alternative [Initiatives for Critique of Reform Measures and Supporting Alternatives]
PRO-GE	Produktionsgewerkschaft [Trade Union for Production Workers]
PROTECTOR	Federatia 'PROTECTOR' a sindicatelor din industria de Securitate [Trade Union Federation 'Protector' for the Security Industry]
PSZ	Postás Szakszervezet [Hungarian Postal Trade Union]
PZZ KADRA	Porozumienie Zwiazków Zawodowych KADRA [Trade Union Agreement 'KADRA']
REX	External Relations Section (EESC Section)
RHSD	Rada pro hospodářské a sociální dohody [Council for Economic and Social Accord]
RO	Romania
ROH	Revoluční odborové hnutí [Revolutionary Trade Union Movement]
RS ČR	Rada seniorů České Republiky [Czech Senior Council]
SGiE	Sekretariat Górnictwa i Energetyki [Mining and Energy Secretariat / National Secretariat of Mine and Energy Workers Union]
SI	Slovenia
SK	Slovakia
SKEI	Sindikata kovinske in elektro industrije Slovenije [Trade Union of Metal and Electro Industry of Slovenia]

SKF	Svenska Kullagerfabriken [Swedish Ball Bearing Factory]
SKGWB	Sekcji Krajowej Górnictwa Węgla Brunatnego [Section of the National Brown Coal Mining]
SKGWK	Sekcji Krajowej Górnictwa Węgla Kamiennego [Section of the National Hard Coal Mining]
SKK	slovenska koruna [Slovak Koruna]
SMEs	small and medium-sized enterprises
SOC	Employment, Social Affairs and Citizenship (EECS Section)
SOZ SP	Slovenský odborový zväz slobodných povolaní [Slovak Trade Union of Liberal Professions]
STICEF	Organizația patronală din industria sticlei și ceramicii fine [Employers' Organization of the Glass and Fine Ceramics Industry]
SZEF	Szakszervezetek Együttműködési Fóruma [The Forum for the Cooperation of Trade Unions]
SZOT	Szakszervezetek Országos Tanácsa [National Council of Trade Unions]
TB-CZ	Typografická Beseda [Czech Trade Union of Printing Producers]
TEN	Transport, Energy, Infrastructure and Information Society
TU	Trade Union
TUAC	Trade Union Advisory Committee to the Organisation for Economic Co-operation and Development
TUC	Trade Union Confederation
TUC	Trade Union Congress
TUF	Trade Union Federation
TUFIB	Trade Union Federation from Insurances and Banks
UGSR	Uniunea Generală a Sindicatelor din România [General Union of Trade Unions of Romania]
UK	United Kingdom
UNI	Union Network International
UNI Europa	Union Network International Europa
UNI Europa MEA	UNI Europa Media and Entertainment and Arts
UNI Global	Union Network International Global
V-4 / V4	Visegrad group: Poland, Slovakia, Czech Republic and Hungary are the Visegrad countries
V-5 / V5	Visegrad 4 plus Slovenia

VASAS	Vasas Szakszervezeti Szövetsé [Metalworkers Federation of Trade Unions]
VAT	value-added tax
VDSZ	Magyar vegyipari, energiaipari és rokon szakmákban dolgozók szakszervezeti szövetsége [Federation of Trade Unions of the Chemical, Energy and Allied Workers]
Ver.di	Vereinte Dienstleistungsgewerkschaft [United Services Union]
VKF	Versenyszféra és a Kormány Állandó Konzultációs Fóruma [Consultative Forum of the Industry and the Government]
VSZSZ	Vagyonvédelmi Szakszervezetek Szövetségének [Trade Union of the Private Security Worker]
VW	Volkswagen
WCL	World Confederation of Labour
WWF	World Wide Fund For Nature
WWF EPO	World Wide Fund For Nature European Policy Office
ZO OS KOVO	základní organizace odborový svaz KOVO [Basic Organisations of Czech Metalworkers´ Federation]
ZOJES	Združenie odborárov jadrovej energetiky Slovenska [Trade Union of Nuclear Power Workers of the Slovak Republic]
ZUWINS	Zukunftsraum Wien-Niederösterreich-Südmähren [European Territorial Co-operation Austria–Czech Republic, Future Region Vienna–Lower Austria–South Moravia]
ZZG w Polsce	Związku Zawodowego Górników w Polsce [Mine Workers Union in Poland]

Preface

This book presents the results of a research project conducted from 2012 to 2014 that examined the integration of trade unions from European Union (EU) member states of the Eastern Enlargement into EU governance as a follow-up to a similar study conducted in 2007. The project examines a total of 50 trade unions from the six largest states that joined in 2004 / 07, namely Bulgaria, the Czech Republic, Hungary, Poland, Romania and Slovakia.

Analysing integration at the EU level, in interregional cooperation and in EU Works Councils, the main objective was to assess to what extent trade unions from the member states of the Eastern Enlargement have been integrated into EU governance structures and how related cooperation is assessed. Based on this assessment, the research project also analysed which strategies the trade unions follow in their EU-related activities and how they developed and discussed these strategies internally.

The research project has been coordinated by the Research Centre for East European Studies at the University of Bremen, Germany, and it has been financially supported by the Hans Böckler Foundation. The project team included Monika Čambáliková (Institute of Sociology, Slovak Academy of Sciences), Klaus Henning (Research Centre for East European Studies at the University of Bremen, now University of Potsdam), Vassil Kirov (Institute for the Study of Societies and Knowledge, Bulgarian Academy of Sciences), Christin Landgraf (Research Centre for East European Studies at the University of Bremen, now Zeppelin University, Friedrichshafen), Aleksandra Lis (Adam Mickiewicz University in Poznań), Zdenka Mansfeldová (Institute of Sociology, Academy of Sciences of the Czech Republic), Heiko Pleines (Research Centre for East European Studies at the University of Bremen) and Leyla Safta-Zecheria (Central European University, Budapest).

We would like to thank our partners at the Hans Böckler Foundation, all members of the project's advisory board and the participants of the project conference conducted in Bremen in April 2014 for their support and helpful advice. Our thanks also go to all respondents who participated in the project survey.

Special thanks go to Anastasia Stoll and Matthias Neumann for the style editing and layout of the book manuscript.

Bremen, March 2015
The Project Team

Introduction

Although the traditional task of trade unions is the representation of workers *vis-à-vis* employers, trade unions regularly seek access to policymaking processes to represent workers' interests in the political arena. In European societies, trade unions are still important interest groups in political decision-making even though their influence is perceived to be in a long-term decline and there are huge differences between European states concerning the actual political role of trade unions.

From a historical perspective, trade unions were one of the first collective actors with a mass following to emerge in the wake of industrialisation, and they therefore received special attention from policymakers. As a result their prerogatives, together with those of employers' associations, were codified in most European countries through special legislation on wage bargaining and social dialogues. Through the European social dialogue they also have—at least de jure—a privileged position in EU-level policymaking.

As more and more policies are regulated in Brussels, trade unions also present their interests at the EU level. As interest groups with a massive membership base in all EU member states and with a privileged role in policymaking, they are an important and interesting case for interest group studies, all the more because they are integrated into EU governance at several levels ranging from the company level, with the European Works Council, to the EU level, with European umbrella trade union organisations in Brussels.

Nonetheless, research on interest groups in the EU addresses mostly business interests and a small group of value-based NGOs from the old EU member states. There are a very limited number of studies that focus on trade unions in EU governance. Moreover, interest group studies tend to select cases from the small group of big, old EU member states.

With the EU's Eastern Enlargement, however, ten post-socialist countries from Central Eastern Europe joined the EU in 2004 and 2007.[1] At that time, many analysts expected the huge expansion in the number of member states with the accompanying increase in the number of decision-makers and interest groups at the EU level to lead to blockades and a breakdown of decision-making processes. While, in retrospect the challenges for EU governance seem to have been exaggerated, the opposite perspective, focusing on the challenges that EU governance poses for the newcomers, has

1 In the first round of Eastern Enlargement the Czech Republic, Estonia, Hungary, Latvia, Lithuania, Poland, Slovakia and Slovenia joined in May 2004. In the second round Bulgaria and Romania joined in January 2007. Additionally, Croatia joined in July 2013.

hardly been taken in academic research. There are a very limited number of empirical studies that draw their attention to the integration of interest groups from the new EU member states into EU governance, and again, trade unions are not a major focus of research on interest groups.

The research project that has led to this book publication has aimed to fill this gap and to add fruitful empirical insights to the theoretical debate on European interest groups. In the following chapter, Christin Landgraf and Heiko Pleines will elaborate on the related state of research in more detail. Then, Heiko Pleines will present the research design of the project, which forms the foundation for all empirical results presented in this book. After that, a chapter by Klaus Henning introduces the respective trade unions and provides basic facts about labour relations in the countries under study.

The presentations of empirical results are grouped into three parts. The first part gives an overview of the three major levels of EU governance in which trade unions are active. Klaus Henning describes the functioning of the trade unions' European umbrella associations, focusing on the integration of trade unions from the member states of Eastern Enlargement. Then, Christin Landgraf analyses the channels of influence used at the EU level by trade unions from EU member states of the Eastern Enlargement. The third chapter of this part, which has been written by Christin Landgraf and Zdenka Mansfeldová, goes on to look at interregional cooperation using the example of the Vienna Memorandum, which brings metal and machine-building trade unions from the Czech Republic, Hungary, Slovakia and Slovenia together with their peers from Austria and Germany. This part concludes with a look at the company level, which is provided by Karoline Mis, on the basis of an analysis of the role of Polish trade unions in European Works Councils.

The second part changes the perspective and gives an overview of the integration of trade unions from selected countries into the full system of EU governance. The respective chapters are to a large degree based on interviews with trade union representatives and are thus able to present not just integration measures taken but also an assessment of successes and failures by the respective trade union representatives. The chapters in this part cover Bulgaria, with Vassil Kirov as author, the Czech Republic (Zdenka Mansfeldová), and Hungary (Christin Landgraf).

Whereas the second part offers a collective profile of all major trade unions from the respective countries, the third part provides detailed case studies of selected trade unions. In the first chapter of this part, Vassil Kirov describes how the Confederation of Independent Trade Unions of Bulgaria (CITUB), the largest national trade union confederation in Bulgaria, integrates into the different levels of EU governance. Zdenka Mansfeldová then continues with a similar case study of the Czech Metalworkers' Federation Trade Union KOVO (OS KOVO). Looking at the Polish trade union Solidarność, Aleksandra Lis focuses in her chapter on the challenges and tensions that have resulted from integration into EU-wide umbrella organisations. In the same vein, Leyla Safta-Zecheria looks at Alfa Cartel, a major Romanian trade union confederation. Finally, Monika Čambáliková, in her case study of the Slovak Metalworkers' Federation OZ KOVO, includes an analysis of a company-level conflict with a foreign investor from another EU member state.

Analytical Framework

Christin Landgraf and Heiko Pleines

1. Research Questions and Research Context

1.1. Research Objectives

Due to the extended competences of the European Union (EU), trade unions are also present at the EU level in order to participate in decision-making processes. However, there are a very limited number of studies focusing on trade unions in EU governance structures. Relevant studies include Gollbach (2005), Hoffmann (2010), Kovacs (2008), Kusznir and Pleines (2008). Empirical studies that focus on the EU-level integration of interest groups from new EU member states and in EU governance structures are also rare (for notable exceptions, see Einbock/Lis 2007; Pleines 2010; Cianciara 2013), and trade unions are again not a major focus for research on interest groups.

Therefore, our research project aimed to fill this research gap by adding fruitful empirical insights to the theoretical debate on interest groups in EU governance and on the Europeanisation of interest groups. The project examined the integration of trade unions from Central and Southeast European member states, namely Bulgaria, the Czech Republic, Hungary, Poland, Romania, and Slovakia, into EU governance structures. The major objective was to assess how far trade unions from the new EU member states have been integrated at the EU level, in the European Works Councils (EWCs) and in interregional trade union councils. Furthermore, the research project analysed the strategies that trade unions use in their EU-related activities and how they develop and discuss these strategies internally.

The core of the project was the examination of three working hypotheses:

1. The trade unions from the member states of Eastern Enlargement are not active participants in decision-making processes at the EU level. The major aim of their presence at the EU level is to utilise the information and experience that they gather there to improve their political representation at the national level.
2. Accordingly, the trade unions from the member states of Eastern Enlargement do not provide much input to EU-level umbrella organisations and, in turn, only have a marginal impact on decisions made in these umbrella organisations.
3. The trade unions from the member states of Eastern Enlargement do not engage in substantial internal debates about EU-related positions and strategies. In organisational terms, different EU-related activities are not brought together in a systematic way. Accordingly, these trade unions cannot be understood as collective actors. Instead, individual representatives determine their EU-related work.

In order to provide the context for the research questions addressed in this book, this chapter gives an overview of current research on European interest groups by focussing on two major fields: interest groups in EU multi-level governance, on the one hand, and the Europeanisation of interests groups and interest intermediation, on the other. In a further step, the literature on trade unions in Central and Eastern European EU member states will be reviewed, complemented by some basic data on labour relations and trade unions in the six largest countries of Eastern Enlargement that will be covered in this book.

1.2. European Interest Group Research

The following paragraphs will give an overview of current European interest group research. The research thus focuses on two major fields: interest groups in the EU and the Europeanisation of interest groups and domestic interest intermediation systems. In the following paragraphs, major theoretical and empirical findings in these two research branches will be summarised and presented.

1.2.1. Research on Interest Groups in EU Governance Structures

The EU's competencies are a powerful incentive for interest organisations to participate in the EU's decision-making processes (Eising 2008: 15). This incentive also appeals to trade unions, as the EU's competences in the field of social policy have been extended (Treib/Falkner 2009: 261). Thus, social policy issues, such as occupational health, or gender equality, are parts of EU policy-making (Treib/Falkner 2009:261).

There are several theories that attempt to explain interest representation in the EU (for an overview, see Michalowitz 2007: 25–50). One major approach is the multi-level governance concept that describes the growing complexity and interdependency of policy processes between the European, national and subnational levels as a result of European integration (Eising 2008: 10; Marks/Hooghe/Blank 1996; for an overview, see Stephenson 2013). Studies of European industrial relations have also adopted the multi-level governance approach in order to describe employment developments in the EU (Müller/Platzer 2003, Platzer 2009). Thus, European politics consists of numerous venues of interest representation that interest groups can use in order to participate in decision-making processes:

> As a result, we no longer see EU interest politics in terms of 'bottom–up' national interests feeding into the EU, or 'top-down' coordination of EU lobbying, rather we see a managed multilevel process with numerous feedback loops and entry points constrained by the size of the interest group, lobbying budgets, origin, and the policy area. (Coen/Richardson 2009: 7)

Greenwood differentiates between two major venues that interest groups can use to receive access to EU-level decision-makers, namely the 'national route' and the 'Brussels route'. Via the 'national route', interest groups can use interest representation venues at the domestic level in order to exert influence on EU-level decision-makers. On the other hand, via the 'Brussels route', interest groups can directly exert EU-level influence by lobbying EU institutions, such as the Commission or the European Parliament. (Greenwood 2011: 23–52) There are several EU-level interest representation venues that trade unions can use to gain access, including consultations with EU institutions and via the European Social Dialogue, the European Economic and Social Committee and European umbrella organisations for trade unions (Pleines 2008: 11).

However, access to the EU policymaking process is demanding. Eising

> define[s] access as the frequency of contacts between interest organizations and EU institutions. These contacts range from informal bilateral meetings with EU officials and politicians to institutionalized committee proceedings (Eising 2007: 386).

However, according to Bouwen (2002), having access to decision-makers does not automatically result in influence on the legislative process. Nonetheless, access may be an 'indicator of influence' (Bouwen 2002: 366; for measuring the influence of interest groups, also see Dür 2008a, 2008b). Interest groups' access to and influence on EU decision-makers is largely determined by financial and economic capacities, membership size and information (Eising 2008: 15), but also by the strategies and tactics that interest groups use to exert influence. Studies on strategies and tactics can be found in, e.g., Beyers 2004, 2008, Binderkrantz 2008, Chalmers 2013, Dür/Mateo 2013. For example, it is argued by Dür/Mateo (2012) that resource-rich organisations (foremost, business interests) can more frequently access EU level decision-makers. However, the recent study of Dür, Bernhagen, and Marshall (2013) shows that business interests, despite their good access at the EU level, have less influence on EU policy decisions than civil society organisations.

The resource exchange theory of Bouwen (2002) is often used in the literature to study the relationship between EU-level decision-makers and organised interests (Bunea/Baumgartner 2014: 1421). Bouwen perceives the relationships between interest groups (i.e., business interests) and EU institutions 'as an exchange relation between two groups of interdependent organizations. It is a mistake to regard business lobbying as a unidirectional activity of private actors *vis-à-vis* the EU institutions' (Bouwen 2002: 368). In order to receive access to decision-making processes, interest groups must offer 'access goods' (certain types of information) that EU institutions need in order to fulfil their roles (Bouwen 2002).

1.2.2. Europeanisation and Interest Group Research

European interest group research also focuses on the effects that EU-level activities have on domestic interest groups and interest representation (Eising 2008: 11). This research has been carried out under the concept of Europeanisation and has produced comprehensive studies (e.g., Cowles/Caporaso/Risse 2001, Featherstone/Radaelli 2003; for the Europeanisation of Eastern Europe, see Schimmelfennig/Sedelmeier 2005).

However, the debate about the conceptualisation of Europeanisation is still ongoing in the literature, and has resulted in a multitude of definitions and understandings of Europeanisation, either as a top–down process (e.g., Radaelli 2000, 2004) or as a development that also includes bottom–up processes (e.g., Börzel 2002, Saurugger 2005). For instance, Radaelli (2004: 3) conceptualises Europeanisation as

> [...] processes of a) construction, b) diffusion and c) institutionalisation of formal and informal rules, procedures, policy paradigms, styles, 'ways of doing things' and shared beliefs and norms which are first defined and consolidated in the EU policy process and then incorporated in the logic of domestic (national and subnational) discourse, political structures and public policies.

In addition, Börzel (2002: 193) argues the following:

> Europeanization is a two-way process. It entails a 'bottom–up' and a 'top-down' dimension. The former emphasizes the evolution of European institutions as a set of new norms, rules and practices, whereas the latter refers to the impact of these new institutions on political structures and processes of the Member States.

Concerning EU Enlargement, Héritier (2005) even differentiates between 'Europeanization East' and 'Europeanization West'. She argues that the Europeanisation of the new EU member states is different compared with the EU-15. She suggests that the Europeanisation of the new EU member states should instead be seen as a 'one-way street', as these countries are usually unable to influence EU policies. In contrast, Héritier perceives the Europeanisation of old EU member states as a 'two-way street'. (Héritier 2005: 207f.)

Leaving aside the question of conceptualisation, there are also a number of methodological challenges regarding Europeanisation research. Saurugger (2005) provides an overview of how to study the Europeanisation of interest groups; she highlights three major methodological difficulties. According to Saurugger, the 'cause and effect' of Europeanisation are difficult to identify, as Europeanisation is a 'circular movement' (2005: 291) that consists of uploads and downloads of policy ideas or practices. Second, it is challenging to differentiate between domestic and EU-level developments that influence domestic actors, as they may occur simultaneously. Third, Europeanisation is difficult to measure, especially with regard to domestic actors, as they may only adapt their activities for strategic reasons. (Saurugger 2005: 291–292)

In addition, it is difficult to explain why domestic non-state actors Europeanise. One explanation assumes that huge differences between the EU level and the member states regarding 'processes, policies, and institutions' (Börzel/Risse 2000: 5) increase the pressure for domestic actors to Europeanise (Börzel/Risse 2000: 5). Another explanation assumes that the high integration of interest groups into domestic networks and structures constrains the Europeanisation of interest groups (Beyers 2002, Beyers/Kerremans 2007).

Moreover, Europeanisation research has produced far-reaching studies in recent years (e.g., on the Europeanisation of domestic institutions and administrations, see

Knill 2001, Lippert/Umbach 2005; for a systematic review of the Europeanisation literature on institutions and administrations, see Goetz/Meyer-Sahling 2008). However, research on the Europeanisation of national interest organisations from different European member states is rare, often focussing only on Western European countries (as also observed by Eising 2008: 11; on business interests from Western European countries, see, e.g., Fairbrass 2003, Quittkat 2006, Wilts 2001).

1.3. Trade Unions from the EU Member States of the Eastern Enlargement

1.3.1. Trade Unions and Labour Relations in Central Eastern Europe

With the Eastern Enlargement of the European Union, ten post-socialist countries were incorporated from 2004 to 2007. In this context, it has been argued that interest representation in the EU governance system poses formidable challenges to trade unions in post-socialist countries. Shortly after the first wave of the EU's Eastern Enlargement, the quantitative representation of non-governmental organisations from the new member states was still weak. While German, Belgian, French, and Italian organisations were represented in 90% of the relevant European umbrella organisations for social policy, the new member states lay at the other end of the spectrum with only 40–50%, as an analysis by Wasner (2005) demonstrated.

Many analyses of trade unions and labour relations in post-socialist EU member states have been conducted to date. Kohl and Platzer (2004) present an overview of this topic. More important, however, are the numerous individual studies, which together provide a rather comprehensive body of knowledge–first of all for Poland but also for the Czech Republic and partly for Hungary and Slovakia. These studies include Mansfeldová (1999), Myant and Smith (1999), Cox and Mason (2000), Frege (2000), Myant et al. (2000), Čambáliková (2001), Crowley and Ost (2001), Ost (2001, 2006), Pańków and Gąciarz (2001), Pollert (2001), Deppe and Tatur (2002), Dvorakova (2003), Kroupa and Mansfeldová (2003), Crowley (2004), Kubicek (2004), Avdagic (2005), Bohle and Greskovits (2006), Gąsior-Niemiec (2007), Meardi (2007), Vanhuysse (2007), Krzywdzinski (2008), Makó (2010), Pulignano, Mrozowicki, and Van Hootegem (2010), Krén (2011), Stegemann (2011), Meardi and Trappmann (2013), Sznajder-Lee and Trappmann (2014). This literature focuses on post-socialist developments in an attempt to explain trade unions' weaknesses.

Due to their socialist legacy, several trade unions in the new, post-socialist EU member states still have relatively large numbers of members, but they are organisationally limited in terms of their ability to represent interests in the political arena. At the national level, the trade unions are only organised in comparatively loose umbrella associations.

Trade union representatives often shy away from political responsibility and have barely any experience in working with supranational committees. The weakness of the post-socialist trade unions is also demonstrated by the fact that none of the national-level tri-partite committees in the new member states has led to successful trade union participation in political decision-making processes in the new EU member states (Reutter 1996; Kurtan 1999; Casale 2000; Mailand/Due 2004). The trade unions' influence on national politics is generally perceived as minimal (Sil/Candland 2001; Pleines 2003; Avdagic 2005; Matthes/Terletzki 2005; Ost 2006; Meardi/Trappmann 2013). On the basis of a comprehensive study, Stephen Crowley (2004; similar to Vanhuysse 2007) concludes that labour relations in the new EU member states tend to resemble the American model and thus might not be compatible with the EU's system.

In a systematic comparison, Lis concluded that the standard indicators on labour relations show:

> [...] the new EU member states from Central and Eastern Europe to be a relatively coherent region with Slovenia as an explicit outlier whose welfare model bears similarities to the continental version. Meanwhile, the Baltic States' systems most closely resemble the Anglo-Saxon model. The remaining post-socialist member states, which joined in 2004 (the Czech Republic, Hungary, Poland and Slovakia) all demonstrate a relatively weak labour scenario characterized by low trade union density, low collective bargaining coverage, a low degree of bargaining centralization and a low level of strike activity. (2008: 52)

After the first round of the EU's Eastern Enlargement, some publications also look at the (expected) impact of EU membership on trade unions in the new member countries. Bluhm (2006) identifies a 'dilemma of liberalization', pointing out that the deregulation of the national economies in the wake of EU integration will further strengthen the position of employers' organisations *vis-à-vis* trade unions. Trappmann (2013) presents a detailed case study arguing this point.

In contrast, Meardi (2007) and Kaminska and Kahancovà (2011) argue that labour migration from new member states to old ones will lead to labour shortages in the new member countries, which will, in turn, strengthen workers and thus trade unions.

Empirical studies of the actual impact of Eastern Enlargement on trade unions in the new member states, and more specifically studies of the integration of these trade unions into the EU governance system, are very limited in number and scope. Kusznir and Pleines (2008) offer the first study of the EU-level activities of major trade unions from the Czech Republic, Poland, and Slovakia. European Works Councils in the member states of the Eastern Enlargement have also been analysed (see Voss 2006; Tholen 2007; Rudolf/Stegmann 2009; Traxler et al. 2010).

In summary, it can be stated that a systematic account of the integration of trade unions from the member states of the Eastern Enlargement into the EU governance system and related Europeanisation effects has not yet been conducted. The research project that led to this book publication has aimed to fill this gap.

1.3.2. Trade Unions in the Studied Countries

As has been elaborated above, the project covers the most important trade unions from the six largest member states that joined during the Eastern Enlargement (namely Bulgaria, the Czech Republic, Hungary, Poland, Romania, and Slovakia). In terms of their labour relations, all belong to the core group of post-socialist countries that

> demonstrate a relatively weak labour scenario characterized by low trade union density, low collective bargaining coverage, a low degree of bargaining centralization and a low level of strike activity (Lis 2008: 52).

According to an analysis by the European Trade Union Institute (ETUI), trade union density in Central Eastern Europe stood at an average of 20%, and collective bargaining covered 36% of the workforce from 2000 to 2009. Both figures were lowest among the EU's macro-regions (ETUI 2012: 57). Strike participation has also been considerably lower in post-socialist EU member states than in the older EU member states. From 2004 until 2008, strike participation never rose above 10%, while it oscillated between 15% and 25% for the 15 old member states (European Commission 2013: 63).

Among the six countries studied in this book, Romania has the highest proportion of employees in trade unions (33%), followed by Bulgaria (20%), the Czech Republic (17%), and Slovakia (17%). Hungary and Poland are at the bottom with 12%, while the EU average stands at 23% (ETUI/Fulton 2013).

The weakness of trade unions in these countries is also confirmed by relatively low public trust. In 2004, only about a quarter of the populations in these countries claimed that they 'tend to trust' trade unions. In Bulgaria, this figure was substantially lower (14%). In the same year, the average value for all EU member states stood at 41%[1]. However, while the EU average stood somewhat lower in 2010 (38%), trust figures were higher in 2010 than in 2004 for the countries covered here, with the exception of Romania. The Czech Republic had the highest value (52%), followed by Slovakia (40%). In Hungary and Poland, a third of the population tended to trust trade unions (compared with a quarter in 2004); in Bulgaria and Romania, a mere 20% declared trust in trade unions (Eurobarometer 2011).

Within the six studied countries, the structure of national umbrella trade unions differs substantially. In Bulgaria, the Czech Republic, and Slovakia, the successors to the old socialist trade unions—the Confederation of Independent Trade Unions of Bulgaria (CITUB), the Czech-Moravian Confederation of Trade Unions (ČMKOS), and the Confederation of the Trade Unions of Slovak Republic (KOZ SR), respectively—dominate, with a share of at least two thirds of trade union members. In Bulgaria and the Czech Republic, small alternative trade unions have been established: the Confederation of Labour Podkrepa (CL Podkrepa) and the Association of Independent Trade Unions of the Czech Republic

1 Eurobarometer public opinion polls, http://ec.europa.eu/public_opinion/cf/index.cfm?lang=en.

(ASO), respectively. Poland used to be marked by a sharp trade union dualism between Solidarność, which was at the core of the oppositional movement under socialism, and the All-Poland Alliance of Trade Unions (OPZZ), which was the communist trade union. Both were highly politicised, directly supporting political parties and sending members to parliament and government positions. Widespread disappointment with this situation led to the establishment of the Trade Unions Forum (FZZ) as an alternative trade union. The first two trade unions each have a share of a bit more than a quarter of the total trade union membership, though the latter has a somewhat smaller share, with the remaining quarter of trade union members belonging to smaller specialised unions. At the other end of the spectrum, Hungary and Romania are marked by trade union pluralism, with five bigger trade unions and several smaller ones in both cases.

The large national trade union confederations named above are nearly all formally integrated into EU-related governance structures. They are members of the European Trade Union Confederation (ETUC), except for ASO in the Czech Republic and Meridian in Romania[2]. Most of them are also represented in the European Economic and Social Committee (EESC)[3]. Trade unionists from Hungary and Poland have regularly been especially active as rapporteurs to the EESC, while those from Bulgaria and Slovakia have not been active in this role[4]. Czech and Polish trade unions are also members of Interregional Trade Union Councils[5].

The research design of the project described in this book has been developed based on this assessment of the relative weakness of trade unions in the EU member states of Eastern Enlargement. The research design will be presented in the following chapter.

1.4. References

Avdagic, Sabina: State-Labour Relations in East Central Europe. Explaining Variations in Union Effectiveness, in: Socio-Economic Review, 2005 (vol. 3), no. 1, pp. 25–53.

Beyers, Jan: Gaining and Seeking Access: The European Adaptation of Domestic Interest Associations, in: European Journal of Political Research, 2002 (vol. 41), no. 5, pp. 585–612.

Beyers, Jan: Voice and Access: Political Practices of European Interest Associations, in: European Union Politics, 2004 (vol. 5), no. 2, pp. 211–240.

Beyers, Jan: Policy Issues, Organisational Format and the Political Strategies of Interest Organisations, in: West European Politics, 2008 (vol. 31), no. 6, pp. 1188–1211.

2 http://www.etuc.org/a/82 (data as of December 2013).

3 One can find a list of members on the European Economic and Social Committee webpage, available at: http://memberspage.eesc.europa.eu. Data as of December 2013.

4 Data for the period from 2004 to 2012 (rapporteurs to a total of 2020 plenary sessions).

5 ETUC 2010: The Interregional Trade Union Councils, Brussels 2010, available online at: http://www.etuc.org/a/1642.

Beyers, Jan / Kerremans, Bart: Critical Resource Dependencies and the Europeanization of Domestic Interest Groups, in: Journal of European Public Policy, 2007 (vol. 14), no. 3, pp. 460–481.

Binderkrantz, Anne: Different Groups, Different Strategies: How Interest Groups Pursue their Political Ambitions, in: Scandinavian Political Studies, 2008 (vol. 31), no. 2, pp. 173–200.

Bluhm, Katharina: Auflösung des Liberalisierungsdilemmas. Arbeitsbeziehungen in Mittelosteuropa im Kontext des EU-Beitritts, in: Berliner Journal für Soziologie, 2006 (vol. 16), no. 2, pp. 171–186.

Börzel, Tanja: Pace-Setting, Foot-Dragging, and Fence-Sitting: Member State Responses to Europeanization, in: Journal of Common Market Studies, 2002 (vol. 40), no. 2, pp. 193–214.

Börzel, Tanja / Risse, Thomas: When Europe Hits Home: Europeanization and Domestic Change, in: European Integration online Papers, 2000 (vol. 4), no. 15, online available at: http://eiop.or.at/eiop/texte/2000-015a.htm. Accessed 10 November 2014.

Bohle, Dorothee / Greskovits, Béla: Capitalism without Compromise: Strong Business and Weak Labor in Eastern Europe's New Transnational Industries, in: Studies in Comparative International Development, 2006, (vol. 41), no. 1, pp. 3–25.

Bouwen, Pieter: Corporate Lobbying in the European Union: The Logic of Access, in: Journal of European Public Policy, 2002 (vol. 9), no. 3, pp. 365–390.

Bunea, Adriana / Baumgartner, Frank: The State of the Discipline: Authorship, Research Designs, and Citation Patterns in Studies of EU Interest Groups and Lobbying, in: Journal of European Public Policy, 2014 (vol. 21), no. 10, pp. 1412–1434.

Čambáliková, Monika: Tripartismus in der Slowakei. Leere Struktur oder außerparlamentarische Form der Interessenvertretung? in: Zeitschrift für Gemeinwirtschaft, 2001 (vol. 38), no. 6, pp. 27–46.

Casale, Giuseppe: Experiences of Tripartite Relations in Central and Eastern European Countries, in: International Journal of Comparative Labour Law and Industrial Relations, 2000 (vol. 16), no. 2, pp. 129–142.

Chalmers, Adam: Trading Information for Access: Informational Lobbying Strategies and Interest Group Access to the European Union, in: Journal of European Public Policy, 2013 (vol. 20), no. 1, pp. 39–58.

Cianciara, Agnieszka: Polish Business Lobbying in the EU 2004–2009: Examining the Patterns of Influence, in: Perspectives on European Politics and Society, 2013 (vol. 14), no. 1, pp. 63–79.

Coen, David / Richardson, Jeremy: Learning to Lobby the European Union: 20 Years of Change, in: Coen, David / Richardson, Jeremy (eds.): Lobbying the European Union: Institutions, Actors, and Issues, Oxford: Oxford Univ. Press, 2009, pp. 3–15.

Cowles, Maria / Caporaso, James / Risse, Thomas (eds.): Transforming Europe: Europeanization and Domestic Change, Ithaca: Cornell Univ. Press, 2001.

Cox, Terry M. / Mason, Robert: Interest Groups and the Development of Tripartism in East Central Europe, in: European Journal of Industrial Relations, 2000 (vol. 6), no. 3, pp. 325–347.

Crowley, Stephan: Explaining Labor Weakness in Post-Communist Europe, in: East European Politics and Society, 2004 (vol. 18), no. 3, pp. 394–429.

Crowley, Stephen / Ost, David (eds.): Workers after Workers' States. Labor and Politics in Postcommunist Eastern Europe, Lanham: Rowman & Littlefield, 2001.

Deppe, Rainer / Tatur, Melanie: Rekonstitution und Marginalisierung. Transformationsprozesse und Gewerkschaften in Ungarn und Polen, Frankfurt/M.: Campus, 2002.

Dür, Andreas: Interest Groups in the European Union: How Powerful Are They? in: West European Politics, 2008a (vol. 31), no. 6, pp. 1212–1230.

Dür, Andreas: Measuring Interest Group Influence in the EU: A Note on Methodology, in: European Union Politics, 2008b (vol. 9), no. 4, pp. 559–576.

Dür, Andreas / Mateo, Gemma: Who Lobbies the European Union? National Interest Groups in a Multilevel Polity, in: Journal of European Public Policy, 2012 (vol. 19), no. 7, pp. 969–987.

Dür, Andreas / Mateo, Gemma: Gaining Access or Going Public? Interest Group Strategies in Five European Countries, in: European Journal of Political Research, 2013 (vol. 52), no. 5, pp. 660–686.

Dür, Andreas / Bernhagen, Patrick / Marshall, David: Interest Group Success in the European Union: When (and Why) Does Business Lose?, 2013, http://www.intereuro.eu/public/downloads/publications/IGInfluence_paper1_031213.pdf?phpMyAdmin=bc921356f086070c90aa893e9eb2bead. Accessed 19 November 2014.

Dvorakova, Z.: Trade Unions, Works Councils and Staff Involvement in the Modernising Czech Republic, in: International Journal of Public Sector Management, 2003 (vol. 16), no. 6, pp. 424–433.

Einbock, Joanna / Lis, Aleksandra: Polish Trade Unions in EU Governance, in: KICES Working Papers, 2007, no. 11.

Eising, Rainer: Institutional Context, Organizational Resources and Strategic Choices: Explaining Interest Group Access in the European Union, in: European Union Politics, 2007 (vol. 8), no. 3, pp. 329–362.

Eising, Rainer: Interests Groups in EU Policy-Making, in: Living Rev. Euro. Gov., 2008 (vol. 3), no. 4, online available at: http://europeangovernance.livingreviews.org/Articles/lreg-2008-4/. Accessed 22 September 2011.

ETUI: Benchmarking Working Europe, Brussels, 2012, online available at: http://www.etui.org/Publications2/Books/Benchmarking-Working-Europe-2012.

ETUI / Fulton, L.: Worker representation in Europe, in worker-participation.eu, Labour Research Department and ETUI, produced with the assistance of the SEEurope Network, 2013, online available at: http://www.worker-participation.eu/National-Industrial-Relations/Across-Europe/Trade-Unions2. Accessed April 2013.

Eurobarometer: Annex. Table of Results. Standard Eurobarometer 74. Public Opinion in the European Union, in: europa.eu, online available at: http://ec.europa.eu/pub lic_opinion/archives/eb/ eb74/eb74_anx_full_fr.pdf. Accessed 14 September 2014.

European Commission: Industrial Relations in Europe 2012, Luxembourg: Publications Office of the European Union, 2013.

Fairbrass, Jenny: The Europeanization of Business Interest Representation: UK and French Firms Compared, in: Comparative European Politics, 2003 (vol. 1), no. 3, pp. 313–334.

Featherstone, Kevin / Radaelli, Claudio (eds.): The Politics of Europeanization, Oxford: Oxford Univ. Press, 2003.

Frege, Carola M.: The Illusion of Union-Management Cooperation in Postcommunist Central Eastern Europe, in: East European Politics and Societies, 2000 (vol. 13), no. 3, pp. 636–660.

Gąsior-Niemiec, Anna: Civil Society and New Modes of Governance in Poland, in: Polish Sociological Review, 2007, no. 157, pp. 65–85.

Goetz, Klaus / Meyer-Sahling, Jan-Hinrik: The Europeanisation of National Political Systems: Parliaments and Executives, in: Living Rev. Euro. Gov., 2008 (vol. 3), no. 2, online available at: http://europeangovernance.livingreviews.org/Articles/lreg-2008-2/. Accessed 17 September 2014.

Gollbach, Jochen: Europäisierung der Gewerkschaften: Praktische Ansätze im Spannungsverhältnis nationaler und europäischer Strukturen und Traditionen, Hamburg: VSA-Verl., 2005.

Greenwood, Justin: Interest Representation in the European Union, 3. ed., Basingstoke: Palgrave Macmillan, 2011.

Héritier, Adrienne: Europeanization Research East and West: A Comparative Assessment, in: Schimmelfennig, Frank / Sedelmeier, Ulrich (eds.): The Europeanization of Central and Eastern Europe, Ithaca, NY: Cornell Univ. Press, 2005, pp. 199–209.

Hoffmann, Jürgen: Perspektiven der europäischen Arbeitsbeziehungen und Gewerkschaften zwischen Modernisierung, Europäisierung und Globalisierung, in: Leviathan, 2010 (vol. 38), no. 1, pp. 89–102.

Kaminska, Monica / Kahancová, Marta: Emigration and Labour Shortages: An Opportunity for Trade Unions in the New member states, in: European Journal of Industrial Relations, 2011 (vol. 17), no. 2, pp. 189–203.

Knill, Christoph: The Europeanisation of National Administrations: Patterns of Institutional Change and Persistence, Cambridge: Cambridge Univ. Press, 2001.

Kohl, Heribert / Platzer, Hans-Wolfgang: Arbeitsbeziehungen in Mittelosteuropa. Transformation und Integration. Die acht neuen EU-Mitgliedsländer im Vergleich, 2nd ed., Baden-Baden: Nomos, 2004.

Kovacs, Marton: How Do Trade Unions Interact with the European Parliament? A Descriptive Analysis, Brussels: ETUI-REHS Printshop, 2008.

Krén, Ildikó: Thesen zur Standortbestimmung der Gewerkschaften in Ungarn, Friedrich-Ebert-Stiftung Budapest, 2011, online available at: http://library.fes.de/pdf-files/id/07790.pdf. Accessed 14 November 2014.

Kroupa, Aleš / Mansfeldová, Zdenka: The Democratisation of Industrial Relations in the Czech Republic. Work Organisation and Employee Representation. Case Study from the Electronic Industry, in: Smith, S. (eds.): Local Communities and Post-communist Transformation. Czechoslovakia, the Czech Republic and Slovakia, London: Routledge, 2003, pp. 126–142.

Krzywdzinski, Martin: Arbeits- und Sozialpolitik in Polen. Interessenvermittlung und politischer Tausch in einem umkämpften Politikfeld, Wiesbaden: VS Verlag für Sozialwissenschaften, 2008.

Kubicek, Paul J.: Organized Labor in Postcommunist States. From Solidarity to Infirmity, Pittsburgh: University of Pittsburgh Press, 2004.

Kurtan, Sándor: Gewerkschaften und Tripartismus im ostmitteleuropäischen Systemwechsel, in: Merkel, Wolfgang / Sandschneider, Eberhard (eds.): Systemwechsel 4. Die Rolle von Verbänden in Transformationsprozessen, Opladen: Leske+Budrich, 1999, pp. 115–135.

Kusznir, Julia / Pleines, Heiko (eds.): Trade Unions from Post-Socialist Member States in EU Governance, Stuttgart: Ibidem Publishers, 2008.

Lippert, Barbara / Umbach, Gaby: The Pressure of Europeanisation: From Post-Communist State Administrations to Normal Players in the EU System, Baden-Baden: Nomos, 2005.

Lis, Aleksandra: Trade union strength in an EU-wide comparison, in: Kusznir, Julia / Pleines, Heiko (eds.): Trade Unions from Post-Socialist member states in EU Governance, Stuttgart: Ibidem Publishers, 2008, pp. 43–56.

Mailand, Mikkel / Due, Jesper: Social Dialogue in Central and Eastern Europe. Present State and Future Development, in: European Journal of Industrial Relations, 2004 (vol. 10), no. 2, pp. 179–197.

Makó, Csaba: Gewerkschaften im erstarkenden Kapitalismus. Das Beispiel Ungarn, Budapest: Friedrich-Ebert-Stiftung, 2010.

Mansfeldová, Zdenka: Social Partnership in the Czech Republic, in: Kirschbaum, S. J. (eds.): Historical Reflections on Central Europe, Basingstoke: Macmillan, 1999, pp. 207–218.

Marks, Gary / Hooghe, Liesbet / Blank, Kermit: European Integration from the 1980s: State-Centric v. Multi-Level Governance, in: Journal of Common Market Studies, 1996 (vol. 34), no. 3, pp. 341–378.

Matthes, Claudia-Yvette / Terletzki, Peggy: Tripartite Bargaining and its Impact on Stabilisation Policy in Central and Eastern Europe, in: International Journal of Comparative Labour Law and Industrial Relations, 2005 (vol. 21), no. 3, pp. 369–403.

Meardi, Guglielmo: More voice after more exit? Unstable industrial relations in Central Eastern Europe, in: Industrial Relations Journal, 2007 (vol. 38), no. 6, pp. 502–523.

Meardi, Guglielmo / Trappmann, Vera: Social dialogue in crisis. Evidence from Poland, in: Transfer European Review of Labour and Research, 2013 Special Issue 2 1/2013.

Michalowitz, Irina: Lobbying in der EU, Wien: facultas.wuv, 2007.

Müller, Torsten / Platzer, Hans-Wolfgang: European Works Councils: A New Mode of EU Regulation and the Emergence of a European Multi-Level-Structure of Workplace Industrial Relations, in: Keller, Berndt / Platzer, Hans-Wolfgang (eds.): Industrial Relations and European Integration: Trans- and Supranational Developments and Prospects, Aldershot: Ashgate, 2003, pp. 58–84.

Myant, Martin / Slocock, Brian / Smith, Simon: Tripartism in the Czech and Slovak Republics, in: Europe-Asia Studies, 2000 (vol. 52), no. 4, pp. 723–739.

Myant, Martin / Smith, Simon: Czech Trade Unions in Comparative Perspective, in: European Journal of Industrial Relations, 1999 (vol. 5), no. 3, pp. 265–285.

Ost, David: The Weakness of Symbolic Strength. Labor and Union Identity in Poland, in: Crowley, Stephen / Ost, David (eds.): Workers after Workers' States. Labor and Politics in Postcommunist Eastern Europe, Lanham: Rowman & Littlefield, 2001, pp. 79–96.

Ost, David: After Postcommunism. Legacies and the Future of Unions in Eastern Europe, in: Phelan, Craig (eds.): The Future of Organised Labour. Global Perspectives, Oxford: Lang, 2006, pp. 305–331.

Pańków, Włodzimierz / Gąciarz, Barbara: Industrial Relations in Poland. From Social Partnership to Enlightened Paternalism? in: Blazyca, George / Rapacki, Ryszard (eds.): Poland into the New Millennium, Cheltenham: Edward Elgar, 2001, pp. 72–90.

Platzer, Hans-Wolfgang: Approaching and Theorising European Works Councils: Comments on the Emergence of a European Multi-Level-Structure of Employee Involvement and Participation, in: Hertwig, Markus / Pries, Ludger /Rampeltshammer, Luitpold (eds.): European Works Councils in Complementary Perspectives: New Approaches to the Study of European Interest Regulation, Brussels: ETUI, 2009, pp.47–69.

Pleines, Heiko: Sozialpartner, Oligarchen und graue Eminenzen. Zur Rolle nicht-staatlicher Akteure in wirtschaftspolitischen Entscheidungsprozessen, in: Höhmann, Hans-Hermann / Pleines, Heiko (eds.): Wirtschaftspolitik in Osteuropa zwischen ökonomischer Kultur, Institutionenbildung und Akteursverhalten. Russland, Polen und Tschechische Republik im Vergleich, Bremen: Edition Temmen, 2003, pp. 225–245.

Pleines, Heiko (ed.): Already Arrived in Brussels? Interest Representation of Trade Unions from the New EU Member States at the EU Level. Documentation of Interview Results, Working Paper of the Research Centre for East European Studies no. 91, 2008, http://www.forschungsstelle.uni-bremen.de/UserFiles/file/06-Publikationen/Arbeitspapiere/fsoAP91.pdf. Accessed 19 November 2014.

Pleines, Heiko: Is This the Way to Brussels? CEE Civil Society Involvement in EU Governance, in: Acta Politica, 2010 (vol. 45), no. 1–2, pp. 229–246.

Pollert, Anna: Labor and Trade Unions in the Czech Republic. 1989–2000, in: Crowley, Stephen / Ost, David (eds.): Workers after Workers' States. Labor and Politics in Postcommunist Eastern Europe, Lanham: Rowman & Littlefield, 2001, pp. 13–36.

Pulignano, Valeria / Mrozowicki, Adam / Van Hootegegem, Geert: Work Agency and Trade Union Renewal: The Case of Poland, in: Work, Employment & Society, 2010 (vol. 24), no. 2, pp. 221–240.

Quittkat, Christine: Europäisierung der Interessenvermittlung: Französische Wirtschaftsverbände zwischen Beständigkeit und Wandel, Wiesbaden: VS, Verl. für Sozialwiss., 2006.

Radaelli, Claudio: Whither Europeanization? Concept Stretching and Substantive Change, in: European Integration online Papers, 2000 (vol. 4), no. 8, online available at: http://eiop.or.at/eiop/texte/2000-008a.htm. Accessed 10 July 2011.

Radaelli, Claudio: Europeanisation: Solution or Problem? in: European Integration online Papers, 2004 (vol. 8), no. 16, online available at: http://eiop.or.at/eiop/texte/2004-016a.htm. Accessed 10 July 2011.

Reutter, Werner: Tripartism without Corporatism. Trade Unions in Eastern and Central Europe, in: Agh, Attila / Ilonszki, Gabriella (eds.): Parliaments and Organized Interests. The Second Steps, Budapest: Hungarian Centre of Democracy Studies, 1996, pp. 59–78.

Rudolf, Stanislaw / Stegmann, Katherina: European Works Councils Activity in Poland, in: Hertwig, Markus / Pries, Ludger / Rampeltshammer, Luitpold (eds.): European Works Councils in Complementary Perspectives, Brussels: ETUI-Printshop, 2009, pp. 101–125.

Saurugger, Sabine: Europeanization as a Methodological Challenge: The Case of Interest Groups, in: Journal of Comparative Policy Analysis: Research and Practice, 2005 (vol. 7), no. 4, pp. 291–312.

Schimmelfennig, Frank / Sedelmeier, Ulrich (eds.): The Europeanization of Central and Eastern Europe, Ithaca, NY: Cornell Univ. Press, 2005.

Schüttpelz, Anne: Die Europäisierung der Beschäftigungspolitik in Mittel- und Osteuropa vor dem EU Beitritt. Anpassungsprozesse in Tschechien, Berlin: Freie Universität Berlin, 2009.

Sil, Rudra / Candland, Christopher: Institutional Legacies and the Transformation of Labour. Late-Industrializing and Post-Socialist Economies in Comparative-Historical Perspective, in: Candland, Christopher / Sil, Rudra (eds.): The Politics of Labor in a Global Age. Continuity and Change in Late-Industrializing and Post-Socialist Economies, Oxford: Oxford University Press, 2001, pp. 285–308.

Stegemann, Karolina: Gewerkschaften und kollektives Arbeitsrecht in Polen: Wechselbeziehungen im geschichtlichen Kontext, Baden-Baden: Nomos, 2011.

Stephenson, Paul: Twenty Years of Multi-Level Governance: 'Where Does It Come From? What Is It? Where Is It Going?', in: Journal of European Public Policy, 2013 (vol. 20), no. 6, pp. 817–837.

Sznajder-Lee, A. / Trappmann, V.: Labour Union Regeneration in Central and Eastern Europe: Overcoming Postcommunist Weakness through External Pressures? in: European Journal of Industrial Relations, forthcoming 2014.

Tholen, Jochen: Labour relations in Central Europe: the impact of multinationals' money, Aldershot: Ashgate, 2007.

Trappmann, Vera: Fallen heroes in global capitalism. Workers and the restructuring of the Polish Steel Industry. Houndsmill: Palgrave MacMillan (Series Studies in Economic Transition), 2013.

Traxler, Franz / Strohmer, Sonja / Meardi, Guglielmo: The Barriers to Effective EWCs in Central Eastern Europe: An Analysis of Sector Effects in the Czech Republic, 2010, online available at: http://www2.warwick.ac.uk/fac/soc/wbs/research/irru/publi cations/recentconf/gm_-_parma .pdf. Accessed 20 September 2011.

Treib, Oliver / Falkner, Gerda: Bargaining and Lobbying in EU Social Policy, in: Coen, David / Richardson, Jeremy (eds.): Lobbying the European Union: Institutions, Actors, and Issues, Oxford: Oxford Univ. Press, 2009, pp. 256–276.

Umbach, Gaby: Intent and Reality of the European Employment Strategy. Europeanisation of National Employment Policies and Policy-Making? Baden-Baden: Nomos Verlags-Gesellschaft, 2009.

Vanhuysse, Pieter: Workers without Powers. Agency, Legacies and Labour Decline in East European Varieties of Capitalism, in: Czech Sociological Review, 2007 (vol. 43), no. 3, pp. 459–522.

Voss, Eckhard: The Experience of European Works Councils in the new EU member states, Dublin: European Foundation for the Improvement of Living and Working Conditions, Luxembourg: Office for Official Publications of the European Communities, 2006.

Wasner, Barbara: Europäische Institutionenpolitik und die Vernetzung sozialpolitischer Verbände, in: Knodt, M. / Finke, B. (eds.): Europäische Zivilgesellschaft. Konzepte, Akteure, Strategien, Wiesbaden: Verlag für Sozialwissenschaften, 2005, pp. 129–152.

Wilts, Arnold: Europeanization and Means of Interest Representation by National Business Associations, in: European Journal of Industrial Relations, 2001 (vol. 7), no. 3, pp. 269–286.

2. Research Design[1]

2.1. Case Selection

Because the project cannot cover all trade unions in all Central East European countries that joined the European Union (EU) during its Eastern Enlargement in 2004 / 07, the project team has opted for a focused comparison. Focused comparisons 'have proved to be the success story of comparative politics in recent decades'[2] because they are seen as a good compromise between individual case studies and macro-statistical analysis.

Because trade unions in Central Eastern Europe are generally perceived to be weak in terms of resources, membership support and political representation, and because smaller trade unions are not even formally represented at the EU level, the project team has decided to include only the strongest trade unions in the analysis. Accordingly, the analysis is not meant to give a representative view of trade unions from Central East European countries in general but is explicitly designed as the best case scenario for trade unions from the EU member states of the Eastern Enlargement.

Accordingly, small countries (with a population of less than 4 million) have been excluded. In the bigger countries, all general national trade union associations have been selected in addition to especially strong and influential national branch associations, namely mining and metals. To cover the service sector, branch unions for trade and the financial sector have also been included, although they tend to be weaker.

As a result, the project covers the most important trade unions from the six largest member states that joined during the Eastern Enlargement (namely Bulgaria, Czech Republic, Hungary, Poland, Romania and Slovakia). It includes all general national trade union associations plus national branch associations for metals, mining, retail trade / commerce, and banking / finance. Small trade unions of only local relevance are not included. Based on these criteria, 50 trade unions from the countries under study have been included in the analysis.

To enrich the analysis of the integration into EU governance, the project also covers the respective European umbrella organisations of trade unions[3], representatives of EU institutions and the Vienna Memorandum as an example of interregional cooperation,

1 A more detailed description of the research design is available on the project website at http://www.forschungsstelle.uni-bremen.de/UserFiles/file/04-Forschung/research-design.pdf.

2 Rod Hague / Martin Harrop: Comparative Government and Politics, Basingstoke [a.o.]: Palgrave Macmillan, 2001, p. 73.

3 The European Trade Union Confederation (ETUC) as a general union, IndustriAll for metals / mining and UNI-Europa for retail trade / commerce and banking / finance.

including, in this case, metals trade unions from the Czech Republic, Hungary, and Slovakia as well as Austria and Germany. Accordingly, Austrian and German trade union representatives have also been interviewed to capture their perception of the cooperation with the respective trade unions from the countries under study. Moreover, European Works Councils have been studied on the example of participating trade union representatives from Poland.[4]

Data collection within the project consisted of four major elements:

- desktop research to assemble background data;
- semi-structured interviews to document the activities and views of trade union representatives in the countries under study and at the EU level;
- case studies to examine in detail the decision-making processes in national trade unions and their strategies towards integration into EU governance;
- case studies of trade union cooperation at the different levels of EU governance, namely European umbrella organisations, the Vienna Memorandum group and European Works Councils.

2.2. Desktop Research

Using databases and publications, the research team has collected data on three major topics, namely national labour relations, trade unions in the countries under study and finally their representation at the EU level.

Major sources were data on national labour relations from the European Trade Union Institute (ETUI) and the European Commission, representative polls from the Eurofound survey of European managers and employee representatives, the World Value Survey, European Bank for Reconstruction and Development (EBRD) Life in Transition Survey and Eurobarometer as well as information provided by ETUC.

2.3. Interviews

2.3.1. Selection of Respondents

For the analysis of trade unions from the six countries under study, interviews have been conducted with representatives of national trade union confederations plus national branch associations for metals, mining, retail trade / commerce, and banking / finance. Small trade unions of only local relevance have not been included in the sample.

Altogether, 56 trade unions have been identified that meet the selection criteria. 50 trade unions could be covered through standardised interviews with their

4 The study of European Works Councils has been conducted by Karoline Mis outside the project context and has been integrated into the project at the analytical stage.

representatives. Of the six missing trade unions, three are national confederations, among them two Hungarian ones which are currently in negotiations about a merger. Two are trade unions from the service sector and one trade union from the metal industry could also not be included.

The Romanian report on the conduction of interviews, written by Leyla Safta-Zecheria, illustrates this process:

> The list of trade unions to be included in the project was put together starting from the suggested list of respondents, adding information from the reports funded by the Friedrich-Ebert-Foundation on the Social Dialogue in Romania, as well as from files on 'representativeness' provided by the Romanian Ministry of Labour, Family, Social Protection and the Elderly. First, the trade union confederations were contacted. They were asked to suggest trade union federations which fit the project's selection criteria. As a result of this approach two trade unions were added and one excluded. Moreover, two trade union federations were excluded on the basis of their invisibility, as contact details were not listed in any online or print registers.[5]

In summary, excluding Hungarian trade unions that were soon to be merged, the standardised interviews cover 34 out of 35 confederations plus all but of one of the branch unions for mining and metals in the six countries under study. Additionally, the interviews cover 14 out of 16 branch unions for retail trade / commerce and banking / finance. Thus, trade / finance trade unions from Bulgaria and the Czech Republic are not fully represented. The degree of coverage should be taken into consideration when interpreting the results.

Full coverage is important not only at the level of trade union organisations but also at the level of representatives of individual trade unions. In the project's interview guidelines, the respective selection criteria read:

> For each trade union, all representatives responsible for EU affairs, EU Works Councils and cross-border cooperation plus one member of the governing board with overall responsibilities are interviewed.

The full coverage of trade union representatives with responsibility for issues covered in the research project is especially important for gaining an understanding of the trade unions' internal cohesion in relation to European issues and their internal decision-making processes. This aspect is all the more relevant as the impression of the project team was that the trade unions' work in relation to the EU is often determined by individual representatives and not through collective decision-making processes.

5 The full country reports on the conduction of interviews have been made available to the project's advisory board. Because they contain personal information about the respondents that cannot be anonymised due to the respondents' specific profiles, the reports cannot be published.

2.3.2. The Interview Process

Because the organisational structure of most trade unions included in the analysis is not publicly available and in many cases the division of labour within the trade union leadership does not seem to be precisely defined, the project partners developed different strategies to identify all trade union representatives that fulfil the selection criteria.

Most trade unions, especially branch federations, have only a very small number of professional staff members. In Bulgaria, for example, most of the federations employ only one president and one administrative employee. (Among the six federations covered in Bulgaria, the only exception was a metals trade union, which has a total staff of nine experts.) Even in Poland, which has some of the biggest trade unions among the countries under study, branch unions are usually very small and they employ only the president, the vice-presidents and the secretaries. However, the three major confederations in Poland have a differentiated organisational structure with a special department responsible for international relations, as in the case of Niezależny Samorządny Związek Zawodowy (NSZZ) Solidarność, which has several employees and in the cases of Ogólnopolskie Porozumienie Związków Zawodowych (OPZZ) and Forum Związków Zawodowych (FZZ), which each have only one employee. In Slovakia, there are only two trade unions that have an employee directly responsible for EU affairs. As a result of the very small staff, the president, a vice-president or a secretary is usually also the trade union's representative in most EU-level organisations and institutions both on the confederate and on the branch union level.

The following excerpts from the Czech country report on the conduction of interviews, which has been authored by Zdenka Mansfeldová, illustrate the situation:

> The websites of the trade unions often give very limited or unreliable information about the organisational structure and possible contact persons. Some trade unions do not even have their own website. The snowball method worked only in cases where there had been personal contacts established previously within the respective trade union. The interview process moved forward very slowly. The willingness of trade union representatives to cooperate was worse than in the preceding project five years ago.
>
> The trade unions are losing their membership and, with that, also financial resources. As a result, some have a very small staff without a functioning secretary (administrative assistance). Accordingly, some trade unions do not have an employee who is available to answer phone calls and to arrange meetings or to give information about the availability of trade union representatives. The practice of shared administrative assistance is not used yet.
>
> From the list of originally selected respondents, eight refused to give an interview for different reasons, namely long-time illness, changed portfolio and retirement. Because of a shortage of staff and a high workload in two cases the trade union chairpersons decided that only one representative from the respective union will be available for an interview. In these cases, the selection of the actual respondent was discussed with the trade union leader in a joint effort to identify the most competent trade union representative.[6]

---

6 The full country reports on the conduction of interviews have been made available to the project's advisory board. Because they contain personal information about the respondents

In Romania, as Leyla Safta-Zecheria explains:

> [T]he secretary (administrative staff) was contacted first, since there is little information available on the trade unions' websites about their organisational structure. Contacting the secretary proved to be helpful, because in most organisations the secretary would contact the trade union president in order to get approval for the interviews and the president usually offered to do the first interview himself. Generally, the president then suggested other potential interview partners. The president, vice-president or the secretary general are usually also the representatives of the trade union in most European level organisations and institutions.
>
> This method has the weakness, though, of not allowing me to decide which interview partners are most appropriate, as I had to accept the president's suggestions. This is not per se due to the method itself, but to the lack of information publicly available about the activities of the respective trade unions.

In Poland, however, the interview process went much more smoothly, as the following passage from the report by Aleksandra Lis shows:

> In general, I encountered no problems in contacting the trade union leaders, using contact data available on their websites. The leaders answered the phone or replied to my emails themselves. They scheduled interviews with me individually and I usually did not have to wait for a long time for the meeting. Among the branch trade unions, the mining and metals unions are better-off and in these cases the meeting was usually arranged through secretaries. Moreover, the leaders of these unions were busier, travelling to Brussels more often and I had to wait for an appointment much longer.

2.3.3. Outcome

In the first half of 2013, the project team conducted a total of 101 interviews with representatives of trade unions from the six countries under study. The interviews consisted of closed questions with predefined answers and open questions.[7] The interviews covered seven topics: (1) Importance of the EU, (2) Channels of influence at the EU level, (3) European umbrella organisations of trade unions, (4) Links between the EU and the national level, (5) Cooperation with trade unions from the old EU member states, (6) Cooperation with neighbouring countries in Interregional Trade Union Councils (IRTUCs) and (7) European Works Councils. In addition, standard personal data about the respondents were collected.

All interviews were conducted face-to-face by the responsible project partners or by trained interviewers working for them (with the exception of eight interviews by telephone in the case of Poland). In nearly all cases, interviews were conducted at the headquarters of the respective trade union. The average length of each interview was

---

that cannot be anonymised due to the respondents' specific profiles, the reports cannot be published.

7 The original questionnaire is reproduced in the more detailed description of the research design, which is available on the project website at http://www.forschungsstelle.uni-bremen.de/UserFiles/file/04-Forschung/ research-design.pdf.

approximately 60 minutes. All interviews, with only three exceptions, were recorded electronically with the explicit consent of the respective respondent.[8]

Concerning the reliability of the respondents' individual answers, it is important to take into consideration that they are all professionals. During the interviews, they talked about their major professional tasks (in most cases in their normal office environment). They answered questions on issues they have been managing for a long time. The high number of 'I don't know' answers (more than 50% in the case of several very specific questions) also indicates that the respondents were not willing to share spontaneous views on issues with which they were not familiar. It should also be kept in mind that most respondents have experience with interview situations, most of all through contacts with journalists. Accordingly, we assume that the interviews present the established professional view of the respondents as they would also express it in a public statement.

In addition, individualised guided interviews have been conducted for the case studies of European umbrella organisations (in total 22 interviews), for the incorporation of the views of trade union representatives from Austria and Germany (10 interviews), for the analysis of European Works Councils (3 interviews conducted outside the project context by Karoline Mis) and for the case studies of individual trade unions from the six countries under study (19 additional interviews).

The additional interviews conducted for the case studies of different levels of EU governance, i.e. European umbrella associations, interregional cooperation and European Works Councils, will be introduced in the respective chapters in part 1 of this book.

2.4. Case Studies of Individual Trade Unions

For selected national trade unions—one in each country under study—detailed case studies have been conducted. While the 101 standardised interviews capture the position of the respective trade union representatives on a broad range of EU-related issues, the case studies intended to examine the internal decision-making processes and specific strategies towards the different levels of EU governance.

8 The answers of all 101 respondents to the 48 closed questions have been entered into one Excel data sheet. The answers to questions that had also been asked in the preceding survey in 2007 (which is the case for 17 questions) have been added in a separate data sheet in the same file. The answers to the 17 open questions (plus elaborations added to the closed questions) from all 101 respondents comprise a total of approximately 250 000 words. To allow for systematic analysis, the free answers have been imported into a MAXQDA file. The conducted interviews (audio files and scanned questionnaires) are archived at the Research Centre for East European Studies at the University of Bremen. All original questionnaires remain with the responsible project partner.

The case studies were conducted as explorative studies and were informed first of all by the empirical data and not by our external analytical framework. However, for all case studies, the focus has been kept on interaction with the EU, interregional cooperation and European Works Councils.

The case studies have been based on all available evidence, including additional interviews with trade union representatives and experts, minutes of trade union meetings, information material from trade unions and EU institutions, mass media reports, and all other relevant sources including expert analyses, opinion polls and statistical data.

3. Trade Unions and Industrial Relations in the EU Member States of Eastern Enlargement

Relying on quantitative figures from cross-national statistics and representative opinion polls, this chapter will give a short overview of the general characteristics of trade union organisation in the new member states (NMS) and will outline the basic characteristics of the industrial relations systems. In addition, it will look at challenges and changes since the financial and economic crisis of 2008.

3.1. Organisational Features and Status in Labour Relations

Of course, there are important differences between the union landscapes of the individual countries that are analysed in this study. However, the countries have similarity not only in the historic experience of centralised state economies and their transformation to liberal capitalist systems but also in the development of their own systems of industrial relations.[1] According to most scholars, during the transformation period, the transformation countries tended less to import models of industrial relations from the west and more to develop specific labour relations models that were comparable with neither any southern, western or continental systems in Europe.[2] This model suggests a special configuration of NMS trade unions' organisational and institutional power resources that shape the role they can play in the process of the Europeanization of trade union policy.

Today, there are three important characteristics of industrial relations in NMS:

1. Compared with other regions in Europe, trade unions are small and weak; the degree of unionisation is low. Trade union organisation is decentralised and relies on the company level.
2. The collective bargaining structures are weak, the coverage by collective agreements is limited and the focus of collective bargaining is the company level.
3. Workplace representation of employees is mostly based on trade union organisation at the company level. Statuary worker representation bodies (works councils) rarely exist.

The political changes in post-communist societies after 1989 led very rapidly to a fundamental change in trade union systems in these societies' beginning transitions. The most important common elements of these new systems of industrial relations were

1 Trif, Aurora / Koch, Karl: Strategic unionism in Eastern Europe, in: MPIfG working paper, 2005, no. 05 / 7, here p. 6.

2 Fichter, Michael: Industrial relations and European integration, in: Industrielle Beziehungen: Zeitschrift für Arbeit, Organisation und Management, 2006, no. 13, 2, here p. 182.

(1) the emergence of independent trade unions and (2) the democratisation of communist trade unions and the decentralisation of their structures.[3]

In most NMS, there is a duality of 'old' federations, which have their roots in communist professional unions, and 'new' federations, founded after the fall of communism, or, in the case of Niezależny Samorządny Związek Zawodowy Solidarność (NZZ Solidarność) in Poland, in opposition to the communist state.[4] However, the transformation period led to an approximation of the character of these two types of unions. Whereas 'new' trade unions (with the exception of NZZ Solidarność) remained small and weak, the 'old' did not succeed in using their political and financial resources to strengthen their organisational capacities. One reason for this was the decentralisation of their structures, which were 'often pushed to extremes, which tangibly reduced their capacity to mobilize resources.'[5]

The following table (Table 3-1) shows recent figures on trade union density in the NMS that were analysed in this study. Union density is the most important indicator of trade union strength. The data are based on Eurostat's observations of European industrial relations[6].

Table 3-1: Trade Union Density in the Countries Under Study (most recent figures as of September 2014)

Country	**Bulgaria**	**Czech Republic**	**Hungary**	**Poland**	**Romania**	**Slovak Republic**	**EU average**
Proportion of Employees in Unions	18%	16%	11%	12%	40%	16%	23%

Source: Eurofund: EurWORK European Observatory of Working Life, in: eurofund.europa.eu, http://www.eurofound. europa.eu/eiro/, accessed 21 September 2014.

The numbers show that the general degree of unionisation is very low compared with the EU average, varying from some 40% (Romania) to 11% (Hungary, Poland). In all countries, with the exception of Romania, the degree of unionisation is below the

3 Mielke, Siegfried / Peter Rütters: Die neuen Gewerkschaftsbewegungen in Mittel- und Osteuropa und ihre Auswirkungen auf die internationale Gewerkschaftsbewegung [The new trade union movements in Central Eastern Europe and their impact on the international trade union movement], in: Aus Politik und Zeitgeschichte, 1991, B 13, pp. 35–46.

4 Schroeder, Wolfgang: Arbeitsbeziehungen in Mittel- und Osteuropa. Weder wilder Osten noch europäisches Sozialmodell [Industrial Relations in Central Eastern Europe. Neither wild East nor the European social model], in: Schmid, Josef / Harald Kohler (eds): Arbeitsbeziehungen und Sozialer Dialog im alten und neuen Europa. Unterschiede, Gemeinsamkeiten, Kooperationen [Industrial Relations and Social Dialogue in old and new Europe. Differences, similarities, collaborations], Baden Baden: Nomos, 2009, pp. 309–329, here p. 316.

5 Genov, Nikolai: State and economy in Eastern Europe. trends in establishing social dialogue, in: Mansfeldova, Zdenka / Vera Sparschuh / Agnieszka Wenninger (eds): Patterns of Europeanisation in Central and Eastern Europe, Hamburg: Kräemer, 2005, pp. 95–115, here p. 102.

6 Eurofund: EurWORK European Observatory of Working Life, in: eurofund.europa.eu, http://www.eurofound. europa.eu/eiro/, accessed 21 September 2014.

European Union average. However, even these numbers do not exactly describe the reality because there are also large differences between sectors and companies; in some sectors and companies, there are no trade unions at all.

This low union density meets a landscape of small and weak trade unions (in some cases only existing at the company level) . The trade union movement is divided along different lines on different levels. This fragmentation is particularly strong in Bulgaria, Romania, Poland and Hungary. Only in the Czech Republic and Slovakia is the situation better because there are united national confederations. The Annex to this chapter shows the most important trade unions in the NMS that are affiliated with the European federations: European Trade Union Confederation (ETUC), the umbrella federation, IndustriAll (industrial unions) and Union Network International (UNI, service sector unions) that will be analysed in the following chapter. Apart from the general weakness, the table in the appendix of this chapter gives an indication of the fragmentation of the trade union landscape.

In Romania, for example, there are five umbrella organisations (Fratia, Blocul National Sindical (BNS), Confederaţia Sindicatelor Democratice din România (CSDR), Cartel Alfa, and Meridian). In Bulgaria, there are large competing confederations: Podkrepa and Confederation of Independent Trade Unions of Bulgaria (CITUB). In Hungary, there have been six confederations. Four, Magyar Szakszervezetek Országos Szövetsége (MSZOSZ), Autonóm Szakszervezetek Szövetsége (ASZSZ), Szakszervezetek Együttműködési Fóruma (SZEF), and Értelmiségi Szakszervezeti Tömörülés (ÉSZT), emerged as reformed organisations from the unified trade union confederation Szakszervezetek Országos Tanácsa (SZOT), which existed before 1989, and two, Független Szakszervezetek Demokratikus Ligája (LIGA) and Mozdonyvezetők Szakszervezete (MOSZ), grew out of a combination of anti-communist activists and local protest movements. In addition to these confederations, there are also a large number of independent unions.[7] Only recently, there was a merger by the reformed trade unions MSZOSZ, ASZSZ and SZEF to a single Hungarian Trade Union Confederation.[8] However, the trade union landscape remains plural mostly because of the division between 'old', 'new' and 'independent' unions but also because of political divisions.

The fragmentation is also based on different political orientations. With the exception of the Czech and Slovak Republics, there is trade union plurality in all new member states.[9] In Romania, for example, there are two trade union confederations (Fratia

7 Fulton, L.: Worker representation in Europe, in: worker-participation.eu, 2013, http://www.worker-participation.eu/Nationale-Arbeitsbeziehungen/Laender/Ungarn/Gewerkschaften, accessed 16 March 2014.

8 MSZOSZ: We did it!—Hungarian Trade Union Confederation established!, in: mszosz.hu, 7 December 2013, http://www.mszosz.hu/en/news/874-we-did-it-hungarian-trade-union-con federation-established, accessed 16 March 2014.

9 Lecher, Wolfgang / Optenhögel, Uwe: Wirtschaft, Gesellschaft und Gewerkschaften in Mittel- und Osteuropa [Economy, Society and Trade Unions in Central East Europe], Köln: Bund-Verlag,

and BNS) that are close to the Socialists and one that is close to the Christian Democrats (Cartel Alfa). In addition, there is also strong sectorial fragmentation: There are different unions for different sectors, and some unions are only strong in one segment of a sector. According to officials in Brussels, in some new member states (Bulgaria, Romania), there is the additional problem that some unions not only belong to a political party but are also involved in a system of competing networks of business and politics. The competition between these elites' networks is then transferred into the competition between different trade unions.[10]

Unlike in any other country of the EU, in most NMS, there is a 'bottom–up system' of trade union organisation. The basis of trade union organisation is the company level. At the company level, unions collect membership fees, and only a small part of this money goes 'up' to the sectorial and then national levels of trade unions. The majority of the money remains at the company level, and the union leaders can make offers to workers and thereby gain popularity and support. With this control over the money, company-level unions have an 'exit option', and thus, sectorial unions are very weak.[11] There are trade unions that only exist in one company.

The Central Eastern European model of industrial relations implies politically and financially weak unions. Officials in the secretariats in Brussels consider this form of organisation the most important problem in developing trade unions in new member states. This consideration certainly has something to do with the fact that owing to the lack of money, the Central Eastern European trade unions have fewer opportunities to engage and pay for European trade union work. The European Trade Union Federations, therefore, promote more cooperation between trade unions and support projects to change the trade union structures to a stronger sectorial approach. Until now, these approaches have had, however, only limited success.[12]

The fragmentation and decentralisation of trade union structures suggests a lack of centralised actors in the industrial relation systems that could play the role of collective bargaining partners. On the other side, there is the same problem—there is a lack of centralised and representative employers' associations.[13] Another factor is that trade unions in NMS are often present only in state-owned or formerly state-owned

---

1995, here p. 28.

10 Interview with IndustriALL official, Belgium, LT/IA1 21 May 2013.

11 Lecher, Wolfgang / Optenhögel, Uwe: Wirtschaft, Gesellschaft und Gewerkschaften in Mittel- und Osteuropa [Economy, Society and Trade Unions in Central East Europe], Köln: Bund-Verlag, 1995, here p. 28.

12 According to a Brussels official, the Slovak Metalworker's Union KOVO decided in 2013 that all membership fees in case of a founding of a trade union must first be sent to the central level, which then returns a part of it to the company.

13 Slomp, Hans / Hoof, Jacques van / Moerel, Hans: The transformation of industrial relations in some Central and Eastern European countries, in: Ruysseveldt, Joris van / Visser, Jelle: Industrial Relations in Europe, Heerlen, 1995, here p. 345.

companies. In small and medium-sized enterprises, they are not present at all. This is not unique to Central Eastern Europe, but the unions in the NMS are in general too weak to enter into sectorial collective agreements. Thus, these small and medium-sized enterprises are not covered by collective agreements at all. As a result, the social partnership and union influence at the national and sectorial levels remains weak, and the density of collective agreement coverage remains low.[14]

Table 3-2: Collective Bargaining Coverage,* Degree of Collective Bargaining Centralisation (1–5)** and the Existence of Minimum Wages*** (most recent data as of September 2014)

Country	Bulgaria	Czech Republic	Hungary	Poland	Romania	Slovak Republic	EU average
Collective bargaining coverage	33%	34%	23%	20%	35–40%	35%	62%
Centralisation of collective bargaining	2 (2)	1 (1)	1 (1)	1 (1)	1 (3)	2(2)	
Minimum wages	Yes (5)	Yes (8)	Yes (4)	Yes (8)	Yes (8)	Yes (8)	

* *Eurofund: EurWORK European Observatory of Working Life, in: eurofund.europa.eu, http://www.eurofound. europa.eu/eiro/, accessed 21 September 2014.*

** *Visser, Jelle: ICTWSS. Database on Institutional Characteristics of Trade Unions, Wage Setting, State Intervention and Social Pacts in 34 countries between 1960 and 2012, in: Amsterdam Institute for Advanced Labour Studies (AIAS), 2013, http://www.uva-aias.net/207, accessed 21 September 2014. Ordinal scale between 1 and 5: 5 = bargaining predominantly at the central or cross-industry level and there are centrally determined binding norms or ceilings to be respected by agreements negotiated at lower levels; 4 = intermediate or alternating between central and industry bargaining; 3 = bargaining predominantly takes place at the sector or industry level; 2 = intermediate or alternating between sector and company bargaining; 1 = bargaining predominantly takes place at the local or company level.*

*** *Ibid. Numbers describe the type of minimum wages: 4 = National minimum wage is set through tripartite negotiations; 5 = National minimum wage is set by the government, but after (non-binding) tripartite consultations; 8 = Minimum wage is set by government, with no fixed rules.*

Table 3-2 underlines this assertion; it shows the collective bargaining coverage, the degree of collective bargaining centralisation, and the existence of minimum wages. The collective bargaining coverage figures come from European industrial relations observations,[15] the degrees of decentralisation come from the Database on Institutional Characteristics of Trade Unions, Wage Setting, State Intervention and Social Pacts

14 Kohl, Heribert: Wo stehen die Gewerkschaften in Osteuropa heute? Eine Zwischenbilanz nach der EU-Erweiterung [Where Do Trade Unions Stand in Eastern Europe Today? Stock-taking after EU Enlargement], in: FES Kurzberichte, 2008, no. 5, here p. 4.

15 Eurofund: EurWORK European Observatory of Working Life, in: eurofund.europa.eu, http://www.eurofound. europa.eu/eiro/, accessed 21 September 2014.

ICTWSS-4.0-Survey by Jelle Visser (2013).[16] The latter uses an ordinal scale ranging between 1 (bargaining predominantly at the local or company level) and 5 (bargaining predominantly centrally or cross-industry). The figures are from 2011 (2010). The numbers on minimum wages are also according to Visser.

The first row shows that collective bargaining coverage is low, between 30% and 38%, and is some 50% below the EU average. The second row shows that the most important and dominant level of collective bargaining is the company level. Sectorial collective bargaining plays a subordinate role, with the exception of Bulgaria and Slovakia, where sectorial collective agreements exist on a larger scale. The general trend in these countries, however, is towards a more decentralised collective bargaining structure. What is notable are the figures for Romania, where the degree of centralisation fell from a rating of 3 (primarily sector-level) in 2010 to 1 (primarily company-level) in 2011.

Because of the weak industrial relations structures, the state plays a more important role in regulating wages and working conditions. The state regulates industrial relations mainly through labour laws and minimum wages. In all NMS, there are statuary minimum wages. Additionally, the state provides institutional frameworks of consultation through social dialogue structures. Thus, for instance, in Bulgaria and Hungary, trade unions are involved in setting minimum wages.

However, although there have been attempts to strengthen the social partners through participation in the policymaking in economic and social councils, the role of the state remains strong because of the weakness of the social actors. In general, social dialogue has been less an instrument for codetermination and more for legitimising government policy. Social dialogue in Central Eastern Europe was and is until today not comparable with social partnership in other parts of Europe.[17] In addition, there has been a further weakening of the already weak elements of social dialogue since 2008. During the crisis, there were labour law and social partnership reforms in a number of NMS. In some countries, such as Hungary and Romania, central levels of social dialogue were weakened in favour of the company level.

Figure 3-1 shows a comparison of the two indicators *trade union density* and *collective bargaining coverage* for all EU member states and Switzerland. The figure reflects the general weakness of trade unions in the NMS. With the notable exception of Slovenia,

---

16 Visser, Jelle: ICTWSS. Database on Institutional Characteristics of Trade Unions, Wage Setting, State Intervention and Social Pacts in 34 countries between 1960 and 2012, in: Amsterdam Institute for Advanced Labour Studies (AIAS), 2013, http://www.uva-aias.net/207, accessed 21 September 2014.

17 Schröder, Wolfgang / Kalass, Viktoria: Sozialdemokratie und Gewerkschaften in Osteuropa [Social Democracy and Trade Unions in Eastern Europe], in: FES–Internationale Politikanalyse, 2010 May, here p. 5.

Figure 3-1: Proportion of Employees in Unions in Relation to Collective Bargaining Coverage

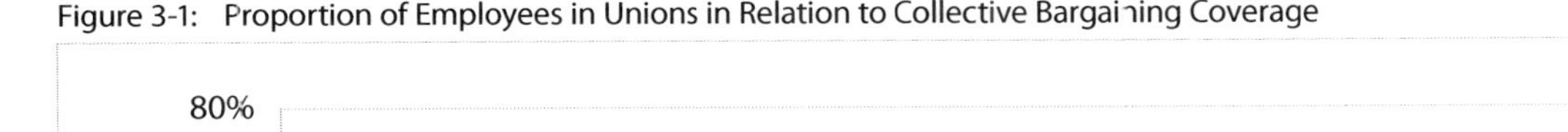

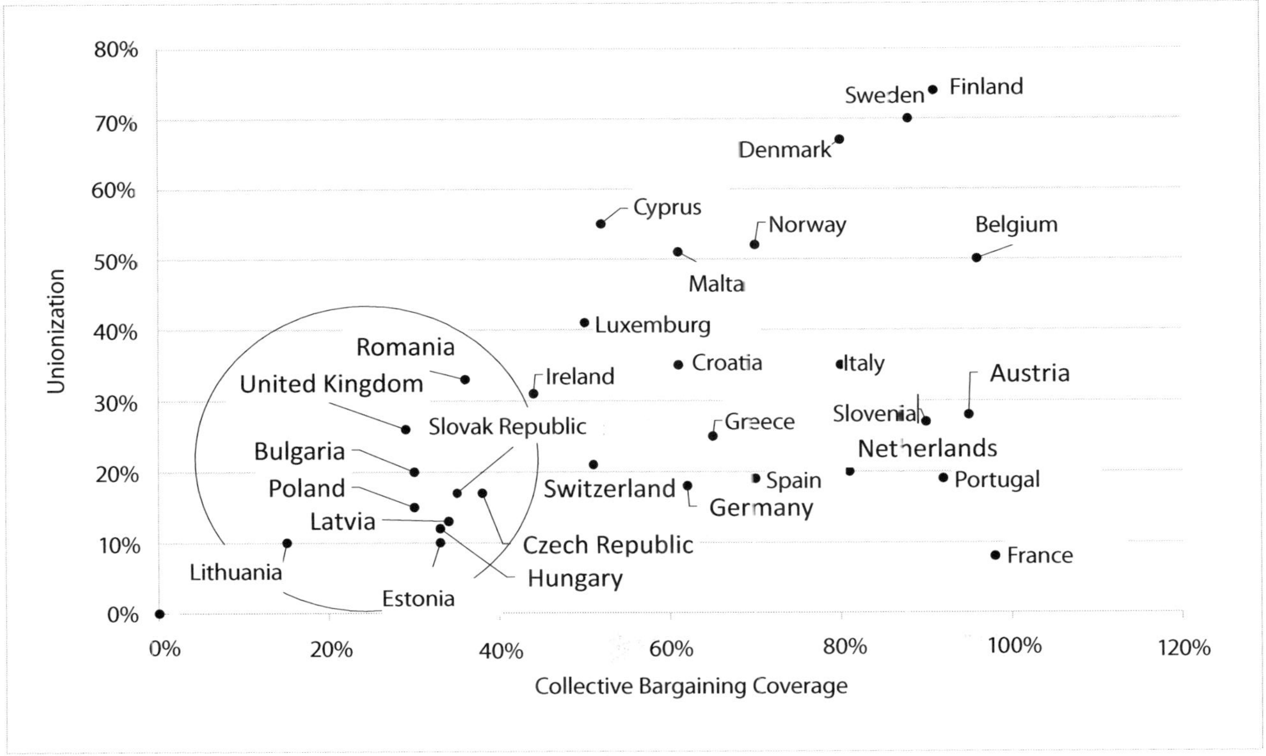

Source: Fulton, L.: Worker representation in Europe, in: worker-participation.eu, 2013, http://www.worker-participation.eu/Nationale-Arbeitsbeziehungen/Laender/Ungarn/Gewerkschaften, accessed 21 September 2014.

industrial relations in the new member states form, together with the United Kingdom, the lower end of a line whose upper end is formed by the Scandinavian countries.

Facing a lack of organisational and institutional resources, 'old' and 'new' trade union federations both often moved straight towards a strategy of purely political representation rather than building capacities in workplaces. A trade union official in Brussels criticised the strategy of many affiliates in NMS: to only 'flirt with political parties, to look on ministries and to swim in the wake of politicians with the hope to get imposed their demands in the case of a change of government'[18].

Another important aspect of the industrial relations systems in NMS is the fact that employee workplace representation is mostly based on company-level trade union organisation. Although by law, the establishment of employee representation bodies in all NMS is possible, representative statuary worker bodies (such as 'works councils') beyond unions until now rarely exist. If they do exist, they are subordinated *vis-à-vis* union representation. However, according to Fulton[19], a tendency is visible for government focus to move more and more towards strengthening and supporting the concept of works councils:

- In Poland, the only representation until now was by company unions. However, changes in legislation after the implementation of the EU directive on information and consultation provided the possibility to establish a large number of works councils.
- In Hungary, there was until now a duality between company unions and works councils, which had equal rights. However, with the implementation of the new labour law, company unions lost their monitoring powers and their right to be consulted. This right now remains only for works councils.
- In Slovakia, there have been major changes in legislation that favour works councils over workplace trade union bodies. Both can now exist in the same place, and powers are to be divided between them.

3.2. Public Trust

Public trust and support for trade unions in NMS are generally low, as Table 3-3 shows. The numbers are average values that rely on the European Value Survey (EVS) 2008 and 1999, and are on a scale between 1 (a great deal) and 4 (not at all). The numbers in the first row show that trust in trade unions in NMS is generally low. The lowest level of trust is observed in Bulgaria, and the highest in the Slovak Republic. Nevertheless,

18 Interview with European Metalworkers Federation (EMF) representative, Germany, EMF4/PS 20 September 2010.

19 Fulton, L.: Worker representation in Europe, in: worker-participation.eu, 2013, http://www.worker-participation.eu/Nationale-Arbeitsbeziehungen/Laender/Ungarn/Gewerkschaften, accessed 21 September 2014.

in all new member states, trust is lower than the average in old member states. The difference becomes clear in any comparison with the Nordic states: In Denmark, for instance, there is 'quite a lot' of confidence in trade unions.

Table 3-3: Confidence in Institutions in New Member States According to the European Value Survey 2008 (1999)

How much confidence is there in	Bulgaria	Czech Republic	Hungary	Poland	Romania	Slovak Republic	old member states	Denmark
Trade Unions (1999)	3.39 (3.20)	2.92 (3.02)	2.99 (3.09)	2.86 (2.78)	2.78 (2.88)	2.75 (2.69)	2.67	2.39
Political Parties	3.46	3.21	3.32	3.33	3.20	2.97	3.00	2.59
Government	3.34	3.09	3.23	3.08	3.04	2.56	2.80	2.46
EU	2.41	2.68	2.52	2.46	2.31	2.35	2.58	2.63

Source: EVS: EVS—European Values Study various years and countries, in: Gesellschaft Sozialwissenschaftlicher Infrastruktureinrichtungen (GESIS) Data Archive, Cologne, https://dbk.gesis.org/dbksearch/GDESC2.asp?no =0009&DB=E, accessed 21 September 2011. Average values on a scale between 1 and 4: 1 = a great deal, 2 = quite a lot, 3 = not very much, 4 = none at all.

However, the gap between the NMS and EU averages is not as significant as the figures for the average of all old member states show. The relativity becomes much clearer if compared with trust in other political institutions in NMS. In nearly all NMS, the trust in trade unions is low, but it is higher than the trust in governments or political parties. Regarding comparisons with other institutions, it is interesting to note that in all NMS, confidence in the European Union is higher than that in trade unions.

In addition, the European Value Survey does not show a common temporal trend in confidence changes for the period before 2008. In Bulgaria, Poland and the Slovak Republic, public trust decreased, but in the Czech Republic, Hungary and Romania, it increased. Available data from the European Value Survey do not track the development of public trust since the economic crisis of 2008/9. Recent results from other surveys, however, show evidence that the trust in trade unions in most new member states could have increased since the crisis.

The Life in Transition survey (Table 3-4) concludes that in the period of 2007–2010, trust rose in Bulgaria, the Czech Republic, Poland and the Slovak Republic. Eurobarometer figures (Table 3-5) also show an increase in trust in trade unions in Hungary. This increase in trust is accompanied simultaneously by a growing distrust in trade unions. This contradiction could be an expression of increasing differentiation and polarisation in the NMS societies during the crisis.

Table 3-4: Trust in Trade Unions in New Member States, 2007 and 2010, According to the Life in Transition Survey in %

	Bulgaria		Czech Republic		Hungary		Poland		Romania		Slovakia	
	2007	2010	2007	2010	2007	2010	2007	2010	2007	2010	2007	2010
Complete distrust (1)	36.29	23.13	8.64	6.04	21.56	24.27	12.26	4.95	21.13	29.41	15.14	7.17
Some distrust (2)	20.70	23.76	16.65	15.04	14.83	19.82	14.29	21.12	17.93	20.20	17.16	20.36
Neither trust nor distrust (3)	19.64	19.77	29.14	33.69	25.08	27.10	32.09	34.46	27.64	21.19	31.02	37.13
Some trust (4)	5.98	8.62	22.63	32.20	18.36	10.01	18.12	25.87	18.78	13.76	16.42	20.78
Complete trust (5)	1.07	1.05	4.80	4.45	4.17	2.73	4.48	2.77	4.91	2.18	1.92	3.59

Source: data available in: http://www.ebrd.com/pages/research/economics/data/lits.shtml, accessed 25 November 2014

Table 3-5: Trust in Trade Unions in New Member States, 2007* and 2010**, According to Eurobarometer in %

	Bulgaria		Czech Republic		Hungary		Poland		Romania		Slovakia	
	2007	2010	2007	2010	2007	2010	2007	2010	2007	2010	2007	2010
Tend to trust	12	21	39	52	23	31	29	31	27	21	30	40
Tend not to trust	55	60	47	37	54	54	37	47	48	63	54	51
Don't know	33	19	14	11	23	15	34	22	25	16	16	9

** European Commission: public opinion report 2007, in: europa.eu, http://ec.europa.eu/public_opinion/cf/showchart_column.cfm?keyID=2188&nationID=27,17,22,24,29,26,&startdate=2004.10&enddate=2007.10, accessed 21 September 2014.*

***European Commission: primary data of Eurobarometer 74.2 2010, in: GESIS Data catalogue, https://dbk.gesis. org/dbksearch/download.asp?db=E&id=49619, accessed 21 September 2014.*

3.3. Trade Unions in New Member States. Facing the Crisis

To explain current trade union developments in new member states, it is important to mention that the global financial and economic crisis marked a radical break in the social and economic development of countries in Central Eastern Europe. According to some scholars, Central Eastern Europe was hit harder by the economic downturn than even Southern Europe. Taken together as a whole, Drahokopil argued, the former transition countries were (in all country-specific differences) more affected by the

2008 global crisis and subsequent related political measures than any other comparable group of countries.[20]

The NMS had high economic growth rates in the pre-crisis period before 2008. However, they had their starting point after the post-transformation crises in the 1990s, when the NMS economies lay immobilised. Therefore, the high growth rates, between 4 and 10%, contributed mainly to merely neutralising the effects of the economic collapse in the early 1990s.

This development stopped abruptly with the global financial and economic crisis. In 2009, economies collapsed in all countries with the exception of Poland (where the economy did, however, stagnate). The collapse was comparable with those in other countries in the European Union but, in contrast to Germany, in the NMS, there was no sustainable growth after 2009 that could have neutralised the economic breakdowns. Rather, there are signs of an ongoing period of economic stagnation.

The economic slump fundamentally changed the environments in which unions operate in the NMS. Unemployment, which had been falling slowly but steadily before 2008, rose again to two-digit numbers.[21] In addition, European Industrial Relations Observatory (EIRO) figures show that the common Increase in labour disputes in the pre crisis period declined and then stopped after 2008.[22]

Unions from NMS were affected by political measures against workers' rights that were enacted in other parts of Europe as well; all unions were affected by labour law reforms. According to Schömann / Clauwaertmost, the important measures have been:[23]

- the deregulation of working time (Czech Republic, Poland) and the extension of fixed-term contracts and temporary or agency work (Czech Republic, Poland, Romania, Slovakia);
- the weakening of employment protection and the degradation of redundancy payments (Slovakia, Czech Republic, Poland);
- the decentralisation of collective bargaining and weakening of the rights of trade unions (Romania and Slovakia) as well as attacks on the system of social dialogues (Romania, Hungary). There were also attacks on existing collective agreements and attempts to reduce minimum wages (Slovenia).

---

20 Drahokoupil, Jan / Myant, Martin: Transition Economies after the Crisis of 2008. Actors and Policies, in: Europe-Asia Studies, 2013 (vol. 65), no. 3, here p. 373.

21 Eurostat: Unemployment rate, by sex, in: Eurostat.ec.europa.eu, http://epp.eurostat.ec.europa.eu/tgm/ download.do?tab=table&plugin=1&language=en&pcode=tsdec450, accessed 21 August 2014.

22 EurWORK: Developments in industrial action 2005–2009, in: Eurofund, 25 August 2010, http://www.euro found.europa.eu/eiro/studies/tn1004049s/tn1004049s.htm#hd5, accessed 21 September 2014.

23 Schömann, Isabelle / Clauwaert, Stefan: The crisis and national labour law reforms. A mapping exercise, Brussels: ETUI Working Paper, 2012, here p. 8 ff.

Table 3-6: Real GDP Growth Rates (Percentage Change from the Previous Year) and Unemployment Rates (In Percentages)* According to Eurostat, Number Of Industrial Disputes 2005–2009 According to EIRO**

	2005	2006	2007	2008	2009	2010	2011	2012	2013	
Bulgaria	6.4	6.5	6.4	6.2	-5.5	0.4	1.8	0.6	0.9	GDP growth rate
	10.1	9	6.9	5.6	6.8	10.3	11.3	12.3	13	Unemployment rate
	2	2	n.a.	3	2					Number of disputes
Czech Republic	6.8	7	5.7	3.1	-4.5	2.5	1.8	-1	-0.9	GDP growth rate
	7.9	7.1	5.3	4.4	6.7	7.3	6.7	7	7	Unemployment rate
	15	14	10	26	7					Number of disputes
Hungary	4	3.9	0.1	0.9	-6.8	1.1	1.6	-1.7	1.1	GDP growth rate
	7.2	7.5	7.4	7.8	10	11.2	10.9	10.9	10.2	Unemployment rate
	28	36	59	38	52					Number of disputes
Poland	3.6	6.2	6.8	5.1	1.6	3.9	4.5	2	1.6	GDP growth rate
	17.9	13.9	9.6	7.1	8.1	9.7	9.7	10.1	10.3	Unemployment rate
	8	27	1736	12800	49					Number of disputes
Romania	4.2	7.9	6.3	7.3	-6.6	-1.1	2.3	0.6	3.5	GDP growth rate
	7.2	7.3	6.4	5.8	6.9	7.3	7.4	7	7.3	Unemployment rate
	98	95	86	116	75					Number of disputes
Slovakia	6.7	8.3	10.5	5.8	-4.9	4.4	3	1.8	0.9	GDP growth rate
	16.4	13.5	11.2	9.6	12.1	14.5	13.7	14	14.2	Unemployment Rate
	0	4	1	1	0					Number of disputes

* *Eurostat: Unemployment rate, by sex, in: Eurostat.ec.europa.eu, http://epp.eurostat.ec.europa.eu/tgm/download.do?tab=table&plugin=1&language=en&pcode=tsdec450, accessed 21 August 2014.*

** *EurWORK: Developments in industrial action 2005–2009, in: Eurofund, 25 August 2010, http://www.euro found.europa.eu/eiro/studies/tn1004049s/tn1004049s.htm#hd5, accessed 21 September 2014.*

Additionally, there were a number of cuts in public spending, reductions in welfare state benefits and direct state regulation of wages.[24]

- Freezes or cuts in minimum wages (Czech Republic, Hungary);

24 European Foundation for the Improvement of Living and Working Conditions. Impact of the crisis on industrial relations, Dublin, 2013, here p. 9.

- public-sector pay freezes (Hungary, Poland, Slovak Republic);
- public-sector pay cuts (Romania);
- welfare benefit cuts and changes to pensions (Poland, Romania, Slovak Republic).

Regarding the case of Hungary, Andras Toth et al. argued that the cuts in public services and governments' changes to labour legislation and labour market regulation are of a new variety that is a 'major break with the policies of the past 20 years and would create a completely new societal model in an EU member state'[25].

These measures have major consequences for trade unions and the possibilities for worker participation. According to Schömann / Clauwaert,[26] recent labour policies in many NMS were similar in dimension to the measures in Southern Europe. However, this was not reflected as much in public awareness in comparison with the events in Southern Europe, where trade unions organised huge protests and general strikes against austerity measures. However, there have been protest actions against austerity measures by trade unions in NMS.

- In October 2010, several thousand trade unionists marched through the Slovak capital, Bratislava, in protest of public spending cuts and increases in the value-added tax (VAT).[27] Rising opposition against anti-crisis measures forced the Slovak government to resign in 2011.
- In April 2011, Hungarian and European trade unions organised a demonstration against austerity measures and the conclusion of the Euro-Plus-Pact with some 45,000 participants in Budapest.[28]
- In Romania, multiple waves of protests against austerity measures took place beginning in 2010. In February 2012, the Romanian government of Emil Boc was forced to resign after three weeks of spontaneous uprising. The trade unions backed the protests.[29]

---

25 Toth, Andras / Neumann, Laszlo / Hosszu, Hortenzia: Hungary's full-blown malaise, in: Lehndorf, Steffen (eds): A triumph of failed ideas. European models of capitalism in the crisis, Brussels: ETUI aisbl, 2012, pp. 137–154.

26 Schömann, Isabelle / Clauwaert, Stefan: The crisis and national labour law reforms. A mapping exercise, Brussels: ETUI Working Paper, 2012, here p. 8ff.

27 Sita / ČTK / Tasr: Protest odborárov sa skončil poeticky: Vypustili farebné balóny [The trade unionist's protest ends poetically: Let loose colored balloons], in: Čas SK, 12 October 2010, http://www.cas.sk/clanok/182471/ protest-odborarov-sa-skoncil-poeticky-vypustili-farebne-balony.html, accessed 21 September 2014.

28 Balazs, Eszter / Agence France-Presse: Tens of Thousands Against European Austerity Measures, in: commondreams.org, 9 April 2011, http://www.commondreams.org/news/2011/04/09/tens-thousands-against-european-austerity-measures, accessed 21 September 2014.

29 PG / JR / Press TV: Romania's prime minster resigns following anti-austerity protest, in: presstv.com, 6 February 2012, http://www.presstv.com/detail/225262.html, accessed 21 September 2014.

- In November 2012, Czech trade unions organised a demonstration against pension reform and cuts in health care with 20,000 participants in Prague.[30]
- In February 2013, the Bulgarian centre-right government of Bojko Borisov had to resign after protests against energy price increases and other austerity measures. The protests were preceded by trade union protests and strikes beginning in 2010.[31]
- In September 2013, the three main confederations in Poland overcame their division and organised a common protest march against pension reforms and working time deregulation with 200,000 participants, which was the largest demonstration in Poland since 1989.[32]

The picture is therefore more complex. The weakness of trade unions and the decrease in labour disputes at the company level during the crisis (see above) is one side of the picture. The shift in union activity to political mass action and, in part, the growing reputation of trade unions in NMS societies is the other. This contradiction is not unique to the NMS, however; rather, it is similar to general developments one can see in Western Europe.[33]

In most cases, concrete measures followed the general objectives of the European institutions. For instance, the weakening of social dialogue structures, decentralisation of collective bargaining systems and cuts in public spending correspond to the explicit objectives of the 'Euro-Plus-Pact' and the 'Fiscal Pact'. Whereas trade unions from new member states had a positive image of the EU and strongly supported the accession of their countries until recently, the question arises now of the extent to which the developments since the crisis have led to differing trade union views and strategies regarding European policy in NMS.

30 Czech-Moravian Confederation of Trade Unions: Demonstration of Trade Unions and Civic Associations in Prague on 17th November 2012, in: official website of ČMKOS, 20 November 2012, http://www.cmkos.cz/ homepage/3523-3/demonstration-of-trade-unions-and-civic-associations-in-prague-on-17th-november-2012, accessed 21 September 2014.

31 Pop, Valentina: Bulgarian government to resign amid austerity protests, in: euobserver.com, 20 February 2013, http://euobserver.com/economic/119128, accessed 21 September 2014.

32 Slk / Ch / Associated Press / Agence France-Presse: Tens of thousands protest labor reforms in Poland, in: dw.de, 14 September 2013, http://www.dw.de/tens-of-thousands-protest-labor-reforms-in-poland/a-17088977, accessed 21 September 2014.

33 Hamann, Kerstin / Johnston, Alison / Kelly, John: Unions against governments. General strikes in Western Europe 1980–2006, in: Comparative Political Studies, 2013 (vol. 46), no. 9, here p. 1030.

3.4. Appendix: Affiliates of ETUC, IndustriALL, UNI Europa from New Member States

	ETUC	IndustriAll Europe	UNI Europa
Bulgaria	CITUB / KNSB (Confederation of independent trade unions)	- Federation of Independent Syndicates of Miners - Fosil - Metalicy - Chemistry and Industry - Metal-Electro	- Trade Union Federation of Communications
	PODKREPA	- Chemical Workers' Federation - Light Industry - Nuclear Energy workers - Metallurgy CL	- Guards and Security Employees Union - Post, Telegraphs and Communications Union
Czech Republic	CMK OS (Czech Moravian Confederation of Trade Unions)	- OS KOVO - OS TOK - OS Echo, Chemical and Energy Workers - OS SKP Trade Union of Glass, Ceramics and Porcelain	- Echo-CZ - ITU-CZ Czech Television - OS MEDIA-CZ National Union of Mass Media - OS PPP-CZ Banking and Insurance Employees - OS ZPTNS-CZ Workers in Postal, Telecommunication and Newspaper Services - OSPO-CZ Commercial Workers - TB-CZ Typografická Beseda
Hungary	LIGA Democratic League of Independent Trade Unions	- EVDSZ Villamosenerg-iaipari Dolgozók Szakszervezeti Szövetsége	
	MOSz National Federation of Workers' Councils	- Munkastanasok Federation of Textile and Clothing Workers	- ÉŐDSZ Trade Union of Value Transportation and Security Workers

	ETUC	IndustriAll Europe	UNI Europa
Hungary (continued)	MSZOSZ National Confederation of Hungarian Trade Unions	- MOL Bányász Szakszervezet - VDSZ Federation of Unions of Chemical, Energy & allied Workers - BDSZ Mining and Energy Workers' Union - EFEDOSZSZ Trade Union of Building Materials workers - HOPWTU Trade Union of Hungarian Oil- and Gas Workers - VASAS	- BBDSZ Federation of Unions of the Finance Sector - BBDSZ SZ Bankok, Biztositok-DolgozoiSzakszervezeteinek-Szovetsege - KASZ Trade Union of Commercial Employees - VSZSZ Trade Union of the Private Security Worker - FFSZ Syndicat des Auteurs et des Employés du Cinéma Hongrois - HGWU Hungarian Graphical Workers' Trade Union - PSZ Hungarian Postal Trade Union
	ÉSZT Confederation of Unions of Professionals		
Poland	NSZZ Solidarność Independent and Self-Governing Trade Union 'Solidarność'	- Chemiesekretariat - Federacja Przemysłu Lekkiego - Metalowców - Sekretariat Górnictwa Energetyki	- Pracowników Bankowości 'BANKOWIEC' - Pracowników Ochrony - National Secretariat Commerce Workers Union - Krajow a SekcjaNauki - National Section of Bank Workers
	OPZZ All-Poland Alliance of Trade Unions	- OPZZ Metalworkers TUC of Poland - OZZGNIG – T.U. Fed. of Polish Oil and Gas Companies - Związku Zawodowego Górników w Polsce (Miners)	- ZPPP Związek Zawodowy Pracowników Przemysłu Poligraficznego - FZZ PKIS Federation of Trade Unions of Culture and Arts Workers
	FZZ Trade Unions Forum	- FZZP T.U. Fed. of Chemical, Glass & Ceramic Industries - KADRA Porozumienie Zwiazków Zawodowych	
Romania	BNS The National Trade Unions Block	- Federatia Sindicala a Lucratorilor din Industrie – Metal	- FSCOM Trade Union Federation of Communication - FSPCOM Federatia Sindicatelor din Posta si Comunicatii

	ETUC	IndustriAll Europe	UNI Europa
Romania (continued)	Cartel Alfa National Trade Union Confederation	- FSS Metarom - FNS Solidaritatea Metal - Federatia Sindicatelor UNICONF - Pielarul (Confpeltex) - Federatia Nationala Mine Energie	- FSRT Federatia Sindicatelor din Romtelecom - FSC Trade Union Federation of Commerce - PROTECTOR Trade Union Federation 'Protector' for the Security Industry - TUFIB Trade Union Federation from Insurances and Banks
	CNSLR-Fratia National Confederation of Free Trade Unions of Romania - FRATIA	- Sindicatul National Petrom-Energie - ATLAS Uniunea - Fratia Peltricontex - Federatia Sindicatelor Gaz - Federatia Sindicatelor Libere din Chimiesi Petrochimie	
	CSDR Democratic Trade Union Confederation of Romania		
		- Conftex - Craimodex craiova - Federatia Sindicala Hidroelectrica	
Slovak Republic	KOZ SR	- ECHOZ Energy – Chemical Trade Union - IOZ Integrovaný odborový zväz - OZ KOVO Slovak Metalworkers' Federation - ZOJES Trade Union of Nuclear Power Workers of Slovak Republic	- OZ PAL Posts and Logistics - OZ PPA P Pracovníkov Peňažníctva a Poisťovníctva - OZ POCR Commerce and Tourism - OZT – Telekom - SOZ SP Arts & Entertainment

For abbreviations see 'List of Abbreviations and Acronyms' on p. 9.

Part I: Forms of International Cooperation

Klaus Henning

4. Not Dominant but Existent. Involvement of Trade Unions from EU Member States of Eastern Enlargement in European Trade Union Federations

4.1. Introduction

The process that Radaelli described as 'Europeanization' is not a development in only one direction, in which national actors take over 'formal and informal rules, procedures, policy paradigms, styles or "ways of doing things"' on a European level. Rather, it is a double-sided process whereby, in the first step, national actors create European rules, structures, views and policy paradigms that they later acquire at a national level.[1] For research that analyses the Europeanization of trade unions, it is, therefore, of great importance to examine the role played by trade unions from new member states (NMS) in the trade union federations at the European level.

This study examines the integration and involvement of trade unions from NMS in three European trade union federations. It investigates what the participation and cooperation of trade unions from NMS looks like, in what specific forms they communicate with the European federations, which priorities and positions they bring into account and to what degree they influence the policy of the federations. The focus is, according to the research design of the research-project, on confederations and branch unions in the fields of mining, metal, commerce and finance in Poland, the Czech and Slovak Republics, Hungary, Romania and Bulgaria.[2]

The chapter begins with a description of the research objects: the profiles of European trade union federations. Then, the specific involvement of the trade unions from NMS in the internal structures and in the policy fields of the European federations will be analysed. At the end, the results are summarised.

There has been an increased research interest in European Trade Union Federations (ETUFs) recently, as shown by, for example, works by Hans Wolfgang Platzer, Torsten

1 Auel, Katrin: Die Europäisierung nationaler Politik [The Europeanization of national policy], in: Bieling, Hans-Jürgen / Lerch, Marika (eds): Theorien der Europäischen Integration [Theories of European Integration], Wiesbaden: VS Verlag für Sozialwissenschaften, 2005, pp. 293–318, here p. 296.

2 I would like to thank Magdalena Bernaciak from the European Trade Union Institute Brussels, Michael Fichter from Freie Universität Berlin, Martina Hartung from Uni Europa Youth / Hans Boeckler Foundation and the members of the project team and advisory board for their help and comments on this paper.

Müller,[3] and Rainer Fattmann.[4] There are also historical books about European trade union federations that have appeared primarily on anniversaries.[5] However, there is no specific literature on the involvement of trade unions from NMS in the European Trade Union Federations.

This study relies on data and results obtained in several research projects.

- Primary results obtained in research projects on the Europeanization of trade unions in the countries of the Eastern Enlargement, led by Heiko Pleines at the Research Centre for East European Studies / University of Bremen 2007–2008 and 2012–2014.[6]
- Additional results from a project on the history of the European Metalworkers' Federation, conducted by a research team led by Siegfried Mielke at the Free University Berlin, 2009–2012.[7]

The database includes documents written by the federations that are available primarily on websites and in the archive of social democracy in Bonn and expert interviews. Written documents primarily include public statements, position papers, annual reports, work programs, and a number of internal protocols ('minutes') of committee meetings. A total of 16 recorded interviews with members of the European Trade Union Confederation (ETUC) secretariat, the IndustriAll secretariat, and the European Metalworkers Federation (EMF) secretariat and officials from Industriegewerkschaft Metall (IG Metall) are used in this study. The interviews were conducted from 2010 to 2013. All interviews followed an open, semi-structured and problem-centred method. I chose this method to gain information and used assessments that were not in the range of prior knowledge and could not be accessed by other sources.

The interviews with the members of the secretariats in Brussels reflect, to a certain degree, the views of the European associations *vis-à-vis* trade unions of the NMS.

---

3 Platzer, Hans-Wolfgang / Müller, Torsten: Die globalen und europäischen Gewerkschaftsverbände [Global and European Trade Union Federations], Berlin: edition sigma, 2009.

4 Fattmann, Rainer: Für ein soziales Europa. Der Agrar-, Lebensmittel- und Tourismusbereich in der europäischen Gewerkschaftspolitik seit der Gründung der europäischen Wirtschaftsgemeinschaft [For a social Europe. Agriculture, food and tourism sectors in the European trade union policy since the founding of the European Economic Community], Münster: Westfälisches Dampfboot, 2013.

5 Degryse, Christophe / Tilly, Pierre: History of the European Trade Union Confederation, Brussels: European Trade Union Institute, 2013.

6 Kusznir, Julia / Pleines, Heiko (eds): Trade Unions from Post-Socialist Member States in EU Governance, Stuttgart: ibidem-Verlag, 2008.

7 Henning, Klaus: Europäische Integration und Gewerkschaften. Der EMB zwischen Interessenvertretung und transnationaler Solidarität [European integration and trade unions. The EMF between advocacy and transnational solidarity], Wiesbaden: Springer, 2013. Clairmont, Yves: Vom europäischen Verbindungsbüro zur transnationalen Gewerkschaftsorganisation. Organisation, Strategien und Machtpotentiale des Europäischen Metallgewerkschaftsbundes bis 1990 [From European liaison office to transnational trade union organisation. Organisation, strategies and power potential of the European Metalworkers' Federation until 1990], Stuttgart: Steiner, 2014.

However, one should note that the statements of secretaries in Brussels reflected not only the views of the European associations but also national views, expectations and experiences because members of the secretariats in Brussels usually have a professional history in the national unions of their countries of origin.

To question assessments critically and to verify information, selected results of the survey of union officials from new member states ('the other side') were included in this study. This survey was part of the research project 'Europeanization of Trade Unions in the Countries of the Eastern Enlargement', led by Heiko Pleines. The data were obtained through 101 interviews with national officers of trade unions from Bulgaria, the Czech Republic, Hungary, Poland, Romania, and Slovakia, conducted by the project team as described in Chapter 2.

4.2. European Trade Union Federations. Historical Roots and Current Structure

This chapter analyses the involvement of trade unions from NMS into three European trade union federations: ETUC, the trade unions' umbrella federation, IndustriAll, the European federation of trade unions in the industrial sectors, and Union Network International Europa (UNI Europa), the European federation of trade unions in the service sectors.[8] It is only a selection because there are now approximately twelve trade union federations at the European level. However, the selected federations are the largest and most important.

Figure 4-1: Logos of ETUC, IndustriAll Europe, and UNI Europa

ETUC (founded in 1973) has approximately 85 affiliates from 36 countries, with 34 affiliates and observers from NMS. IndustriAll Europe (founded in 2012) now has 192 affiliates from 38 countries, with 84 affiliates and observers from Central Eastern Europe.

8 For information on the federations, see their websites: www.etuc.org, www.industriall-europe.eu, www.uniglobalunion.org/regions/uni-europa/.

UNI Europa (founded in 2000) has 330 affiliates from 50 countries, with 88 affiliates from Central Eastern Europe.

The historical roots of all European trade union federations go back to the 1950s. In reaction to the development of political integration in Western Europe, trade unions in the European Coal and Steel Community (ECSC) and later the European Economic Community (EEC) created European Trade Union Committees for several branches and a European Committee for the national umbrella organisations. The first was a committee called 'Committee of the 21'. It was a committee of sectorial and umbrella federations to represent trade union policies *vis-à-vis* the ECSC institutions. After 1958, with the creation of the European Economic Community, European trade union committees (ETUCs) for several branches and the European Trade Union Secretariat (ETUS) for the national umbrella organisations were founded. Since the 1970s, the sectorial committees were expanded to the European trade union federations (ETUFs), and in 1973, the trade union secretariat was transformed into the European Trade Union Congress (ETUC). The ETUC is the federation of national umbrella organisations, but since the 1990s, the European Trade Union Federations have also been members of the ETUC executive committee. The ETUC therefore has both a federational and a sectorial structure.

The task of these committees was to represent the interest of workers *vis-à-vis* European institutions, employer organisations, and multinational companies. These committees also gave the Western European trade unions the opportunity to coordinate their policies and to organise practical solidarity with each other.

The current structure of European Trade Union Federations is also a result of an ongoing process of restructurings and mergers at the European level, particularly since the 1990s. These mergers often followed similar restructurings at national levels. UNI Europe was formed in 2000 by a merger of four European regional organisations in the service sector (International Federation of Employees, technicians and managers (FIET), Communications International (CI), International Graphical Federation (IGF), Media and Entertainment International (MEI)). The last large merger was in 2012, when three European Industry Federations (European Mine, Chemical and Energy Workers' Federation (EMCEF), Metalworkers' European Federation (EMF), European Trade Union Federation-Textiles Clothing and Leather (ETUC-TCL)) formed the new federation IndustriAll Europe. The following diagram (Figure 4-2 opposite) illustrates the historical development of the federations analysed in this chapter.

The political decision-making process and the institutional system in the EU were described as multi-level governance.[9] This concept is also helpful to describe the European system of industrial relations and the European system of trade union

9 Marks, Gary et al.: European Integration since the 1980s. State-Centric vs. Multi-Level Governance, in: Journal of Common Market Studies, 1996, no. 3, p. 34 f.

Figure 4-2: Historical Genesis of the Three Federations Analysed in this Study

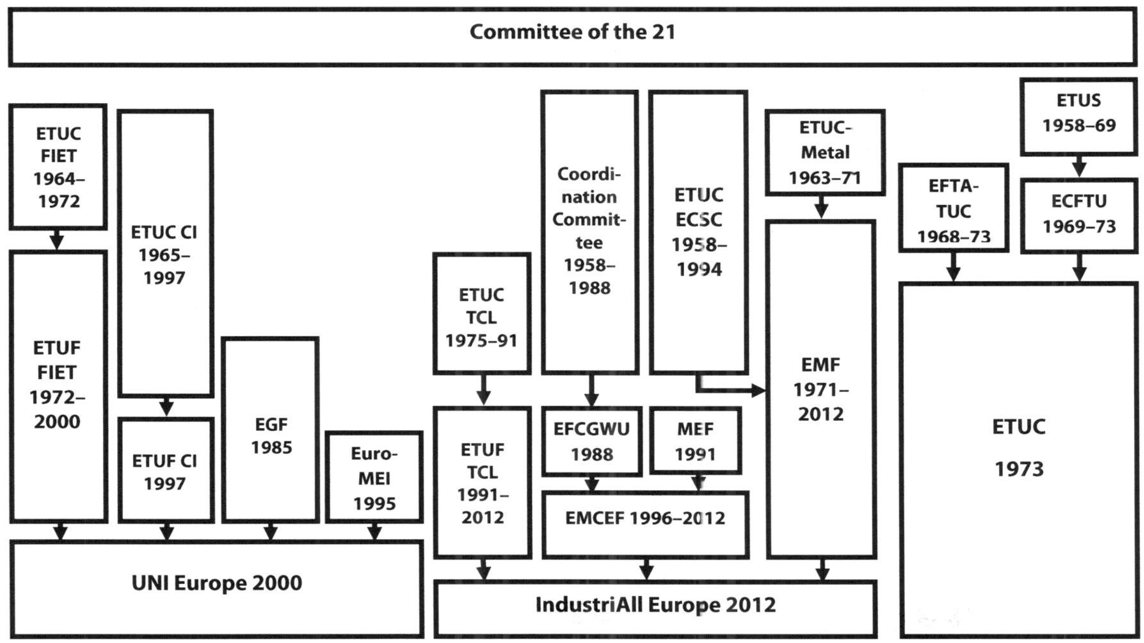

Source: own picture, based on Buschak, Willy: Der Europäische Gewerkschaftsbund und die Europäischen Gewerkschaftsverbände [The European Trade Union Confederation and the European Industry Federations], in: Optenhögel, Uwe / Schneider, Michael / Zimmermann, Rüdiger (eds): Europäische Gewerkschaftsorganisationen. Bestände im Archiv der sozialen Demokratie und in der Bibliothek der Friedrich-Ebert-Stiftung [European trade union organisations. Stocks in the archives of Social Democracy and in the library of the Friedrich Ebert Foundation], Bonn: Friedrich-Ebert-Stiftung, 2003, pp. 9–19.

representation. Regarding trade union organisations, there is a specific competence distribution between national, European, and international levels of governance on one side and company, sectorial, and interprofessional levels on the other side. For instance, the ETUC is not a regional organisation of the International Trade Union Confederation (ITUC) (the Pan European Regional Council) but an autonomous trade union federation. 'IndustriALL Europe' is also not a regional organisation of the international industry federation, 'IndustriAll global union'. On the contrary, UNI Europa is a purely regional organisation of Union Network International Global (UNI Global), integrated in its structures and activities.

It is important to note that because the competencies of trade unions are distributed between national and European levels, there are both supranational and international modes of cooperation. For instance, on one hand, the 'classical' collective bargaining is the competency of national trade unions and, therefore, is coordinated among national trade unions. On the other hand, there is a social dialogue on the European level in some areas, where the competencies are in the hands of European federations (ETUC on interprofessional and ETUFs on sectorial levels). A similar multi-level distribution exists at the company level between European and national works councils.

Table 4-1: Competencies of Trade Unions at National, European, and Global Levels

	Company Level	Sectorial Level	Interprofessional Level
Global	International Works Councils	Global Union Federations (GUFs)	International Trade Union Confederation (ITUC)
EU	European Works Councils (EWC)	European Trade Union Federations (ETUFs)	European Trade Union Confederation (ETUC)
National	Works Councils / Union Delegates / company unions	Trade unions of specific branches	National Confederations

There is also a specific distribution of competencies at the European level. The ETUC is the umbrella federation within the European Union. It is responsible for all interprofessional questions. It includes not only national federations but also the sectorial European trade union federations (ETUFs), such as IndustriAll and UNI Europa. These sectorial ETUFs are responsible for all sectorial questions, sectorial social dialogue, and collective bargaining at the sectorial level. They are, in turn, in charge of the European Works Councils (EWCs) covered by their sectors. The EWCs are responsible for European policies and coordination in single companies.

The internal structure of the three federations analysed in this study can be classified into four types of bodies. (1) The highest bodies are general assemblies, which are usually held every four years. They consist of delegates of the national trade unions.

In the ETUC and IndustriAll Europe, they are called 'congresses' and in UNI Europa, 'regional conferences'.

Figure 4-3: The Internal Structure of the Trade Union Federations

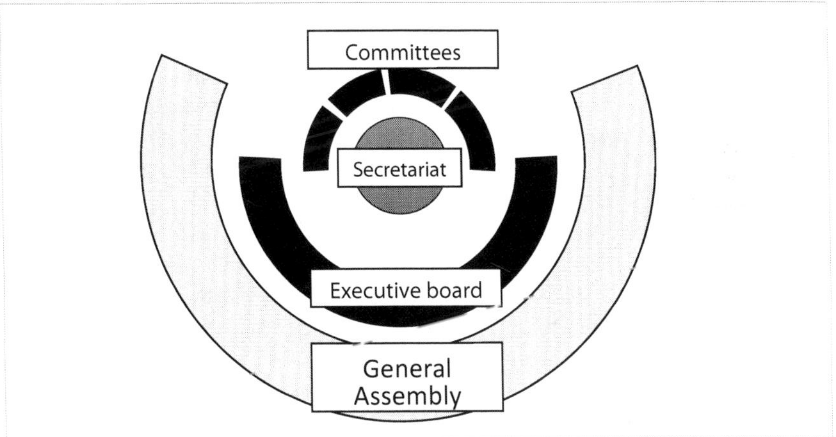

(2) Then, there are executive boards that make the decisions between the meetings of these assemblies: the *executive committees* of ETUC and IndustriAll and the *regional board* of UNI Europa. (3) The federation's *secretariats* in Brussels are responsible for the day-to-day business, the implementations of work programs, representation and the organising of meetings and events. In the case of ETUC, approximately 52 persons are working for the secretariat, 24 for IndustriAll, and 18 for UNI Europa. (4) The fourth type of body characterizes smaller working groups or committees for special political, sectorial or geographical responsibilities. They consist of representatives from affiliates, meet at least twice a year and are the core of what can be called the work structure of the federations because political and organisational decisions that reach the executive boards are usually discussed and prepared in these committees.

The structures of all European federations seem to be similar at first glance. However, there are important differences in these work structures. The committees of the ETUC consist of different working groups that are primarily structured by the current priorities of policies in the European Union. Some working groups are purely ETUC bodies; others are part of tripartite bodies (social dialogue committees, advisory bodies). Now, there are approximately 28 working groups or committees in the ETUC.[10]

10 Working groups and committees on: (1) Economic and Social crisis; (2) Monetary and Fiscal Policies; (3) Economic and Social Cohesion / Structural Funds; (4) Financial Transaction Tax (FTT); (5) European Social Dialogue; (6) Industrial Policy; (7) European Corporate Governance; (8) Collective Bargaining and Wage Policy; (9) EWC / Workers' Rights Information and Consultation;

The work structure of IndustriAll relies on three pillars: policy committees, sectorial committees, and regional committees. In the field of policy, there are three policy committees[11] and four 'horizontal' committees.[12] Additionally, IndustriAll is a social partner in joint bodies with employer federations of special branches. There are now 11 sectorial social committees and 1 intersectorial social dialogue where IndustriAll is involved.[13] There are at least 12 sectorial committees[14] and eight regional committees.[15]

In contrast, the work structure of UNI Europa relies on different sectors. Now, there are 13 sectorial sub-organisations.[16] The biggest of these sectorial organisations are UNI Europa Finance (1.2 million members) and UNI Europa Commerce (2.2 million members). The primary difference in the sectorial structure of IndustriAll is that these sectors are not subcommittees but relatively autonomous organisations with their own names, their own decision bodies and their own subcommittees. The confederation UNI Europa is only a clip that unites relatively autonomous sectorial organisations on a regional level. The reason for this structure is the history of UNI Global as a merger of many very different Global union federations. Because UNI Europa is the regional organisation of UNI Global in Europe, the sectorial organisations in Europe are also regional sub-organisations of the sectorial organisations of UNI Global. Therefore, UNI Europa Finance is both a sectorial organisation of UNI Europa and a regional organisation of UNI Global Finance. The sectorial organisations are also social partners in the sectorial social dialogues. UNI Europa Finance is, for instance, a social partner in three social dialogue committees,[17] UNI Europa Media and Entertainment and Arts (MEA)

---

(10) Restructuring; (11) Labour Market Policy; (12) Education, Training and Lifelong Learning; (13) Youth and Employment; (14) Free Movement of Workers; (15) Migration; (16) Interregional Trade Union Councils (IRTUCs) and Interregional Cooperation; (17) Smart Regulation; (18) Public Procurement; (19) Public Services; (20) Posting of Workers; (21) Social Progress Protocol; (22) Temporary Agency Work; (23) Gender Equality; (24) Lesbian, Gay, Bisexual and Transgender Rights; (25) Disability; (26) Social Protection; (27) Health & Safety; (28) Energy Climate Change.

11 (1) Collective Bargaining Committee; (2) Industrial Policy Committee; (3) Company Policy Committee.

12 (1) Equal Opportunities: (2) Youth: (3) Training and Education; (4) Health and Safety.

13 Sectorial Social Committees: (1) Textile Clothing; (2) Footwear; (3) Tanning Leather; (4) Steel; (5) Metal Industry; (6) Shipbuilding; (7) Chemical Industry; (8) Extractive Industries; (9) Paper; (10) Electricity; (11) Gas; Intersectorial Committee: European Network for Silica (NEPSI).

14 Permanent: (1) Textile, Leather, Clothing; (2) Basic Metals; (3) Pharma; (4) Information and Communication Technology (ICT); (5) Mechanical Engineering; (6) Automotive, (7) Aerospace; (8) Shipbuilding; (9) Chemical and Basic Materials; (10) Energy, and ad-hoc: (1) Defence and (2) Rail.

15 (1) Benelux; (2) British Irish; (3) Central Region; (4) Eastern Region; (5) Nordic Baltic; (6) South; (7) Southeast; (8) Southwest.

16 Sectorial Organisations: (1) Cleaning / Security; (2) Commerce; (3) Finance; (4) Gaming; (5) Graphical & Packaging; (6) Hair & Beauty; (7) ICTs; (8) Media—Entertainment & Arts; (9) Post & Logistics; (10) Sport; (11) Temp & Agency Workers; (12) Tourism; (13) Health and Care.

17 I.e. social dialogues in the banking sector and insurance industry; Social Dialogue with central banks.

are partners in two.[18] In total, all sectorial organisations currently cover approximately ten sectorial social dialogues.[19]

4.3. Historical Integration of Trade Unions from New Member States

For decades, ETUC and ETUFs were geographically limited to the region west of the 'Iron curtain', but after 1990, they also integrated trade unions in Central Eastern and Southeastern Europe. Therefore, these trade unions had the potential opportunity to participate in the decision-making processes of the European federations. A question arises regarding how this integration was specifically designed and what consequences it had on the cooperation of trade unions in Europe and on the politics of the European Trade Union Federations.

Historically, one of the predecessors of IndustriAll, the European Metalworkers' Federation (EMF), has played an important pioneering role in the integration of trade unions from Central Eastern Europe. In contrast to the ETUC and to other ETUFs, the EMF integrated Central Eastern Europe's trade unions shortly after 1990 as full members. Between 1990 and 1991, Vasas Szakszervezeti Szövetsé (VASAS) from Hungary, the metalworkers' branch of Niezależny Samorządny Związek Zawodowy Solidarność (NZZ Solidarność) from Poland, and Odborový svaz KOVO (OS KOVO), the Czechoslovakian metalworkers' union joined the EMF.[20] There were, however, also disputes about this relatively fast enlargement. In some trade unions, there was a concern that the full integration of these trade unions could complicate the approach of a common collective bargaining policy in Europe because of the very large differences in wages, working times and working conditions.[21] Another dispute was about the competencies: British trade unions wanted to see the involvement of American trade unions through the International Metalworkers' Federation (IMF) because they were concerned about the dominance of the large German union IG Metall and feared an attempt to expand the very specific German system of industrial relations to Central Eastern Europe.[22] EMCEF, the second biggest predecessor of IndustriAll, enlarged its structures in the second half of the 1990s. This federation was not founded until 1996. However, one of the predecessors of EMCEF, the European Miners' Federation, developed strong cooperation

18 Social dialogues in performing arts and audiovisual branches.

19 In addition to those already mentioned: commerce, hairdressing services, post services, private security services, cleaning services.

20 Interview with the former general secretary of EMF, Germany, BT/EMF1 13 October 2010.

21 Minutes of the 59th meeting of the EMF executive committee, 90/03/22, 5/EMBA 030011.

22 Minutes of the 67th meeting of the EMF executive committee, 91/11/21, 5/EMBA 030011.

with trade unions from Central Eastern Europe because they had partnered early the International Miners' Federation.[23]

The ETUC contained no members from Central Eastern Europe in the first half of the 1990s. Although it created a committee (the 'Forum Eastern Europe') where the trade unions could cooperate,[24] the ETUC was not willing to give Central Eastern European trade unions full membership until the congress of 1995. The reason for this reluctance was a discussion on the geographical coverage of ETUC and, thus, of the sectorial ETUFs. Both very narrow (only trade unions from European Community member states) and very wide (Russia and Commonwealth of Independent States (CIS)-States)[25] concepts were advanced. Finally, a compromise was reached, stating that trade unions could join if their countries had pre-accession agreements with the EU. Other federations, such as EMF and EMCEF, adapted this compromise later.[26] According to this compromise, ETUC and IndustriAll unite trade unions from all enlargement countries and also from the candidate (Turkey, Serbia, Macedonia, Montenegro) and potential candidate countries (Bosnia, Albania, Kosovo). Unions from former Soviet Union countries who are not candidates for EU membership are explicitly not included (Ukraine, Moldova, Russia, Georgia).[27]

According to an ETUC official, there was a conflict between trade unions from Central Eastern Europe and the ETUC secretariat about their competencies in the European Social Dialogue in the 1990s. Central Eastern European unions, after they became members after 1995, demanded full access and full decision rights in the European Social Dialogue. However, ETUC officials did not share this position; they thought that these rights were only possible based on EU rules. Such participation could be possible only after an EU-accession of their countries, not before.[28] Another ETUC official also reported about the difficulties to integrate trade unions from Central Eastern Europe into the work of the Economic and Social Committee. Officially, there was no possibility until the accession of their countries. However, there were attempts

23 Rütters, Peter: Skizze zur Geschichte der Bergarbeiter- und der Lebensmittelarbeiter-Internationale [Sketch of history of miners and food workers' international], in: Friedrich-Ebert-Stiftung, IUL und IB, Protokolle und Berichte, Bonn: Friedrich-Ebert-Stiftung, 2001, here .p. 25.

24 Gläser, Cyril: Europäische Einheitsgewerkschaft zwischen lähmender Überdehnung und umfassender Repräsentativität, EGB-Strukturen und die Herausforderung der Erweiterung [European united trade union between paralyzing overstretching and comprehensive representativeness, ETUC structures and the challenge of enlargement], in: Mittag, Jürgen (eds): Deutsche Gewerkschaften und europäische Integration im 20. Jahrhundert, Mitteilungsblatt des Instituts für soziale Bewegungen, 2009, no. 42, here p. 228.

25 Dürmeier, Silvia / Grundheber-Pilgram, Alfons: Der Europäische Gewerkschaftsbund und die Europäisierung der industriellen Beziehungen. Handbuch der Gewerkschaften in Europa [The European Trade Union Confederation and the Europeanization of industrial relations. Handbook of Trade Unions in Europe], Brussels, 1998, here p. 14.

26 Minutes of the 72nd meeting of EMF executive committee, 94/07/01, 5/EMBA 030013.

27 These trade unions cooperate in the framework of Pan European Regional Council in the ITUC

28 Interview with the deputy general secretary of ETUC, Belgium, JN/ETUC1 3 October 2013.

to cooperate before enlargement, and the focus was on a good preparation of the accession process. Joint committees were created to support the founding of accession countries' own economic and social committees.[29]

With respect to the disputes between political orientations or the 'new' vs. 'old' trade union division, the European federations took no position for one side. They cooperated with and integrated all unions alike under the condition that they were democratic and independent from the state and the employers.[30]

With the accession of trade unions from Central Eastern Europe, the number of members in the European Federations increased significantly and doubled almost in the case of EMF in the 1990s. This led to problems of the homogenisation of trade union structures at the European level which particularly concerned the policies of fees: the trade unions from Central Eastern Europe negotiated in the cases of both industrial federations (EMF, EMCEF and ETUC-TCL) and ETUC special membership fees because of the substantial differences in wages and prices in their countries.

European federations existed in a complex situation: On one hand, they did not want to have financial barriers to cooperation with Central Eastern European trade unions. On the other hand, they did not want to have a patchwork of membership fees or to make exceptions to the standard fees.[31] There were also trade unions in Western Europe that had financial problems. The lack of financial resources was one of the barriers for a fast accession of Central Eastern European trade unions. In the case of ETUC, the financial question was also described as one reason for the reluctance of ETUC concerning a fast membership of Central Eastern European trade unions described before. In the case of EMF, only in 2005 did the first Bulgarian trade unions join the federation, primarily for financial reasons. The accession of Baltic unions was delayed until the year of the dissolution of the EMF in 2012 because the Baltic unions could not pay the minimum fee of 5,200 Euros per year.[32]

The increase of members also led to an increase in the plurality of different interests within the federations. To both encourage the participation of as many members as possible and not to affect an effective policymaking within the federation, a reform of decision-making structures was needed. In EMF and EMCEF, a number of reforms in the internal structure were implemented. To tighten the decision-making, 'Steering Committees' were founded to represent regions rather than national unions.

The enlargement of European trade union federations intensified the discussions on the structure of these associations in the 1990s. Against the background of new integration initiatives by the commission under Jacques Delors, trade unions from

29 Interview with ETUC secretary, formerly responsible for European Economic and Social Committee, Belgium, TJ/ETUC4 3 October 2013.
30 Interview with the former general secretary of EMF, Germany, RK/EMF3 15 October 2010.
31 Interview with the former general secretary of EMF, Germany, PS/EMF4 20 September 2010.
32 Ibid.

southern Europe tended to promote more centralised supranational associations. In this concept, national trade unions should have fewer competencies and should play a more subordinate role *vis-à-vis* European federation levels. Trade unions from central and northern Europe, however, promoted a more federalist concept in which European federations should only improve their competencies in specific areas, and new competencies and possibilities should be created by the commission (e.g., European Works Councils). From this perspective, national member organisations should have dominant decision-making competencies.[33] The Central Eastern European trade unions tended to support the side of the 'federalists', who could realise their concept in this dispute. However, they did not play a dominant role in these discussions.[34]

The difficulties that resulted from an increased number of member organisations, on one hand, and a stagnating financial basis, on the other hand, led to increased pressure to merge European industry federations. According to Platzer / Müller, the financial and structural dilemma that resulted from the accession of Central Eastern European trade unions was an important reason for the creation of EMCEF.[35] In addition, these dilemmas could be seen as one of the reasons for the merger of EMCEF, EMF and ETUC-TCL in 2012.

The integration of trade unions from Central Eastern Europe was completely different in the case of UNI Europa. Their accession took place in the framework of the International Trade Union Federations that merged in 2000 to create UNI Global.[36] UNI Europa is currently a regional organisation of UNI Global, and it also includes trade unions from Armenia, Azerbaijan, Belarus, Georgia, Russia and Ukraine.

4.4. Affiliates from NMS and their Reasons for Membership

Officials in the secretariats in Brussels see the most important reason for weakness and fragmentation rooted in the organisational model of trade unions in NMS. As described in the preceding chapter on 'Trade Unions and Industrial Relations in the EU Member States of Eastern Enlargement', in most NMS, there is a 'bottom–up-system' of trade union organisation that hinders the development of stronger unions at sectorial or national levels.

---

33 Among the controversial issues within the EMF were a European direct membership for trade unionists, the size and composition of the executive committee and the political competencies of the steering committee.

34 See for, example, the so called 'Rome-process' in the EMF, the paper on the evaluation and discussions at the seminar in Rome, in: Documents of the 88th meeting of EMF executive committee, 2000/09/16, 5/EMBA 030017.

35 Platzer, Hans-Wolfgang / Müller Torsten: Die globalen und europäischen Gewerkschaftsverbände [Global and European Trade Union Federations], Berlin: edition sigma, 2009, here p. 485.

36 Lecher, Wolfgang / Optenhögel, Uwe: Wirtschaft, Gesellschaft und Gewerkschaften in Mittel- und Osteuropa [Economy, Society and Trade Unions in Central East Europe], Köln: Bund-Verlag, 1995, here p 363.

As was described, trade unions in many NMS are divided between different lines. Based on a system of trade union pluralism, there is fragmentation based on political orientations, between 'old' and 'new' unions, and on the company level because the strength of sectorial organisations is limited. However, it must be mentioned that interviewed officials in the secretariats regard the differences that may be rooted in the different history between 'old' and 'new' trade unions to be irrelevant. Thus, there are old trade unions that are seen as much more independent in the representation of worker interests than trade unions that call themselves independent.[37]

There is another important aspect regarding the involvement of trade unions from NMS in European trade union federations: Some trade unions are more strongly organised on an interprofessional level and some on a sectorial level. For instance, according to an ETUC official responsible for NMS, NZZ Solidarność is stronger at an interprofessional level; thus, their participation in ETUC is stronger, whereas Ogólnopolskie Porozumienie Związków Zawodowych (OPZZ) is stronger at sectorial levels and more involved in the sectorial ETUFs.[38]

Officials in the secretariats in Brussels see the strong desire and reason for membership of trade unions from NMS in ideology and, in fact, that their officials are convinced that European cooperation is important and that the growing role of the EU in national policy requires an adequate association on the trade union side.[39]

According to officials in the secretariats in Brussels, the most important substantial benefit is the fact that the trade unions gain access to the policy making process in Brussels. In most cases, they only receive information about policies in Europe. For small and financially weak unions, this access via European federations is even more important than for large unions. In contrast to large unions (for example, German ones), affiliates from NMS have no resources to pay for their own liaison offices in Brussels.[40]

These assessments correspond to the results of the survey. Most see the access to information and experiences as one of the most important advantages of the collaboration with European umbrella organisations.[41] Most state, in addition, that their unions indirectly consult the European Commission and Parliament through ETUC and that their union represents the interests at the European level among other (42 respondents) or exclusively (19 respondents) via European umbrella federations.[42] According to trade union officials from NMS, the ETUC and ETUFs are the most important instruments to influence the EU level because direct links to EU institutions, beyond contacts

37 Interview with the deputy general secretary of IndustriALL, responsible for the area of Central Eastern Europe, Belgium, LT/IA1 21 May 2013.
38 Interview with the deputy general secretary of ETUC, Belgium, JN/ETUC1 3 October 2010.
39 Interview with the deputy general secretary of ETUC, Belgium, JN/ETUC1 3 October 2010.
40 Ibid.
41 Results of the questionnaire national trade unions, Q28 2013. The results are from the research project 'Europeanization of Trade Unions in the Countries of the Eastern Enlargement'.
42 Results of the questionnaire national trade unions, Q19 2013.

with European politicians from their country, particularly in the case of smaller unions, hardly exist.[43]

According to officials in the secretariats in Brussels, unions from NMS are increasingly interested in information about planned directives and about how to address these policies. This interest includes information regarding the experiences of other trade unions in the implementation of new directives.[44] At the same time, the ETUFs offer the opportunity to exchange experiences and obtain support from other trade unions in building up the trade union organisations. There is extensive support for the development of trade union structures in Central Eastern Europe both on a multilateral level via the European associations and on a bilateral level, where European associations are not involved. This support is often organised in the framework of common projects that are also sometimes co-sponsored by other institutions (for instance, EU, International Labour Organisation (ILO), and national and European Foundations).

In a sense, membership helps unions to obtain financial support from the EU; if trade unions from NMS want to conduct projects sponsored by the EU, a 'letter of support' from the federations helps in the applications. Some officials in Brussels, however, consider this strategy—to apply for EU projects and gain from financial EU support—to be underdeveloped. Therefore, in an interview, an official in Brussels with Italian origin asked why trade unions from new member states compared with other unions do not use this instrument more often.[45] This assessment corresponds with results of the survey: Only trade union officials from Bulgaria and Romania mentioned EU funding as a positive effect on the work of their unions.[46]

One explanation could be the fact that the applicant union has to co-finance at least 20% of any project. Thus, these projects can be seen as a provision of additional support but not as a free 'source of income' because the unions are required to pay their share.

4.5. Political Preferences and Focus of Activities

For officials in Brussels, it was difficult to make statements about specific claims and demands and political preferences and priorities of trade unions from the NMS because they described their participation in the federations as on the whole 'upgradeable'

43 Results of the questionnaire national trade unions, Q8 and Q10 2013.

44 Interview with the deputy general secretary of IndustriALL, responsible for the area of Central Eastern Europe, Belgium, LT/IA1 21 May 2013.

45 Interview with ETUC's secretary, responsible for migration policy, collective bargaining coordination, Belgium, MC/ETUC5 3 October 2013.

46 Results of the questionnaire national trade unions, Romania, Gn11 Q4 and Bulgaria, Gn03 Q4 2013.

or not very active.[47] Another problem emphasised by ETUC officials is the fact that trade unions in the NMS are marked by union pluralism and a division of unions along political lines. For example, in the case of Poland, political positions held by representatives of OPZZ (the old communist union) were seen as more radical than those of NZZ Solidarność. In Hungary, there is a whole spectrum of political directions in the trade union movement, similar to southern and Western Europe (Italy, France, etc.).[48]

According to ETUC and ETUF officials in Brussels, trade unions from NMS consider campaigns against political attacks on workers' rights as important. Trade union representatives from NMS also strongly support campaigns against precarious work; measures against the crisis were connected with a liberalisation of labour market regulation since 2008.[49]

The central focus of trade unions from NMS is on wage policy because incomes are so low that workers can barely pay for their basic needs. In relation to wage policy, all other questions (such as working time, vocational training, health and safety at work) are second-rate. In this context, trade unions from NMS strongly support a further Europeanization of wage policy and the concept of a statutory minimum wage. As a Romanian trade union official expressed it:

> From my point of view, a policy area in which the European Union should be more present in the member states is the wage policy. We think there should be a minimum wage established by Brussels and adopted by all member states.[50]

A controversial discussion inside the ETUC pertained to the demand for a European minimum wage. A growing number of affiliates saw the need for the European regulation of minimum wages. In this discussion, there were supporters (among other unions from Germany and Spain) and critics (unions from Italy and Nordic countries) of such an initiative.[51] According to an ETUC official in Brussels, trade unions from NMS mostly sided with the supporters of European minimum wages in this discussion:

> Eastern European trade unions strongly supported statutory minimum wages. However, they also realised that there is resistance from unions that support a negotiation model. Therefore, they supported the final document of the ETUC. In the internal debates, however, they were strong advocates of statutory minimum wages[52].

47 Interview with the deputy general secretary of IndustriALL, responsible for the area of Central Eastern Europe, Belgium, LT/IA1 21 May 2013.

48 Interview with ETUC's secretary, responsible for Workers Participation and European Works Councils, Belgium, WK/ETUC2 3 October 2013.

49 Interview with the deputy general secretary of ETUC, Belgium, JN/ETUC1 3 October 2013.

50 Results of the questionnaire national trade unions, Romania, Gn26 Q5 2013.

51 Eldring, Line / Alsos, Kristin: European Minimum Wage. A Nordic Outlook FAFO-report 2012/17, Oslo, 2012, here p. 58. The reason for opposition by Italian and Nordic trade unions against a European minimum wage is a general rejection of state intervention in wage negotiations and the favouring of autonomous agreements between trade unions and employers.

52 Interview with the deputy general secretary of ETUC, Belgium, JN/ETUC1 3 October 2013.

According to Kohl / Platzer, the reason for the support of statutory minimum wages is the weak structure of sectorial collective bargaining in most NMS and the important substitute role for collective agreements that statuary minimum wages play in NMS.[53] Statements of Romanian and Bulgarian trade union officials, who demanded an EU-wide equal minimum wage, show, in addition, that there is hope that a European regulation on wages could support an increase of wages in NMS and close the immense gap of wages between Central Eastern and Western Europe.[54] For most trade union officials in the survey, the coordination of bargaining policy with the aim of harmonisation is also the most important area, where European collaboration between trade unions should be intensified.[55]

According to ETUF officials, trade unions from NMS strongly support a further Europeanization of collective bargaining in other areas, and they are strong supporters of the European social dialogue. This statement corresponds to results of our survey that shows that many union officials from NMS see participation in the social dialogue as one of the most important positive influences of the EU:

> An example of the positive impact of EU is the existence of the European social dialogue[56].

This assessment also corresponds to the results of another study, which found that unions from NMS have a much more positive attitude toward the results of the European social dialogue than unions from other parts of Europe.[57]

The common explanation for favouring the European social dialogue by trade unions from NMS is observed in the fact that its outcomes could substitute the lack of standards in NMS.[58] However, according to officials in Brussels, this is a less important reason because topics discussed in the European social dialogue are primarily not the priorities of trade unions from NMS. The most important reason, therefore, is that the European social dialogue negotiations can also open the door for a national social dialogue in NMS on other subjects. Employers in NMS are more willing to talk about the implementation of European initiatives on a national level if a European agreement with European employers is in place. According to an ETUC official, the Social

53 Kohl, Heribert / Platzer, Hans Wolfgang: Mindestlöhne in Mittelosteuropa [Minimum Wages in Central Eastern Europe], in: Schulten, Thorsten / Bispinck, Reinhard / Schäfer, Claus (eds): Mindestlöhne in Europa [Minimum Wages in Europe], Hamburg: VSA, 2006, here p. 173.

54 Results of the questionnaire national trade unions, Romania, Gn09 Q38, Gn14 Q21, Gn20 Q28, Gn23 Q33, Gn26 Q5 and Q6, Bulgaria, Gn05 Q6 2013.

55 Results of the questionnaire national trade unions, Q8 2013.

56 Results of the questionnaire national trade unions, Slovakia, Gn04 Q4 2013.

57 Busemeyer, Marius / Kellermann, Christian / Petring, Alexander / Stuchlik, Andrej: Politische Positionen zum Europäischen Wirtschafts- und Sozialmodell. eine Landkarte der Interessen [Political Positions on the European Economic and Social Model. A Map of Interests], in: Internationale Politikanalyse Europäische Politik, 2006, August.

58 Lafoucrière, Cèline / Magnusson, Lars: Social Dialogue. The last guardian of European solidarity?, in: Magnusson, Lars / Stråth, Bo (eds): European Solidarities. Tension and contentions of a concept, Brussels: Peter Lang, 2007.

Dialogue topic of work-related 'stress' was not as important for trade unions from new member states because they have to fight first for wages and working times that allow workers to live. However, the discussions on stress were important for them to contact employers in their countries.[59]

Another interesting aspect is the fact that according to ETUC officials, unions from NMS prefer a tripartite social dialogue. A bipartite, autonomous dialogue between trade unions and employer associations hardly exists in NMS. Therefore, for these unions, a dialogue without the commission was something completely new, and there was scepticism about the development of such an autonomous social dialogue in Europe.[60]

Trade unions from NMS were always more sceptical about protectionist approaches. Thus, even in the 1990s, unions from the Czech Republic and Slovakia were strong supporters of trade liberalisation in Europe, whereas unions in Western Europe were more afraid of wage and social dumping and wanted to prevent such tendencies through protection measures and transitional rules.[61]

A controversial issue was the free movement of workers. The conflicts at Viking, Rueffert and Laval ended at the European Court of Justice in Brussels, which made some decisions that were strongly criticised by trade unions.[62] Viking was the first decision in which the Court took a position on the relationship between the right to strike and the freedom of capital. The decision on Laval and Rueffert, in contrast, was an interpretation of the so-called posting directive of 1996 and directed the focus of European trade unions to a revision of this directive.

According to an official of IndustriAll who manages collective bargaining policies, a majority of trade unionists in NMS took the position that the directive on posted workers should not be changed.[63] However, this position had no influence on the policy of the federation because in the meetings of the collective bargaining committee, trade unionists from these countries were rarely present. At the end, there was a common position supported also by trade unions from NMS. In contrast, an official of the ETUC stated that a common position existed right from the beginning, and there was no division between west and east in the ETUC.[64]

A similar controversial subject was the 'directive on services in the internal market' (Bolkestein directive). According to an ETUC official, at the beginning of the discussion

59 Interview with ETUC's secretary, responsible for migration policy, collective bargaining coordination, Belgium, MC/ETUC5 3 October 2013.

60 Interview with ETUC's secretary, responsible for European Social Dialogue and gender equality, non-discrimination policies, Belgium, CS/ETUC6 3 October 2013.

61 Minutes of the 70th meeting of EMF executive committee, 93/11/04, 5/EMBA 030011.

62 Warneck, Wiebke: The ECJ decisions, in: Bücker, Andreas / Warneck, Wiebke (eds): Viking–Laval–Rüffert. Consequences and policy perspectives, Brussels: ETUI ailbl, 2010, here p. 7.

63 Interview with IndustriALL's secretary, responsible for collective bargaining coordination, Belgium, EH/IA3 21 May 2013.

64 Interview with the deputy general secretary of ETUC, Belgium, JN/ETUC1 3 October 2013.

in the ETUC, there were also voices from NMS that supported the removal of barriers for service providers without the demand of minimum standards.[65] However, in the subsequent discussions, it was possible to come to a common position that the directive would not be supported without minimum standards. Later, at the demonstrations against the directive, trade unions from NMS were present. Reluctant at the beginning, they became forerunners in the ETUC campaign against the directive.[66]

Regarding further political preferences, a study by Stuchlik, Kellermann et al. in 2006 found that trade unions from NMS are strong supporters of a European tax coordination to prevent a 'race to the bottom'. Furthermore, trade unions from NMS support a more expensive fiscal policy to allow for more investments.[67] However, the results of our survey show that some trade union officials from NMS, on the contrary, support some austerity measures to reduce public debt:

> Unless we (Slovakia) were member of the EU, we would have much bigger economic problems than we have; EU teaches us about the discipline in public finances. That is a positive impact[68].

An ETUC official stated that for trade unions from NMS, especially from Poland, climate policy was an important question. Polish trade unions tried actively to influence and change the ETUC's policy regarding climate and carbon to protect their industrial workplaces. In this process, Polish trade unions cooperated with other trade unions from the region to actively change the decision made by ETUC.[69]

In addition, there is a rising interest in other subjects. According to officials in Brussels, an important subject that trade unions from Central Eastern Europe stress in the Social Dialogue meetings is the lack of systems for vocational trainings in their

65 Interview with ETUC's secretary, responsible for Workers Participation and European Works Councils, Belgium, WK/ETUC2 3 October 2013. Furthermore, trade unions officials from NMS mentioned 'intense discussions' on the directives of services and posting workers: Results of the questionnaire national trade unions, Czech Republic, Gn14 Q38, 2013. Furthermore, it was 'difficult to establish a common position': Results of the questionnaire national trade unions, Poland, Gn11 45, 2013. However, they are stretching the fact that at the end, 'division between the old and the new member states was overcome', and a common position was found: Results of the questionnaire national trade unions, Poland, Gn11 Q45, 2013.

66 Bernaciak, Magdalena: East-West European labour transnationalisms. Rivalry or joint mobilization? in: Bieler, Andreas / Lindberg, Ingemar (eds): Global restructuring, labour and the challenges for transnational solidarity, London: Routledge, 2011, here p. 35.

67 Busemeyer, Marius / Kellermann, Christian / Petring, Alexander / Stuchlik, Andrej: Politische Positionen zum Europäischen Wirtschafts- und Sozialmodell. eine Landkarte der Interessen [Political Positions on the European Economic and Social Model. A Map of Interests], in: Internationale Politikanalyse Europäische Politik, 2006, August.

68 Results of the questionnaire national trade unions, Slovakia, Gn12 4 2013.

69 Interview with the deputy general secretary of ETUC, Belgium, JN/ETUC1 3 October 2013.

countries.[70] There was a wide interest and active participation in the process of the revision of the EWC directive.[71]

According to ETUC officials, migration policies have become a more important focus of the political activities of Polish, Czech and Hungarian trade unions. The reason is seen in the fact that these countries are confronted with the increased immigration of workers from non EU-countries.[72]

4.6. Involvement in the Structures of the Federations

According to a majority of trade union officials from NMS, the cooperation with European umbrella federations functions well. In addition, the survey shows that they are satisfied with the work of their union in the European federations.[73] Further results show that the most important means of communication between Brussels and the national affiliates is contact via email.[74] This is an expression of the two most important difficulties in the personal participation of trade union representatives from NMS in the work of the federations: the problem of travel costs and the problem of language fluency. Communication via email can solve these problems because there are no associated travel costs, and easy electronic translation is possible.

Union officials from NMS also believe that their union provides an important contribution to the overall interest representation of trade unions at the EU level.[75] This assessment, however, is in contrast to the assessment of officials of the European federations. Although they see differences between the various work structures and fields of activities, most respondents in Brussels described the general involvement and the attitude towards the development of political positions from NMS trade unions as not very active or significant.[76] It makes sense, therefore, to move from a general assessment to a concrete analysis of participation in the working structures and activity areas.

The influence of affiliated unions in the European umbrella organisations is determined by their size because the delegates in the highest bodies, such as congresses, correspond with the number of members they have. Therefore, the Deutscher

70 Interview with ETUC's secretary, responsible for migration policy, collective bargaining coordination, Belgium, MC/ETUC5 3 October 2013.

71 Interview with ETUC's secretary, responsible for Workers Participation and European Works Councils, Belgium, WK/ETUC2 3 October 2013.

72 The rising number of people from 'third countries' entering the EU via NMS. Poland is becoming a migration country; in the last three years, more than one million people came to Poland (mostly from Ukraine) to work in the EU.

73 Results of the questionnaire national trade unions, Q32 and Q22 2013.

74 Results of the questionnaire national trade unions, Q24a, b, c 2013.

75 In 2013, 66% of respondents think that their union provides an important contribution; only 15% think not. In the 2007 survey, these figures were 71% and 29%: Results of the questionnaire national trade unions, Q30 2007 and 2013.

76 Interview with the deputy general secretary of IndustriALL, responsible for the area of Central Eastern Europe, Belgium, LT/IA1 21 May 2013.

Gewerkschaftsbund (DGB), with approximately 6 million members, has more delegates and influence in the ETUC than the Bulgarian federation CL Podkrepa, with approximately 150,000 affiliated workers. The same is true for IndustriAll, where IG Metall has approximately 2 million members and the sections of CL Podkrepa have together approximately 13,000 affiliated workers. However, the number of delegates does not fully reflect the membership rise in the countries because there is a special balancing key. Therefore, countries with several small unions have an advantage here. A country with a plurality of trade unions will have more delegates because every organisation has the right to send at least one delegate. Therefore, countries with trade union pluralism have more delegates.

Table 4-2: Number of Delegates in the Congress / Regional Conference

	ETUC	IndustriAll	Uni Europa
Bulgaria	6	9	0
Czech Republic	4	9	1
Hungary	16	8	4
Poland	10	11	6
Romania	13	17	0
Slovak Republic	3	5	5

Without observers, according to lists of delegates of the last congresses (Athens 2011, Toulouse 2011, Brussels 2012), thanks to officials for ETUC, IndustriAll and Martina Hartung for Uni Europa.

The secretariats in Brussels handle daily business. They coordinate the activities of the associations, prepare meetings (in particular, executive committee meetings) and are responsible for implementing all tasks that are given by the executive bodies of the associations. They also represent the association to the 'outside', holding contact to European institutions, employer organisations, and other institutions and multinational companies. In the ETUC secretariat, there are approximately 50 employees (7 officials, 12 consultants and the rest administrative personnel). Only one of them, Josef Niemiec (NZZ Solidarność / Poland), is from an NMS. He is, however, in the rank of Deputy General Secretary. In the secretariat of IndustriALL, there are 24 employees but none from an NMS.

Finally, yet importantly, the decision-making of the federations is in the hands of the executive committees. These bodies are also responsible for creating a mandate body in cases of transnational negotiations, for instance, in the Social Dialogue. They hold meetings regularly twice a year (Uni Europa once a year).

The Executive Committee of ETUC is composed of representatives from the affiliates (in proportion to their membership between 1–5 representatives per affiliate) and from sectorial ETUFs. The Executive Committee of IndustriALL is also open for every affiliate. The structure is currently in a transition period because of the merger in 2012.[77] Although the executive committees of these federations are open for all affiliates, the participation of trade unions from NMS was described as weak by officials in Brussels.[78] The lack of financial resources to pay for travel costs is seen as the most important reason for weak participation. For all trade unionists from NMS, but especially for Bulgarians and Romanians, travel costs are a significant barrier to strong participation. For the ETUC executive committee, in contrast with political committees and working groups, there is no financial support for travel costs from the European Union. As Romanian and Slovakian trade union officials stated:

> I only participate when the travel funding is granted, and this is happening less and less recently.[79]
>
> ...we do not have activities at the EU level—only if we were invited to participate in a particular meeting or activity and at least travel costs would be repaid to us[80].

The second most important reason is the language barrier. The commission provides translation services for only six languages. Sometimes, Czech or Polish are among these languages, but trade unionists from other NMS have to bring their own translators if they cannot speak one of these languages, which imposes an additional financial burden.

The Executive Committee of UNI Europa has a completely different structure. It consists of (1) regional representatives, (2) the presidents of the sectorial organisations and (3) representatives of special groups. There are now five representatives from NMS out of 70 total representatives: one for the UNI graphical section, three for the area (Central Europe, South Eastern Europe and the Baltic States) and one from the UNI Europa women's committee.

The participation in the other working structures of the federations is very different and depends on many factors, particularly on the aforementioned different shape of working structures of the ETUFs. It makes sense, here, to go into more detail.

In ETUC, the working structure relies on working groups and subcommittees accepted by the executive committee. There are permanent working groups and ad hoc working groups. Meetings occur between two and four times per year. The subjects of the working groups rely on the political priorities of the commission. Some committees are pure ETUC working groups, some are part of a tripartite body or are advisory boards of the commission.

---

77 Because of a transition rule, every affiliate (even very small unions with some 100 affiliated workers) is allowed to send delegates to the executive committee.

78 In IndustriALL, only five of 45 organisations from Southeastern Europe sent somebody to the first executive meeting in 2013. From the Eastern region, the participation was better, but even here, not all affiliates sent delegates. Only 78 of 200 delegates came to the meeting in Brussels.

79 Results of the questionnaire national trade unions, Romania, Gn03 Q23 2013.

80 Results of the questionnaire national trade unions, Slovakia, Gn12 Q18 2013.

As mentioned previously, in the ETUC, there are currently 28 committees or working groups. In some committees, the presence is stronger; in some, weaker. An extraordinarily strong presence was observed for collective bargaining committees and for gender equality groups; a somewhat weaker presence has been observed until now in the migration policy group. Other than these relatively unimportant differences, the presence of representatives from NMS is generally strong in every committee according to ETUC officials. This is because there is a large difference between the executive committee and these subgroups. In the executive committee, the number of trade union representatives depends on the size of the confederation. The representatives have to pay for travel costs. In the working groups and committees, in contrast, there is only one representative per country, but the commission pays the travel and accommodation costs. This is, on one hand, a problem for countries with trade union pluralism, as in NMS. In these countries, the unions have to agree on one representative. These unions criticise this regulation, saying it supports the Northern and Central European model of trade union unity. On the other hand, the commission's financial support gives unions from NMS the opportunity to participate. That is why participation from NMS in ETUC working groups is, in general, much better than in the executive committee.

There is also a type of regional committee in ETUC. For Central Eastern Europe, it is the so-called 'Visegrad cooperation', an annual meeting that takes place contemporaneously with the meeting of the governments of this region.[81] In addition, there is the cooperation of trade unions in Western Balkans. However, the regional cooperation in ETUC is not as strong as the regional committees in IndustriAll.

The working structure of IndustriALL is, as was mentioned, organised in three pillars: policy committees, sectorial committees and regional committees. In stark contrast to the ETUC structure, the commission does not pay travel costs for IndustriAll committees or working groups. The only exceptions here are the committees of sectorial social dialogue (see below) and meetings in connection with some programs or workshops supported by the European Union.

The policy committees are open to all members. Trade unions from NMS have the opportunity, here, to participate and to shape the policies of the federation. However, the participation is very different. There is the same problem with travel expenses and languages as with participation in executive committees. The policy committees are held in smaller rooms with fewer translation cabins, so the number of translated languages is very limited.

According to officials in Brussels, in the company policy committee, only one delegate from Romania, the Czech Republic and Slovakia participates somewhat regularly. Sometimes, a representative comes from Hungary and Poland, but no representatives

81 Interview with the deputy general secretary of ETUC, Be, JN/ETUC1 3 October 2013.

come from Slovenia, Bulgaria or the Western Balkan Countries. Therefore, officials describe the participation as low:

> Participation is still low, and we hope for the future, really, that every country in Eastern Europe can be represented in the company policy committee[82].

According to officials in Brussels, the most involved unions are OS KOVO from the Czech Republic, OZ KOVO from Slovakia and NZZ Solidarność from Poland. Officials from VASAS no longer attend, but recently, colleagues from Magyar Olaj- és Gázipari Bányász Szakszervezet (MOL), a small Hungarian company union, have attended. The reason for the participation is that this committee is working with European Works Councils. Trade unions from these countries are more affected than, for example, Bulgaria because multinational companies, covered by EWCs, are present there and the trade unions have to send representative to the EWC bodies. Nevertheless, the participation of these trade unions seems to have a more passive characteristic: '... [T]hey are there more to listen and to get information'[83].

Trade unions from NMS are not involved in the active preparation of the meetings of company policy committees. They have never participated in meetings of the steering committee of the company policy committee, the so-called 'selected working group'. As for meetings of the full committee, participants have to pay travel and accommodation costs in this body. Trade unions from NMS are, however, involved in the development of positions and documents in the area of company policy through email communication.

One reason for this reluctant participation could be that countries in Central Eastern Europe have been covered only since their accession to the EU in 2004 by the directive. Another reason could be the fact that whereas multinational companies have dependence on Central Eastern Europe, their headquarters are in Western Europe and so is the residence of the EWC body. Despite the less active role, according to officials of IndustriALL, it is very important that the trade unions from NMS participate in the company policy committee. Even merely 'listening' enables these unions to play a more active role in national debates. Therefore, they participated in debates on implementation of the revised EWC directive in their countries.

Similarly, in the Committee for Collective Bargaining (CCB) there is the problem of languages and travel expenses. Currently, there is an agreement in place that once a year, the meeting of the committee is organised in a new member state to ensure a greater involvement of trade unions in Central Eastern Europe. Meetings have been held in Prague, Sofia and other capitals in the NMS. Trade unions from NMS are participating in the committee for collective bargaining, but their involvement is also weak:

---

82 Interview with IndustriALL's secretary, responsible for European Works Councils, Belgium, CC/IA2 21 May 2013.

83 Ibid.

'They are the minority; they are not dominant, but they are there.'[84] The most involved union is, again, the Czech trade union OS KOVO; OZ KOVO and VASAS also attend the meetings relatively regularly. Representatives from Poland are rare. There are specialised subcommittees for special groups of workers, but trade unions from NMS are not involved in these subgroups. Like in the Committee for Collective Bargaining, there is a selected working group inside the Committee for Collective Bargaining that prepares the meetings and develops the political debates and positions. OS KOVO is the only trade union from NMS that participates in this board.

The involvement of trade unions from NMS in the sectorial social dialogue committees is much better than in the policy committees. This is (as was mentioned) because financial problems are not a factor; the European Commission pays for travel costs and even for hotel accommodation. The meetings of the social dialogue are therefore also important for policy making in IndustriALL because they also serve as places where coordination among trade unions and European meetings of their representatives is possible. Prior to every official committee meeting, there is another meeting, where participating trade unions meet to discuss not only the meeting but also other issues and topics concerning the policy of the federation. However, there is one problem with the social dialogue committees: There is only translation into three languages: English, French and a third language. This third language changes but is usually not a language from NMS, but a language, that is spoken by more people (like Spanish, Italian, German etc). The participation of trade unions from NMS is therefore dependent on whether they can send an official who speaks English or French:

> The Social Dialogues, they function, but participation depends on language ability.[85]

The obvious problems of participation in the policy committees are also factors in all sectorial and horizontal committees. As elsewhere, participation from NMS is generally weak and depends on the political issue. In the Sectorial Committee for Shipbuilding, the Polish trade unions are present because of the importance of the shipbuilding industry in Poland. In the Sectorial Committee for Information and Communication Technology (ICT), Romanian and Hungarian trade unions are involved because of the importance of this industry in their countries. Additionally, members of UNI Europa Finance describe the involvement of NMS trade unions in the sectorial social dialogue as strongly positive.[86]

According to officials of IndustriALL, the influence of trade unions from NMS on policy making in the sectorial social dialogue committees is very weak. 'Documents

84 Interview with IndustriALL's secretary, responsible for collective bargaining coordination, Belgium, EH/IA3 21 May 2013.
85 Interview with the deputy general secretary of IndustriALL, responsible for the area of Central Eastern Europe, Belgium, LT/IA1 21 May 2013.
86 Results of the questionnaire national trade unions, Poland, Gn01 Q10 2013.

sent by the committee are at the best taken note of, but there is hardly any feedback from NMS.'[87] Like for the policy committees, sectorial committees seem to have low significance and importance for trade unions from NMS.

In the IndustriALL regional committees, trade unions from NMS can participate in a better way because meetings take place in their region. There are three regional committees in which trade unions from NMS are involved: Northern Europe (Baltic states), Eastern Europe (unions from Poland, Hungary, the Czech Republic and Slovakia) and South Eastern Europe (unions from Bulgaria and Romania). The work of these committees is organised not by the secretariat in Brussels but by the trade unions in the region. It is, therefore, their decision how to organise the practical work.

IndustriAll officials described the work of the regional committee Eastern Europe as very good. The presidency is in the hands of OS KOVO, there are meetings every six months, and at the recent meetings, almost all trade unions were present. In the South East regional committee, the cooperation is not yet so intensive. The secretariat has to give more support and assistance. The presidency was, in 2013, in the hands of Federația Sindicală a Siderurgiștilor METAROM (FSS Metarom, Romania), and it was planned for Sindikalna Federazia Metalicy (SF Metalicy, Bulgaria) in 2014. The cooperation there is in the stage of building a more institutionalised structure. There are preparation meetings for a steering committee, and a first meeting took place in Bucharest. Romanian trade unions are dominant, but there were also representatives from Bulgaria and the Western Balkans.

UNI Europa is, as was mentioned, organised by sectors. Every sector's organisation has its own executive committee and subcommittees. This structure is different from sector to sector. In the steering committees, there are delegates from every region, and NMS trade unions have their places in this framework.[88]

Recently, some sectorial organisations of UNI Europa reinforced their activities to strengthen the participation of trade unions from NMS in the activities of European trade union federations. These activities had two focuses: the first was on the educational and training support of trade unions in NMS, and the second was on the support to build trade union structures in the NMS. For this task, sectorial organisations of UNI Europa organised a large number of seminars and projects on subjects such as organising, social dialogue, information and consultation, and collective bargaining. The other pillar of activities aimed to increase the involvement of trade unions

87 Interview with IndustriALL's secretary, responsible for collective bargaining coordination, Belgium, EH/IA3 21 May 2013.

88 UNI Global Union Commerce: Global Steering Committee 2013–2017, in: uniglobalunion.com, http://www.uniglobalunion.org/sites/default/files/images/globalsteeringcommittee2013-2017.pdf, accessed 15 January 2014.

from NMS into the working structures and practical activities of the sectorial organisations of UNI Europa.[89]

The sector organisations are also responsible for the sectorial social dialogue committees. Because the commission also pays for travel costs and accommodation, the participation of unions from NMS should also be better, for example, in the policy committees.

4.7. Membership Fees

Since the integration of trade unions from Central Eastern Europe, exceptions were made regarding membership fees, yet today, there are large differences in the fees that trade unions from new member states pay:

> Unions from the NMS still pay a reduced membership fee. Also the Turkish confederations. Then, we also have confederations that have only observer status, which do not pay any contributions.[90]

In general, fees depend on the number of members that a national union claims to have. This number does not always correspond with the real number of members a union has. Some unions say they have more members to have more influence in the association; others say they have fewer to pay lower fees. For Central Eastern European trade unions, the first case is rare; the only case is the Romanian union FSS Metarom in IndustriAll. The latter case is more common. For example, an official of IndustriAll Europe said that NZZ Solidarność pays for fewer members in the federation because the fees are too high for them.[91]

According to European trade union officials, trade unions from NMS are willing to pay their membership fees, and in that willingness, there are no differences compared to unions from other parts of Europe. The main problem, however, is not the willingness to pay but the precarious financial situation of trade unions from NMS. Even a small membership fee is, for them, a high price and could be equal to the salary of a fulltime union official in their countries.[92]

From the perspective of trade unions from NMS, the fees are a genuine burden and are the only 'downside' of membership in the European umbrella organisations, an argument that was stressed mainly by Polish trade unionists.[93] The advantages outweigh this disadvantage, however.

---

89 Platzer, Hans-Wolfgang / Müller, Torsten: Die globalen und europäischen Gewerkschaftsverbände [Global and European Trade Union Federations], Berlin: edition sigma, 2009, here p. 597.

90 Interview with ETUC's secretary, responsible for Workers Participation and European Works Councils, Belgium, WK/ETUC2 3 October 2013.

91 Interview with the deputy general secretary of ETUC, Belgium, JN/ETUC1 3 October 2013.

92 Interview with the deputy general secretary of IndustriALL, responsible for the area of Central Eastern Europe, Belgium, LT/IA1 21 May 2013.

93 Results of the questionnaire national trade unions, Poland, Gn02, Gn04, Gn08, Gn 11, Gn13, Gn14 Q29 2013.

4.8. Participation in Fields of Activities

4.8.1. European Social Dialogue

As was agreed upon in the early 1990s, ETUC is responsible for the interprofessional Social Dialogue, whereas sectorial ETUFs are social partners in the sectorial Social Dialogues. The focus in both is to have talks with the European employers' associations, to create joint statements or even negotiate European agreements, to implement them and to monitor the implementation of outcomes. However, it is important to know that the European social dialogue is not a type of collective bargaining on the European level. It is primarily a place where European 'social partners' can exchange information. The character of the meetings is therefore less confrontational but cooperative.

The social dialogue committee of ETUC meets 3–4 times per year. According to ETUC officials, the participation of trade unions from NMS is 'average'[94]. There is one representative per country, but there are smaller differences in the regular presence. The Polish attendance is best; the attendance of Czechs, Slovenians and Hungarians is good. Romanian and Slovakian unions are less frequently present.[95] The committee has subgroups that address special subjects. Due to the trade union pluralism in most NMS, the different unions of a country coordinate positions in individual subgroups among themselves.[96]

The most important problem of participation in the European social dialogue is, however, not the participation of trade unions from NMS but the implementation of agreements made by this committee. In the 1990s, there was a tripartite social dialogue at the European level, and the implementation in the member states on a national level was also tripartite. Under the initiative of the European commission, the social partners negotiated three agreements in this time (part-time work, fixed term contracts, parental leave), but these agreements were implemented as national legislation by the European directive. Since the end of the 1990s, however, the focus was on 'autonomous agreements' (on telework, stress, inclusion, harassment). These agreements were not converted into directives. The national social partners should implement these 'autonomous' agreements on the national level. This could be realised by different means, for instance, by collective agreements, by joint declarations or by joint projects. At this point, it is obvious that the weak industrial relation systems in NMS are a problem for the good implementation of European social dialogue

94 Interview with ETUC's secretary, responsible for European Social Dialogue and gender equality, non-discrimination policies, Belgium, CS/ETUC6 3 October 2013.
95 Ibid.
96 Results of the questionnaire national trade unions, Hungary, Gn06 Q8 2013.

outcomes. According to ETUC officials, the national implementation of social dialogue agreements was relatively strong in Poland and the Czech Republic, but in other new member states, implementation was weak.[97]

As described above, the participation in sectorial social dialogue committees in IndustriAll is stronger than in many other committees. This is primarily because of the payment of travel and accommodation costs by the commission. However, the weakness of unions from NMS means that they cannot take an active part in the discussions and actions. The underdevelopment of sectorial and national industrial relations also affects the implementation of social dialogue outcomes on the national level because this implementation is in the hands of national social partners. For instance, in the case of IndustriAll, there is an approach to create Sector Skill Councils that are bipartite bodies in the countries, where national social partners discuss the need for skills and suitable professional trainings. At the European level, there is coordination between these councils. Until now, NMS have not been present in the Sector Skill Councils because the construction of such bipartite councils at the national level has not been successful.

On the one hand, the lack of bipartite social dialogue structures in NMS seems to be a barrier for stronger political participation in the European Social Dialogue. On the other hand, trade unions from NMS are strongly in favour of an extension of the European Social Dialogue. They advocate further European negotiations with the hope of using European agreements to build a Social Dialogue on the national level. In this context, trade unions from NMS seem to be more involved in tripartite approaches of social partnership on a European level. One example is the strong participation in the activities of the European Social Fund (ESF). According to an ETUC official, the involvement of trade unions from NMS is strong in the ETUC working group and in the national or regional monitoring committees created by the governments.[98] Another example is participation in the European Economic and Social Committee (EESC). According to an ETUC official, the participation of trade unions from NMS is very good. One reason for their good participation is the payment of travel costs, as the commission pays for the meetings of European Economic and Social Committees. According to officials in Brussels, trade unions from NMS use this opportunity to come to Brussels and to participate contemporaneously at other ETUC meetings.[99]

As mentioned by Brussels' officials, trade unionists from NMS try to use their work in the EESC not primarily to shape EU social policy; they try to use the model of this advisory committee to strengthen social dialogue bodies in their countries because

97 Interview with the deputy general secretary of ETUC, Belgium, JN/ETUC1 3 October 2013.
98 Interview with ETUC's secretary, responsible for cohesion-, social- and economic policy, European social fund, EU budget policy, Belgium, CD/ETUC3 3 October 2013.
99 Interview with ETUC's secretary, formerly responsible for European Economic and Social Committee, Belgium, TJ/ETUC4 3 October 2013.

they are also primarily tripartite advisory bodies for shaping governmental policymaking.[100] In this sense, the preference for tripartite social dialogue at the European level by the trade unions from new member states could also reflect the important role of tripartism in their countries.[101]

4.8.2. European Collective Bargaining Coordination

Because European collective bargaining negotiations do not exist, and negotiations of the European social dialogue cover only 'soft' issues of common interests (occupational health and safety, innovation, industrial policy, trainings), ETUC and ETUFs have tried to coordinate of national collective bargaining policies.[102] The aim of this strategy is not to wait for European collective agreements with employers' associations but to create common minimum standards that will be implemented by the members at the national level. This strategy was initiated by the ETUC with the 'Doorn Initiative' in 1997 but was later implemented by the sectorial ETUFs.

Whereas the coordination is fully developed in IndustriAll (the EMF has been the forerunner of the collective bargaining coordination since 1998), it is just at the beginning stage in UNI Europa. Only two sectorial organisations, UNI Europa Graphical and UNI Europa Finance, show real attempts to introduce a European coordination of collective bargaining. Actually, a real wage coordination is only in place in UNI Europa Graphical.[103]

There is a collective bargaining committee in the ETUC. It is a permanent committee open to all members. It is not responsible for wage coordination, which is the competency of sectorial ETUFs. The task of the ETUC committee is, rather, to discuss general trends in collective bargaining policy. According to ETUC officials, the participation of unions from NMS in this committee is very good. Normally, most NMS trade unions are coming to the committee, even countries with very weak unions, such as Lithuania.[104] Unions from NMS are not only there, but they also give reports about their national situations. They are very interested to learn how collective bargaining structures in other countries function. The main subject they stress in the meetings is the

100 Ibid.

101 Fichter, Michael: Modernisierung und EU-Beitritt in Mittelosteuropa. Herausforderungen für die Gewerkschaften [Modernization and EU accession in Central Eastern Europe. Challenges for trade unions], in: Koch-Baumgarten, Sigrid / Rütters Peter (eds): Pluralismus und Demokratie. Interessenverbände – Länderparlamentarismus – Föderalismus – Widerstand [Pluralism and democracy. Interest groups, states parliamentarism, federalism, resistance, Frankfurt am Main: Bund-Verlag, 2006, here p. 188.

102 Schulten, Thorsten: Solidarische Lohnpolitik in Europa. Zur politischen Ökonomie der Gewerkschaften [Solidary wage policy in Europe. On the political economy of trade unions], Hamburg: VSA-Verlag, 2004, here p. 280 ff.

103 Ibid., here p. 295

104 Interview with ETUC's secretary, responsible for migration policy, collective bargaining coordination, Belgium, MC/ETUC5 3 October 2013.

weakness of their own collective bargaining structures. They report about their national problems and about the attacks on collective bargaining and social dialogue structures in their countries. Often, they demand support in the engagement to strengthen collective bargaining and help to build trade union capacities. They argue that the weakness of trade unions and the lack of collective bargaining structures is the reason for the large gap between wages in old and new member states.[105]

Furthermore, in IndustriALL and in two sectorial organisations of UNI Europa (Graphical and Finance), the collective bargaining committee plays an important role. In the case of IndustriAll Europe and UNI Europa Graphical, trade unions not only discuss trends in wages and collective bargaining policy but are responsible for a European collective bargaining coordination. As described above, the participation of unions from NMS in the collective bargaining committee of IndustriALL is moderate.

IndustriALL also includes a summer school, an annual meeting where participants come together for one week to discuss the agenda for the next year in the field of collective bargaining policy. The participation of unions from NMS is again very low, although travel expenses are paid and the summer school takes place in 'attractive places' (sunny places in southern Europe).

There is a similar obstacle to good participation in the field of common collective bargaining policy, such as in the European social dialogue: The lack of sectorial or national collective bargaining structures in NMS makes it hardly possible to transfer the common wage demands adopted in the collective bargaining committee to the national level. Although there are successes at the level of some individual companies, the unions in NMS are often too weak to gain contracts with the public or private employers for a whole sector.[106] Therefore, it is difficult to implement the coordination rules, even if unions from NMS strongly support these rules. Particularly in this field, it is obvious that the dominance of the company level governance in industrial relations is a real barrier for a stronger Europeanization of trade unions from NMS.

However, trade unions from NMS try to participate. To monitor the implementation of common demands and to monitor trends in national collective bargaining policies, European collective bargaining networks (EUCOBAN) were established. These include databases with information about national collective agreements and forums to discuss and to exchange information. In the case of IndustriALL, the assessment of participation of unions from NMS was very positive. According to officials, they participate very well in the surveys and regularly give all information to the network.[107]

105 Interview with ETUC's secretary, formerly responsible for European Economic and Social Committee, Belgium, TJ/ETUC4 3 October 2013.

106 Aro, Pekka O. / Repo, Paula: Trade Union experiences in collective bargaining in central Europe, Geneva: International Labour Office, 1997, here p. 153.

107 Interview with IndustriALL's secretary, responsible for collective bargaining coordination, Belgium, EH/IA3 21 May 2013.

Another strategy to answer the problem of collective bargaining in NMS is to put the focus on the company-level governance. For several years, but particularly since the crisis of the European wage coordination after the outbreak of the global finance crisis in 2008, there have been debates on ideas about how to support trade unions in the NMS on the company level against pressure to reduce wages.[108]

4.8.3. Company Policy

Participation in the area of company policy is highly relevant for unions from NMS because, today, transnational corporations usually have locations in Central Eastern Europe. Especially in the eastern border regions of Germany, Austria and Italy (Poland, the Czech Republic, Slovakia, Hungary, Slovenia), companies from Western Europe have invested in and taken over production locations.

ETUC is responsible for all general questions of company policy in Europe. For instance, the confederation manages directives concerning company policy, participation, and information and consultation rights on the company level, such as the framework on Information and Consultation, Collective Redundancies, Transfer of Undertakings, European Works Councils, European Company Statute, European Cooperative Society, cross-border mergers, and Transnational Company Agreements. There are two important ETUC working groups: one on European corporate governance and one on European Works Councils.

As part of a revision initiative ('fitness check'), there have been three political focuses in recent time: the framework on information and consultation, collective redundancies and the transfer of undertakings. According to an ETUC official, confederations from NMS were less involved in these activities than others. However, the EWC directive was revised in recent years, and confederations from NMS were heavily involved in the revision.[109]

Another important focus of the ETUC's company policy is the coordination of EWCs. Historically, the directive on workers' information and consultation in 1994 accelerated the development of trade union cooperation. This directive forced transnational companies to create European Works Councils if they fall under the regulation of the directive. Until the accession of 2004, however, the directive did not cover

108 Interview with IG Metall's secretary at the Department for Collective Bargaining Policy at the national board, member of the collective bargaining committee and small working group of this committee, Germany, UF/IGM3 19 September 2011. Henning, Klaus: Europäisierung der Gewerkschaftspolitik. Eine Antwort auf die Krise? [Europeanization of trade union policy. A response to the crisis?], in: Dörre, Klaus / Schmalz Stefan (eds): Comeback der Gewerkschaften? Machtressourcen, innovative Praktiken, internationale Perspektiven [The comeback of trade unions? Power resources, innovative practices, international perspectives], Frankfurt am Main: Campus, 2013, here p. 111.

109 Interview with ETUC's secretary, responsible for Workers Participation and European Works Councils, Belgium, WK/ETUC2 3 October 2013.

locations in Central Eastern Europe. However, in this period, the policy of ETUFs was to push for the inclusion of Central Eastern European locations on a voluntary basis. Thus, the EMF adopted in 1995 'binding rules' whereby union officials from Western Europe were forced to include Central Eastern European locations in the negotiations on EWC agreements. Therefore, the enlargement of the EWC structures functioned very well. The database of the European Trade Union Institute supports this assessment. It shows that of all 1017 existing EWCs, 229 have members from the NMS that joined the EU in 2004 (Poland, the Czech Republic, Slovakia, Hungary, Slovenia) and 56 members from the 2007 member states (Romania, Bulgaria).[110]

However, the ETUC is only responsible for a cross-sectorial framework coordination of sectorial EWCs policy. The direct responsibility of EWC coordination lies with sectorial ETUFs. The sectorial ETUFs are an important part of the EWC working group. Every year, the ETUC organises, in cooperation with sectorial ETUFs, a cross-sectorial EWC conference. According to ETUC officials, the participation from NMS is 'pretty good'.[111]

Participation from NMS in the company policy committee of IndustriAll is, according to officials, varying. Officials describe the participation of Czech and Slovakian unions as 'very good' and that of Polish unions as 'good'. The relationship with Hungarian unions qualifies as 'rare' and 'complicated'. With the Slovenian unions, there is 'a lack of good relationships' in the field of company policy.[112] Cooperation with trade unions from Romania and Bulgaria is growing now. The interest of these unions in cooperation also depends on the actual presence of transnational companies in these countries. There are good examples for the inclusion of local unions (Confederation of Independent Trade Unions of Bulgaria and CL Podkrepa in Bulgaria) in the work of the European Works Councils and in company policy activities of IndustriAll.

IndustriAll is responsible for approximately 500 EWCs, all sector organisations of UNI Europa for approximately 180.[113] The overwhelming majority of companies are headquartered either in Germany or in France. There is only one multinational company with headquarters in a NMS within the responsibility of IndustriAll that meets the criteria of the directive on EWC: the Hungarian gas and fuel producer MOL.[114] The support of EWCs' work within the responsibility of IndustriAll is the most important

110 See the website with the database: http://www.ewcdb.eu/, accessed 09 December 2014.

111 Interview with ETUC's secretary, responsible for Workers Participation and European Works Councils, Belgium, WK/ETUC2 3 October 2013.

112 Interview with IndustriALL's secretary, responsible for European Works Councils, Belgium, CC/IA2 21 May 2013.

113 The most are in finance (54), graphics (45), and commerce (28). Platzer, Hans-Wolfgang / Müller, Torsten: Die globalen und europäischen Gewerkschaftsverbände [Global and European Trade Union Federations], Berlin: edition sigma, 2009, here p. 601.

114 The Czech energy company České energetické závody (CEZ), which exports electricity from the nuclear power plants Temelin and Dukovany to the Eastern member countries and has power plants in Poland, Bulgaria and Romania, is another rare example. However, for this company, the European Federation of Public Service Unions (EPSU) is responsible.

pillar of company policy activities. For example, the federation supports the renegotiation of EWC agreements and supplies the EWCs with information and recommendations based on the evaluation of the experiences of other EWCs. Primarily, the so-called trade union coordinators organise this support in IndustriAll.

Among the 500 EWCs that are the responsibility of IndustriAll, there are only two with EWC coordinators from NMS. This is the case for the EWC in Ideal Standard, an international company for sanitary and bathroom ceramics, where two Bulgarian trade unionists were mandated as coordinators in 2012, and for the EWC in the aforementioned company MOL in Hungary (fuels and chemical products).[115] According to officials in the secretariat of IndustriAll, cooperation with EWC coordinators from NMS is good. They want to play an active role in their EWC bodies, and the willingness to cooperate is described as high.[116]

In addition to the coordinators, trade unions from NMS participate in EWC works in sending representatives of their national locations to meetings of the EWC. Most of the multinational companies covered by IndustriAll have locations in NMS. IndustriAll actively supported the creation of election bodies in NMS so that colleagues from NMS could participate from the first day of accession. The inclusion functioned very well, according to the IndustriAll official, responsible for European Works Councils[117], and NMS were as well represented as other countries. However, according to this official, there are two problems:

- a lack of participation from NMS in the boards of the EWCs (smaller working groups);
- problems with what officials call a 'good nomination' of EWC delegates.

Smaller working groups or executive boards of EWC play an important role in the practical work of the EWCs. Their role was even strengthened with the recent revision of the EWC directive. Whereas locations in NMS are important in terms of the number of workers employed there, these locations did not play, until now, an important role in the executive bodies of the EWCs. The most important reason for that was, according to IndustriAll officials, the lack of experiences in EWC work by trade unionists from NMS, which did not allow them to take over responsibility in the executive bodies. Even today, the problem of representation in the smaller working groups continues; however, the situation has improved recently:

115 Although the majority of the workers of this company work in Croatia, the EWC's headquarters was in Hungary. After the accession of Croatia in 2013, it planned to relocate its headquarters to Croatia.

116 Interview with IndustriALL's secretary, responsible for European Works Councils, Belgium, CC/IA2 21 May 2013.

117 Ibid.

> We see more colleagues from Eastern Europe who are involved in the smaller committees, and this is really a good development.[118]

The second problem, according to officials, is the nomination of delegates from NMS. Problems with democratic standards in the choice of EWC delegates is an issue not only in Central Eastern Europe but also in Western countries. However, according to officials, this problem is more common in Central Eastern Europe.[119] This 'bad' nomination causes the problem that trade union representatives participate only once or twice in EWC meetings and are then not seen any more. There is also a problem with the personnel continuity of representatives from Central Eastern Europe, according to IndustriAll officials. As a result, some EWC delegates are nominated by employers, who use EWC nominations as a bonus system for the loyal behaviour of workers' representatives. There are even cases where the employers send their own representatives, who are members of the management.

Trade unions in Central Eastern Europe recognise the problem of 'bad nominations' and take it seriously; this issue is, once again, the result of their own weakness. The 'bad nominations' take place in companies where unions are weak or not present and therefore have no influence on the nominations. Where unions are present, a good nomination is enforced in line with legal regulation.

One of the biggest challenges for the work of the EWC is to find a common and solidary strategy in cases of transnational relocation and restructuring. In such situations, where jobs are up for grabs, the solidarity of workers can collapse in favour of securing 'national locations'. The main task, therefore, is to develop a common strategy of employee representatives.

The relocation of production from Western to Central Eastern Europe was and is still a challenge. According to Brussels officials, it was not always easy to obtain solidarity from NMS trade unions against such relocations because their members profited from these relocations. This assessment corresponds with results of studies about trade union responses that showed that there were several disagreements about production relocations between trade unions from old and new member states before and during the crisis of 2008–10.[120]

---

118 Interview with IndustriALL's secretary, responsible for European Works Councils, Belgium, CC/IA2 21 May 2013.

119 Ibid.

120 Bernaciak, Magdalena: Labour solidarity in crisis? Lessons from General Motors, in: Industrial Relations Journal, 2013 (vol. 44), no. 2, pp. 139–153. Bernaciak, Magdalena: East-West European labour transnationalisms. Rivalry or joint mobilization?, in: Bieler, Andreas / Lindberg, Ingemar (eds): Global restructuring, labour and the challenges for transnational solidarity, London: Routledge, 2011, here p. 37.

However, according to the IndustriAll official responsible for the European Works Councils in Brussels secretariat[121] trade unions from NMS have recognised that workers across Europe have the same interests. The problem of relocation to the 'east' is no longer just a problem of employees in France, Germany, etc. Meanwhile, Polish, Czech or Hungarian workers are also affected by relocations to countries with even lower wages, so they know that they can be the next and that they, too, rely on the solidarity of trade unions in other countries:

> In the beginning, in 2004–2005, it was harder. In general, they were the winners of restructuring. Only the winners. And the losers were workers in Western Europe. However, nowadays this is more mixed. Therefore, that is why I would say they understand the problems and have the same behaviour as in the West.[122]

According to the IndustriAll official, responsible for European Works Councils, trade unionists from NMS are currently more convinced that the role of EWCs must be strengthened.[123] Whereas they were previously seen as passive bodies that were 'waiting' for information from the management, they are now seen as bodies that are shaping the policy of the company and influencing the decisions of the management.

Another task related to that strategy is the negotiation of the European framework agreement with the management. These agreements play an important role in the respect of trade union rights, particularly in NMS. Negotiations on the company level could also help to strengthen trade unions and to build up social dialogue structures in NMS. That is because the need for implementation of these agreements opens a framework, where trade unions can contact employers.

A popular example provided by IndustriAll was the framework agreement on collective bargaining rights at Volkswagen. This agreement was also implemented in Poland and achieved additional consultation rights for employees' representatives. Another example noted by UNI Europa Finance are the negotiations with UniCredit regarding a framework agreement on social dialogue. UniCredit is strongly involved in the NMS, so such an agreement could greatly improve the consultation rights of trade unions in NMS. According to officials, trade unions from the region are strongly in favour of this approach, and they want a strengthening of this strategy. They also took part in the meetings and negotiations.[124]

An interesting aspect of the strategy, to strengthen co-determination in NMS in company policy through EU-level institutions, is the competing approaches of

121 Interview with IndustriALL's secretary, responsible for European Works Councils, Belgium, CC/IA2 21 May 2013.

122 Interview with IndustriALL's secretary, responsible for European Works Councils, Belgium, CC/IA2 21 May 2013.

123 Ibid.

124 Interview with ETUC's secretary, responsible for migration policy, collective bargaining coordination, Belgium, MC/ETUC5 3 October 2013.

company-level participation. In the case of the implementation of the consultation and information framework directive, many governments in NMS decided not to use the existing bodies of co-determination in the companies but to create new bodies. Because these bodies are also elected, they become a second actor in industrial relations at the company level and, therefore, enter competition with the existing works councils. This development is dangerous for trade unions because trade unions could lose consultation and information rights to these new bodies.[125]

Another strategy at the company level is to put pressure on the customers of companies that violate the rights of workers. There were cases where trade union rights have been violated in Central Eastern Europe and where EWC client companies were pressured to distance themselves from these practices. This strategy was partly successful. Unions from NMS have been involved in these measures because they also had members in the EWC.

4.8.4. Cross-Border Cooperation

Another field of activity is cross national trade union cooperation in border regions. The ETUC has now 45 Interregional Trade Union Counsels (IRTUCs). These bodies are cross-border cooperation networks between confederations in a specific border region. Since the 1990s, even before EU enlargement, ETUC created IRTUCs in the Eastern border region. Now, there are approximately 20 IRTUCs in the border regions of NMS. The majority of IRTUCs including trade unions from NMS have been, until now, in the Eastern border regions of Germany and Austria. There are also, however, IRTUCs at the Italian–Slovenian, Hungarian–Slovenian–Croatian, Hungarian–Romanian–Serbian[126], and more recently in the Bulgarian–Romanian border regions.[127]

Much support was given to the IRTUCs by German unions, in the Hans Boeckler Foundation and the Friedrich Ebert Foundation. The internal organisation faces difficulties (the degree of cooperation depends on the work of local unions because the IRTUCs work autonomously), but the general participation of unions from NMS is described as 'quite good'[128].

In this context, there is currently cooperation in the local European Employment Services (EURES) activities, a network of public employment services. There are EURES

125 Ibid.

126 ETUC: The Interregional Trade Union Councils. IRTUC, in: etuc.org, October 2013, http://www.etuc.org/sites/www.etuc.org/files/CSI-Ft_A3_2013.pdf, accessed 09 December 2014.

127 Tomev, Lyuben. Unions in Bulgaria and Romania establish interregional council, in: EurWORK European Observatory of Working Life, 10 May 2013, http://eurofound.europa.eu/observatories/eurwork/articles/industrial-relations-other/unions-in-bulgaria-and-romania-establish-interregional-council, accessed 09 December 2014.

128 Interview with ETUC's secretary, responsible for cohesion-, social- and economic policy, European social fund, EU budget policy, Belgium, CD/ETUC3 3 October 2013.

cross-border partnerships where not only the regional employment administrations but also local social partners cooperate. The main subject there is the coordination of labour market policies, and educational and vocational training initiatives. Trade unions from NMS are becoming more involved in these initiatives.[129]

At a sectorial level, there were also attempts to build cross-border networks between national trade unions. Since the 1990s, IG Metall has established so-called 'collective bargaining networks' at its border regions. The idea was to exchange information about developments in the field of collective agreements and to have a cross-national exchange of observers in the regional collective bargaining negotiations. There is now only one network with participation from NMS: between Poland and Germany.[130] However, a similar example of this strategy was the establishment of the so-called 'Vienna Memorandum Group' in 1999 between unions from Germany (IG Metall), Austria (Produktionsgewerkschaft PRO-GE), Slovakia (OZ KOVO), the Czech Republic (OS KOVO), Hungary (VASAS) and Slovenia (Sindikat kovinske in elektro industrije Slovenije-SKEI). This network still exists and has enlarged its activities recently beyond the founding subjects of employment and collective bargaining policy.[131]

4.8.5. European Action Days

Since the 1990s, there has been a growing focus on ETUC and European trade union federations as well as on the mobilisation and organisation of coordinated European action days. Since the outbreak of the global financial crisis in 2008, ETUC and ETUFs have organised more than ten European action days and Euro demonstrations against austerity measures. Three of the central actions were also in new member states; there were Euro-demonstrations in Ljubljana, Prague and Budapest. The mobilisation was remarkable. In Budapest in April 2011, 40,000 workers gathered on the occasion of an EU summit where new austerity measures were adopted. It was one of the biggest protests in the country in a long time. In addition to central demonstrations, the number of decentralised action days is increasing.

These action days are coordinated across Europe both by ETUC or by ETUFs for special sectors or companies. According to officials in Brussels, the participation of the Central Eastern European trade unions in these coordinated action days is quite strong on both sectorial and company levels. This assessment corresponds with the statements of national union officials from NMS. A large majority of respondents in our survey (86 of 101) reported that their trade union supported European-wide protest

129 Ibid.

130 Gollbach, Jochen: Europäisierung der Gewerkschaften. Praktische Ansätze im Spannungsfeld nationaler und europäischer Strukturen und Traditionen [Europeanization of trade unions. Practical approaches in the conflict between national and European structures and traditions], Hamburg: VS-Verlag, 2005, here p. 71.

131 See the chapter of Christin Landgraf and Zdenka Mansfeldova in this book.

actions organised by European umbrella organisations. Only some Romanian and one Bulgarian sectorial union reported that they had not yet participated.[132]

4.9. Conclusion

The participation in ETUC and European trade union federations shows a significant variance. There are differences in participation between the ETUFs, resulting from the different working structure of the associations but also between confederations and unions from NMS. However, the general weakness of trade union structures in Central Eastern and South Eastern Europe is an obstacle for a successful integration of the organisations into the ETUFs.

These problems start with the membership fees, where trade unions from Central Eastern Europe are 'out of the system' and have paid, until now, less than other trade unions in Europe. Organisational and financial weakness is another major obstacle to participation in the structures of the federations. Trade unions from new member states participate in the congresses but have no political weight due to their small size. In the executive committees of ETUC and IndustriALL, the participation of unions from NMS is inadequate; the same is true for political, sectorial and horizontal committees in IndustriALL.

The reasons for the poor participation are, on the one hand, the lack of financial resources for travel and accommodation costs and, on the other hand, the problem of languages; many trade union officials from NMS do not speak English sufficiently enough to communicate without translation in the meetings. The low participation in the internal structures of the associations means that trade unions from NMS are hardly in a position to bring independent positions and priorities into account. One result of the language problem is that the most important form of communication is communication via email, where electronic translators can be used.

However, there are some positive developments. With respect to participation in the federations, there are areas in which the unions are now better integrated. In the ETUC, the participation in working groups and committees is better than in the executive committee because in these groups, they can take part without having to pay for the travel costs. The same is true in the sectorial social dialogues in IndustriALL. The meetings of committees in the working groups in the ETUC and the sectorial social dialogue in IndustriALL show a good participation rate of representatives from NMS. Trade unions from NMS also use these events to participate in additional meetings of federations in Brussels. Additionally, regional cooperation seems to be more effective and successful. The participation in regional committees is easier because committee meetings take place in geographical proximity. A further regionalisation

132 Questionnaire national trade unions, Q26 2013.

of activities of the federation seems to be a good way to involve the unions in a more active European cooperation.

The cooperation between the associations and trade unions from the studied countries is increasing, according to officials. Networks, such as the collective bargaining network and the EWC coordinator network, are important. In the field of the collective bargaining network, existing EUCOBAN networks offer an effective channel for communication. In the area of cooperation at the enterprise level, officials also see progresses because of the rising number of EWCs, in which trade unions from NMS are included. More and more unions from NMS are now taking part in the selection committees of the EWCs. The employee representatives and trade unions from NMS are much more aware today that the EWCs must be active and that European solidarity and common action are necessary in cases of production relocation.

Finally, the confederations and unions from NMS are also increasingly involved in Europe-wide campaigns and European days of action. The participation often does not run via central manifestations in Brussels but through decentralised coordinated actions in the member states or at the company level. The willingness to participate in these campaigns and days of action also reflects the fact that the trade unions from NMS are now facing the same economic, social and political developments (unemployment, precarious work, worsening working conditions, pension reforms and cuts in social services, etc.) as other trade unions in the EU in the wake of the global financial crisis.

Christin Landgraf

5. EU-Level Activities of Trade Unions from the New EU Member States

5.1. Introduction

'The "social partners" are the civil society players which have achieved most access to intergovernmental European Union (EU) decision-making.'[1] However, despite their privileged position in EU policy-making, trade unions and their lobbying activities at the EU level are less researched[2] compared with detailed studies on business Interests in EU multilevel governance.[3] Furthermore, a major research gap exists regarding the lobbying activities of interest groups from the new EU member states. Therefore, this chapter analyses the Integration of trade unions from the countries of the Eastern Enlargement at the EU level.

Trade unions from the new EU member states have been facing broad challenges after 1989/90 regarding interest representation. 'They had to build up new structures of industrial relations in a short period of time—something that had taken Western Europe decades to develop.'[4] During that time, according to Kohl, trade unions were placed under significant pressure. This pressure was caused first by the introduction and adaptation to new market economic rules and the process of determining new

---

1 Greenwood, Justin: Interest Representation in the European Union, 3. ed., Basingstoke: Palgrave Macmillan, 2011, p. 28.

2 For exceptions, see Kovacs, Marton: How Do Trade Unions Interact with the European Parliament? A Descriptive Analysis, Brussels: ETUI-REHS Printshop, 2008. The following authors include trade unions in their studies in addition to other types of interests: Beyers, Jan: Voice and Access. Political Practices of European Interest Associations, in: European Union Politics, 2004 (vol. 5), no. 2, pp. 211–240; Chalmers, Adam: Interests, Influence and Information. Comparing the Influence of Interest Groups in the European Union, in: Journal of European Integration, 2011 (vol. 33), no. 4, pp. 471–486; Chalmers, Adam: Trading Information for Access: Informational Lobbying Strategies and Interest Group Access to the European Union, in: Journal of European Public Policy, 2013 (vol. 20), no. 1, pp. 39–58.

3 For example, Bouwen, Pieter: Exchanging Access Goods for Access. A Comparative Study of Business Lobbying in the European Union Institutions, in: European Journal of Political Research, 2004 (vol. 43), no. 3, pp. 337–369; Bouwen, Pieter: The Logic of Access to the European Parliament. Business Lobbying in the Committee on Economic and Monetary Affairs, in: Journal of Common Market Studies, 2004 (vol. 42), no. 3, pp. 473–495; Eising, Rainer: Multilevel Governance and Business Interests in the European Union, in: Governance, 2004 (vol. 17), no. 2, pp. 211–245; Eising, Rainer: Institutional Context, Organizational Resources and Strategic Choices. Explaining Interest Group Access in the European Union, in: European Union Politics, 2007 (vol. 8), no. 3, pp. 329–362.

4 Kohl, Heribert: Where Do Trade Unions Stand in Eastern Europe Today? Stock-Taking after EU Enlargement, 2008, http://library.fes.de/pdf-files/ipg/ipg-2008-3/09_a_kohl_gb.pdf, accessed 19 November 2014, here p. 107.

salary and employment conditions for employees and second, by the introduction of the acquis communautaire and EU accession.[5] These developments progressed with a tremendous decrease of trade union density in Central Eastern Europe.[6] Furthermore, rivalries emerged between unions that succeeded the former socialist trade unions and unions that had been founded in opposition to the socialist state resulting in a pluralistic system in Bulgaria, the Czech Republic, Hungary, Poland and Romania.[7]

Since EU Enlargement in 2004 and 2007, trade unions from Central Eastern Europe have opportunities to participate in the EU-level decision-making process. However, the study Pleines et al. conducted on trade unions in Poland, the Czech Republic and Slovakia demonstrated that the interest representation of trade unions from these countries at the EU level was weak. Trade unions from these countries seldom had direct access to the institutions of the EU, and they largely represented interests indirectly through either the European umbrella organisations of trade unions or the European Economic and Social Committee (EESC).[8]

Therefore, this chapter contributes empirically to the research on interest groups in EU multilevel governance by examining at the EU level the interest representation of trade unions from Bulgaria, the Czech Republic, Hungary, Poland, Romania and Slovakia. This chapter will analyse what venues of interest representation trade unions from the new EU member states use to participate at the EU level, what type of access they have to EU institutions and how they assess their work and activities at the EU level.

This chapter is based on interviews conducted by the project team with union representatives of confederations and branch unions in the fields of metal, mining, commerce and finance from the new EU member states. In total, the project team conducted 101 interviews with union representatives from Bulgaria (10), the Czech Republic (15), Hungary (12), Poland (16), Romania (34) and Slovakia (14). However, as the number of interviews show, the sample is too small to calculate statistical correlations. Nonetheless, for the confederations and branch unions we have studied, we can identify tendencies of their EU-level activities.

In identifying these tendencies, this chapter will proceed as follows. The second section of this chapter will present some important empirical and theoretical findings

---

5 Ibid.

6 See, for example, Ost, David: The End of Postcommunism. Trade Unions in Eastern Europe's Future, in: East European Politics and Societies, 2009 (vol. 23), no. 1, pp. 13–33, here p. 14.

7 ETUI / Fulton L.: Worker Representation in Europe. Labour Research Department and ETUI. Produced with the Assistance of the SEEurope Network, in worker-participation.eu, 2013, http://www.worker-participation.eu/National-Industrial-Relations/Across-Europe/Trade-Unions2, accessed 19 November 2014.

8 Pleines, Heiko: Representing Workers or Presenting EU Prescriptions? Trade Unions from Post-Socialist Member States in EU Multi-Level Governance, in: Kröger, Sandra / Friedrich, Dawid (eds): The Challenge of Democratic Representation in the European Union, Basingstoke: Palgrave Macmillan, 2012, pp. 241–255, here pp. 246–247.

of research on interest groups in EU governance, namely, the venues of interest representation and access at the EU level (section 5-2). A detailed analysis of the data is conducted in sections 5-3 and 5-4. The results will be summarised in section 5-5.

5.2. Interest Representation at the EU Level

5.2.1. Venues of Interest Representation for Trade Unions

The legal competence of the EU is a significant incentive for interest groups to participate in the EU's decision-making processes.[9] According to Pleines, there are several venues of interest representation at the EU level that trade unions can use to exert influence. These venues include consultations with EU institutions as well as access through the European Social Dialogue, the European Economic and Social Committee and the European umbrella organisations of trade unions.[10]

The European Commission is the most important EU-level access point for interest groups.[11] As Bouwen summarises, the Commission is the EU's agenda setter. Because it drafts all proposals, the Commission must have a considerable understanding of policy issues.[12] The European Parliament is the second most important channel to influence decision-making at the EU level.[13] As Greenwood argues:

> The absence of an in-built majority to the European Parliament makes it highly oriented towards coalition building and consensus, and thus heightens its importance as a venue of interest representation.[14]

9 Eising, Rainer: Interest Groups in EU Policy-Making, in: Living Reviews in European Governance, 2008 (vol. 3), no. 4, http://europeangovernance.livingreviews.org/Articles/lreg-2008-4/, accessed 22 September 2011, here p. 15.

10 Pleines, Heiko (eds): Already Arrived in Brussels? Interest Representation of Trade Unions from the New EU Member States at the EU Level. Documentation of Interview Results, in: Working Paper of the Research Centre for East European Studies no. 91, 2008, http://www.forschungsstelle.uni-bremen.de/UserFiles/file/06-Publikationen/Arbeitspapiere/fsoAP91.pdf, accessed 19 November 2014, here p. 11.

11 Greenwood, Justin: Interest Representation in the European Union, 3rd ed., Basingstoke: Palgrave Macmillan, 2011, here p. 24.

12 Bouwen, Pieter: Corporate Lobbying in the European Union. The Logic of Access, in: Journal of European Public Policy, 2002 (vol. 9), no. 3, pp. 365–390, here p. 379.

13 Greenwood, Justin: Interest Representation in the European Union, 3. ed., Basingstoke: Palgrave Macmillan, 2011, here p. 24. Eising, Rainer: Der Zugang von Interessengruppen zu den Organen der Europäischen Union. Eine organisationstheoretische Analyse [Stakeholders' Access on the Institutions of the European Union. An Organisational-Theoretic Analysis], in: Politische Vierteljahresschrift, 2004 (vol. 45), no. 4, pp. 494–518, here p. 498.

14 Greenwood, Justin: Interest Representation in the European Union, 2. ed., Basingstoke: Palgrave Macmillan, 2007, here p. 36.

Important access points are the members of the committees as well as the representatives.[15] The Council of Ministers is the third most relevant access point at the EU level for interest groups.[16] According to Eising, the Council has an important position in the legislative process. However, the Council is seldom lobbied by interest organisations because particularly domestic interest organisations represent their interests at the domestic level through national contacts instead of lobbying the Council directly.[17]

Another venue for interest representation for trade unions is the European Social Dialogue.[18] As Hix summarises, the introduction of the Maastricht Treaty and the Maastricht Social Agreement was an important step for the social partners.[19] Thus, a collective agreement by the social partners 'can serve as a direct substitute for EU legislation.'[20] However, employer organisations often refuse to conclude EU-level agreements.[21]

The European Economic and Social Committee was created by the Rome Treaties in 1957 to integrate interests in EU policy-making. The EESC members comprise employers, employees and other interests. The EESC has an advisory function: it must be consulted by the Commission or the Council in various policy fields. With the Treaty of Amsterdam, the European Parliament has been allowed to consult the EESC. The issues for referral have been extended over the years.[22] Therefore, the EESC is consulted in numerous policy fields, such as employment, education, and health issues for employ-

---

15 Eising, Rainer: Der Zugang von Interessengruppen zu den Organen der Europäischen Union. Eine organisationstheoretische Analyse [Stakeholders' Access on the Institutions of the European Union. An Organisational-Theoretic Analysis], in: Politische Vierteljahresschrift, 2004 (vol. 45), no. 4, pp. 494–518, here p. 498.

16 Greenwood, Justin: Interest Representation in the European Union, 3. ed., Basingstoke: Palgrave Macmillan, 2011, here p. 25. Eising, Rainer: Der Zugang von Interessengruppen zu den Organen der Europäischen Union: Eine organisationstheoretische Analyse [Stakeholders' Access on the Institutions of the European Union. An Organisational-Theoretic Analysis], in: Politische Vierteljahresschrift, 2004 (vol. 45), no. 4, pp. 494–518, here p. 498.

17 Eising, Rainer: Der Zugang von Interessengruppen zu den Organen der Europäischen Union: Eine organisationstheoretische Analyse [Stakeholders' Access on the Institutions of the European Union. An Organisational-Theoretic Analysis], in: Politische Vierteljahresschrift, 2004 (vol. 45), no. 4, pp. 494–518, here p. 498.

18 Pleines, Heiko (eds): Already Arrived in Brussels? Interest Representation of Trade Unions from the New EU Member States at the EU Level. Documentation of Interview Results, in: Working Paper of the Research Centre for East European Studies no. 91, 2008, http://www.forschungs stelle.uni-bremen.de/UserFiles/file/06-Publikationen/Arbeitspapiere/fsoAP91.pdf, accessed 19 November 2014, here p. 11.

19 Hix, Simon: The Political System of the European Union, 2. ed., Basingstoke: Palgrave Macmillan, 2005, here p. 217.

20 Ibid.

21 Hoffmann, Jürgen: Perspektiven der europäischen Arbeitsbeziehungen und Gewerkschaften zwischen Modernisierung, Europäisierung und Globalisierung [Prospects for European Industrial Relations and Trade Unions in the Midst of Modernization, Europeanization and Globalization], in: Leviathan, 2010 (vol. 38), no. 1, pp. 89–102, here p. 100.

22 European Economic and Social Committee: Regarding the Committee: in: eesc.europa.eu, http://www.eesc.europa.eu/?i=portal.en.about-the-committee, accessed 19 November 2014.

ees.[23] However, the EESC cannot vote on legislation; it cannot adopt binding opinions or recommendations.[24] Because of its limited influence, Nugent argues that the EESC is not the foremost access point for interest groups to exert influence at the EU level. According to Nugent, interest groups consider access to the Commission or the Council a more effective venue of interest representation at the EU level.[25] The same observation is suggested by Eising: 'It is generally considered to be of marginal importance for the representation of interests within the EU.'[26]

Moreover, according to Pleines, the European umbrella organisations of trade unions are another venue of interest representation for trade unions at the EU level,[27] such as the European Trade Union Confederation (ETUC), IndustriAll and Union Network International Europa (Uni Europa).

5.2.2. Access to EU Institutions

Explaining the access and influence of interest groups through an exchange of resources between actors and institutions is a central approach in European interest group research.[28] According to Bouwen, interest groups and EU institutions trade resources, namely, interest groups obtain access to the decision-making process at the EU level in exchange for 'access goods', (policy) information that EU institutions need to fulfil their duties.[29]

Access is defined here 'as the frequency of contacts between interest organizations and EU institutions. These contacts range from informal bilateral meetings with EU officials and politicians to institutionalized committee proceedings.'[30]

---

23 Smismans, Stijn: The European Economic and Social Committee. Towards Deliberative Democracy via a Functional Assembly, in: European Integration online Papers (EIoP), 2000 (vol. 4), no. 12, http://eiop.or.at/eiop/texte/2000-012a.htm, accessed 19 November 2014, here p. 2.

24 Hönnige, Christoph / Panke, Diana: The Committee of the Regions and the European Economic and Social Committee. How Influential are Consultative Committees in the European Union?, in: Journal of Common Market Studies, 2013 (vol. 51), no. 3, pp. 452–471, here p. 452.

25 Nugent, Neill: The Government and Politics of the European Union, 7. ed., Basingstoke: Palgrave Macmillan, 2010, here p. 230.

26 Eising, Rainer: Interest Groups in EU Policy-Making, in: Living Reviews in European Governance, 2008 (vol. 3), no. 4, http://europeangovernance.livingreviews.org/Articles/lreg-2008-4/, accessed 22 September 2011, here p. 13.

27 Pleines, Heiko (eds): Already Arrived in Brussels? Interest Representation of Trade Unions from the New EU Member States at the EU Level. Documentation of Interview Results, in: Working Paper of the Research Centre for East European Studies no. 91, 2008, http://www.forschungsstelle.uni-bremen.de/UserFiles/file/06-Publikationen/Arbeitspapiere/fsoAP91.pdf, accessed 19 November 2014, here p. 11.

28 Princen, Sebastiaan / Kerremans, Bart: Opportunity Structures in the EU Multi-Level System, In: West European Politics, 2008 (vol. 31), no. 6, pp. 1129–1146, here p. 1134.

29 Bouwen, Pieter: Corporate Lobbying in the European Union. The Logic of Access, in: Journal of European Public Policy, 2002 (vol. 9), no. 3, pp. 365–390.

30 Eising, Rainer: Institutional Context, Organizational Resources and Strategic Choices. Explaining Interest Group Access in the European Union, in: European Union Politics, 2007 (vol. 8), no. 3, pp. 329–362, here p. 331.

In addition to information, a profound knowledge, a large membership and economic and financial capacities are important resources for interest groups.[31] According to Dür, the resource capacities of interest groups are determined by, e.g., the organisational structure and type of constituency. For example, a large membership may endow an interest group with more legitimacy.[32]

However, what we know concerning the trade unions of the new EU member states regarding resources and resource endowment appears more challenging. An immense decrease of trade union density worsened the financial situation of trade unions in the countries of the EU Eastern Enlargement and their capacity to act after 1989/90. The organisational and internal financial structures of unions in Central Eastern Europe also have a negative impact on the financial resources of the unions. According to Kohl, the plant-level unions receive the major portion of membership fees whereas only between 10–30% reach the level of the branch unions and only 2–10% of the membership fees reach the confederations. Although unions from Central Eastern Europe have a well-educated staff, the number of employees at the trade union headquarters is too low for the work and tasks of the unions.[33] This insufficiency is also reflected in the following numbers. Among the countries included in our study, only Romania (33%) lies above the EU average of 23% (proportion of employed union representatives), followed by Bulgaria (20%), the Czech Republic and Slovakia (each 17%), as well as Hungary and Poland (each with 12%).[34]

At the EU level, all of these factors may influence the interest representation of trade unions from Bulgaria, the Czech Republic, Hungary, Poland, Romania and Slovakia. One result of the previous study of the project team (Pleines et al. 2008) was that interest representation of trade unions from Poland, the Czech Republic and Slovakia was weak at the EU level. These trade unions seldom had direct access to EU institutions. The trade unions studied represented their interests mostly through either the European umbrella organisations of trade unions or the European Economic and Social Committee.[35]

---

31 Dür, Andreas: Interest Groups in the European Union. How Powerful are They?, in: West European Politics, 2008 (vol. 31), no. 6, pp. 1212–1230, here p. 1214. Eising, Rainer: Interest Groups in EU Policy-Making, in: Living Reviews in European Governance, 2008 (vol. 3), no. 4, http://europeangovernance.livingreviews.org/Articles/lreg-2008-4/, accessed 22 September 2011, here p. 15.

32 Dür, Andreas: Interest Groups in the European Union. How Powerful are They?, in: West European Politics, 2008 (vol. 31), no. 6, pp. 1212–1230, here p. 1214.

33 Kohl, Heribert: Where Do Trade Unions Stand in Eastern Europe Today? Stock-Taking after EU Enlargement, 2008, http://library.fes.de/pdf-files/ipg/ipg-2008-3/09_a_kohl_gb.pdf, accessed 16 August 2014, here p. 114.

34 ETUI / Fulton L.: Worker Representation in Europe. Labour Research Department and ETUI. Produced with the Assistance of the SEEurope Network, in worker-participation.eu, 2013, http://www.worker-participation.eu/National-Industrial-Relations/Across-Europe/Trade-Unions2, accessed 19 November 2014.

35 Pleines, Heiko: Representing Workers or Presenting EU Prescriptions? Trade Unions from Post-Socialist Member States in EU Multi-Level Governance, in: Kröger, Sandra / Friedrich, Dawid (eds):

Therefore, we can assume from the theoretical insights presented and from the results of the previous study that the unions will primarily use the European umbrella organisations of trade unions to indirectly represent interests at the EU level whereas the unions will have less frequent access to EU institutions.

5.3. EU-Level Activities of the Unions from the New EU Member States

Generally, we can assume that interest groups are active at the EU level when they believe that EU regulation is important for their activities. Therefore, in our study, we wanted to capture the attitudes of the respondents concerning the EU and its influence on national politics to better explain interest representation at the EU level. Thus, we asked our respondents to assess the importance of the EU for their trade union in comparison with national politics. The majority of the respondents stated that the EU is equally important or even more important than national-level politics. Only a minority of the respondents thought that European-level politics would be less important than the domestic level.[36] We also wanted to know what future role of the EU our respondents believe would be desirable. Regarding this question, the majority of the respondents in all countries under study stated that the influence of the EU on domestic politics should increase.[37] We also asked our respondents regarding the impact of the EU on the work of their trade unions. Again, the majority of the respondents of all countries we have studied mentioned that the EU has a positive effect on the work of the trade union.[38] Regarding these results, we can assume that many respondents consider the EU a reference framework for the activities and interest representation of their trade unions.

As observed in section 5-2 of this chapter, trade unions can use different venues of interest representation to participate in the decision-making process of the EU and to have access to decision-makers. These channels include contacts and consultations with the European Commission, the European Parliament and the Council of Ministers. Furthermore, these channels also include access through the Social Dialogue or the EESC, or indirectly through the European umbrella organisation of trade unions, such as the ETUC, IndustriAll or UNI Europa. As observed, the respondents from all countries under study use all venues of interest representation at the EU level that I identified in section 5-2 of this chapter, including consultations with the Commission, the

The Challenge of Democratic Representation in the European Union, Basingstoke: Palgrave Macmillan, 2012, pp. 241–255, here pp. 246–247.

36 Results of the questionnaire national trade unions, Q1 2013. The results are from the research project 'Europeanization of Trade Unions in the Countries of the Eastern Enlargement'.

37 Ibid., Q2 2013.

38 Ibid., Q3 2013.

European Parliament and the Council. However, union access to the institutions of the EU varies to a large degree. In general, the respondents had less direct contacts to the Commission, the European Parliament or the Council.[39] As indicated in the literature on interest groups in EU governance,[40] interest groups may have more frequent access to the European Commission, followed by the European Parliament and the Council of Ministers. These considerations cannot be verified by our data.

As expected, the interviewed trade unionists tried more frequently to influence decision-making through the Social Dialogue and the EESC, although access varies in the countries we studied.[41] However, as observed in section 5-2 of this chapter, receiving access to the EU decision-making process through the EESC only seldom results in direct influence on the decision-making process of the EU because the EESC plays only a consultative role.[42]

Moreover, the data show that the European umbrella organisations of trade unions are extensively used by the respondents to indirectly exert influence at the EU level.[43] These results were also similar when we asked the respondents if they represent interests alone or in cooperation. A lot of respondents mentioned that they represent interests in cooperation with European umbrella organisations. Only a minority of the respondents stated that they represent interest at the EU level alone. Furthermore, respondents stated that they represent interests with other unions and other partners.[44]

These results show that the respondents use various venues of interest representation at the EU level to participate in the decision-making process. The respondents also use several strategies to gain access to decision-makers. One method includes networking with European umbrella organisations to influence decision-makers indirectly. Second, the unionists find partners and engage in EU-level networks to exert influence at the EU level. Third, the unionists try to gain access to EU institutions directly to exert direct influence on the decision-making process. However, the study shows that the venues of interest representation the respondents use at the EU level and access to EU institutions is not balanced.

5.4. Satisfaction with the Work at the EU Level

To gain a more detailed picture of interest representation of the trade unions, we asked our respondents regarding their satisfaction with the activities of their trade unions

39 Ibid., Q8 2013.
40 See section 5-2 of this chapter.
41 Results of the questionnaire national trade unions, Q8 2013.
42 For example, Eising, Rainer: Interest Groups in EU Policy-Making, in: Living Reviews in European Governance, 2008 (vol. 3), no. 4, http://europeangovernance.livingreviews.org/Articles/lreg-2008-4/, accessed 22 September 2011, here p. 13.
43 Results of the questionnaire national trade unions, Q8 2013.
44 Ibid., Q19 2013.

in the European umbrella organisations and at the EU level in general. This approach considers the individual perceptions of the trade unionists that may give us a better explanation for the chosen venues of interest representation and access at the EU level as well as the perceived influence of the respondents.

According to the data, cooperation with the European umbrella organisations is assessed positively.[45] The majority of the respondents stated that they were satisfied or very satisfied with the work of their unions in the European umbrella organisations.[46] This result is illustrated by the following description of one respondent who emphasises the intensive activity of the umbrella organisations:

> I think that trade unions are extremely active—ETUC and its organisations are constantly campaigning for something. The campaigns consist of protest actions, which are visible, but also of everyday work such as cooperation with the Commission, as they try to influence all processes at the place of their origin, which is in the Commission.[47]

However, being only indirectly active at the EU level through the European umbrella organisations has also been named by respondents as a reason for dissatisfaction. One respondent, for example, argues that the European umbrella organisations can only represent the more general interests of trade unions without representing the issues and needs of the single member branches in more detail:

> We are unsatisfied because we cannot get involved directly in influencing decisions that could be applied to our activity sector. The participation in decision-making is mostly done through institutions we are affiliated to and in most cases they can only address general issues at the EU level and not our specific issues.[48]

This problem of internal interest formulation, decision-making and representation has also been identified in the literature.[49] When we asked our respondents regarding their satisfaction with the work of their trade union in general at the EU level, the results were more diverse.[50] Many respondents stated that they were satisfied or very satisfied with the activities of their trade union at the EU level.[51] One respondent, for example, argued that there are many possibilities for unions to participate at the EU level:

> We have enough opportunities to voice our opinions and defend our interests.[52]

45 Ibid., Q21 2013.

46 Ibid., Q22 2013.

47 Interview with trade union representative, Czech Republic, Gn09 23 April 2013.

48 Interview with trade union representative, Romania, Gn27 05 July 2013.

49 See, for example, Hoffmann, Jürgen: Perspektiven der europäischen Arbeitsbeziehungen und Gewerkschaften zwischen Modernisierung, Europäisierung und Globalisierung [Prospects for European Industrial Relations and Trade Unions in the Midst of Modernization, Europeanization and Globalization], in: Leviathan, 2010 (vol. 38), no. 1, pp. 89–102, here p. 100.

50 Results of the questionnaire national trade unions, Q16 2013.

51 Ibid.

52 Interview with trade union representative, Czech Republic, Gn13 15 May 2013.

Another respondent illustrates that unions could use the existing venues of interest representation according to their possibilities, although there are differences regarding the work of more influential unions:

> It is not 100% satisfaction, but taking into account our possibilities, I am satisfied. But there are completely different players such as Germany and so on.[53]

One respondent also emphasised that by being active at the EU level, trade unions have many ways to accumulate new contacts and gather information:

> We have new opportunities, contacts, knowledge.[54]

Another respondent stresses the opportunity to engage in networks and to gain experience:

> We are able to represent broader interests, we have a lot of contacts and we can exchange experience.[55]

However, many respondents also answered that they were neither satisfied nor dissatisfied or they were even unsatisfied.[56] Here, some respondents argued that the lack of financial means and resources of their unions greatly affect interest representation negatively. As observed in section 5-2 of this chapter, access to EU institutions is demanding and largely determined by money, expertise and knowledge as well as staff. One respondent also emphasised the importance of financial resources, equipment and foreign language competence to be able to be active at the EU level:

> The participation is very low, because of the lack of financial means to support our participation, but in the rare case that we do participate at organized meetings—apart from being heard, our position is not really taken into consideration as opposed to that of other federations from Europe, for the simple fact that we are not taken seriously with the problems we have here. This is also due to the fact that we cannot make our position clear by attending these debates, there are many which we miss out on mainly because of the lack of financial means and at the same time there would be the possibility to inform about our position and the situation in Romania via the electronic channel, but here as well it doesn't work because we have a very backward informatics system and we are not very well equipped in this field. It is difficult to work, the lack of thorough knowledge of a foreign language of European circulation, no one in our federation has this knowledge, so we are suffering because of the lack of adaptation to the new requirements of the European Social Dialogue, of European participation and information. Through three points: lack of financial means, of informatics training, of linguistic training. We have many problems, which we would like to make known, but we are not succeeding.[57]

Because of a lack of staff and language competence, internal working processes seem to be slower. This slowness obstructs swift information transmission to the EU level. As illustrated by one respondent, statements or documents coming from the EU level

53 Interview with trade union representative, Slovakia, Gn05 16 April 2013.
54 Interview with trade union representative, Poland, Gn06 23 June 2013.
55 Interview with trade union representative, Poland, Gn14 08 May 2013.
56 Results of the questionnaire national trade unions, Q16 2013.
57 Interview with trade union representative, Romania, Gn07 23 April 2013.

must be translated before they can be discussed. Then, the position of the union must be formulated and translated again. Because of a lack of foreign language competence, the trade union member who speaks the meeting language attends the EU-level meetings, not the trade union experts.

> It means many things. In order to be able to participate at the European level you need to have financial capacity. You need to have expert potential, which we have, we have the necessary experts. But then, there is also linguistic...[capacity]. For example, when the Committee for Social Dialogue meets and I need to send the expert who is most qualified for that, it turns out he doesn't know a second [EU] language. So, I must personally participate and I must translate the information, so that I can give it to him. He needs to understand it, respond to me and then I must translate it again and present it. That is a huge difficulty, which originates from the lack of financial capacity. It's a hindrance for us and our active participation. And I'd like to be more active....[58]

Another respondent emphasised that the costs of lobbying, being active at the EU level, and sending in documents and statements are often high and do not correspond with the benefits:

> Because the results are disproportionate to the effort. The effort is very high, not only intellectually, to write up the document, edit it and translate it....[59]

In addition to the lack of resources and financial means, it has also been mentioned by some respondents that the current developments and the political environment in Europe does not favour trade unions' ideas and interests. This has an influence on the interest representation of the unions at the EU level:

> Both at the European and national level, trade unions are not taken seriously. To put it in a better way: they listen to us but then do it their way anyhow....[60]

Another respondent similarly argues that business interests currently have more influence:

> [The] [c]urrent situation is not in favour of employees' representatives, the lobbyism of the employers also at the EU level is currently more successful.[61]

As these statements show, the perceptions of the unionists representing interests in a political environment considered disadvantageous for unions as far as interest representation is concerned also create dissatisfaction. In contrast, respondents also emphasised the good relations between the unions and umbrella organisations and the EU institutions:

> I think that there is a positive view about social partners in the EU. My sources say that ETUC is often invited to many advisory meetings to discuss issues with social partners,

58 Interview with trade union representative, Bulgaria, Gn04 26 March 2013.
59 Interview with trade union representative, Romania, Gn09 31 March 2013.
60 Interview with trade union representative, Czech Republic, Gn05 28 March 2013.
61 Interview with trade union representative, Slovakia, Gn10 06 May 2013.

with ECOSOC, the European Parliament, and the European Commission.[62] (ECOSOC—Economic and Social Council)

The perceptions of the unionists appear to be rather diverse. This variation suggests that a more detailed analysis regarding issues and policy fields is needed to gain a better understanding of the interest representation and influence of unions at the EU level. However, the study shows that many respondents are satisfied with the work of their unions at the EU level. Conversely, there are still organisational and contextual factors that are perceived as disadvantageous for interest representation and the exertion of influence at the EU level.

5.5. Conclusion

In our study, we analysed the integration of trade unions from the new EU member states in EU governance structures. To assess the integration at the EU level, we conducted 101 interviews with union representatives from national confederations and branch unions in the fields of mining, metal, commerce and finance in Bulgaria, the Czech Republic, Hungary, Poland, Romania and Slovakia. As shown in this chapter, the trade unions we studied made use of several venues of interest representation at the EU level, including direct consultations with the EU institutions or membership in the Social Dialogue, EESC or European umbrella organisations. However, access to EU institutions and consultative bodies differed to a large degree. The respondents had less direct contacts to the Commission, the European Parliament or the Council, and more access through the EESC and the European Social Dialogue to decision-making processes at the EU level.

In general, many respondents were satisfied with the activities of their union at the EU level. However, a lot of respondents also stated that they were neither satisfied, nor dissatisfied or they were dissatisfied arguing that because of the lack of financial resources and language competence, they could not effectively represent their interests at the EU level.

In addition, the European umbrella organisations of trade unions seem to play a major role in the unions' interest representation at the EU level. Umbrella organisations were extensively used to exert influence at the EU level. Collaboration with European umbrella organisations was assessed positively. Thus, a deeper analysis of trade union integration by the new EU member states and how they exert influence in European umbrella organisations, such as the analysis conducted by Klaus Henning in this book, will help achieve a broader understanding of union representation by the new EU member states at the EU level.

62 Interview with trade union representative, Czech Republic, Gn15 29 May 2013.

Christin Landgraf and Zdenka Mansfeldová

6. Trade Unions from the New EU Member States that Are in Multilateral Cooperation. The Example of the Vienna Memorandum Group

6.1. Introduction

One of the aims of our project was to assess the integration of trade unions from the new European Union (EU) member states that are in bilateral and multilateral cooperation. We chose the Vienna Memorandum Group as one example of multilateral cooperation between trade unions, from both the new and the old EU member states, for several reasons. First, this network contains branch trade unions from a few major countries in our study, namely the Czech Republic, Slovakia and Hungary, in the metal industry field. Second, it is a cooperation that can provide insights into the cooperation between unions from Central Eastern and Western European countries and into interest formulation and representation beyond the EU level. Thus, by providing insights into the work of the Vienna Memorandum Group, this paper attempts to answer the following questions. How do trade unions from the new and old EU member states work together in this trade union network? What are the major activities of the Vienna Memorandum Group? How is the network perceived? What is the noteworthiness and the concrete use of this network?

The data for this paper are based on semi-structured elite-interviews that were conducted with responsible trade unionists of the member organisations in Germany and Austria. We also considered interviews with respondents from the Czech Republic, Hungary and Slovakia in this project. To complement this picture, documents of the Vienna Memorandum Group have been included in the analysis. The information booklet of the network provides a good overview of the Vienna Memorandum and its activities.[1]

To answer our research questions, this chapter will proceed as follows. The next part of this chapter (Section 6.2.) will present more information about the broad political and economic contexts that led to the foundation of the Vienna Memorandum Group. It will also outline the development of the network. Section 6.3. will present the member unions of this trade union network in more detail. Section 6.4. will focus on the internal organisation and activities of the Vienna Memorandum Group; in

1 IG Metall Bayern et al. (eds): 10 Jahre Wiener Memorandum 1999 – 2009 [10 Years of Vienna Memorandum 1999–2009], Kösching: Druckerei Hage GmbH, 2009.

Section 6.5., we will assess the work of the network, with regard to the other levels in EU Multilevel Governance. Section 6.6. will provide a short summary and a conclusion.

6.2. Foundation and Aims of the Vienna Memorandum Group

The introduction of the Maastricht Treaty and the Maastricht Social Agreement was an important step for European trade unions.[2] There was the hope that on the basis of the Social Agreement, a transnational tariff system could be initiated within the EU.[3] However, as Kohl / Platzer argue, employer organisations often refused to negotiate EU-level collective agreements. As a result, trade unions were forced to find new ways to cope with different wage standards in Europe, namely by implementing transnational tariff coordination among the European trade unions.[4]

In 1997, the German Industriegewerkschaft Metall (IG Metall) decided to set up transnational tariff partnerships with branch trade unions from neighbouring countries.[5] This resulted in the establishment of tariff partnerships with branch unions in the metal field, e.g., the foundation of the cooperation between IG Metall Bavaria, the Austrian Gewerkschaft Metall-Bergbau-Energie (GMBE), the Czech Odborový svaz KOVO (OS KOVO), the Slovak Odborový Zväz Kováckých Odborech (OZ KOVO), the Hungarian Vasas Szakszervezeti Szövetség (VASAS) and the Slovenian Sindikata kovinske in elektro industrije Slovenije (SKEI).

Cooperation within the Vienna Memorandum Group goes back to the bilateral contacts that the member unions had maintained since the fall of the iron curtain or before: IG Metall maintained bilateral contact with the branch trade unions from Czechoslovakia and Slovenia, and the Czechoslovakian, Slovenian and Austrian unions also had good relations with the Hungarian branch union.[6]

---

2 Hix, Simon: The Political System of the European Union, 2nd ed., Basingstoke: Palgrave Macmillan, 2005, here p. 217.

3 Schulten, Thorsten: Europäisierung der Tarifpolitik. Der Koordinierungsansatz des Europäischen Metallgewerkschaftsbundes (EMB) [Europeanization of Collective Bargaining. The Coordination Approach of the European Metalworkers' Federation (EMF)], in: Schulten, Thorsten / Bispinck, Reinhard (eds): Tarifpolitik unter dem Euro. Perspektiven einer europäischen Koordinierung. das Beispiel Metallindustrie, Hamburg: VSA-Verlag, 1999, pp. 197–226, here p. 197–198.

4 Kohl, Heribert / Platzer, Hans-Wolfgang: Arbeitsbeziehungen in Mittelosteuropa. Transformation und Integration. Die acht neuen EU-Mitgliedsländer im Vergleich [Industrial Relations in Central and Eastern Europe. Transformation and Integration. A Comparison of the Eight New EU Member States], 2. ed., Baden-Baden: Nomos-Verlags-Gesellschaft, 2004, here p. 272.

5 Schulten, Thorsten: Europäisierung der Tarifpolitik. Der Koordinierungsansatz des Europäischen Metallgewerkschaftsbundes (EMB) [Europeanization of Collective Bargaining. The Coordination Approach of the European Metalworkers' Federation (EMF)], in: Schulten, Thorsten / Bispinck, Reinhard (eds): Tarifpolitik unter dem Euro. Perspektiven einer europäischen Koordinierung. Das Beispiel Metallindustrie, Hamburg: VSA-Verlag, 1999, pp. 197–226, here p. 214.

6 Neugebauer, Werner / Jena, Matthias: 10 Jahre zuhören, lernen und helfen für die gemeinsamen Ziele [10 Years of Listening, Learning and Helping for Common Goals], in: IG Metall Bayern

During that time, the cooperation between trade unions from Central Europe, on one site, and Germany and Austria, on the other site, was a single-track process. Thus, cooperation first consisted of education, training trade union officials and transmitting know-how concerning wage and salary negotiations.

However, this single-track process was not always free of conflicts among the unions that later formed the Vienna Memorandum Group, as Werner Neugebauer, one of the founders of the Vienna Memorandum Group,[7] states:

> When the borders were opened, our works council members—I only report, and I do not criticise that—visited our colleagues, and they thought they had to tell them about the works constitution and about German labour laws. The colleagues of the trade union KOVO, for instance, were seriously angry. They asserted that the German colleagues would behave like during the German reunification process. But they appreciate that they can decide what to do on their own. This should be seen in the light of the fact that the colleagues in the Czech Republic did not have works councils, but plant-level unions. Until today, they attach great importance to the preservation of this structure. In short, massive conflicts developed. We then said that we first had to inform ourselves about their situation and their organisation.[8]

Based on these bilateral contacts, in 1999, the Vienna Memorandum Group was founded to implement the Wage Coordination Rule of the European Metalworkers Federation (EMF).[9] The Vienna Memorandum presented a new quality of cooperation in Central Europe, in the form of a multilateral process. The network's primary objective was an intensive exchange of information, particularly with regard to tariff politics and wage and salary negotiations, but the cooperation also aimed to support an exchange of information about the general political and economic developments in the member countries of the Vienna Memorandum.[10]

After the four Central Eastern European countries (Slovakia, Slovenia, the Czech Republic and Hungary) joined the European Union in 2004 and became regular members of EU bodies, the regional grouping did not lose its meaning. Shortly after the EU Enlargement, the Group renewed its declaration and cooperation in 2005.[11]

---

et al. (eds): 10 Jahre Wiener Memorandum 1999 – 2009, Kösching: Druckerei Hage GmbH, 2009, pp. 34–36, here p. 34.

7 Wiener Memorandum, März 1999 [Vienna Memorandum, March 1999], in: IG Metall Bayern et al. (eds): 10 Jahre Wiener Memorandum 1999 – 2009, Kösching: Druckerei Hage GmbH, 2009, pp. 3–5, here p. 5.

8 Neugebauer, Werner: Wiener Memorandum. Gelebte Zusammenarbeit von unten [Vienna Memorandum. Active Cooperation from Below], in: Otto-Brenner-Stiftung (eds): Mehr und bessere Arbeitsplätze durch Europa. Markt contra Staat, Hamburg: VSA-Verlag, 2007, pp. 80–89, here p. 81, Translation by the authors.

9 Interview with trade union representative, Austria, Gn01 29 January 2014.

10 Wiener Memorandum, März 1999 [Vienna Memorandum, March 1999], in: IG Metall Bayern et al. (eds): 10 Jahre Wiener Memorandum 1999 – 2009, Kösching: Druckerei Hage GmbH, 2009, pp. 3–5, here p. 5.

11 Memorandum. InterregionaleTarifpolitik. Kooperationsnetzwerke der Gewerkschaften (in der Fassung vom 7. November 2005) [Memorandum. Inter-regional Tariff Policy. Cooperation

The economic crisis of 2008 / 2009 had a deep impact on the discussions and activities of the network. Issues, such as the opening of the labour markets in Austria and Germany for the new member states from Central Eastern Europe, were replaced or completed as new problems emerged. Issues that were connected to the preservation and creation of jobs and a strengthening of the social dialogue and employees' rights in times of crisis were now in the foreground.[12]

According to Hoffmann, the financial crises also challenged the solidarity between the unions from the old and new EU member states. They had been confronted with opposing trends. On the one hand, countries from the EU Enlargement benefit from the relocation of workplaces. On the other hand, the economic crisis even further pushed the countries of the EU Enlargement to the periphery, while countries from Central Europe profited from the export of goods to the new EU member states.[13] The tension between competition and solidarity is also visible, in our case, based on the dislocation of production to another country within the Vienna Memorandum Group. However, we have to consider that the concept of solidarity may and will differ based on the national partners. Klemm, Kraetsch and Weyand noticed that there is a difference between the general perception of solidarity and the real practice by the trade union members, and there are also country specifics.[14]

6.3. Member Unions of the Vienna Memorandum Group

The Vienna Memorandum unites branch unions in the metal field from Central Eastern and Western European countries, namely the German IG Metall Bavaria, the Austrian Produktionsgewerkschaft (PRO-GE), the Hungarian VASAS, the Czech OS KOVO, the Slovak OZ KOVO and the Slovenian SKEI. All of the unions in the Vienna Memorandum Group are present at the EU level and are members of the European umbrella organisation, IndustriAll Europe.[15]

Networks of Trade Unions (in the Version of 7 November 2005], in: IG Metall Bayern et al. (eds): 10 Jahre Wiener Memorandum 1999–2009, Kösching: Druckerei Hage GmbH, 2009, p. 39–43.

12 Positionspapier. Wiener Memorandum Gruppe (Präsidententreffen, 20. April 2009) [Position Paper. Vienna Memorandum Group (Presidents' Meeting, 20 April 2009)], in: IG Metall Bayern et al. (eds): 10 Jahre Wiener Memorandum 1999 – 2009, Kösching: Druckerei Hage GmbH, 2009, pp. 46–48.

13 Hoffmann, Jürgen: Perspektiven der europäischen Arbeitsbeziehungen und Gewerkschaften zwischen Modernisierung, Europäisierung und Globalisierung [Prospects for European Industrial Relations and Trade Unions in the Midst of Modernization, Europeanization and Globalization], in: Leviathan, 2010 (vol. 38), no. 1, pp. 89–102, here p. 99.

14 Klemm, Matthias / Kraetsch, Clemens / Weyand, Jan: Kultur und Solidarität in der betrieblichen Arbeitnehmerinteressenvertretung [Culture and Solidarity in the Workplace Employee Representation], Ms. Nürnberg: Friedrich-Alexander-Universität Erlangen-Nürnberg, Institut für Soziologie, Juli 2010, here p. 128–129.

15 IndustriAll Europe's affiliates' list, in: industriall-europe.eu, http://www.industriall-europe.eu/about/about.asp?mloc=puba&abo=aff, accessed 16 September 2014.

However, the background of the unions that form the Vienna Memorandum and their history and experience, as well as their resources and collective bargaining power, are quite diverse, which may affect cooperation within the network. Thus, the trade unions from the new EU member states have faced various challenges. The transformation from a socialist state economy to a market economy created new tasks for the trade unions in that region. However, a rapid decrease in membership after the system change dramatically reduced their capacity to act.[16] Thus, although IG Metall Bavaria consists of more than 366.000 members today[17], and the Austrian PRO-GE consists of approximately 250.000 members[18], the Czech OS KOVO consists of, in contrast, 107.000 members[19], and the Hungarian VASAS has approximately 40.000 members[20].

According to Kohl, the internal financial structure contributes to the lack of financial resources in most trade unions from Central Eastern Europe. The major portion of the membership fees stays at the level of company unions; only a small part of the fees reaches the branch trade unions or the confederations. Under these conditions, it has been very difficult for unions in that region to finance experts and staff.[21]

The coverage of collective agreements, the heart of the cooperation in the Vienna Memorandum, still differs to a large degree between the member countries of the network. The collective agreement coverage in Slovenia was at 95%, in Slovakia was at 45%, in Hungary was at 40% and in the Czech Republic was at 36% in 2009.[22] The dominant level for the negotiation of collective agreements is in Slovakia, and it is in Slovenia at the sectoral level and in Hungary and the Czech Republic at the company level.[23] On the other hand, the collective bargaining coverage for sectoral collective agreements in Germany was at 53% (West Germany) and 36% (East Germany) in 2012;

16 Ost, David: The End of Postcommunism. Trade Unions in Eastern Europe's Future, in: East European Politics and Societies, 2009 (vol. 23), no. 1, pp. 13–33, here p. 14.

17 Die IG Metall in Bayern, in: igmetall-bayern.de, http://www.igmetall-bayern.de/ig-metall-bayern/, accessed 4 July 2014.

18 Branchen, in: proge.at, 2009, http://www.proge.at/servlet/ContentServer?pagename=P01/Page/Index&n=P01_8.a&cid=1258991418657, accssed 4 July 2014.

19 Odborový svaz KOVO, in: oskovo.cz, 2014, http://www.oskovo.cz/odborovy-svaz-kovo, accessed 4 July 2014.

20 Krén, Ildikó: Hungary – Labour Relations and Social Dialogue, Annual Review 2013, in: Friedrich-Ebert-Stiftung, http://library.fes.de/pdf-files/bueros/warschau/10436-20140107.pdf, accessed 4 July 2014, here p. 20.

21 Kohl, Heribert: Where Do Trade Unions Stand in Eastern Europe Today? Stock-Taking after EU Enlargement, 2008, in: Friedrich-Ebert-Stiftung, http://library.fes.de/pdf-files/ipg/ipg-2008-3/09_a_kohl_gb.pdf, accessed 16 August 2014, here p. 114.

22 Kohl, Heribert: Freedom of Association, Employees' Rights and Social Dialogue in Central and Eastern Europe and the Western Balkans. Results of a Survey of 16 Formerly Socialist Countries in Eastern Europe, Berlin: Friedrich-Ebert-Stiftung, Division for International Dialogue, Department of Central and Eastern Europe, 2009, http://library.fes.de/pdf-files/id/06606.pdf, accessed 19 September 2014, here p. 31, figure 12.

23 Ibid., here p. 29, figure 11.

for collective bargaining, the sectoral level is predominant.[24] In Austria, the collective bargaining coverage rate is at approximately 95%–98%, and again, the sectoral level is the predominant level of collective bargaining.[25] The different levels of collective bargaining, particularly with regard to Hungary and the Czech Republic, may cause problems for the trade unions in the case of German or Austrian investment because the foreign companies are less limited by collective bargaining. Therefore, cooperation between the unions of the Vienna Memorandum Group is important to promote harmony and exert pressure.

Cooperation within the Vienna Memorandum Group mainly occurs in the metal field, although all of the member unions represent other branches as well. The German IG Metall Bavaria also represents employees from, for example, the textile industry and the high-tech, plastics and wood industry.[26] The Austrian branch union of PRO-GE was formed after a merger of branch unions in the fields of metal, food, textiles and chemistry in 2009.[27] All of the unions of the Vienna Memorandum have, therefore, had to cope with declining branches, which can increase tensions within the unions themselves, such as in the field of OS KOVO.[28]

However, what all of the unions of the Vienna Memorandum have in common is that they are active in countries that are highly economically dependent on and connected by the automobile industry. Thus, at a conference on the Europäische Automobilkonferenz (AUTOglobal) project that was held in June 2014 in Nürnberg, Germany, the member unions stated:

> The automobile and sub-contractor industry is in these countries one of the most important industries and makes an important contribution to the overall economy. The automobile and sub-contractor industry offer hundreds of thousands of employees directly employment and secure the livelihood of millions of people.[29]

24 Vogel, Sandra: Germany. Industrial Relations Profile, in: EurWORK European Observatory of Working Life, 23 October 2014, http://eurofound.europa.eu/observatories/eurwork/comparative-information/national-contributions/germany/germany-industrial-relations-profile, accessed 12 November 2014.

25 Allinger, Bernadette: Austria. Industrial Relations Profile, in: EurWORK European Observatory of Working Life, 23 October 2014, http://eurofound.europa.eu/observatories/eurwork/comparative-information/national-contributions/austria/austria-industrial-relations-profile, accessed 12 November 2014.

26 Die IG Metall in Bayern [The IG Metall in Bavaria], in: igmetall-bayern.de, http://www.igmetall-bayern.de/ig-metall-bayern/, accessed 4 July 2014.

27 2009. Gewerkschaft PRO-GE gegründet [2009. Trade Union PRO-GE Founded], in: proge.at, http://www.proge.at/servlet/ContentServer?pagename=P01/Page/Index&n=P01_1.1.2.a&cid=1258991427746, accessed 4 July 2014.

28 See the case study on OS Kovo in this book publication.

29 Resolution der Konferenz AUTOGlobal [Resolution of the AUTOGlobal Conference], in: igmetall-bayern.de, http://www.igmetall-bayern.de/uploads/media/Resolution.pdf, accessed 4 July 2014, translation by the authors.

The participants also noted the danger of part of the production being moved to Asia. In their resolution, they asked their governments and the European Union to take measures to keep the automobile industry and its exceptional position in Europe.[30]

6.4. Work of the Vienna Memorandum Group

6.4.1. Organisation and Activities

The work of the Vienna Memorandum consists mainly of an exchange of information and experiences, as well as support regarding collective bargaining and strikes. A good overview of the Vienna Memorandum and its activities, hereby, provides the information booklet of the network.[31]

According to one of our respondents, there are three regular contacts that form the basis for the work of the network. Firstly, once a year, the presidents of the respective trade unions alternate meeting in the member countries. These meetings are mainly meant to inform the partner unions about the current socio-political and economic developments in the member countries of the network (e.g., about labour market developments, on-going wage and salary negotiations and current topics, such as parliamentary elections). In addition, the presidential meetings are also used to review urgent issues in more detail, such as youth unemployment, the employment situation of elderly employees or the development of right wing parties in the member countries.[32]

The presidential meetings are supported by additional meetings that occur once a year, where experts and other unionists of the member unions meet.[33] Their major task is to prepare or reinforce the presidential meetings by reviewing topics that will be discussed at the next presidential meeting or by reviewing ideas that were discussed at the last presidential meeting.[34]

Furthermore, there are international seminars in Bavaria; the trade unions from the new EU member states propose the topics of these seminars, which can include, e.g., working time accounts, company pension or temporary work.[35] In addition to these institutionalised meetings and activities, the members of the Vienna Memorandum

30 Ibid.

31 IG Metall Bayern et al. (eds): 10 Jahre Wiener Memorandum 1999 – 2009 [10 years of Vienna Memorandum 1999–2009], Kösching: Druckerei Hage GmbH, 2009.

32 Interview with trade union representative, Germany, Gn09 16 April 2013.

33 Interview with trade union representative, Austria, Gn01 29 January 2014.

34 Interview with trade union representative, Germany, Gn09 16 April 2013.

35 Neugebauer, Werner / Jena, Matthias: 10 Jahre zuhören, lernen und helfen für die gemeinsamen Ziele [10 Years of Listening, Learning and Helping for Common Goals], in: IG Metall Bayern et al. (eds): 10 Jahre Wiener Memorandum 1999 – 2009, Kösching: Druckerei Hage GmbH, 2009, pp. 34–36, here p. 35.

Group support each other during international strikes, such as in Munich in 2006,[36] or they support each other through expressions of solidarity and through consultations in the case of company or factory closures, such as, for instance, in the case of the factory closure of Siemens in the Czech Republic.[37]

In addition to the regular meetings, the Vienna Memorandum Group organises additional projects, such as the AUTOglobal project. Motivated by the different situations of the social dialogues and wage standards in the member countries of the Vienna Memorandum, the project was born at the presidential meeting in 2012.[38] Major objectives of this project included 'a critical assessment of the current developments of the automobile industry within the countries of the Vienna Memorandum, with the aim to enter a tariff and social-political dialogue'[39] and 'to support the development and improvement of a social dialogue within the automobile industry of Central Eastern Europe.'[40] The project was funded by the EU and IG Metall Bavaria was responsible for project management.[41]

The trade unions from the Central Eastern European member countries of the Vienna Memorandum were fully integrated into this project. The member unions organised national workshops to analyse and discuss the current developments of the automobile industry in their countries, including the development and importance of the automobile industry for Eastern Europe[42] or the situation of the contractor firms and their lack of financial resources.[43] Works council representatives, as well as trade unionists from different companies, also attended these workshops.[44] External

36 München 2006. Internationale Demonstration (Deutschland) [Munich 2006. International Demonstration (Germany)], in: IG Metall Bayern et al. (eds): 10 Jahre Wiener Memorandum 1999 – 2009, Kösching: Druckerei Hage GmbH, 2009.

37 Josef Středula. Siemens Prag. Beispiel einer grenzüberschreitenden Solidarität [Josef Středula. Siemens Prague. Instance of a Cross-Border Solidarity], in: IG Metall Bayern et al. (eds): 10 Jahre Wiener Memorandum 1999 – 2009, Kösching: Druckerei Hage GmbH, 2009, pp. 19–23.

38 Das EU-Projekt AUTOglobal [The EU-project AUTOglobal], in: projekt-autoglobal.de, http://www.projekt-autoglobal.de/eu-projekt-autoglobal/, accessed 4 July 2014.

39 Ibid., translation by the authors.

40 Ibid.

41 IG Metall: AUTOglobal. Newsletter des EU Projekts VP/2013/001/0004 [AUTOglobal. Newsletter of the EU-Project VP/2013/001/0004], in: autoglobal.de, 14 November 2013, http://www.projekt-autoglobal.de/fileadmin/04_Admin/Autog/downloads/Newsletter-2013-11-14.pdf, accessed 4 July 2014.

42 IG Metall: AUTOglobal. Newsletter des EU Projekts VP/2013/001/0004 [AUTOglobal. Newsletter of the EU-Project VP/2013/001/0004], in: autoglobal.de, 7 March 2014, http://www.projekt-autoglobal.de/fileadmin/04_Admin/Autog/downloads/Newsletter-2014-03-07.pdf, accessed 4 July 2014.

43 IG Metall: AUTOglobal. Newsletter des EU Projekts VP/2013/001/0004 [AUTOglobal. Newsletter of the EU-Project VP/2013/001/0004], in: autoglobal.de, 2 April 2014, http://www.projekt-autoglo bal.de/fileadmin/04_Admin/Autog/downloads/Newsletter-2014-04-02.pdf, accessed 4 July 2014.

44 Ibid. IG Metall: AUTOglobal. Newsletter des EU Projekts VP/2013/001/0004 [AUTOglobal. Newsletter of the EU-Project VP/2013/001/0004], in: autoglobal.de, 31 March 2014, http://www.

experts were also present at the workshops.[45] The results of these workshops were discussed at a general conference that was held in June 2014 in Germany with trade unionists and works council representatives from the member countries of the Vienna Memorandum Group.[46]

The AUTOglobal project has been assessed as useful.[47] The project again showed the importance of the automobile industry within the discussions, the activities and the cooperation of the Vienna Memorandum Group.

6.4.2. Resources and Flow of Communication

As observed in the previous section, the Vienna Memorandum Group meets on a regular basis to exchange information and experiences. However, different than other networks, the Group does not employ its own secretary or a standing committee that organises its work.

According to one of our respondents, the activities of the Vienna Memorandum are, rather, additional tasks that are fulfilled by representatives of the member unions themselves. In most cases, there is no external funding for the meetings and seminars. The seminars and activities are financed by the branch unions' own resources. The member organisations alternate hosting and organising the meetings and use their own human resources for them.[48] However, this may be a challenge for unions that have less financial resources, and this issue also addresses the question of solidarity, if unions have to support each other to make the meetings and the participation of resource-poor unions possible.

Nonetheless, besides limited financial and human resources, information and the exchange of experiences, as well as certain flexibility in agenda setting for the meetings, seem to be the concrete uses of this trade union network for the member organisations. As known from the literature on interest representation at the EU level,

---

projekt-autoglobal.de/fileadmin/04_Admin/Autog/downloads/Newsletter-2014-03-31.pdf, accessed 4 July 2014.

45 IG Metall: AUTOglobal. Newsletter des EU Projekts VP/2013/001/0004 [AUTOglobal. Newsletter of the EU-Project VP/2013/001/0004], in: autoglobal.de, 7 March 2014, http://www.projekt-autoglobal.de/fileadmin/04_Admin/Autog/downloads/Newsletter-2014-03-07.pdf, accessed 4 July 2014.

46 Resolution der Konferenz AUTOGlobal [Resolution of the AUTOGlobal Conference], in: igmetall-bayern.de, http://www.igmetall-bayern.de/uploads/media/Resolution.pdf, accessed 4 July 2014.

47 For example: Budapesten tanácskoztak a „Bécsi Memorandum" régiós együttműködés szakszervezeteinek elnökei [The Presidents of the Trade Unions from the 'Vienna Memorandum' Regional Cooperation Deliberated in Budapest], in: vasasszakszervezet.hu, 25 March 2013, http://www.vasasszakszervezet.hu/hirek/1-hirek/720-budapesten-tanacskoztak-a-becsi-memorandum-regios-egyuttmukodes-szakszervezeteinek-elnokei, accessed 4 July 2014.

48 Interview with trade union representative, Germany, Gn09 16 April 2013.

'information is the currency of lobbying in the EU.'[49] We can assume that this is also true for the national or subnational levels because the unions can use the information and experience that they gain through cooperation for interest representation in the national arena against employers and the state. However, the Vienna Memorandum Group has no real power to act on or enforce the implementation of its decisions. They cannot go beyond the discussion stage.

Because we assume that the exchange of information and experiences is a very important use of the network, the dissemination of information among and within the unions is also an important point. Regarding this question, the flow of communication within the network is perceived by the member unions to work well:

> In general, I can say: After the first few years that contained an atmosphere of a gold rush, much has been improved. Locally, the employee and trade union structures have been considerably enhanced and have been adapted to the current requests. And the flow of information is better at all of the levels, thus we can more quickly and more effectively react to new developments. In addition, we regularly change the information, and we have common seminars. These are important cornerstones of this development.[50]
> What we also do, usually after the presidential meeting, is that we report in the respective bodies so that we do not only meet and exchange views.[51]

The exchange of information does not only occur in the headquarters of the member unions. In addition to the formal meetings and contacts, there are further contacts that help support the work of the member unions and the works council members by quickly gaining and exchanging information, as the following statement illustrates:

> The advantage is that the information exchange is very important, I mean, in regard to gaining insight into what questions are really on the daily agenda of the trade unions and what wage agreements have been concluded. This leads to a quick exchange of information, which works quite well during the single meetings and beyond. Recently, we have also received requests from our work council members...Recently, I received a request from an installation company concerning the working time regulations in Slovakia. We were able to quickly receive information due to the good contacts of the Vienna Memorandum.[52]

However, language is one major challenge regarding the organisational work of the network. To reduce the costs of translations and interpreters, German is the working language of the meetings and the documents.[53] Nonetheless, finding interpreters who are familiar with the work of trade unions, so that they can provide proper translations

49 Chalmers, Adam: Interests, Influence and Information. Comparing the Influence of Interest Groups in the European Union, in: Journal of European Integration, 2011 (vol. 33), no. 4, pp. 471–486, here p. 471.
50 Neugebauer, Werner / Jena, Matthias: 10 Jahre zuhören, lernen und helfen für die gemeinsamen Ziele [10 Years of Listening, Learning and Helping for Common Goals], in: IG Metall Bayern et al. (eds): 10 Jahre Wiener Memorandum 1999 – 2009, Kösching: Druckerei Hage GmbH, 2009, pp. 34–36, here p. 36, translation by the authors.
51 Interview with trade union representative, Germany, Gn09 16 April 2013.
52 Interview with trade union representative, Austria, Gn01 29 January 2014.
53 Interview with trade union representative, Germany, Gn09 16 April 2013.

that include all of the technical details, may be challenging. Furthermore, it seems to be problematic that the communication language within the Vienna Memorandum Group is German, and the communication language in IndustriAll Europe is English. After taking into account the insufficient language knowledge of trade union representatives in general and the limited size of trade unions' executive bodies in the member organisations of the new EU member states, it can be observed that it is not easy, first, to find enough representatives for these international bodies and, second, to find the financial sources so that at least the basic documents can be translated to the native language of the national trade union executive. Thus, problems of intercultural communication, which exist due to the countries' different historical, political and cultural experiences, may be strengthened by the language barrier.

6.5. Interactions between the Vienna Memorandum Group and the Other Levels

We can imagine the cooperation in a hierarchical complementary system between the target groups on different levels of universality. It corresponds to the internal organisation of cooperation and division of responsibility within the particular national trade unions.

Bilateral (in a few cases, trilateral) regional cooperation in border regions, or Interregional Trade Union Councils, is on the lower level. Interregional Trade Union Council's (IRTUC) aim is the regulation of cross-border work, concentrating on specific sectors and the problems of the cross-border region or on one sector, such as the mining industry in the IRTUC Elbe-Neiße. Themes of industrial relations, collective agreement issues and the legal fundamentals of the countries could also be involved, depending on the individual IRTUCs and the needs that they have. Mutual participation in the demonstrations on wage and trade union demands or, in individual cases, cross-border support, such as wage campaigns, is also part of the cooperation. The activities are coordinated at the regional level, and methodical help from the centre is available, when needed.

The Vienna Memorandum Group, however, is perceived as the cooperation between the Visegrad countries (Visegrad group (V4 or V5)), plus Bavaria and Austria, which is often mentioned in the interviews with the member organisations from Central Europe. This is the more common perception of the Vienna Memorandum Group cooperation. We have to mention that for the Visegrad countries, both Germany (Bavaria) and Austria are the closest partners historically, in spite of the former existence of the iron curtain. For example, when we asked the Czech and Slovak respondents with whom they have the closest cooperation regarding the old member states, in Slovakia, 57% of the respondents mentioned Germany, and 86% mentioned Austria. In the Czech Republic, Germany was first (79%), and Austria was second (63%). This explanation could be the origin of the mother companies of Foreign Direct Investment (FDI), the industrial branch where cooperation is the most important or the region where the labour force / pedlars / commuters go. The strong orientation toward the automobile industry in the Czech Republic and Slovakia may be one of the explanations for this.

The Vienna Memorandum Group was originally a voluntary grouping, an initiative from the bottom and a response to an existing need, and these circumstances have had a positive impact on its functioning. It seems to be closer to the problems in the branches and less formal than the overall European level. The network did not lose its relevance after the creation of the IndustriAll Eastern region. When compared to IndustriAll Europe, the Vienna Memorandum Group's scope is still narrower, and its communication is less formal.[54] It is easier for the Group to influence the agenda for the next meeting and to react to the changing economic situation. The contact is more frequent and more intensive. The former scope (employment and tariff policy) was enlarged, and today, it also includes social policy, agency work and its impact on employment. Experience exchange and know-how transfer are highly appreciated. As mentioned by one Czech representative, in the area of collective bargaining or agency work, the Western European partners are more experienced, and they address problems for a longer time so that they can learn from their experiences and mistakes.[55]

IndustriAll Europe, the regional group, covers more countries and more branches (metal, textile, chemical and energy), so the scope of its problems, as well as the scope of the particular national or branch specific interests, is broader. The countries that are united in the Vienna Memorandum Group are divided into two regional groups within IndustriAll Europe. The Czech Republic, Hungary, Slovakia and Slovenia, together with Poland, create the Eastern Region; Germany and Austria belong to the Central Region with Switzerland. The combination of Eastern European countries and their immediate Western European neighbours of Bavaria and Austria is an 'added value' of the Vienna Memorandum Group, with respect to economic interests.

Could the Vienna Memorandum Group deliver incentives for IndustriAll Europe's activities and vice versa? According to our experts and the available documents, there is a mutual thematical influence. It concerns, first of all, the wage tariff policy, wage coordination, precarious work, agency work and similar topics. The original objectives (tariff coordination) also correspond to the strategy of IndustriAll. The goals of the regional networks, such as the Vienna Memorandum Group, which is specific to the metal industry, are also important for other branches, such as the chemical industry because they enforce wage coordination and standards throughout Europe, which is the aim and interest of the confederations and the European level umbrella organisations.[56]

54 Interview with trade union representative, Czech Republic, Gn18 30 January 2014.
55 Interview with trade union representative, Czech Republic, Gn03 25 February 2013.
56 Interview with trade union representative, Austria, Gn01 29 January 2014.

The Vienna Memorandum Group is not a step / specific level on the vertical line from the national level to the EU level; however, it offers a platform for cooperation and joined action. We need to keep in mind that in small countries, the number of representatives in different international and EU boards and committees is not large, and personal contacts could be used as a bridge. What is discussed within regional groupings is then transferred to the European level. As mentioned by one of our respondents, the transfer is realised through various channels. When the Vienna Memorandum Group is not suitable, action occurs via the country's own trade union institutions.[57]

6.6. Conclusion

The Vienna Memorandum was founded before EU Enlargement and presented a new quality of cooperation in Central Europe. The Vienna Memorandum Group was based on former bilateral contacts that were created between trade unions from Central Eastern European countries, and Germany and Austria, and was created to consolidate and strengthen these contacts. It has been an initiative from the bottom and a response to existing needs. The idea was to also introduce a social dimension to the EU Enlargement. Despite the different types of Europe-wide trade union representations and multiple memberships by trade union experts, the Vienna Memorandum Group seems to have its place in the system of international cooperation and networks. It is perceived as a cooperation of the Visegrad countries (V4 or V5), plus Bavaria and Austria, and we have to mention that for the Visegrad countries, both Germany (Bavaria) and Austria are the closest partners historically, in spite of the former existence of the iron curtain. This regional grouping is a good example of the close cooperation between the trade unions from the old and new EU member states, which is maintained by the partners' own resources and is organised by them.

In light of the fact that in a few member states, collective bargaining exclusively / mostly occurs on the company level, the information on the transnational tariff partnership and wage and salary negotiations is assessed very positively by the participating trade unions and their representatives.

The goals and topics of the Vienna Memorandum Group correspond to the goals and objectives of IndustriAll Europe; however, the small and less formal format provides the members with more opportunities to influence agenda setting.

57 Interview with trade union representative, Austria, Gn01 29 January 2014.

Karoline Mis

7. European Works Councils in Poland and the Europeanization of the Niezależny Samorządny Związek Zawodowy Solidarność (NSZZ Solidarność) Trade Union

7.1. Introduction

With the adoption of the council directive 94/45/EC of 22 September 1994—on 'the establishment of a European Works Council (EWC) or a procedure in Community-scale undertakings and Community-scale groups of undertakings for the purposes of informing and consulting employees'—European legislators finally implemented a compulsory transnational framework for the representation of workers' interests in multinational companies, despite vehement resistance from the European Employers' Federation. Accordingly, this new directive was considered one of the most important European Union (EU) decisions in the social policy field, opening a path for the emergence of transnational and EU-level industrial relations.[1]

The directive applies to all transnational companies that are active in Europe and have at least 1,000 employees, while operating in a minimum of two EU countries with more than 150 workers in each country. Since the implementation of the directive, 1,030 of these transnational information and consultation bodies have been installed, which corresponds to a coverage rate of approximately 47% by taking into account the 2,200 companies that came under the directive (status: 2011).[2] After the recast of the directive in 2009 (2009/38/EC), some of the main conflicts regarding the interpretation of 'information and consultation' or the question of which matters should be considered 'transnational', could be resolved through a better definition of EWCs' competencies.[3]

Since their conception, the EWC's quite unique construction as complex national, supranational and company-level organisational networks has inspired wide-rang-

1 Müller, Torsten / Platzer, Hans-Wolfgang: European Works Councils. A new Mode of EU Regulation and the Emergence of European Multi-level Structure of Workplace Industrial Relations, in: Keller, Berndt / Platzer, Hans-Wolfgang (eds): Industrial Relations and European Integration. Trans- and Supranational Developments and Aspects, Aldershot: Ashgate, 2003, pp. 58–84, here p. 58.

2 European Trade Union Institute (ETUI): EWC Database 5/2012, in: ewcdb.eu, http://www.ewcdb.eu/statistics_graphs.php, accessed 29 November 2014. It should be noted, that these data are ratings, because the exact number of EWC couldn't be identified due to lack of legal obligations to inform about EWC creations.

3 Jagodzinski, Romuald: Review, Revision or Recast? The quest for an amended EWC Directive, in: Dorssemont, Filip / Blanke, Thomas (eds): The Recast of the European Works Council Directive, Antwerp: Intersentia, 2010, pp. 293–311.

ing research interest in the European scientific community.[4] However, EWC research has been complicated by the character of each individual EWC body, which is based

> on the different national transposition laws of the countries where the corresponding companies are active and the individual negotiated agreements between management and labour representatives.[5]

In view of this divergent nature, it is not surprising that a controversial scientific debate about the role of EWCs in the Europeanization of industrial relations is ongoing. While 'pessimistic' authors argue that EWCs 'are neither European, nor Works Councils',[6] 'optimistic' observers see in 'EWCs currently the most dynamic pole within the transnationalisation of industrial relations'[7]. On the basis of an EWC typology, some authors identified different developmental stages of European Works Councils and, using evidence from sporadic EWC case studies,[8] asserted that 'participative' EWCs are the only channel of Europeanization.[9]

Although categories provide initial orientation to EWC practice, they are only partially able to explain the full picture of EWC realities—especially in the context of Central Eastern Europe. Because of the small number of negotiating EWCs and fewer EWC members from Central Eastern Europe in these participative European Works Councils, their Europeanization impact should not be visible when following the established research literature. Thus, it is essential to clearly define the term 'Europeanization' itself—which is frequently used in industrial relations research, though it is not always clear on which levels it has taken effect. When focusing on possible Europeanization

---

4 For an extensive literature review, see the following sources: Müller, Torsten / Hoffmann, Aline: EWC Research. A Review of the Literature, in: Warwick Papers in Industrial Relations (65), 2001, pp. 1–143. Waddington, Jeremy: European works councils. A transnational industrial relations institution in the making, New York: Routledge, 2011.

5 Hertwig, Markus / Pries, Ludger / Rampeltshammer, Luitpold: European Works Councils as international non-profit organisations. An organisational research approach to a crucial element of Europeanisation, in: Hertwig, Markus / Pries, Ludger / Rampeltshammer, Luitpold (eds): European Works Councils in complementary perspectives, Brussels: European Trade Union Institute, 2009, pp. 13–46, here p. 13.

6 Streeck, Wolfgang: Neither European nor works councils. a reply to Paul Knutsen, in: Economic and Industrial Democracy, 1997 (vol. 18), no. 2, pp. 325–337.

7 Lecher, Wolfgang / Platzer, Hans-Wolfgang / Rüb, Stefan / Weiner, Klaus Peter (eds): European Works Councils. Development, Types and Networking, Aldershot: Ashgate, 2001, here p. 120.

8 According to estimates, only 5% of all existing EWCs had negotiated an international agreement with their management, which is seen as a main indicator for categorizing them as participative EWCs. Rüb, Stefan / Platzer, Hans-Wolfgang / Müller, Torsten: Transnationale Unternehmensvereinbarungen. Zur Neuordnung der Arbeitsbeziehungen in Europa [Transnational company agreements. Restructuring industrial relations in Europe], Berlin: Edition Sigma, 2000, here p. 235.

9 For a recent recapitulation, see: Platzer, Hans-Wolfgang: Approaching and theorising European Works Councils. comments on the emergence of a European multi-level structure of employee involvement and participation, in: Hertwig, Markus / Pries, Ludger / Rampeltshammer Luitpold (eds): European Works Councils in complementary perspectives, Brussels: European Trade Union Institute, 2009, pp. 47–69, here p. 58 f.

processes on the national level, namely in Poland, the EWC category becomes secondary because the national actors, such as trade unions, are the centre of interest. Following Börzel and Risse's conceptualisation of Europeanization,[10] this paper argues that a mismatch between European and national industrial relations practices leads to domestic change in Poland. This forces national actors to oppose domestic change (as veto points) or support it (as change agents). Because industrial relations in Central Eastern Europe are generally characterised as weak—Poland in particular was accused of being a 'Trojan horse of Americanisation'[11]—the mismatch between European and national standards in the social dialogue appears high, and accordingly, this is attributed to the resistance of the national actors against change. Analysing the Polish trade union NSZZ Solidarność under Europeanization pressures via the implementation process of the EWC directive, evidence shows that, although the mismatch is quite high, the trade union, surprisingly, acts as a 'change agent'.

The purpose of this paper is to explain how Europeanization processes initiated by the EWC directive affect the NSZZ Solidarność and why it acted as a 'change agent'. For this reason, the second section provides a theoretical framework and explains the methodology. Empirical data about European Works Councils in Poland are presented in the third section. The fourth section analyses the NSZZ Solidarność strategies compared to the EWC directive, and derived from these, Europeanization effects will be outlined. In the fifth section, all results will be summarised and further research questions enunciated.

7.2. Theoretical Framework and Methodology

One main argument of this paper is that Europeanization processes must be analysed in a complex multi-level system,[12] in which national trade unions are only one possible field of interest. Just considering the national context, this means that other possible Europeanization objects are, for instance: the system of industrial relations or individual European Works Council members (see the following Figure 7-1). Europeanization must be understood as differentiated and overlapping processes within national borders that result from the impact of EU membership or EU accession. It must be noted that Europeanization processes changed dramatically for the new member states after EU accession because they became involved in European decision-making and had to

10 Börzel, Tanja A. / Risse, Thomas: Conceptualizing the Domestic Impact of Europe, in: Featherstone, Kevin / Radaelli, Claudio M. (eds): The Politics of Europeanization, Oxford: University Press, 2003, pp. 57–82.

11 Meardi, Guglielmo: The Trojan Horse for the Americanization of Europe? Polish Industrial Relations towards the EU, in: Journal of Industrial Relations, 2002 (vol. 8), no. 1, pp. 77–99.

12 Müller, Torsten / Platzer, Hans-Wolfgang / Rüb, Stefan: Transnational company agreements and the role of European Works Councils in negotiations. A quantitative analysis in the metalworking sector. Report 127, Brussels: European Trade Union Institute, 2013, here p. 19 ff.

take responsibility for the outcomes of these decisions. This is why Europeanization has not only a vertical dimension, which is implemented top–down in each EU member state, through the European legislation, but also a horizontal dimension. Transferred to industrial relations, horizontal Europeanization processes can be observed, for example, between national trade unions and EWC members or within EWCs. To complete the picture of Europeanization effects triggered by EWCs in EU member states, their impact also needs to be analysed via case studies with the focus on the national (Polish) EWC members as well as the EWC directive's national legislative transposition process.[13] This chapter concentrates only on Europeanization effects at the national level, using the example of trade union activists from the Foreign Department of the NSZZ Solidarność headquarters in Gdańsk.

Figure 7-1: Analytical Framework for Europeanization Processes Caused by European Works Councils

Europeanization objects / Level	System of industrial relations	Social partners / trade unions	EWC and its members
EU	↑ vertical Europeanization		
National		*Focus of the chapter*	
Local	↓	← horizontal Europeanization →	

Own conceptualization.

7.2.1. What Does Europeanization Mean?

Europeanization has become quite a popular term in recent academic literature, namely in political science as well as in industrial relations research. While political science developed some useful definitions and concepts of Europeanization, these are lacking in EWC research literature, although the term is extensively utilised.[14] Without a systematic theoretical conceptualisation of EWCs in Europeanization processes, the exist-

13 Mis, Karoline: Transformations- und Europäisierungsprozesse der industriellen Beziehungen Polens am Beispiel von Europäischen Betriebsräten [Transformation and Europeanization of industrial relations in Poland based on the example of European Works Councils], PhD thesis, Kassel, 2014.

14 This applies also to the 'organisational fit' approach of Hauser-Ditz / Hertwig / Pries, where methodical deficits (only automobile sector, German bias, unclear empirical data) lead ultimately to more confusion than theoretical clarity. Hauser-Ditz, Axel / Hertwig, Markus/ Pries, Ludger / Rampeltshammer, Luitpold: Transnationale Mitbestimmung? Zur Praxis Europäischer Betriebsräte in der Automobilindustrie [Transnational participation? European Works Councils' practice in the automotive industry], Frankfurt am Main: Campus Verlag, 2010, pp. 35–63.

ing definitions often remain vague. Marginson and Sisson propose using the term in two ways:

> The first is to describe an end-state, which takes the form of a vertically integrated system equivalent to that which exists at national levels….The other is to describe a tendency or trend in which there is discernible movement with common policies leading to common outcomes achieved by common processes.[15]

Other authors warn us not to reduce Europeanization to the question of an increasing convergence of the systems of industrial relations.[16] However, Platzer follows the convergence paradigm and defines this as one of three possible dimensions of Europeanization. In this view—adding the term 'systemic transformation'—Europeanization has occurred when 'EWC practice led to a dominance of monistic or single channel industrial relations that affect and transform dualistic national IR systems.'[17] (IR—industrial relations). The second dimension is defined as 'horizontal' Europeanization, where transnational exchange and learning processes change the national behaviour of the EWC members 'from above'.[18] Finally, in accordance with Platzer, 'vertical' Europeanization can be observed in the negotiating practices of the participative-oriented EWCs, which go far beyond the primary intention of the EWC directive.

This short overview shows the diverse aspects of Europeanization, which mostly refer to the development of a European system—or to changes in national systems—of industrial relations. That is problematic insofar as nothing is said about the mechanism of these changing processes within national contexts, why Europeanization occurs or how it can be measured. To clarify the underlying understanding of Europeanization, the following definition from Kutter and Trappmann is used:

> Europeanization can be defined as the outcome of the social partners in industrial (EU) multi-level system processes, in which the rules, discourses and practices that have evolved in the context of European integration as EU specifically are incorporated in the context of nationally operating institutions and political systems.[19]

15 Marginson, Paul/ Sisson, Keith: European integration and industrial relations. Multi-level governance in the making. Basingstoke: Palgrave, 2005, here p. 8.

16 Eberwein, Wilhelm / Tholen, Jochen / Schuster, Joachim: The Europeanisation of Industrial Relations. National and European processes in Germany, UK, Italy and France. Aldershot: Ashgate, 2002, here p. 157.

17 Platzer, Hans-Wolfgang: Approaching and theorizing European Works Councils. comments on the emergence of a European multi-level structure of employee involvement and participation, in: Hertwig, Markus / Pries, Ludger / Rampeltshammer, Luitpold (eds): European Works Councils in complementary perspectives, Brussels: European Trade Union Institute, 2009, pp. 47–69, here p. 52.

18 Ibid., here p. 54.

19 Kutter, Amelie / Trappmann, Vera (eds): Das Erbe des Beitritts. Europäisierung in Mittel- und Osteuropa [The legacy of accession. Europeanization of Central Eastern Europe], Baden-Baden: Nomos, 2006, p. 16.

For a deeper understanding of the mechanism of Europeanization and the outlined mismatch, the following top–down Europeanization concept[20], developed by Börzel and Risse, will be explained in detail.

7.2.2. Where Is the Mismatch and How Does Europeanization Work?

The starting point for this analysis of Europeanization processes is the already mentioned 'mismatch-approach'. The theory underlies the general assumption that there is a mismatch between the European and national levels, which is the reason for domestic change processes.

Defining the mismatch in the case of industrial relations requires deep historical and cultural insight into national social dialogue practices, especially because of different path dependencies in the former communist states and their transformation. It is beyond controversy that the Polish society had undergone dramatic change after the fall of communism. Thus, the last 20 years can be characterised by efforts to catch up politically, socially and economically.[21] During this transformative time, Polish industrial relations had been a testing ground for democratic negotiations due to the NSZZ Solidarność's role as key political actor in the revolutionary protest movement of civil society.[22] Unfortunately, Polish trade unions failed to establish a capable industrial relations system in the face of privatisation and globalisation pressures. Consequently, some authors see the Polish case as an example of 'deregulated, marketised, short-term and fragmented industrial relations, which with much approximation could be labelled as "Americanisation"'[23]. Comparing all types of industrial relations in Central Eastern Europe, Kohl and Platzer propose separating them into two categories based on transformation and speed, where the Polish system is in the weaker, slower and

20 Börzel, Tanja A. / Risse, Thomas: Conceptualizing the Domestic Impact of Europe, in: Featherstone, Kevin / Radaelli, Claudio M. (eds): The Politics of Europeanization, Oxford: University Press, 2003, pp. 57–82.

21 Hardy, Jane: Poland's new capitalism. London: Pluto Press, 2009. Bohle, Dorothee: Europas neue Peripherie. Polens Transformation und transnationale Integration [Europe's new peripheral. Poland's transformation and transnational integration], Münster: Westfälisches Dampfboot, 2002.

22 Ost, David: The Defeat of Solidarity. Anger and Politics in Postcommunist Europe, New York: Cornell University Press, 2005.

23 Meardi, Guglielmo: Neo-liberal Models and Mirages in Polish Industrial Relations, in: Labour Focus on Eastern Europe, 2001, no. 69, pp. 23–46, here p. 30. Steger, Thomas: Auf dem Weg zum Neo-Liberalismus? Ein kritischer Blick auf die Entwicklung der industriellen Beziehungen in Mittel- und Osteuropa [On the way to neo-liberalism? A critical look at the development of industrial relations in Central Eastern Europe], in: Jurczek, Peter / Niedobitek, Matthias (eds): Europäische Forschungsperspektiven. Elemente einer Europawissenschaft, Chemnitzer Europastudien Band 8 [European research perspectives. Elements of European Science, Chemnitz European Studies Volume 8], Berlin: Duncker & Humblot, 2008, pp. 153–174.

inherently conservative group.[24] Without going too far into the details, the general rating of Polish industrial relations triggered appropriate doubts about their adaptability relative to Western European standards.[25]

Adopting the EWC directive during the EU accession process in the course of the acquis communautaire did not cause fundamental changes in Poland's industrial relations. Despite the already mentioned shortcomings of Polish industrial relations, the social dialogue is highly regulated by law, so that the existing framework between the social partners can certainly compete with Western European standards. However, 'Polish labour suffers from an imbalance due to overregulation on one side and a plethora of vague formulations on the other, which enable the employers' side to dilute standards.'[26] That is why the mismatch cannot be described as absence of legal regulations at the national level.

Although information and consultation rights did exist formally before the EWC directive, this was not seen as desirable practice for Polish trade unions on the local level, which is their main arena of activity. Participation in economic or strategic management decisions stands contrary to the trade unions self-understanding as local provider and preserver of social services. Of course, the unwillingness of employers to allow forms of co-determination presents the other side of the same problem. This rather 'confrontational behaviour' is undoubtedly a result of former experiences in the communist era (path dependency) and explains, moreover, the rejection of trade unions against works councils. For that reason employee interest representation is highly dependent on the existence of a local trade union organisation, which nevertheless excludes the vast majority of Polish workers from these rights.

To sum up, there are different factors which generate the mismatch in social dialogue among the European, national and local company levels. For instance, on the national level there is also a significant lack of consensual negotiation among the partners in the tripartite commissions, so that cooperative communication between employer and employee representation can be seen as relatively unusual in this country.

---

24 Kohl, Heribert / Platzer, Hans-Wolfgang: Arbeitsbeziehungen in Mittelosteuropa. Transformation und Integration. Die acht neuen EU-Mitgliedsstaaten im Vergleich [Industrial relations in Central and Eastern Europe. Transformation and integration. A comparison of the eight new EU member states], Baden-Baden: Nomos, 2004, here p. 281.

25 Ladó, Mária: EU-Enlargement. Reshaping European and National Industrial Relations?, in: The International Journal of Comparative Labour Law and Industrial Relations, 2002 (vol. 18), no. 1, pp. 101–124. Marginson, Paul: Europeanisation and Regime Competition. Industrial Relations and EU Enlargement, in: Industrielle Beziehungen, 2006 (vol. 13), no. 2, pp. 97–117. Keune, Maarten: EU enlargement and social standards. exporting the European Social Model?, Working Paper 2008.01, Brussels: European Trade Union Institute for Research, Education and Health and Safety (ETUI-REHS), 2008. Vaughan-Whitehead, Daniel C.: EU enlargement versus social Europe? The uncertain future of the European social model. Cheltenham: Elgar, 2003.

26 Trappmann, Vera: Trade Unions in Poland. Current Situation, Organisation and Challenges, Berlin, Bonn: Friedrich Ebert Foundation, 2012, here p. 5.

In this sense, the mismatch between Polish labour relations and European requirements can be seen on one hand both as institutional and as a formal lack of information and consultation opportunities for Polish workers; on the other hand, the mismatch can be seen as culturally inadequate negotiation practices and conflict-oriented attitudes among the social partners.

Returning to the theoretical concept of Europeanization defined above, mismatches provoke domestic change. Börzel and Risse identified two ways that these changes within the nation state. First, they see a redistribution of resources (rational institutionalism) as a sufficient condition for domestic change; and second, the change process may occur as socialisation and a learning process.[27] In the first case national actors are provided with additional opportunities and they have also the capacities to exploit such new options.[28] In the second case, 'the emergence of new rules, norms, practises and structures of meaning to which member states are exposed and which they have to incorporate into their domestic practises and structures' are leading to domestic changes.[29] If national actors serve as 'change agents' or 'norm entrepreneurs', domestic change is more likely at the time when national 'veto points' do exist. Finally, the outcome of domestic change in response to Europeanization can be distinguished in three ways, namely 'absorption' (low change), 'accommodation' (middle change) and 'transformation' (high change).[30] As the authors note, both processes can overlap.

Transferring this concept to our object of investigation—NSZZ Solidarność—this would signify the following assumptions:

1. There is a significant mismatch between the European level of industrial relations and the national (Polish) one, which the EU tries to harmonise by means of several instruments, such as the EWC directive.
2. Over the course of the implementation of the directive, Polish trade union actors saw new opportunities to force their influence.
3. They invested staff and financial resources in promoting EWCs in Poland and served hence as 'change agents'.

Before delving into the quantitative and qualitative empirical findings, the following section explains the underlying methodology.

7.2.3. Methodology

In this chapter Europeanization processes had been analysed within the already presented multi-level framework (see Figure 7-1) and where the emphasis was on the

27 Börzel, Tanja A. / Risse, Thomas: Conceptualizing the Domestic Impact of Europe, in: Featherstone, Kevin / Radaelli, Claudio M. (eds): The Politics of Europeanization, Oxford: University Press, 2003, pp. 57–82, here p. 63 ff.
28 Ibid., here p. 64.
29 Ibid., here p. 66.
30 Ibid., here p. 69 f.

national and local (Polish) level. Beyond the five 'most-different-case-studies' (EWCs) carried out with focus on the Polish EWC members, three key actors from the NSZZ Solidarność foreign department had been interviewed as experts.[31] All interviews had been recorded, transcribed and translated into German (by the author) and served afterwards as qualitative data.

A quantitative overview of European Works Councils was possible through a database that was developed and maintained by one of the NSZZ Solidarność interview partners. This data source was provided complete to the author. The development of this database was made possible by an EU-founded project, namely 'ERZ i rada pracowników jako platforma dialogu autonomicznego w poznawaniu i określaniu wspólnych interesów pracodawców i pracowników'[32]. The results of this project are still available on a special website,[33] where they are no longer up to date. The analysis of these data will be presented in the following section.

To complete the methods section, it should be mentioned that—in contrast to most Western European EWC studies—at this time almost all existing Polish research literature and documents of the trade union could be integrated into the research, so that a comprehensive perspective of the different perceptions of EWCs is possible.

7.3. European Works Councils in Poland

From the beginning European Works Councils have been observed by the Polish trade union NSZZ Solidarność and a number of scientists. Although Poland and other Central Eastern Europe countries aroused relatively little attention in Western European research contexts, national (Polish) dedication enables comparatively satisfying data, as presented in the following section.

7.3.1. Quantitative Overview. Facts and Figures

In Poland and in the rest of Central Eastern Europe the EWC coverage rate is much higher than in Western Europe, comparing the coverage rate of potential multinational companies (MNU) that come under the directive and operate in Central Eastern Europe with those companies which are active in at least one of the Central Eastern Europe countries and where a European Works Council is already established. While the EWC coverage rate in all EU member states is up to approximately 35%,[34] the data

31 This was accomplished during the author's two-month research stay at the foreign department of the NSZZ Solidarność in Gdańsk (September and October 2011).

32 Own translation: 'EWC and Workers' Councils as platforms of an autonomous dialogue to identify common interests for employers and employees.'

33 See the project's website at http://erz.solidarnosc.org.pl/.

34 Tholen, Jochen: Zur Bedeutung von Europäischen Betriebsräten für »gute Arbeit« in Mittel / Osteuropa [On the importance of European Works Councils for 'good work' in Central

from the following Figure 7-2 indicate that this value is approximately 54% in Central Eastern Europe.

Figure 7-2: Multinational Enterprises Under EWC Directive with Subsidiary Companies in NMS (by Country of Establishment)

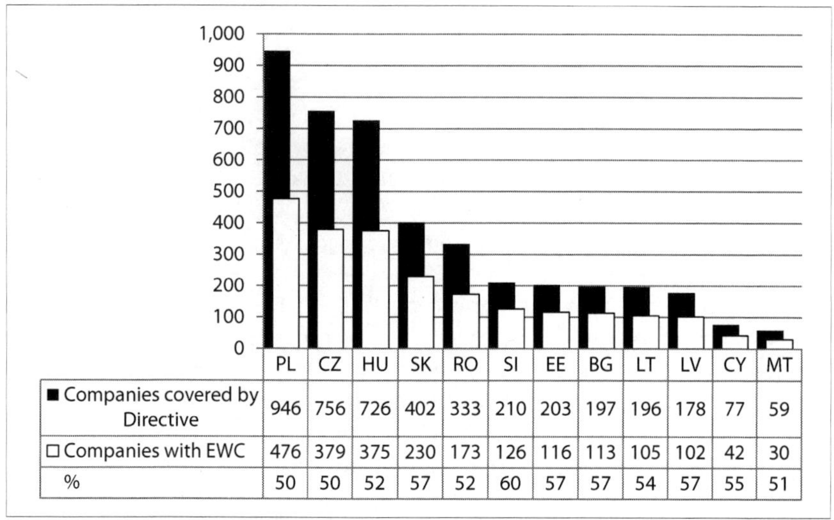

	PL	CZ	HU	SK	RO	SI	EE	BG	LT	LV	CY	MT
■ Companies covered by Directive	946	756	726	402	333	210	203	197	196	178	77	59
□ Companies with EWC	476	379	375	230	173	126	116	113	105	102	42	30
%	50	50	52	57	52	60	57	57	54	57	55	51

Source: Weiler, Anni: European Works Councils in practice. Key research findings. Background paper, Dublin: European Foundation for the Improvement of Living and Working Conditions, 2008, here p. 7. Figures from the European Works Councils database, ETUI-REHS, March 2008.

Based on these data, there seems to be evidence for the presumption that European Works Councils represent a significant factor in industrial relations in Central Eastern Europe because those economies are pervaded by foreign capital. However, these figures do not mean an automatic integration of Central Eastern Europe representatives in all established EWCs which are operating in this region. For Poland, the first estimates from 2006 assessed that only 130 to 140 EWC bodies had one or more Polish delegates—of the 425 companies with an EWC that are active in Poland. Because there might also be more than one Polish member in the several EWCs, the evaluated total number of Polish EWC members was approximately 300.[35] More recent figures from the NSZZ Solidarność database (with data through 2011) rate 187 EWCs with Polish

Eastern Europe], in: Becke, Guido / Bleses, Peter / Ritter, Wolfgang et al. (eds): »Decent Work«. Arbeitspolitische Gestaltungsperspektive für eine globalisierte und flexibilisierte Arbeitswelt ['Decent Work'. Labour-policy perspectives for a globalized and flexible working life], Wiesbaden: VS Verlag für Sozialwissenschaften, pp. 77–95, here p. 83.

35 Matla, Andrzej: Nieodkryty potencjał europejskich rad zakładowych – milowy krok na drodze budowania europejskiego wymiaru zbiorowych stosunków pracy [The undiscovered potential of the European Works Councils—a milestone on the road to European collective industrial

participation and more than 280 Polish members. From these data, summarised in the following graphic, it appears that 120 EWCs have one Polish member, 50 bodies have two Polish representatives, 10 EWC have three Polish delegates, while there are four EWCs with five Polish members and one EWC with nine members:

Figure 7-3: Number of Polish EWC Members Per EWC

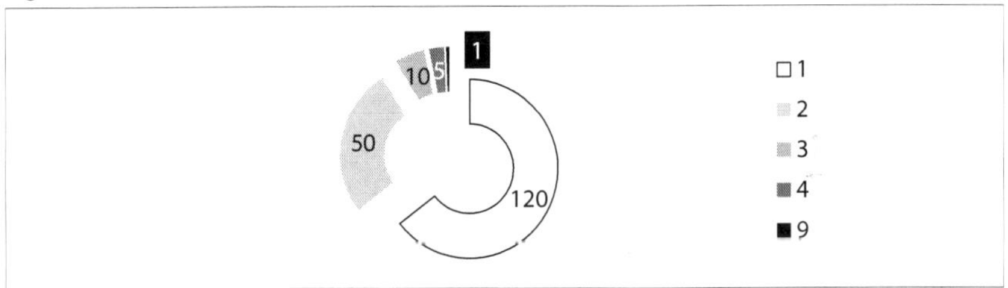

Source: Own figure according to the NSZZ Solidarność database.

With regard to the parent companies' country of origin or the country whose national legislation was the basis for the EWC agreement, most bodies are based on a German agreement (36), followed by France (34), Belgium (19) and the UK (18).[36] Non-European companies are missing from this analysis because they are only covered indirectly by the EWC directive and therefore no data are available. Surprisingly, there is still no EWC under Polish law, although there are between six and eleven Polish companies which fall under the EWC directive.[37]

Referring to pan-European developments, a significant decrease in the dynamics of establishing EWCs after 1996 is obvious, as demonstrated by the following figure:

Figure 7-4: Year of EWC Establishment

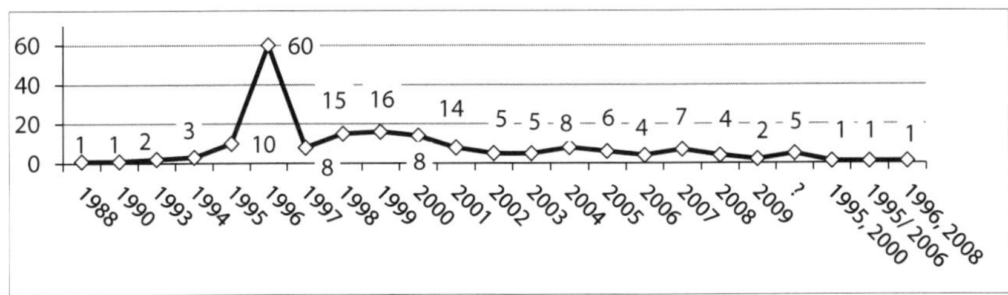

Source: Own figure according to the NSZZ Solidarność database.

relations], in: Nieodkryty Potencjał Europejskich Rad Zakładowych [The undiscovered potential of European Works Councils] Conference materials, Warsaw, 2006, pp. 7–14, here p. 12.

36 Own figure according to the NSZZ Solidarność database.

37 Rudolf, Stanislaw / Stegemann, Karolina: European Works Councils activity in Poland, in: Hertwig, Markus / Pries, Ludger / Rampeltshammer, Luitpold (eds): European Works Councils in complementary perspectives, Brussels: European Trade Union Institute, 2009, pp. 101–125, here p. 109.

In only a few cases was there a renegotiation of the agreement and a subsequent change in the legal status. In 5 cases the year of EWC establishment is unknown. The majority of EWC agreements (59%) must have been founded under Article 6 of the EWC directive, but there are no exact data available, the year of EWC foundation is the only possible source for this assumption.

In terms of the correlation of EWCs with the responsible European trade union federations, there is some noticeable overlap in associational responsibilities:

Figure 7-5: Classification According to Trade Union Federations

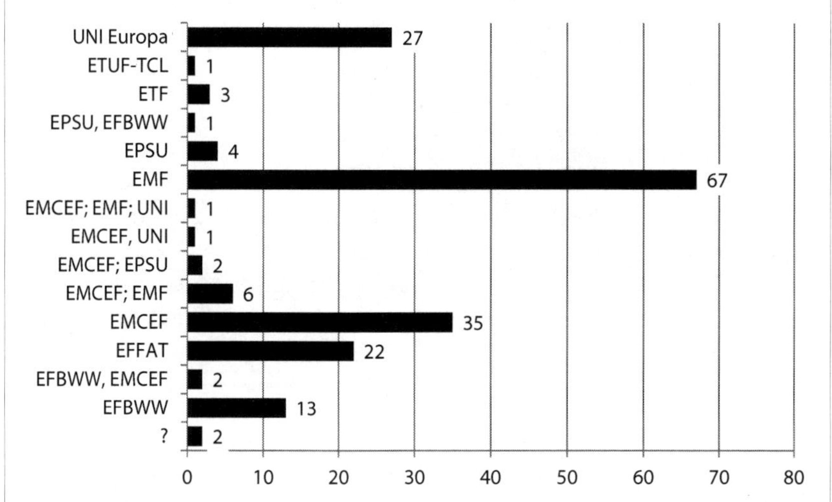

Source: Own figure according to the NSZZ Solidarność database.

The vast majority of European Works Councils with Polish participation come from manufacturing, where the metal sector is by far the largest group, followed by the chemical industry and the food and agricultural sector. Consequently, the service sector plays a minor role, which corresponds to the generally weak unionisation of this sector in Poland.

Finally, the frequency of the EWC meetings can give a first indication about the qualitative development level of the appropriate European Works Councils (see Figure 7-6 opposite).

This last figure shows that 75% of all EWCs with Polish members have only one annual meeting. Interpreting this fact, it seems unlikely that these bodies are participative-oriented EWCs with above-average information and consultation practices. For the Polish delegates this means that in practice, if the individual member is a dedicated trade union representative, he / she could be very dissatisfied with the opportunities generated by European Works Councils.

Figure 7-6: Number of Annual EWC Meetings

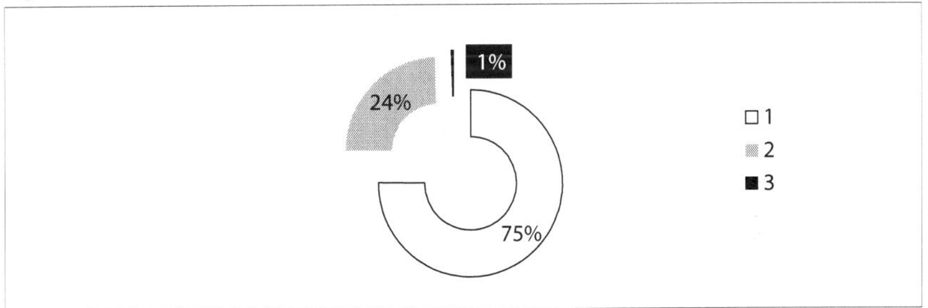

Source: Own figure according to the NSZZ Solidarność database.

The fundamental problem with the underlying data collection is that almost the half of the Polish EWC members are unknown and most likely not unionised. Among the other (known) members, again, 50% belong to the NSZZ Solidarność and the others likely belong to other national trade union federations. Furthermore, the figures indicate that the EU enlargement did not happen automatically in all European Works Councils and that there still seem to be many unknown variables in this data source. To that effect, this database can only be considered an approximation of EWC reality in Poland.

7.3.2. EWCs in the Polish Research Literature

Beyond quantitative data about European Works Councils in Poland, a qualitative approach is possible due to the existence of several studies about EWCs in the Polish context. In contrast to the well-established industrial relations research in Western Europe, this topic is covered in Poland by only a handful of experts, so that industrial relations are very underrepresented at Polish universities. Accordingly, trade union-oriented research institutes or foundations are entirely absent at the national level, so that most information available is at the European level, such as the European Trade Union Institute (ETUI) or European Industrial Relations Observatory (EIRO).

Nevertheless, the first study about European Works Councils in Poland was published in 1999 by Rudolf. He interviewed in nine EWCs their Polish delegates (19 persons) about their—at that time quite fresh—experiences with these European bodies.[38] In principle, this early phase of Polish EWC integration reveals the keen interest

38 Rudolf, Stanisław: Polish Representatives of Company Employees in European Works Councils, Łódź: University Press, 1999.

of the NSZZ Solidarność in being represented in EWCs as much as possible, so that most of these early Polish EWC members had also been union members; and it was the national trade union organisation which built up the first contacts between the employee representatives.[39] A second result of this early research is that the Polish delegates perceived, on the one hand, a lack of negotiation competencies in EWCs, but on the other hand they wondered about the culture of open dialogue between employer and employee representatives:

> The Polish representatives are fascinated by the openness of the top management hardly encountered in Poland, with whom they can talk, who come up to them, for example during a break or an informal meeting and inquire about the existing problems, so that it can be seen that they are truly interested.[40]

A follow-up to this first study was presented by Skorupińska in 2006, in which she tried to cover all known Polish EWC members. Hence, she interviewed 57 Polish members from 50 EWCs. Again, the significant role of the NSZZ Solidarność during the initial phase of the EWCs in Poland was identified as well as the high union membership rate among the interviewed Polish EWC members (90%).[41] However, this number is declining due to more open elections among employees, which is in contrast to the delegation principle of trade union organisations in the early phase of EWCs.

Rudolf, together with Stegemann, repeated his investigation in 2009. In accordance with the results from 1999 and 2006, they again found evidence for the disappointment of some Polish EWC members regarding the effectiveness of the EWC. Expecting a strong, competent and well-organised body with large bargaining power, they were often confronted with inadequate information and consultation procedures.[42] In the eyes of the majority of respondents, nothing useful had been negotiated or decided on in the EWC meetings. According to the authors, the biggest disappointment was expressed by the Polish EWC members about the absent influence of the EWC on (local) management decisions.

In 2007, an extensive study was presented by Gardawski, which is actually the most comprehensive analysis of Polish EWC members in transnational companies.[43] Gardawski questions the impact of European Works Councils on the industrial relations in Poland.[44] For this purpose he primarily uses a questionnaire and seven case

39 Ibid., here p. 9.
40 Ibid., here p. 21.
41 Skorupińska, Katarzyna: Polskie przedstawicielstwo w europejskich radach zakładowych (ERZ) [Polish members in European Works Councils], in: Zarządzanie Zasobami Ludzkimi, 2006, no. 5, pp. 39–52, here p. 42 ff.
42 Rudolf, Stanislaw / Stegemann, Karolina: European Works Councils activity in Poland, in: Hertwig, Markus / Pries, Ludger / Rampeltshammer, Luitpold (eds): European Works Councils in complementary perspectives, Brussels: European Trade Union Institute, 2009, pp. 101–125, here p. 116.
43 This research was supported by the NSZZ Solidarność trade union.
44 Gardawski, Juliusz: Korporacje Transnarodowe a Europejskie Rady Zakładowe w Polsce [Transnational Companies and European Works Councils in Poland), Warsaw: Warsaw School of

studies secondarily. However, his research is limited to the metal sector. The results from the questionnaires (20) indicate that the EWC membership has improved the local situation of the individual EWC (and union) members. The respondents reported that their relationship to the local management improved and that management took them more seriously. They felt better informed and consulted more often, so that the whole company dialogue had progressed.[45]

The case studies illustrated a far more differentiated picture because the EWC had no relevance for some Polish delegates, while others confirmed a very large impact. Moreover, Gardawski identified serious problems that may occur for individual members. Some delegates reported an overwhelming 'flow of English information', which overburdened them. Others became involved in serious conflicts of interest, especially when it came to relocating production to Poland because their European colleagues expected transnational solidarity against the management's decisions. The Polish members reported that they could hardly find arguments for the local employees as to why they should be against more work and products at the Polish sites.[46]

Finally Gardawski found an example of a huge cultural transfer from a German car manufacturer (most likely VW) to the Polish site with regard to social dialogue.[47] The Polish delegate was surprised by a completely new dialogue culture between management and employee representatives, which he was not used to from his national experiences.

Compared to the existing Western European EWC literature, the Polish scientists focus solely on the Polish EWC members and disregard the rest of the institutional EWC body. Hence, a significant impact of European Works Councils on the local industrial relations was confirmed, while negative effects—which could possibly be described as a 'legitimacy dilemma'—have also been identified. Although this literature gives an insight into the perspective of local EWC (and trade union) members, nothing is known about the impact of EWCs at the national trade union level. This will be the content of the following section.

7.4. The NSZZ Solidarność Trade Union and EWCs. Strategies and Learning Processes

As presented in the last section, most of the existing information and literature about European Works Councils in Poland can be attributed to NSZZ Solidarność, so that this trade union must obviously be seen as a pioneer in this issue for the Polish case. Indeed, the first EWC training organised by the NSZZ Solidarność took place in 1995,

Economics Publishing House, 2007, here p. 9.

45 Ibid., here p. 43.

46 Ibid., here pp. 81–89.

47 Ibid., here p. 118.

shortly before the EWC directive came into force in the former EU member states. Since 1996—almost from the beginning—there were Polish members in European Works Councils. In this sense, the NSZZ Solidarność was for a long time the only institution in Poland in which knowledge about European Works Councils had been accumulated. This section tries to explain how the trade union handled the topic of EWCs, why this involvement was remarkable and what effects European Works Councils had per se on the organisation.

7.4.1. Why Were EWCs so Interesting for the Trade Union?

All interviewed NSZZ Solidarność representatives agreed that they initially saw European Works Councils as a new instrument to strengthen the Polish trade unions. Thus, this fascinating 'tool' was observed from its beginning in the early 1990s by the Polish trade unionists. According to one interview partner[48], this interest was justified by the early diagnosis in 1994 that Polish industrial relations would not develop in the desired direction and that an additional source of influence was needed.[49] Referring to the strong international and European commitment of the NSZZ Solidarność, as presented by Lis in this volume, the following statement is not surprising:

> We as a trade union are big proponents of Europeanization and transnational negotiations....This is the only chance for us as a union, but not only in this part of Europe, but generally for all European trade unions. We know and we feel that we will be weak without this additional European level due to the post-transformational weakness of our industrial relations....So, this is in our interest.

Finally the Polish trade unionists believed that in contrast to their Western European colleagues, they would have nothing to lose when a new European level of industrial relations emerged. For them, their situation could only improve. That is why the NSZZ Solidarność's strategic goal had been to place as many Polish members onto existing European Works Councils as quickly as possible.[50] This declared strategy substantiates the already mentioned theoretical assumptions that the mismatch provides the national actors with additional opportunities and that they serve as change promoters when they benefit from these changes. However, the political influence of the NSZZ Solidarność at the national level had been limited in light of the implementation of the directive. Although the NSZZ Solidarność activists followed the process with great interest, they could only interact informally with the respective Ministry of Labour.[51] In contrast, more influence was possible during the revision of the EWC directive, where the trade union was part of the tripartite commission and participated actively.

48 Interview with NSZZ Solidarność representative A, Poland, 14 October 2011.
49 Ibid.
50 Interview with Solidarność representative B, Transcript p. 5, Poland, 13. October 2011.
51 Ibid.

7.4.2. Extern Support and Intern Work. EU-Capacity Building

Beyond internal and external political lobbying, from the beginning, the NSZZ Solidarność offered its own members various training programs, which were supported with EU funds. Following the argument of Börzel and Risse, this European capacity building can be understood as the one of the sufficient conditions for rational institutionalism.[52] Moreover, in this context learning processes can also be observed, as the following conference titles illustrate. They enabled Polish actors to network and frequently exchange information:

- 2001: 'Europejskie Rady Zakładowe: polskie doświadczenia i perspektywy' [European Works Councils: Polish experiences and perspectives] 28–29 May 2001 in Gdansk.
- 2004: '10 Lat Dyrektywy o Europejskich Radach Zakładowych – polska perspektywa.' [10 years of the EWC Directive—Polish perspectives] 7–8 April 2004 in Gdansk.
- 2009: 'Europeizacja stosunków przemysłowych w funkcjonowaniu ERZ i rad pracowników – wymiana dobrych praktyk.' [Europeanization of industrial relations in functioning EWCs and Works Councils—exchange of good practice] 16 March 2009 in Warsaw.
- 2010: 'Rola i formy dialogu społecznego w sytuacji globalnego kryzysu gospodarczego oraz wymiana dobrych praktyk.' [Role and form of the social dialogue in the global economic crisis—exchange of best practices] 25 March 2010 in Warsaw.

Consequently this European capacity building is responsible for the great data collection and scientific knowledge about European Works Councils in Poland as presented in the previous sections. As a result of its extensive commitment, compared to European Works Councils, the NSZZ Solidarność can be described as a 'change agent' that strengthens the acceptance of EWCs in Poland.

7.4.3. The Europeanization of NSZZ Solidarność. Institutional Changes

After the specification of the NSZZ Solidarność's active involvement in promoting European Works Councils in Poland, the next question regards the repercussions of the EWC directive on the organisation and its staff. According to the presented Europeanization definition, this means the incorporation of European rules, discourses and practices into the national context. European Works Councils provoked different Institutional in the trade union, which can also be summarised as learning processes through observation and data collection as well as training of Polish EWC members.

52 Börzel, Tanja A. / Risse, Thomas: Conceptualizing the Domestic Impact of Europe, in: Featherstone, Kevin / Radaelli, Claudio M. (eds): The Politics of Europeanization, Oxford: University Press, 2003, pp. 57–82.

In addition, the regularly successful application and implementation of EU-funded projects provided access to additional financial resources and can therefore be seen as a gain in organisational and technical know-how.

Furthermore, European Works Councils have a direct impact on the sectoral organisational structure of the trade union because Polish EWC members are mainly supported at this level. Due to historical reasons, the sectoral level of the trade union organisation is financially the weakest compared to regional or national organisation structures.[53] This changed a little when questions from local trade union members for assistance in EWC matters were generally referred to the respective sector secretariats. Subsequently, the sectoral secretariats applied for payment of their membership fees and finally received a financial incentive to offer support in EU affairs. Consequently this money helped diverse sectoral secretariats to pay their own membership fees in international trade union federations.[54] As one of the NSZZ Solidarność representatives concedes in the interview, the trade union has a structural problem with its sectoral organisations because they receive only 2% of the total (operational) membership fees and this is not enough to be active at the transnational level.[55] Thus, they are barely able to cover their own staff expenses. Their own membership in European trade union federations such as European Metalworkers' Federation (EMF), International Metalworkers' Federation (IMF), or European Federation of Food, Agriculture and Tourism Trade Unions (EFFAT) is highly dependent on their members' annual contributions, although in contrast to the regional organisation structures, there is no membership constraint. Comparing the different branches, the metal and automobile secretariat has no problems paying European membership fees, while other sectors, such as the food secretariat, have enormous problems. According to the interviewed trade unionist:

> However, in the food sector, the secretary had big problems because he constantly got payment prompts from Brussels and Geneva, but he did not have this money. He acted quite offensive in this matter, when he addressed the problem to his local trade union organisations, for example Danone, Nestle and Philip Morris, and so on. Acting this way he got his financial situation back under control.[56]

To sum up, the EWC directive must be seen as trigger for internal organisational change processes with reference to the formulated Europeanization concept. Through rational institutionalism and learning processes the trade union tried to develop additional options for action in their weak national industrial relations system. Therefore, they used human and technical capacities to gain more influence. In fact, this could only be realised at the sectoral level of the trade union organisation structure, where

53 Gardawski, Juliusz / Mrozowicki, Adam / Czarzasty, Jan: Trade Unions in Poland. Report 123, Brussels: ETUI, 2012, here p. 44.

54 Interview with NSZZ Solidarność representative B, Poland, 13 October 2011.

55 Ibid.

56 Ibid.

the secretariat gained new legitimacy and consequently new financing options due to European Works Councils. Not least in comparison with other national trade union organisations, the identified key actors from the NSZZ Solidarność behaved as 'change agents' and contributed significantly to the trade union acceptance of European Works Councils in Poland. However, there is no automatic acceptance and adoption of new EU regulations in the field of industrial relations. Quite the contrary, the NSZZ Solidarność reacted against the European information and consultation directive (2002/14/EC), which was heavily rejected by the trade union. However, that is another story.

7.5. Summary

Although this chapter highlights the effects of European Works Councils at the national trade union level via the example of NSZZ Solidarność, this is not the whole picture of Europeanization. Due to national organisational structures of employee representation in Poland, the main arena of union activity is the local—or rather the company—level. Furthermore, Polish EWC members act, in most cases, as local trade union representatives at this level, so that their participation in European Works Councils must have additional effects on their local situation.[57] As the national research literature noted, many Polish EWC members are disappointed because of the limited negotiation ability and practice of EWCs. Similar frustrations had been noted by the interviewed national-level NSZZ Solidarność representatives:

> As a trade union we have no benefit from our EWC involvement.[58]

From the national organisation perspective, EWCs did not reinforce the trade union movement through a gain of more individual trade union members, nor did they fundamentally strengthen industrial relations. They could rarely meet the expectations of many trade union representatives as a new transnational negotiation body.

On the other hand, European Works Councils offer the possibility of receiving (international) information, which is normally not available to the Polish members. This information may influence the national negotiation position, when employee representatives know more than their national management. Beyond official management information, horizontal information exchange between the EWC members from the different countries may occur. For example, the EWC members can exchange their local collective agreements and indirectly support their colleagues with useful arguments. Regardless of the small number of truly negotiating European Works Councils, their mere existence has a certifiably Europeanizing impact on trade unions, mainly in Central Eastern Europe.

57 Voss, Eckhard: The experience of European Works Councils in new EU Member States, Luxembourg: Office for Official Publ. of the European Communities, 2006, p. 31.

58 Interview with NSZZ Solidarność representative A, Poland, 12 October 2011.

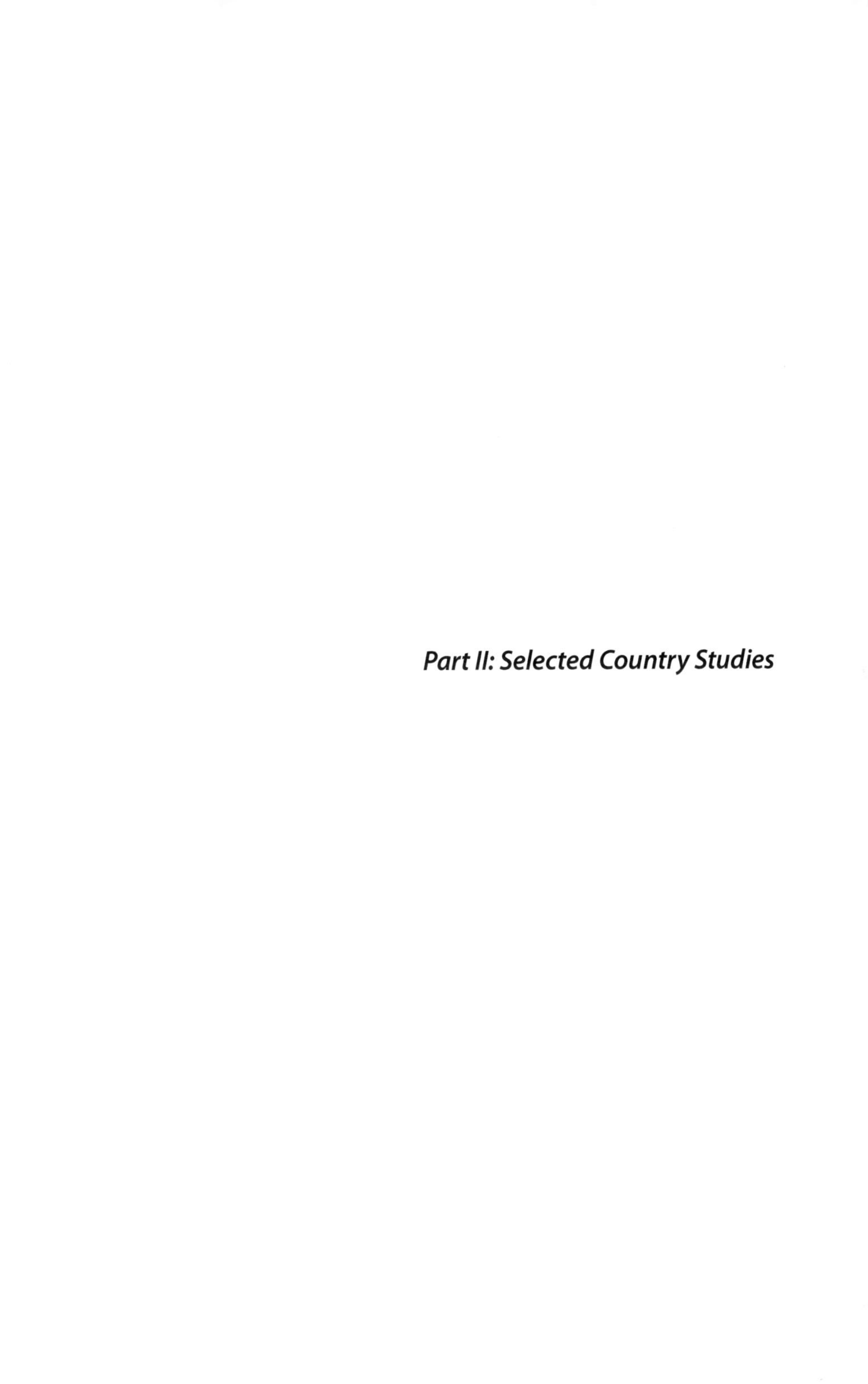

Part II: Selected Country Studies

Vassil Kirov

8. The Europeanization of Bulgarian Trade Unions. Achievements and Challenges

Bulgarian trade unions were important players in the European integration of the country. The main objective of Bulgarian society in the 1990s was to join the European Union (EU) to 'come back' to the European family. For a long time, EU membership was associated with high societal expectations of social justice and economic prosperity, and there was a national consensus about the need to be part of the EU.[1]

However, the European integration of the country was far from a smooth process. Due to the political and economic instability of the 1990s, the prevailing opinion in Bulgarian society was that the country had experienced a delay in the European integration and should catch up quickly. On 10 November 1999, the EU made a decision to start membership negotiations with Bulgaria (and five other candidate countries) and thus put an end to long national discussions and fears that the country would not be among the candidates. The negotiation process was finalised in 2004, and the country became a member of the European Union on 1 January 2007. This EU integration process was carried out quickly, and there was often no place for critical voices or statements because of the fear of hindering the process. However, the lack of criticism and the lack of a comprehensive debate on many societal options before the accession became an important issue on the agenda after the accession.

This chapter presents the main results of the study in Bulgaria, based on the interviews with representatives at the confederational and federational levels from both of Bulgaria's main trade unions, the Confederation of Independent Trade Unions of Bulgaria (CITUB) and the Confederation of Labour Podkrepa (CL Podkrepa).The covered branch unions from both confederations represent the interests of workers and employees of the metallurgy sector, the metal sector, and the mining sector. Those branch unions are representatives for the respective sectors. The metallurgy sector is still highly unionised (57.8% in 2008)[2]. According to a European Foundation for the Improvement of Living and Working Conditions (Eurofound) representativeness study in 2008, the CITUB metallurgy union has 7,387 members, and the CL Podkrepa metallurgy federation has 3,516 members.[3] Membership has decreased since this period, but

1 Kirov, Vassil: Bulgarie [Bulgaria], in: Bertoncini, Y. et al. (eds): Dictionnaire Critique de l'Union Europeenne, Paris: Armand Colin, 2008.

2 Mihaylova, Tatiana: Representativeness of the European social partner organisations. Steel industry—Bulgaria, in: EurWORK European Observatory of Working Life, 22 September 2009, http://www.eurofound.europa.eu/eiro/studies/tn0811027s/bg0811029q.htm, accessed 02 September 2013.

3 Ibid.

data are not available. The metal sector is much less unionised; union membership is approximately 16%, according to a Eurofound representativeness study[4] in 2009, and is much more fragmented compared with the metallurgy union. The metal federation of CITUB had 10,417 members in 2009, and the federation of CL Podkrepa had 6,028 members.[5] Some workers from the metal sector are members of other federations of CITUB or Podkrepa, such as electronics and military production. Since this representativeness study was conducted, the membership has further decreased, but exact data are not available. There are no precise data available about the trade union membership in the mining sector, but union presence is still significant, and unions are strong, as their actions (strikes, lobbying activities) show. A total of 13 interviews were conducted in 2013 with leaders or experts from the two unions. The research was complemented with desk research of internal union documents, reports and agreements.

8.1. The Bulgarian Transition

The concrete socio-economic and political context in the period of the survey should be considered to better understand the specific challenges faced by trade unions in Bulgaria and their role. After a period of instability during the first part of the 1990s, in the winter of 1996–1997, the country was in financial collapse, and the protests on the streets forced the neo-communist government to resign. Since then, the stabilisation efforts have included the establishment of a currency board,[6] the signature of agreements with the international financial institutions (the International Monetary Fund (IMF) and the World Bank) and measures to ensure macroeconomic stabilisation. The economic reforms included also massive privatisation, using different methods (direct sales, mass privatisation, management and employee buy-out (MEBO)), and closures of the enterprises with financial difficulties. This economic policy started to contribute to positive results in terms of growth and confidence for the investors, but it was at a high social cost. Throughout the period of instability and reforms, unions played an important role in working to ensure social peace in the country.

The economic growth was resumed in 1998 and continued until the year 2008. The unemployment trend was reversed: though it was almost 20% in the year 2000, it reached less than 6% in 2008. During the first decade of the 2000s, there was a massive inflow of foreign direct investment (FDI) in the country (attaining almost 33% of the gross domestic project (GDP) in 2007, according the World Bank), in many sectors of the economy, such as industry, real estate, and services. In 2007, the country joined

4 Ibid.
5 Ibid.
6 Avramov, Roumen: Currency board et stabilité macroéconomique. le cas de la Bulgarie [Currency board and macroeconomic stability. The case of Bulgaria], in: Revue de l'OFCE, 2000, no. 72, pp. 71–98.

the European Union, which was one of the long-term goals for the Bulgarian political players and society. In this period, the social dialogue structures were further institutionalised, but at the same time, unions continuously lost membership and influence.

However, since the beginning of the financial crisis, the economic situation in Bulgaria started to deteriorate. The FDI inflows decreased considerably. Many Bulgarian companies were forced to downsize and restructure because of the loss of markets, the diminished order from the Western contractors, and the problematic internal market. Thus, the unemployment level increased to approximately 13% in 2013[7]. The economic difficulties were accompanied by protests by different groups of the population who were unsatisfied with the high cost of living and the corruption. The union movement continued to play a role at the national level and in particular sectors and enterprises, but the outcomes of the social dialogues and collective bargaining were uneven.

8.2. The Bulgarian Trade Union Movement during the Post-Communist Transition

The Bulgarian industrial relations system emancipated from the aegis of the Bulgarian communist party in the years 1989–1990. During the years after 1989, the trade union movement was dominated by the largest trade union, CITUB, and the second largest, CL Podkrepa. In addition to the two largest unions, in different periods during the last 25 years, other unions were recognised as being nationally representative for short periods of time.

The Confederation of Independent Trade Unions of Bulgaria[8] is the largest trade union in Bulgaria. CITUB was established in 1990 based on the old single trade union during the communist period (Balgarski Profesionalni Sauzi (BPS)). On its website, CITUB claims to be the successor to a 100-year trade union tradition. It inherited important resources in terms of members, structures, and experts from the former communist trade union structures, although the union was confronted with the challenges of internal reform and the need to prove its 'independence' from the communist party, which was itself under reform. Under these new conditions, CITUB opted for painful internal reorganisation while trying to participate actively in the establishment of a new industrial relations system and the design of transition reforms. Established in February 1990, CITUB is considered to be one of the best reformed former trade unions

7 Eurostat: Unemployment rate by sex and age groups. annual average, %, in: eurostat.ec, 28 November 2014, http://appsso.eurostat.ec.europa.eu/nui/show.do?dataset=une_rt_a&lang=en, accessed 14 December 2014.

8 Konfederatsiyata na nezavisimite sindikati v Balgariya (KNSB): KNSB official website, in: knsb-bg.org, http://www.knsb-bg.org, accessed 02 September 2013.

in the region of Central Eastern Europe[9] and has been the largest national trade union centre ever since. In the early 1990s, when the trade union membership was quasi-compulsory, CITUB had more than 3 million members. In the middle of the decade 2000, it affiliated 35 federations and had approximately 380,000 members. Its membership continued to decline, and it is currently approximately 275,000[10]. According to the 2012 census of employer and trade union organisations, only two trade union confederations still meet the representation criteria: CITUB, with 275,762 members, and CL Podkrepa, which has 91,738 members.[11] Trade union membership declined significantly in the years of transition following the EU enlargement because of, e.g., high unemployment, privatisation, anti-union behaviour of employers (especially private enterprise employers) and less trust in trade unions.

In 2013, CITUB still affiliated 35 members (federations, unions), which are involved in collective bargaining processes at the sectorial / branch level. At the enterprise level, the confederation has established 6,381 trade union organisations. CITUB has 243 municipal structures (in most of the Bulgarian municipalities).[12] According to the Bulgarian industrial relations profile (prepared for Eurofound), the consolidation process of affiliated federations through mergers continues to be unpopular. Nonetheless, in some sectors, several parallel structures are affiliated to CITUB (e.g., education, transport, energy, and metalworking).[13]

The Confederation of Labour Podkrepa was formed on 8 February 1989 by a small group of dissidents. According to the CL Podkrepa leaders, at the time of its creation, the group was comfortable because the laws were very 'liberal' to trade unions.[14] That was the only way for the organisation to become official and to operate legally. During the initial period of CL Podkrepa (1989–1991), it was very difficult to distinguish its trade union activities because it functioned rather as a political movement. Even its first demands were more political (e.g., free movement of people within the country) than trade unionist. However, CL Podkrepa rapidly became the second strongest trade union confederation in Bulgaria with strong presence in all sectors and regions.

9 Dimitrova, Dimitrina / Vilrokx, Jacques (eds): Trade union strategies in Central and Eastern Europe. Towards decent work, Budapest: International Labour Organisation, 2005. Kirov, Vassil: Facing EU accession. Bulgarian trade unions at the crossroads, in: Dimitrova, D. / Vilrokx, J. (eds): Trade union strategies in Central and Eastern Europe. Towards decent work, Budapest: International Labour Organisation, 2005, pp. 111–151.

10 According to its own documents, e.g., the Report from the 7th Congress, the members are about 250.000. See therefore KNSB: KNSB official website, in: knsb-bg.org, http://www.knsb-bg.org, accessed 02 September 2013.

11 Eurofound: Bugarian industrial relations profile, 2013, in: eurofound.europa.eu, http://www.eurofound.europa.eu/eiro/country/bulgaria_3.htm, accessed 02 September 2013.

12 Ibid.

13 Ibid.

14 Kirov, Vassil: Facing EU accession. Bulgarian trade unions at the crossroads, in: Dimitrova, D. / Vilrokx, J. (eds): Trade union strategies in Central and Eastern Europe. Towards decent work, Budapest: International Labour Organisation, 2005, pp. 111–151.

In the 2000s, this trade union organisation affiliated 36 regional unions and 30 branch unions. Its members numbered approximately 120,000[15]. According to the last available data, CL Podkrepa has 91,738 members.[16]

The data about the development of the trade union membership and structures suggest that Bulgarian trade unions experience a continuous decrease in members and still face important sectorial fragmentation. This fragmentation furthers undermines the existing resources and limits the possibilities for action, especially at sectorial level.

8.3. The Europeanization of Bulgaria and the Challenges for the Unions

The Europeanization of the Bulgarian union movement (in the context of the Europeanization of the Bulgarian state and society) should be examined according to the periods, considering the specific challenges, the role of the European Union and the attitudes in the country towards it. Bulgaria joined the European Union on 1 January 2007, along with Romania, in the last part of the fifth European enlargement. The accession to the EU offered different channels for the representation of Bulgarian citizens within the EU institutions, opened access to the markets, to mobility, and to the structural funds of Europe.[17] However, after seven years of membership, many observers have concluded that the Bulgarian actors in general do not take a proactive role within the European Union.[18]

To what extent could this conclusion be applied to the trade unions? From 1990–2007, or for almost two decades, the challenges that unions faced were related to the post-communism reforms and the entry into the EU. There are different opinions about the role of the trade unions in the pre-accession process. However, we could agree with Gradev that first, the process of Bulgaria's integration into the EU has long been 'the sole domain' of a small group of government experts, and the keyword in this process has been 'speed' at the expense of the content of the agreements. Furthermore, as shown by Gradev, 'the social questions are not a priority in the process of negotiations' [19].

15 Kirov, Vassil: Facing EU accession. Bulgarian trade unions at the crossroads, in: Dimitrova, D. / Vilrokx, J. (eds): Trade union strategies in Central and Eastern Europe. Towards decent work, Budapest: International Labour Organisation, 2005, pp. 111–151.

16 Eurofound: Bugarian industrial relations profile, 2013, in: eurofound.europa.eu, http://www.eurofound.europa.eu/eiro/country/bulgaria_3.htm, accessed 02 September 2014.

17 Kirov, Vassil: Bulgarie [Bulgaria], in: Bertoncini, Y. et al. (eds): Dictionnaire Critique de l'Union Europeenne, Paris: Armand Colin, 2008.

18 Tanasoui, Cosmina: Europeanization post-accession. rule adoption and national political elites in Romania and Bulgaria, in: Southeast European and Black Sea Studies, 2012 (vol. 12), no. 1, pp. 173–193.

19 Gradev, Grigor: Social dialogue and trade unions in enlarging Europe. losers among winners?, in: Dimitrova, D., Vilrokx, J. (eds): Trade union strategies in Central and Eastern Europe. Towards

Since Bulgaria became a full member of the European Union on 1 January, 2007, and the bulk of the transition reforms were completed (e.g., the economy is almost entirely in private hands, new social security institutions are in place), it was an opportunity to reconsider the unions' strategies.[20] What were the new challenges for the unions in the post-accession period? What really changed after the entry into the EU in terms of the social dialogue and collective bargaining? Are unions better 'equipped' to protect the interests of their members? Are they in a better position to formulate and lobby for policies at the EU or national level? What could their role be in the process of using structural funds?

The challenges for the trade unions originate from several components of Europeanization. The promotion of social dialogue and collective bargaining still needs serious efforts at all levels—national, sectorial, and enterprise—and in connection with the EU-level dialogue developments. After the accession, the national social dialogue was stimulated by the establishment of the Social Pact.[21] However, it is difficult to assess the concrete role of this pact. Serious efforts were also required to face the challenges of the sectorial collective bargaining and dialogue. The need for a meaningful sectorial dialogue is even more urgent than it was before in the midst of multiple sectorial challenges and the general lack of skilled labour force (before the crisis of 2008). This task required specific actions to train, retrain and adapt human resources. There was also a need to lobby for the extension of sectorial agreements, which could be a valuable tool to expand the scope of collective bargaining in the country (these agreements were finally extended in 2010 for a small number of sectors). The serious efforts undertaken by employers in human resources development in particular sectors requires a more active and adequate participation of trade unions. Social dialogue within enterprises also needs renewal for two reasons. First, collective bargaining and the conclusion of collective labour agreements is not sufficient; dialogue is important on a broader range of issues. Second, the content of the agreements must be expanded to make them more meaningful for employees.

The information and consultation issues need also more attention from unions. In the wake of decreasing membership, it is important for the unions to address the question of how employees in Bulgaria can be adequately represented. There are two important challenges to be met. The first one is to see how unions can expand their presence and gain new members. The second is related to the need to promote new mechanisms for information and consultation. In this respect, it has been vitally important to analyse the practice of the information and consultation bodies that were established in some enterprises in response to the enforcement of this legislation in

decent work, Budapest: International Labour Organisation, 2005, pp. 229–264.

20 Kirov, Vassil: Trade Unions in CEEs and the Challenges after the EU Accession. The Case of Bulgaria, in: Economia&Lavoro, 2008 (vol. 42), no. 3, pp. 83–94.

21 Ibid.

2007. Subsequently, it could be interesting to see whether these forms and practices could be further promoted. Although unions opposed the second channel (even not openly) for a long time, there has been a change in the unions' attitude over the past 3–4 years, and they have started to campaign for the establishment of information and consultation bodies. The European Works Councils (EWCs) must also take concrete steps to better prepare and accommodate Bulgarian representatives in these structures so that they can make better use of this form of information and consultation in the case of foreign investors.

In addition, the presence of the Bulgarian unions at different European-level trade unions or consultative structures also requires efforts to prepare the Bulgarian representatives for their work, to consolidate positions and to be able to defend them, particularly in situations of divergent interests or specific challenges for Bulgaria and its economy.

8.4. Major Results from the Survey

The following results are part of the study that was conducted. We analyse the importance of the European Union for the Bulgarian trade unions, their channels of influence and involvement at the EU level, their cooperation with European umbrella organisations, the connections between the EU and the national level, and the bilateral and multilateral international cooperation. While reading the results, it is important to remember that the answers represent the opinion of trade union leaders and experts involved in the issues of European integration and not of the ordinary union members.

8.4.1. Importance of the EU

According to the interviewees, the EU is extremely important for Bulgaria. Most of the interviewees consider that the EU is as important for their trades unions as national politics. Furthermore, the majority of the interviewees believe that the effect of the EU's general role on national policy should grow. This is most likely related to the fact that according to all of the interviewees, the EU's effect on their trade union confederation or federation is positive. However, there could be an additional interpretation: that in the context of decreasing resources, they count on the EU to achieve their strategic goals.

There are several examples about the positive effect of the EU on the unions. According to the respondents, the important dimensions of the positive effect are related to the legal instruments (*'you can refer to a directive'*), the use of European good practices in social dialogue, the opportunity to have exchanges with European trade union colleagues, and the fact that rules are clearer in Europe. The following quotation illustrates some positive effects of the EU:

> First, after Bulgaria became a member of the EU, the Bulgarian trade unions became more involved with the Europeans, although ours had previously also been involved on the international level. You can say that they we're already members of the European family. Second, the positive effect is through participation in European projects with European financing. Currently, they work on two projects—one is for the problems of the social activities in the mining industry, and the other is for the information and communication problems in the mining industry. They are also preparing and applying for other projects. These contacts and this participation, they help a lot in the improvement of the qualifications of the trade unions' leaders and activists. Also, the participation in numerous conferences, bilateral and multilateral meetings, where the relationships between the unions' members are open—they inform and help each other with respect to the problems which they must solve[22].

A minority of respondents observe both positive and negative effects of the EU. Thus, the main negative effects are related to the specific EU requirements or norms for particular industries (e.g., environmental requirements, as shown in the citation below). However, in this case, it is difficult to distinguish between the negative effect on the union from the negative effect on the entire sector / industry that could lead to negative consequences for the union(s).

> The European directives and policies with respect to the pollution of the environment (for example, the requirements for desulphurization or green energy), which the rich Western countries impose on the weaker industrialized countries such as Bulgaria, have a negative impact.[23]

Most of the interviewed trade union leaders or experts observe some policy areas where the EU seems to be more important than the nation state, such as the labour relations, the rights of working people, the European social dialogue, or some specific policies (e.g., in the domain of energy). However, in this case, every respondent has different priorities, and they are difficult to generalise.

According to most of the respondents, the representation of interests at the national level is more important than at the EU level. This is because the decisions for many policies in Bulgaria are made at a national level, such as negotiations about wages. As observed in the quotations below, the interviewed trade unionists noted the specific challenges at the national level.

> The national level for us is more important to play a bigger role in the National Council for Tripartite Cooperation…[24].

> There are problems that countries such as Bulgaria must resolve according to the specific conditions and living standard[25].

22 Interview with CITUB representative, Bulgaria, federation leader 1, 02 April 2013.
23 Interview with CITUB representative, Bulgaria, federation leader 3, 04 June 2013.
24 Interview with CITUB representative, Bulgaria, federation leader 2, 02 April 2013.
25 Interview with CITUB representative, Bulgaria, federation leader 1, 02 April 2013.

> At the national level, many issues are more important. Most of the issues are resolved at the national level. The social security system is at the national level. The rights for social security, the increase in wages...all are decisions made at the national level.[26]

> Personally, the national politics is a priority, and after that is the European. There is a lot to be learned from the Europeans, but I have also insisted on the national level as being the leading one.[27]

Finally, many of the interviewees claim that for their organisation, it is extremely important to be present at the level of EU because of labour rights, rules, multinational companies, the participation in European social dialogue, and even the possibility to change the rules through the umbrella organisations:

> The most important is the opportunity to impact the national policies. I think that not only this is important; another important point is the access to information about what is happening within the EU[28].

> I cannot say which is the most important. There are many important issues...because of all policies, which are proposed and defended by the European Trade Union Confederation at the EU level. In fact, all economic and social issues, which concern the employees, for which the EU prepares policies, are important. And they must be presented to the unions first—the ETUC[29] and also in the European Social Dialogue—intersectorial and sectorial, different federations, and also in the European social committee[30].

> Yes, you can say that the contacts with the other European unions, the opportunity to present some problems in our laws, and together with our colleagues to look for ways to change even EU laws[31].

In summarising this paragraph, we can affirm that for the Bulgarian trade unions, the EU is very important and most of its effects are positive. However, it seems that Bulgarian unions are currently rather passive 'consumers' of EU influences in general.

8.4.2. Channels of Influence of the Bulgarian Unions at the EU Level

The second part of the survey investigates the channels of influence that national confederations / federations from Bulgaria could have and use at the EU level. The main channel for influence at the EU level is the European umbrella organisation ETUC, together with Bulgarian representation in the European Economic and Social Committee (EESC), and participation in the European Social Dialogue, again through the trade union structure at EU level. Some of the respondents mention contacts with the European Commission, the European Parliament, and the Council, among others, but these contacts are in most cases sporadic, e.g., meetings with Members of the

26 Interview with CITUB representative, Bulgaria, confederational high official 5, 26 March 2013.
27 Interview with CL Podkrepa representative, Bulgaria, federation leader 8, 02 April 2013.
28 Interview with CITUB representative, Bulgaria, confederational high official 4, 26 March 2013.
29 ETUC—European Trade Union Confederation.
30 Interview with CITUB representative, Bulgaria, confederational high official 5, 26 March 2013.
31 Interview with CL Podkrepa representative, Bulgaria, federation leader 8, 02 April 2013.

European Parliament from Bulgaria for a particular purpose and visits to the European Commission.

Most of the interviewees affirm that there are debates about EU issues in their organisations. They observe that the debates about EU issues within the trade unions often involve large membership. According to the interviewees, these debates focus both on specific and rather narrow issues, and on broader topics and general principles.

The interviewed trade union representatives consider that the policy positions to be represented in EU level organisations are taken by the different governing bodies of the respective unions (e.g., congresses, executive councils, coordination councils) and their statutes describe the decision-making process and the implementation process of those decisions.

The interviewed Bulgarian trade unionists do not have a homogeneous evaluation of the role that their union plays at EU level. Some of them are completely satisfied and others are partially satisfied, or neither satisfied nor unsatisfied. These subjective evaluations depend on the involvement and ambitions of the respective organisation. Concrete reasons for union members' satisfaction could be related to the fact union officials have an important position in the EU structure:

> I can say that we are satisfied. We can include five. Because Mr. I. is vice-president, our vice-president of the European federation. It used to be EMF[32], now IndustriAll. He is also vice-president of IndustriAll and responsible for Southeastern Europe, so we have very serious contacts.[33]

> Yes. Dr. T. was vice-president of ETUC. Yes, we are satisfied. We have a very good co-operation, our experts too[34].

Conversely, some of the respondents have a more critical view of the role of their organisations, particularly considering the organisational resources and capacity:

> It means many things. In order to be able to participate at the European level, you need to have financial capacity. You need to have expert potential, which we have; we have the necessary experts. But then, there is also linguistic…[capacity]. For example, when the committee for social dialogue meets and I need to send the expert who is most qualified for that, it turns out he doesn't know a second [EU] language. So, I must personally participate, and I must translate the information so that I can give it to him. He needs to understand it and respond to me, and then I must translate it again and present it. That is a huge difficulty, which originates from the lack of financial capacity. It's a hindrance for us and our active participation. And I'd like to be more active. You know how it is with the big unions, which have representatives in Brussels. They have several representatives, each specialises in a specific topic and has detailed knowledge. The language barrier is a huge problem[35].

32 EMF—European Metalworkers' Federation

33 Interview with CITUB representative, Bulgaria, federation leader 2, 02 April 2013.

34 Interview with CL Podkrepa representative, Bulgaria, confederational high official 10, 25 March 2013.

35 Interview with CITUB representative, Bulgaria, confederational high official 4, 26 March 2013.

The participation of the Bulgarian trade unions at the EU level is also related to the financial resources that are available to support the activities of the trade union at the EU level. In most cases, the finances originated from two or three sources: the trade union itself, the European umbrella organisations, and participation in specific projects.

Most of the respondents consider that their unions represent interests at the EU level, primarily in cooperation with the European umbrella organisations.

Most of the respondents consider that the influence of their union at the EU level is smaller than the influence at national level. However, there are trade union leaders that consider this influence equal.

In conclusion, the Bulgarian trade unions could influence the EU level primarily through their umbrella organisations (including within the EU-level social dialogue) or through their representatives in the EESC. In many cases, their presence at the EU level is dependent on their resources (e.g., financial resources, language capacity) and the contributions from EU-level organisations or through EU projects, which are important to fill the gap of their own insufficient resources.

8.4.3. Cooperation of the Bulgarian Trade Unions with European Umbrella Organisations

The Bulgarian trade union confederations CL Podkrepa and CITUB joined the ETUC in 1995. As one of the important channels for influence at the EU level, the Bulgarian trade unions' cooperation with the European umbrella organisation ETUC or the respective EU level sectorial organisations was and is extremely important for them. The general assessment of the interviewed union representatives regarding the collaboration with the European umbrella organisations of trade unions is positive.

Most of the respondents are satisfied with the work of their unions in European umbrella organisation of trade unions. However, the answers about their participation in the work of the umbrella organisations vary greatly. In some organisations, participation happens very often, in others (particularly some of the branch federations), it occurs annually or semi-annually.

The confederations and the branch federations have long-lasting relations with their European umbrella organisations. These relations are the basis for the establishment of contacts, e.g., at the enterprise level.

> The Confederation of Independent Trade unions in Bulgaria is a member of ETUC since 1995. It participates in meetings, seminars, conferences, sharing information[36].

The majority of the respondents believe that often (but not always), the position interests of their trade union coincide with those of the European umbrella organisations to which they belong. Almost all of the interviewees declare that their trade union

36 Interview with CITUB representative, Bulgaria, confederational high official 5, 26 March 2013.

has supported Europe-wide protest actions organised by European umbrella organisations. However, when asked to provide specific examples, some respondents are very concrete—as the citation below shows—, whereas others have difficulty pointing out precise examples.

> Under the chairmanship of John Monks, each year, there is a very big demonstration in the country that presides over the EU, during the meeting of the ministers of finance. Many representatives participate from different countries. For example, I have participated in Ljubljana, Prague, Brussels, and Budapest[37].

In some cases, respondents were aware of specific protest actions but were not able to participate personally because of the cost of the trip.

> The idea was to support them either directly by participating there or by organizing forums with appropriate publicity and advertising. In this case, we organised national forums here in Bulgaria. We informed the press, [via] press conferences, about what was happening and why. Otherwise, we have participated at those demonstrations, Euro-demonstrations, when they are organised and when we have had the chance. And when do we have a chance? When [the demonstrations] are organised close to Bulgaria…for example, in Budapest several years ago. It's all a matter of (financial) resources[38].

According to the interviewees, there are multiple advantages to collaborating with European umbrella organisations of trade unions. This collaboration facilitates access to information, the exchange of good practices, and trade union solidarity:

> So the pros are that it gives you access to information as to what is going on in this community. It's up to you how well you can use that information. It gives you a lot of information[39].

> The advantages are solidarity, the ability to support [each other] during demonstrations, access to information, the analysis of good practices from Europe, which help us with collective negotiations, and also the opportunity to participate in the dialogue with the European federation. In addition, the contacts with labour unions in Europe increase the access to information, also pertaining to multi-companies[40].

> The advantages are gaining experience, sharing of practices and ways of solving important problems. Although when I make comparisons, for example, with Spain, it turns out that we are not very far behind. You can see that they have some benefits that we used to have but for many reasons do not have anymore. You can see the benefits of the social state, which they continue to have[41].

> The advantages are that we use the expert potential of ETUC and we are informed about European issues. We know what is going on in Europe and what will happen. That gives us the chance to react quickly before some laws are adopted and to correct national policies. We have the opportunity to act on the adoption of some directives and corrections in some areas. Sometimes, we use their experts by having consultations and asking them for information[42].

---

37 Interview with CITUB representative, Bulgaria, federation leader 3, 04 June 2013.
38 Interview with CITUB representative, Bulgaria, confederational high official 4, 26 March 2013.
39 Interview with CITUB representative, Bulgaria, federation leader 1, 02 April 2013.
40 Interview with CITUB representative, Bulgaria, federation leader 2, 02 April 2013.
41 Interview with CITUB representative, Bulgaria, federation leader 1, 02 April 2013.
42 Interview with CITUB representative, Bulgaria, confederational high official 4, 26 March 2013.

> Very big. There are truly people there who work at a very high level and know many things. But the specifics of the regions must be considered. Because what is best in Sweden is not the best for us[43].

> The advantages are many. For example, sharing good practices or bad practices—this is also very useful. Because if one of the confederations, members of ETUC, has not succeeded, the reasons for that are being investigated, and we learn from their mistakes, and they learn from ours. The most important is the sharing of information among the confederations and ETUC. That information is very useful. It helps us a lot in our work[44].

However, there are some opinions that this collaboration could be both passive (e.g., to receive information or support) and active:

> Participating in the formulation of labour union policies at the EU level[45].

At the same time, some of the respondents are aware of some disadvantages in this collaboration. According to these respondents, the disadvantages are related to the fact that insufficient attention is being paid to the problems of Bulgaria or the region of Southeast Europe within the large trade union organisations at the EU level:

> The cons are that there is not enough attention paid to the problems of the Southeastern region and ours. And we have many big problems. There are mostly efforts done for the third world countries. But that is more valid for the international confederation. As for the European, it seems like it's looking more into the problems of the Central European countries, and we are left behind to deal on our own if we can. And our problems are much bigger than everyone else's—from low wages to high unemployment, etc. And we also have problems with the division in the trade unions [at the national level]. So, there are no priorities being set forth. We should be a priority, but we are not doing so.[46]

There are thoughts about the difficult coordination of interests in the context of regional divisions:

> The disadvantages can be seen in the continuing segmentation of countries—poor or rich, northern or southern, eastern or western. That does not make a good impression[47].

> Different interests, tough coordination sometimes[48].

The establishment of large sectorial organisations (such as IndustriAll) also contributes to deepening the problems of coordination:

> At least to me, too many sectorial representations and trade unions gathered together may cause problems. Because even when we get together in Bulgaria on a national level to discuss specific problems, every sector believes that their problems are the most important[49].

43 Interview with CL Podkrepa representative, Bulgaria, federation leader 7, 04 April 2013.
44 Interview with CL Podkrepa representative, Bulgaria, confederational high official 10, 25 March 2013.
45 Interview with CITUB representative, Bulgaria, confederational high official 5, 26 March 2013.
46 Interview with CITUB representative, Bulgaria, federation leader 2, 02 April 2013.
47 Interview with CITUB representative, Bulgaria, federation leader 3, 04 June 2013.
48 Interview with CITUB representative, Bulgaria, confederational high official 5, 26 March 2013.
49 Interview with CL Podkrepa representative, Bulgaria, federation leader 6, 04 April 2013.

Finally, as one of the respondents said, there is too much information coming from Europe, and it can be difficult to prioritise it.[50]

Most of the interviewees think that the union to which they belong provides an important contribution to the overall interest representation of trade unions at the EU level. However, some respondents do not believe this to be the case.

Almost all of the respondents declare that they have participated in the debate and supported the social progress clause in the Treaty of the European Union (proposed by ETUC at its Congress in 2012). However, most of them were not able to develop their answers or provide details about the respective debates.

In summary, the researched trade unions seem to be well integrated in their umbrella organisations, but they are mostly passive, e.g., receiving information and seeking support but not (or rarely) attempting to change things.

8.4.4. Connections between the EU and the National-Level Policies

In the negotiations period, the EU had already started to significantly influence Bulgaria's political agenda. Since the beginning of the membership, the influence of the EU spread to various spheres. The influence of the European Union on the national policy for Bulgarian trade unions is examined in this section. With only one exception, all of the respondents believe that the activities of their trade union organisation at the EU level often or always influence its work at the national level. However, they do not provide examples of this influence. The interviewees declare that they usually support the implementation of specific EU regulations in Bulgaria.

The European Union is often used as an argument by the different social and political actors in Bulgaria. This is also the case of trade unions: All of the respondents agree that they use the EU as an argument to justify or support the position or activities of their trade union at the national level. The provided examples for this use are very general, though others concern concrete specific issues, e.g., support for organised demonstrations, stress, and renewable energy:

> Mostly in the area of social dialogue. Mostly there because we're lagging so much in all other areas, and we cannot use anything there.[51]
>
> In defending social rights, income, employment…[52].
>
> Yes, always. When it is necessary, we cite directives and regulations, and especially where exactly Bulgaria is not doing well. We also remind the employers.[53]

Some trade union leaders are very concrete, explaining the mechanisms for pressure:

50 Interview with CITUB representative, Bulgaria, federation leader 1, 02 April 2013.
51 Interview with CITUB representative, Bulgaria, federation leader 1, 02 April 2013.
52 Interview with CITUB representative, Bulgaria, confederational high official 5, 26 March 2013.
53 Interview with CL Podkrepa representative, Bulgaria, federation leader 6, 04 April 2013.

> A more recent example is the OZK Kardjali [Lead & Zinc Complex PLC]. When the plant had to stop operating, we asked for the position of the European trade union; we received it and gave it personally to the prime minister, Mr. Boyko Borisov. Those are types of documents that every prime minister must take into consideration[54].

The respondents believe that the EU has a positive effect on Bulgaria in many different policy areas. Again, some leaders give general examples, as in the area of social dialogue, with the fact that the EU creates stability concerning legislation because laws should be harmonised with the EU legislation. Many respondents believe that the EU is positive in 'determining rules of the game'. Other examples concern the labour law, labour market policies, working conditions, and competition policy. Last, but not least, some respondents state that there is a positive effect related to the access to the structural funds, particularly the operational programme 'Human Resource Development'. Some of them note particular sectors where they believe the effect of the EU is positive, such as agriculture and ecology.

Some negative effects of the EU are also noted. Not all of the interviewees provide such negative examples, but it could be observed that union leaders do not have delusions when analysing the situation. The following quotation is important for understanding the reasoning of the respondents, who analyse the country as unprepared for the single market:

> There is no negative effect, but the social standards development lags the integration of the single market[55].

However, in some cases, they could not easily differentiate between the EU's influence and the adaptation of EU policies and decisions in the country:

> In the economic areas. Maybe it's not from the EU only; maybe it's what our politicians managed to negotiate. Here is a specific example. In the programs for European financing for increasing energy efficiency, the melting houses, which are one of the big energy consumers, are not in the priorities of the program. Second are the tax requirements, ecological requirements, working conditions requirements, etc. They are not bad, but the level of development and the capabilities of the government do not allow for them to be implemented in the required timeframe. You know very well that if we do not compromise about the working conditions in some plants, they must stop working. Yes, but with those high unemployment rates, we should also help...we must conform to that[56].

Many other respondents develop the issues of the quotas or restrictions that could lead to the bankruptcy of Bulgarian companies and an increase in unemployment levels. From this perspective, they are not suitable for the level of development of Bulgaria, according to the union leaders. Concrete examples are provided about such negative effects in mining or the steel industry, among others.

---

54 Interview with CL Podkrepa representative, Bulgaria, federation leader 8, 22 April 2013.
55 Interview with CITUB representative, Bulgaria, confederational high official 5, 26 March 2013.
56 Interview with CITUB representative, Bulgaria, federation leader 1, 02 April 2013.

In conclusion, this section shows that the EU provides important arguments and support to the Bulgarian unions that are widely used in the domestic political debate. However, only one respondent noted that Bulgarian unions are also part of the formulation of these EU-level arguments.

8.4.5. Bilateral and Multilateral Trade Union International Cooperation

Over the last 25 years, the Bulgarian trade unions have developed bilateral cooperation with many trade unions from old or new Europe at both the confederational and federational levels. From the beginning of the transition, this cooperation was crucial for the reforming / institutional building of Bulgarian trade union confederations and federations and sometimes even for the support of everyday operations (e.g., contributions to training seminars, printing materials). The respondents provide different examples of such cooperation with trade union organisations from almost all of the old member states of the EU. Those collaborations could be long-term or both long- and short-term.

> We also communicate with Italians and Spaniards and, last year, with Austrians. But overall, we are oriented towards countries with similar problems. Because there is a difference between a country with 40–50 million people and a country with 8, 10, 12 million…from an organizational standpoint[57].
>
> We have with almost all—Belgians, French, with…almost all of the old members of the EU. In addition, we are partnering with most of them on different projects…and especially the Portuguese[58].
>
> Spain, Italy, Germany, Austria…and Norway, although it is not a member of the EU[59].
>
> German, Austrian, Belgian, English (DGB, OEGB, FGTB, TUC[60])[61].
>
> Germany, Italy, England, France, Great Britain, the Netherlands, Greece, Austria, Spain[62].
>
> Yes, currently with the colleagues from Spain. Of course, we have also participated in trainings with colleagues from France, though they were not organised by us but by the confederation[63].
>
> With unions from France (CFDT[64]), Germany (IG Metall[65]), Poland[66].

57 Ibid.
58 Interview with CITUB representative, Bulgaria, federation leader 2, 02 April 2013.
59 Interview with CITUB representative, Bulgaria, federation leader 3, 04 June 2013.
60 DGB—Deutscher Gewerkschaftsbund, OEGB—Österreichischer Gewerkschaftsbund, FGTB—Fédération Générale du Travail de Belgique, TUC—Trade Union Confederation
61 Interview with CITUB representative, Bulgaria, confederational high official 4, 26 March 2013.
62 Interview with CITUB representative, Bulgaria, confederational high official 5, 26 March 2013.
63 Interview with CL Podkrepa representative, Bulgaria, federation leader 6, 04 April 2013.
64 CFDT—Confédération française démocratique du travail
65 IG Metall—Industriegewerkschaft Metall
66 Interview with CL Podkrepa representative, Bulgaria, federation leader 7,s 02 April 2013.

> We work well with the Italian and German unions, with the Czech KOVO[67] and also IG Metall. We work very well with Balkan countries, although some of them are not in the EU. I work well with Serbia, Bosnia, Croatia—we have perfect relations with their unions[68].
>
> Yes, we have cooperation, signed agreements with many confederations from other countries. In the Netherlands, Spain, France, Romania, Macedonia. We have good relations with Turkey, Belgium, Poland (Solidarnost[69]). We have good relations with almost all.[70]

In most cases, this cooperation includes various elements, such as information exchange, projects, or activity coordination; some concrete examples are mentioned below:

> Activity coordination, solidarity, information exchange. This year we are working on two projects. One is for informing and consulting, but it is not in partnership with 'old' member-states, but with the Romanians. We had invited the Germans, but they were late to send us back a partnership letter. In the second project, which is for the youth and is called 'Securing a better future for young Europeans', we are partnering with France, England, Poland, and Romania[71].
>
> Projects with unions from Italy and Ireland on the topics of information and consultation; projects with unions from Greece, the UK, and Spain regarding the free movement of people; projects with Belgium regarding social security systems, regional development, rights of minorities; projects with Austria—for accession to the EU[72].

These partnerships are developed based on specific interests, commonalities, and experiences in particular topics.

The respondents seem divided when asked whether there are differences in the cooperation with organisations from the old and the new member states. Some do not detect significant differences. According to them, the existing differences are due to the different legacies and resources and the level of experience.

> Very small differences. Just the mentality and understanding. Now, with the new member states such as Poland, Czech Republic, Hungary, Slovakia, Slovenia...we have a similar history with them.[73]
>
> Although small, there are several differences. The old member states' representatives have more experience[74].

However, according to a minority of the interviewees, the differences still play a role:

> Yes. The problems of the new member states are almost the same as ours. As for the old member states, we use the information and experience that they have, and how they have dealt with some problems. They have much better legislation and much better experi-

67 OS KOVO—Odborový svaz KOVO
68 Interview with CL Podkrepa representative, Bulgaria, federation leader 8, 22 April 2013.
69 NSZZ Solidarność—Niezależny Samorządny Związek Zawodowy Solidarność
70 Interview with CL Podkrepa representative, Bulgaria, confederational high official 10, 25 March 2013.
71 Interview with CITUB representative, Bulgaria, federation leader 2, 02 April 2013.
72 Interview with CITUB representative, Bulgaria, confederational high official, 26 March 2013.
73 Interview with CITUB representative, Bulgaria, federation leader 1, 02 April 2013.
74 Interview with CITUB representative, Bulgaria, federation leader 3, 04 June 2013.

ence…good practices in the social partnerships, collective agreements, defending the interests[75].

There is a difference because the partnership with the old member states seems to be easier, better structured. These are organisations with more resources, better financial capacity, and a clearer vision of what they want and how it can be achieved[76].

There are differences. Even though Poland, the Czech Republic, and Hungary became members before us, they still feel the difference in comparison to the progress of the unions from the old member states. And the problems that we have are more similar to the ones of the other new member states. We have still not succeeded in dealing with those problems. If we look at Germany, the investments they have made in improving the working conditions are very different from ours, in spite of the fact that we are also an EU member. They are now talking more about health-related issues, and we are still negotiating free protection, food, and other compensatory mechanisms for bad working conditions[77].

There is no difference. In Germany, for example, the unions have a great impact. I have the feeling that if IG Metall wants, they can have a direct influence over Germany's government. It's a huge union. We can only learn from them—the unification, the way they do things, the professionalism in their structures is truly unique[78].

The level of difference does not matter; the respondents consider that Western European unions have difficulty understanding the unions from the new member states and their positions:

Yes, to some degree, the unions from the old member states are more experienced. But they also have a hard time understanding our specifics[79].

Asked to discuss the areas for partnership and the political areas where the partnership should be reinforced, the respondents provide a large variety of answers. According to some, cooperation currently concerns restructuring issues, whereas others see it as occurring in a larger, social area or in collective bargaining, the European Social Dialogue, the free movement of people, the transnationalisation of the industrial relations, trade union solidarity, or corporate social responsibility. The issue of working conditions is also an important one. Some respondents note larger societal challenges, such as demographic changes.

Most of the respondents would like to further develop these topics. However, their answers suggest that some trade union leaders have better knowledge of what could be realistic and what could not, as in this example:

We're not talking about the same amount of wages, but the bonification mechanisms and social benefits should be unified. If there are food vouchers there, there should be food vouchers also in Bulgaria. If there are performance bonuses [in other countries], there should be bonuses also here [in Bulgaria][80].

75 Interview with CITUB representative, Bulgaria, federation leader 2, 02 April 2013.
76 Interview with CITUB representative, Bulgaria, confederational high official 5, 26 March 2013.
77 Interview with CL Podkrepa representative, Bulgaria, federation leader 6, 04 April 2014.
78 Interview with CL Podkrepa representative, Bulgaria, federation leader 8, 02 April 2013.
79 Interview with CITUB representative, Bulgaria, confederational high official 5, 26 March 2013.
80 Interview with CITUB representative, Bulgaria, federation leader 3, 04 June 2013.

Trade union representatives also note that they need to implement projects funded by the EU so that

> our union representatives may gain experience and get acquainted with the practices of the colleagues from the old member states and to gradually apply this knowledge in Bulgaria[81].

The advantages of this cooperation are that the Bulgarian representatives can learn, enter into networks, and exchange experience and good practices. The respondents also mention some disadvantages. Some of them say that the unionists from old member have a specific attitude towards Central Eastern European colleagues:

> The disadvantages arise from the fact that the representatives of the rich countries are looking down on us[82].

For others, a major disadvantage from the past was the 'export' of models:

> And the disadvantage was that sometimes, there was a tendency to impose on us models that cannot be applied here. Just because they are applied successfully in Sweden or elsewhere, it does not mean they will work here. But this was in the past[83].

In summary, the bilateral cooperation with unions from the old or new member states is extremely important for Bulgarian unions. They seem to be active in long- or short-term cooperation projects that cover different spheres. It seems that the development of these partnerships during recent years has been increasingly shaped by pragmatism, and the initiative is increasingly in the hands of the Bulgarian partners.

8.5. Conclusion and Recommendations

Bulgaria entered the EU in 2007. Unions were involved in the integration process, but this involvement could be characterised primarily as 'passive'. The post-accession period brought to the union agenda a number of challenges related to the harmonisation of the EU acquis, such as the development of the social dialogue and collective bargaining, and the introduction of the second channel of information and consultation. At the same time, it should be acknowledged that the role of the European Union, and the perceptions and expectations in Bulgaria concerning the EU are in a process of continuous change.

The results from the interviews conducted in Bulgaria suggest several conclusions.

First, we could affirm that for the Bulgarian trade unions, the EU is very important and that most of its effects are positive. However, it seems that Bulgarian unions are still rather passive 'consumers' of EU influences in general. Most likely, there are a limited number of high trade union officials who are well integrated in the European

81 Ibid.
82 Ibid.
83 Interview with CITUB representative, Bulgaria, confederational high official 4, 26 March 2013.

trade union governance bodies and networks, but this is still not sufficient for a general change of attitudes and proactivity.

The Bulgarian trade unions can influence the EU level mainly through their umbrella organisations (including within the EU-level social dialogue) or through their representatives in the EESC. In many cases, the presence of the Bulgarian trade unionists at EU level is dependent on their resources (e.g., financial resources, language capacity). If these resources are not sufficient, their inclusion risks being limited; for example, there will be few occasions to participate in meetings. From this perspective, the contributions and support from EU-level organisations or through EU projects are still very important to fill the gap of their own insufficient resources.

The researched trade unions seem to be more or less well integrated in their umbrella organisations (intersectorial and sectorial), but they are mostly passive—e.g., receiving information, seeking support—and do not attempt to change things.

The EU provides important arguments and support to the Bulgarian unions that are widely used in the domestic political debate. However, the knowledge of the trade union leaders and experts is not always sufficient for the appropriate analysis of the complex situation.

The bilateral cooperation with unions from the old or new member states is extremely important for Bulgarian unions. They seem to be active in long- or short-term cooperation projects that cover different spheres.

The recommendations that we could formulate for the Bulgarian unions first concern the need for more active participation at the EU level. In the pre-accession period, the passive attitude could be understood from the perspective of quick EU integration. However, since then, the illusions of the Bulgarian unionists seem to have diminished, and most of them now have realistic views of the advantages and disadvantages of the EU-level participation. At the same time, the European Union itself is changing, and the Bulgarian unions should carefully analyse the consequences of this change, e.g., concerning the crisis, the austerity measures and the increasing EU-level monitoring of national agendas and the idea of the equalisation of the working and living conditions in Europe that seem to have deteriorated since 2008–2009.

The fact that there are Bulgarian representatives in the EESC and among the leaders of some European trade union structures is insufficient for setting the agenda. Unions should have clear priorities to better benefit from the cooperation and to be able not only to complain but also to defend their interests.

Zdenka Mansfeldová

9. Between a Rock and a Hard Place. Czech Trade Unions in Domestic and European Arenas

9.1. Introduction

The transition to democracy and a market economy gave the trade unions the opportunity to become a real social partner who can protect the interests of employees and use a broad variety of legally defined methods and procedures. On the other hand, they were confronted with new problems, a drastic decline of membership and the decline of the union voice in the workplace. As noted by D. Ost, 'during the post-communist era, unions lost prestige, resources, and voice'[1]. One reason for this loss was that the union was a weak opponent to the new market elites and unable to protect those who most needed protection from the negative effect of market reforms. Another reason was the radical change of economic system in the country. By the start of economic reforms and privatisation, Czech trade unions were unable to substantially influence the prepared legislation and rules. Unlike in many other Eastern European countries, employee ownership as a form of employee financial participation enjoyed no special treatment in the privatisation process and consequently plays no significant role in the ownership structure of the Czech economy.

The processes of globalisation and Europeanization, together with the ever-increasing internationalisation of capital and free movement of labour, influence and narrow the negotiation space for national trade unions (TUs). Simultaneously with these top–down challenges, TUs are confronted with further bottom–up membership-based challenges, such as declining membership in trade unions and low attractiveness to young people. As mentioned by several authors, 'especially younger workers in CEE[2] often consider the labour movement to be a relic of the communist era, rather than an indispensable component of modern market economies'[3]. Alternative forms of interest representation, protest movements, and new social networks and platforms, such as

1 Ost, David: The Consequences of Postcommunism. Trade Unions in Eastern Europe's Future, in: East European Politics and Societies, 2009 (vol. 23), no. 1, pp. 13–33, here p. 17.

2 CEE—Central Eastern Europe

3 Ladó, M. / Vaughan-Whitehead, D.: Social Dialogue in Candidate Countries. What for?, in: Transfer. European Review of Labour and Research, 2003 (vol. 9), no. 1, pp. 64–87, here p. 69. Mailand, M. / Due, J.: Social Dialogue in Central and Eastern Europe. Present State and Future Development, in: European Journal of Industrial Relations, 2004 (vol. 10), no. 2, pp. 179–97, here p. 181. Quote after Veverková, S.: The case of the Czech Republic, in: Guardiancich, I. (eds): Recovering from the crisis through social dialogue in the new EU Member States. the case of Bulgaria, the Czech Republic, Poland and Slovenia. Budapest: ILO, 2012, pp. 47–70.

Stop the Government (Stop vládě)[4], Iniciativa pro kritiku reforem a na podporu alternativ (ProAlt), Real Democracy (Skutečná demokracie) and others, seem to be more attractive options for civic participation among young people. In the new EU member states of Central Eastern Europe, these issues are further augmented by numerous path-dependent and contextual factors. This chapter tries to demonstrate the extent to which national partners' ideas, values and modes of operation were influenced by their participation in the European process of representation and decision-making.

The chapter attempts to test the hypothesis of the research project, which states the following:

1. The trade unions from the member states of the Eastern Enlargement do not hold substantial internal debates on EU-related positions and strategies.
2. Concerning their organisation, different EU-related activities are not brought together in a systematic way.
3. Accordingly, these trade unions do not act as collective actors. Instead, their work in relation to the EU is determined by individual representatives.

The chapter addresses the function of Czech trade unions in EU governance and their adaptation to a multilevel system of interest representation. First, I briefly review the developments in trade unionism during the last twenty-plus years and give a brief assessment of the role of trade unions in national politics. In the second section, I look at how trade unions prepared for EU membership and also what support and assistance they received from partners and structures in the European Union. Additionally, I cover issues of cooperation with umbrella organisations and analyse networking efforts, ways of exercising influence on the European level and reflections on the role and functioning of trade unions in the EU. In the third section, I address the European and national aspects of interest representation more generally from the viewpoint of trade unionists, the extent to which the European dimension is deemed important for the national trade union centres and the impact 'Europe' has on its local operations. In the sixth section, I turn to bi-and multilateral international cooperation, and cooperation with trade unions from old and new EU member states. The closing section summarises the results.

The chapter is based on the following sources: 19 expert interviews, which cover nine different trade union organisational units, including the two largest confederations. In addition to eight experts representing the largest confederation, the Českomoravská konfederace odborových svazů (ČMKOS), there were representatives from member trade unions—the TU of Banking and Insurance Workers, the Czech Metalworkers' Federation, and the TU of Workers in Mines, Geology and Oil Industry. The second

4 'Stop the Government' (STOP VLÁDĚ) was a common initiative created by ČMKOS, ASO ČR, the Coalition of Transport Trade Union and 21 civic associations with the purpose of protesting against and stopping the government's reforms.

largest confederation, the Asociace Samostatných Odborů České republiky (ASO ČR), was represented in the sample by its members—TUs in the finance sector and of workers in agriculture and nutrition. Among the interviewed experts, there were three current members of the European Economic and Social Committee-Group II (the Workers' group) and one representative in a European Works Council. This gives us a more diverse view of the activities and positions of the trade unions in European affairs.

In addition to expert interviews, primary and secondary sources were used. To the primary sources belong the homepages of the trade unions and printed documents collected during the interviews. As secondary sources, limited literature dealing with Czech trade unions, periodicals published by trade unions and European Industrial Relations Observatory (EIRO) studies were used.

9.2. Czech Trade Unions

Modern trade unions in the Czech Republic (and former Czechoslovakia) were reborn after the disintegration of the Revoluční odborové hnutí (ROH) at the beginning of the 1990s. At the present time, there are five trade union confederations and a number of trade unions or associations (as the Koalice dopravních odborových svazů (KDOS) that have been independent from their establishment or have left some of the confederations, particularly the ČMKOS. No new trade unions with an explicitly political agenda were established and no party has incorporated the labour movement into its agenda. From the five confederations, two (ČMKOS, ASO) are members of the tripartite council and are important social partners in tripartite negotiations in the framework of the Council of Economic and Social Agreements of the Czech Republic.[5]

The Czech and Moravian Confederation of Trade Unions (ČMKOS) is the largest trade union confederation, with 29 trade unions and 407,000 members in 2011. ČMKOS was the successor of the former ROH and initially took over all the members and assets of the former organisation. ČMKOS is still the dominant trade union federation, comprising approximately 70% of all trade union members. ČMKOS works in the regions of the Czech Republic through Regional Councils of Trade Unions and Regional Offices for Legal Assistance. It is a member of the International Trade Union Confederation (ITUC), European Trade Union Confederation (ETUC), Trade Union Advisory Committee to the Organisation for Economic Co-operation and Development (TUAC), European Economic and Social Committee (EESC), Committee for European Social Fund, and some advisory committees.[6]

The Association of Independent Trade Unions (ASO) is the second largest trade union confederation in the Czech Republic. It was established in 1995 and today

5 Hála, Jaroslav et al: Development of social dialogue in the Czech Republic, Prague: RILSA, 2002.
6 For more information about ČMKOS see the trade union's official website on http://www.cmkos.cz/homepage, accessed 28 March 2014.

represents 15 trade unions with approximately 200,000 members in 2014.[7] Trade unions affiliated to ASO are politically independent and have their own identity. The founders of ASO were the Trade Union of Workers in Agriculture and Food of Bohemia and Moravia, the United Confederation of Private Employees, and Trade Union Northwest Power. Over the years, it has acceded to the headquarters of other unions, such as the Trade Union of Railway Workers, Trade Union of Flat Glass, and the Trade Union of Employees of Nuclear Energy and Air Traffic Controllers. Some independent unions or separate basic organisation even cooperate with ASO. ASO represents its members in international organisations and institutions; however, thanks to its more developed capacity and experience, the dominant representative of trade unions at the EU level is ČMKOS. Since 2000, ASO is a member of the Council of Economic and Social Agreements, where it has replaced the Konfederace Umění a Kultury (KUK), which ceased to meet the criteria of representativeness set for the tripartite due to its declining membership.

The **Confederation of Arts and Culture (KUK)** is the third largest trade union organisation in terms of members and importance; in the past, it was a member of the Council of Economic and Social Agreements of the Czech Republic. After the collapse of socialist trade unions in February 1990, the cultural workers' trade unions formed their own confederation, which grouped together 17 autonomous trade unions in 1996. The KUK members strongly advocate the principle of professional association, whereby the individual interests of various professions stand side-by-side with trade union interests. The membership is declining and several member unions have left the organisation. In December 2011, according to its own data, KUK united 13 trade unions with 35,482 members.[8]

The remaining two trade union confederations are the **Trade Union Association of Bohemia, Moravia and Silesia** (Odborové sdružení Čech, Moravy a Slezska, or OS ČMS), which had approximately 6,250 members (2013), and the **Christian Trade Union Coalition** (Křesťanská odborová koalice, or KOK), with 2,800 members (2013). These do not match the large trade union confederations in terms of either size or importance.[9]

In many Central Eastern European countries, the trade unions have been more concerned about competing with each other rather than with trying to collaborate, thus weakening the strength of the labour movement as a whole. It was possible to observe this tendency in the Czech Republic as well, but not with as much intensity as in other

7 For more information about ASO see the trade union's official website on http://www.asocr.cz/cz/portal/cile-a-poslani/, accessed 22 December 2014.

8 Pojer, Petr: Czech Republic. Industrial relations profile, in: EurWORK European Observatory of Working Life, 24 October 2014, http://www.eurofound.europa.eu/observatories/eurwork/comparative-information/national-contributions/czech-republic/czech-republic-industrial-relations-profile, accessed 22 December 2014.

9 Ibid.

Central Eastern European countries. Competition was not an obstacle for the functioning of trade unions. Over time, the acceptance of the role of trade unions in the society has changed and there is development toward increased trust in trade unions. However, trade unions are not perceived by a substantial proportion of society to be strong players in the field of interest representation, as demonstrated in Figure 9-1. The economic crisis has somewhat strengthened trust in trade unions and the acceptance of the different forms of protests they use; on the other side, the high level of distrust has remained.

Figure 9-1: Trust in Czech Trade Unions, 1995–2014

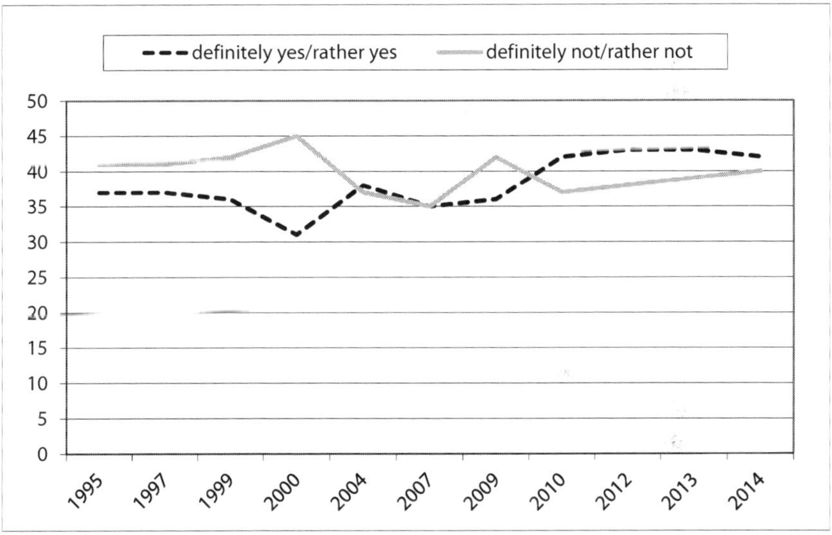

Centre for Public Opinion Research, Institute of Sociology, Academy of Sciences of the Czech Republic: Survey on trust in some public institutions, in: cvvm.soc.cas.cz, various years, http://cvvm.soc.cas.cz, accessed 20 October 2014.

The continuous decline in trade union density has affected the majority of trade unions in the country. By the trade unions' estimation, approximately 16% of the total number of employees in the private sector were unionised in 2011 (down from approximately 20% in 2010 and 22% in 2008). The declining trade union density forces leading union federations to take labour-saving measures. Apart from reduced membership, the fragmentation or merging of trade union associations should be mentioned, even though this has only been the case for a few of the existing trade union organisations. However, reorganisations of trade union organisations and reductions of their professional staff and expenditures were substantially more frequent than mergers.

The crucial task for trade unions is collective bargaining. Collective bargaining is regulated by law, in terms of both process and content. Obligations arising from collective agreements are binding on the contractual parties and the fulfilment of such obligations is legally enforceable. Czech law distinguishes between company-level collective agreements (CLCA), concluded between the relevant trade union body and an employer, and higher-level collective agreements (HLCA), concluded for a greater number of employees by the relevant higher-level trade union body and an organisation or organisations of employers. The most prevalent level of collective bargaining in the Czech Republic is the company level. In 2013, 33.2% of employees were covered by CLCAs and approximately 15% were covered by HLCAs.[10] Nevertheless, collective bargaining was affected by the crisis. According to a ČMKOS report, the economic crisis has halted collective bargaining among some union organisations and worsened its outcomes.[11]

Extensions of the binding nature of HLCAs to another employer are possible under the conditions set by law; the Ministry of Labour and Social Affairs of the Czech Republic possesses the relevant powers. Agreements are extended based on a proposal made by both contractual parties to the agreement, provided that the conditions determined by law are met. There are no voluntary mechanisms of extension. The current legislation of the Czech Republic does not allow an opt-out from an existing collective agreement in force.

ČMKOS coordinates collective bargaining with its members by way of annual targets for wages and verifying their fulfilment. This coordination process takes place in connection with the targets announced by the ETUC. Overall, collective bargaining is relatively stable in the Czech Republic, and centralisation or decentralisation tendencies are not apparent.

Collective agreements, especially at the company level, address a wide range of issues related to labour law, such as the reduction of working hours without reducing wages and leave entitlement. The agreements also cover employment conditions—for example, fixed-term work, part-time work and temporary agency work. Furthermore, the agreements consider social policy, such as employee recreation and transport, as well as continuous vocational training, health and safety, and other matters. Topics such as stress at work and harassment in the workplace are very rarely reflected in

10 Pojer, Petr: Czech Republic. Industrial relations profile, in: EurWORK European Observatory of Working Life, 24 October 2014, http://www.eurofound.europa.eu/observatories/eurwork/comparative-information/national-contributions/czech-republic/czech-republic-industrial-relations-profile, accessed 22 December 2014. The above-mentioned data refers only to ČMKOS, the largest union confederation.

11 ČMKOS: Zpráva o průběhu kolektivního vyjednávání na vyšším stupni a na podnikové úrovni v roce 2009 [Progress report on higher-level and company-level collective bargaining in 2009], paper presented at the ČMKOS Assembly, Prague, 19 October 2009, quoted after Veverková, S.: The case of the Czech Republic, in: Guardiancich, I. (eds): Recovering from the crisis through social dialogue in the new EU Member States. the case of Bulgaria, the Czech Republic, Poland and Slovenia. Budapest: ILO, 2012, pp. 47–70.

collective agreements. On the other hand, arrangements relating to work-life balance tend to be relatively frequent. The topic of lifelong learning rarely, if ever, appeared in collective agreements. In year 2014, general conditions for employees' professional development have been agreed upon in 34% of CLCAs.[12] The importance of lifelong learning is also noted by young TU representatives; for them, it is an important TU activity in situations of unemployment, and youth unemployment more specifically.

There is a gradual rise in the number of CLCAs that contain provisions concerning gender equality and ending discrimination. In 2013 about 30% of company-level collective agreements included measures specifying gender equality and non discrimination. This year such measures are specified in 32.1% of company-level collective agreements (33% in 2012, 30.7% in 2011).[13]

In connection with trade union solidarity and international solidarity, the national regulation of industrial disputes must be mentioned. There is no legally defined reporting duty in relation to industrial conflicts; such activities by social partners have not been centrally monitored since 1997. There must be a legal quorum to call a strike: at least two thirds of the participating employees to whom the collective agreement may apply must vote for a strike, provided that at least half of all such employees took part in the voting. According to Act no. 2/1991 on collective bargaining as subsequently amended, a trade union organisation is obliged to report the number of employees who participate in the strike and list workplaces that will not operate during a strike for the employer. Rather than strikes, which are relatively rare in the Czech Republic, unions tend to declare strike alerts. Strike alerts are announced during collective bargaining as a last means in a dispute over a collective agreement. One example could be the threat of a strike by workers at the car manufacturer Škoda Auto in the Czech Republic,[14] which was lifted when the company and unions agreed on a 4% wage increase on 31 March 2011. The Škoda Auto trade union organisation asked for a 7% raise, with the company originally offering 0.5%. The raise in the end was 3.5% and employees were also given a one-off performance bonus, plus other bonuses. According to the chair of the Škoda Works Council, employees were strongly motivated by hearing that bonuses had been paid in other car factories owned by Volkswagen, Škoda Auto's parent company.

---

12 Ministry of labour and Social Affairs of the Czech Republic: Informační systém o pracovních podmínkách sjednaných v kolektivních smlouvách (ISPP) [Information System on Working Conditions agreed in collective agreements], in: kolektivnismlouvy.cz, http://www.kolektivnismlouvy.cz/download/2014/ISPP_2014.pdf, accessed 22 December 2014, here p. 61.

13 Pojer, Petr: Czech Republic. Industrial relations profile, in: EurWORK European Observatory of Working Life, 24 October 2014, http://www.eurofound.europa.eu/observatories/eurwork/comparative-information/national-contributions/czech-republic/czech-republic-industrial-relations-profile, accessed 22 December 2014.

14 ŠKODA AUTO a.s. is a member of the Volkswagen concern.

Outside the domain of collective bargaining there was, for example, a strike of transportation employees held on 16 June 2011 to protest against government economic reforms, cancellation of employee benefits and the reform of the pension and healthcare systems. The strike affected both passenger and freight railway transport—municipal transport was substantially reduced in several Czech cities, including Prague, and the operation of the Prague underground stopped entirely.

The two largest confederations also act as organisers or initiators of protest actions in situations when the governmental policy affects the standard of living of employees or attempts to restrict welfare. On 21 April 2012, a large demonstration against governmental policy was held in Prague with between 80,000 and 120,000 participants. It was the culmination of the 'Stop the Government' campaign, which had been organised by trade unions in cooperation with civic initiatives. The demonstration was called by trade unions, headed by the largest confederations—ČMKOS and ASO—and supported by other civic initiatives, such as ProAlt, the Czech National Disability Council (Národní rada osob se zdravotním postižením České Republiky (NRZP ČR)), and the Czech Senior Council (Rada Seniorů České Republiky (RS ČR)). Representatives of both trade unions and civic organisations called for the government to resign, asserting that its austerity policies were having a negative impact on the Czech economy and Czech workers' standard of living. The trade unions described the protest event as the largest industrial action in the Czech Republic since 1989.[15]

9.3. Specific Issues Related to Europeanization

To become an influential player or at least an equal partner at the European level requires the development of sufficient capacities and qualified personnel in national organisations as well as the creation of key prerequisites for the representation of trade union interests at the EU level.

First, we must mention the support from the ČMKOS, which has human resources and knowledge for international cooperation and was therefore the leading confederation in the accession period. The preparation activities started early. In 1996, the European Integration Team (EIT) was established as a joint initiative of ČMKOS and ETUC. The EIT was composed of representatives from ČMKOS and member trade unions. During the accession period, the European Integration Team prepared annual summary reports entitled 'ČMKOS and European integration'. Until accession to the EU in 2004, EIT dealt predominantly with preparations for accession; after 1 May 2004, the scope of its activities was transformed. It's most important tasks today include the following:

15 Veverková, Soňa: Trade unions organise biggest demonstration since 1989, in: EurWORK European Observatory of Working Life, 21 June 2012, http://www.eurofound.europa.eu/eiro/2012/05/articles/cz1205019i.htm, accessed 26 March 2014.

- contributing to the acknowledgement of TUs as a social partner that is consulted in the preparation of important documents and actions connected with the activity of the Czech Republic within the EU;
- preparing drafts of TU positions on questions connected with the EU for ČMKOS leadership, which helps give ČMKOS activities a European dimension;
- collecting and distributing information about the EU and its policies among ČMKOS TU members and regional TU councils—especially regarding the positions of ČMKOS and European trade unions on drafts of policies.

These tasks are fulfilled, first of all, by publishing a bulletin, 'Information from EIT ČMKOS'; approximately 20 issues are published per year. The ČMKOS website also includes a page containing EU information, with a special emphasis on the European Social Dialogue. The website contains, for example, all binding joint documents adopted by the European social partners. These information activities are very important because individual trade unions lack sufficient human and financial resources for international activities and there is a lingering problem of insufficient knowledge of foreign languages.

The representatives of ČMKOS are under the institutional aegis of the Czech Republic as EU members of different departmental (ministerial) coordination groups whose task is to prepare the Czech position toward the EU agenda.

ČMKOS has elaborated a standard decision-making procedure for policy positions which need to be represented in EU-level organisations and institutions. The motions should come from the ČMKOS, whose main body consists of representatives of trade unions, i.e. the 29 presidents of the member trade unions. ČMKOS evaluates all proposals of the individual unions and then elaborates (through the expert department) a joint statement, which is discussed and approved. The expert department works with the opinions and views of individual trade unions.[16] During this procedure all the member unions have a chance to express their opinion. The length of negotiation and number of members involved depends on the topic and its importance. In the case of less important topics, it is only the management who approves the joint statement.

9.4. Importance of the EU and Channels of Influence on the EU Level

Accession to the European Union was generally a new challenge for post-communist countries; this applies to trade unions as well. D. Ost described their situation quite pessimistically, noting that '[t]rade unions fared poorly in post-communist Eastern Europe. Everything about them declined: their membership, workplace authority, col-

16 Interview with trade union representative, Czech Republic, Gn14, 14 May 2013.

lective solidarity, sectorial diversity, enterprise responsibilities, and political influence'[17]. Globalisation, Europeanization and internationalisation of capital result in disappearing national borders and narrow the bargaining space for national trade unions as a result. For this reason, it is extremely important for trade unions from new EU member states to participate in discussions on the EU level and in decision-making processes. Czech trade unions passed through a period of transformation and consolidation and were well prepared for integration into European structures.[18] They potentially had the opportunity to participate on decision-making processes, and it is a question as to how far they were able or willing to use that opportunity. Development of sufficient capacities and qualified personnel in national organisations were the key prerequisites for representation of trade union interests at the EU level.

Czech trade unions started to participate in the activity of European institutions through European federations or as observers. For them, it was an important period of gaining information and experience and building social networks. They learned how to create a common position towards employers, especially in sectors where foreign ownership prevailed or in declining sectors. The development of the Czech economy in recent years has confirmed its dependence on external conditions. The economic recession affected the Czech economy as late as 2009, when the GDP growth rate was 4.5%. From 2009 to 2012, the imbalance in the labour market deepened and the registered unemployment rate rose dramatically to 8.0–9.0%. Relations among the social partners were far more consolidated than relations between the social partners and the government from2008 to 2012. The main reason for this relatively close cooperation was the mutual desire to maintain existing jobs.[19]

Comparing the importance of the European and national levels for their own trade unions, almost half of the respondents see the European level as significantly or

---

17 Ost, David: The Consequences of Postcommunism. Trade Unions in Eastern Europe's Future, in: East European Politics and Societies, 2009 (vol. 23), no. 1, pp. 13–33, here p. 14.

18 Fiala, Petr / Hloušek, Vít / Krpec, Oldřich: Evropeizace českých odborových svazů. proměny strategie reprezentace zájmů a okruhu partnerů v procesu evropské integrace [The Europeanization of Czech Trade Unions. Changes in Interest Representation Strategy and Partner Organizations in the European Integration Proces], in: Politologický časopis, 2007, no. 2, pp. 95–109. Mansfeldová, Zdenka: Czech Trade Union in EU Governance, in: Kusznir, Julia / Heiko Pleines (eds): Trade Unions from Post-Socialist Member States in EU Governance, Stuttgart: ibidem Verlag, 2008, pp. 129–139. Pleines, Heiko: Gewerkschaftliche Interessenvertretung auf der EU-Ebene. Eine vergleichende Analyse für Polen, Tschechien und die Slowakei [Trade union representation at the EU level. A comparative analysis for Poland, the Czech Republic and Slovakia], in: Osteuropa Wirtschaft, 2007 (vol. 52), no. 4. pp. 330–346. Pleines, Heiko: Representing workers or presenting EU prescriptions? Trade unions from post-socialist Member States in EU multi-level governance, in: Sandra Kröger / Dawid Friedrich (eds): Democracy and Representation in the EU, Basingstoke: PalgraveMacmillan, 2012, pp. 241–257.

19 Kroupa, Aleš / Pojer, Petr: Czech Republic. Representativeness of the European social partner organisations in the cross-industry social dialogue, in: EurWORK European Observatory of Working Life, 14 March 2014, http://www.eurofound.europa.eu/eiro/studies/tn1302018s/cz1302019q.htm, accessed 28 March 2014.

slightly more important; for one-third, the importance is equal. It is a positive development in comparison with the 2007 survey, when three-fifths evaluated both levels as equally important.

In general, there is no clear opinion whether the role of the EU and its impact on national policy should grow or remain the same, but only a minority of the respondents desire decreased EU impact. When respondents evaluate EU impact on the work of their trade union, more than 89.5% see a positive effect. This partly depends on whether there is a cabinet that is loaded in favour of social dialogue and trade unions—that is, a left-wing cabinet—or instead, a right-wing cabinet that attempts to limit the influence of trade unions. An example of the EU's positive influence could be observed when the right wing government attempted to reduce the participation rights of employees. We must mention that in the period of economic crisis and shortly after, the Czech Republic had two right-wing cabinets (2007–2010 and 2010–2013). In such cases, the EU is used as a benchmark and source for argumentation. One of our respondents has demonstrated the importance of EU regulations in the following example:

> I will say that some European legislation is more advanced than the national ones. One recent example could be the participation of employees in companies. The Czech Republic has changed the law on participation of employees on supervisory boards. [Originally, employees had a third of the seats on the supervisory boards of medium and larger sized public limited companies.] According to the regulation valid until the end of 2013, participation of employees on supervisory boards with more than 50 employees was obligatory. The employees could elect, at minimum, one-third of the board. The new regulation valid since January 1, 2014 has changed the rule towards a voluntary form; the participation is not necessary, but it is possible. This development goes in the opposite direction from the EU[20].

The positive impact of the EU on domestic policy is definitely observed in the social sphere and the protection of employees with its emphasis on functioning social dialogue. In a time of globalisation and internationalisation of capital, the national state lacks many options for influencing the functioning of companies in different countries. Supranational owners could move a company to another country and the national state has no chance to intervene. In the case of supranational companies, the trade unions expect that the EU could to do something and help re-industrialise Europe.

> Just looking at the number of multi-national firms based in this country, it is extremely important to be represented on the European level. I believe that our voice has to be heard in Brussels. Unfortunately the representation of new EU member states on the European level is weak.[21]

The trade union representatives generally share the opinion that it is necessary to be represented on the EU level and participate on EU decision-making processes. In another words, it is necessary to move from the first period of Europeanization and

20 Interview with trade union representative, Czech Republic, Gn18, 30 January 2013.
21 Interview with trade union representative, Czech Republic, Gn03, 25 February 2013.

adaptation to a new political environment to the next step. As mentioned by one respondent, it is important

> ...to be present at everything. We need to be part of all processes, [and] influence all justifications of why we are in the EU and those reasons are political, economic, historical, cultural, and geopolitical. We belong there, full stop. However, because unions also have the right to be part of all these processes according to EU legislation, we would in fact forfeit our rights if we did not participate. If we have this opportunity to be part of everything, why not make use of it? It is our duty![22]

However, there are also some critical comments; first, the overbearing bureaucracy is criticised. It is also possible to mention the directives, which are not in correspondence with the national mentality—or with specific national conditions, at least—or are contradictory because different regulations produced by the EU are not fully meaningful under domestic conditions.

Trade unions and their representatives use different methods to exercise their influence at the EU level and influence decision-making. In the survey, we offered six possible ways that decision-making on the European level could be influenced. The TU representatives could use (1) direct consultations with the European Commission; (2) direct consultations with the European Parliament; (3) consultations with national representatives in the Council of Ministers; or advance their interests (4) via the EU Social Dialogue (including branch dialogues); (5) via the European Economic and Social Committee; or (6) via membership in an European umbrella organisation like the ETUC. In the case of Czech trade unions, according our survey, European trade union structures are preferred to political structures. Membership in the ETUC or one of European industrial unions (83.3%) is most preferred, followed by participation in European Social Dialogue (66.7%). Another channel is the European Economic and Social Committee (61.1%). Noticeably less preferred were direct consulting with the European Commission (38.9%), direct consulting with the European Parliament (38.9%), and consulting with the members of the Council of Ministers (33.3%). Communication with the European Commission, European Parliament or Council of Ministers is used rather on an ad hoc basis. In case of necessity and an actual problem, there is an attempt to contact the respective minister, give him / her the information, and present the trade unions' view. In addition to formal channels, informal channels are also used; it depends on individual contacts with members of the European Parliament or other EU politicians.

9.5. Cooperation with European Umbrella Organisations

Cooperation in European umbrella organisations of trade unions is generally positively evaluated by the respondents. They are satisfied or rather satisfied with this cooperation, and their evaluation is stable over time. The position and interests of their trade

22 Interview with trade union representative, Czech Republic, Gn02, 15 February 2013.

unions often coincide with those of the European umbrella organisations to which they belong. In addition to participation in meetings of European umbrella organisations and personal contacts, there are other modes of communication used, most frequently electronic communication. However, personal contact is seen as very important even with its lower frequency because it creates the conditions for more informal and trustworthy communication via technology. Even if a majority of problems could be solved through emails, some things are better discussed in person. It helps create an atmosphere of confidence and mutual understanding. The younger generation of trade unionists also stress, besides traditional communication channels, the importance of Facebook and Twitter.

The advantage of collaboration with European umbrella organisations of trade unions is seen in the first instance in solidarity, coordination, collaboration, information, and the exchange of good practice and experience. Also important is the coordination of the activities of individual national trade unions and accepting joint opinions. The cooperation also helps Czech trade unions strengthen their position and make use of their national views and experiences.

> Coordinated procedure is a great advantage and always has greater success and weight[23].

The cooperation is evaluated as mainly positive, and European partners are perceived as very helpful. Disadvantages of this cooperation are of an internal character; they are observed in financial costs, which are quite high with the frequency of meetings, especially in situations of declining membership and the ensuing limitation of income sources.

An expression of aforementioned solidarity could be seen in the support of Czech trade unions for European-wide protest actions organised by European umbrella organisations and some national trade unions. All organisations included in the survey have mentioned their regularly demonstrated expressions of solidarity and listed a number of actions, organised either in Brussels or in other member states, in which they took part or at least sent symbolic representation. The Czech trade unions not only express their solidarity and support for events organised by partners, they also receive support from partners in case they organise a protest action. As an example of received support from foreign partners, the large demonstration held in Prague on 21 April 2012 against the government policy could be mentioned. Support for the demonstrators was expressed by foreign trade unions, including the Deutscher Gewerkschaftsbund (DGB), the Österreichischer Gewerkschaftsbund (OEGB) and Poland's Niezależny Samorządny Związek Zawodowy Solidarność (NSZZ Solidarność).[24]

---

23 Interview with trade union representative, Czech Republic, Gn14, 14 May 2013.

24 Veverková, Soňa: Trade unions organise biggest demonstration since 1989, in: EurWORK European Observatory of Working Life, 21 June 2012, http://www.eurofound.europa.eu/eiro/2012/05/articles/cz1205019i.htm, accessed 26 March 2014.

By evaluating their own performance, the trade unions compare their performance on the EU level with the activity of trade unions from other post-communist countries, especially Slovakia, Hungary and Poland. By this comparison, the Czech TUs are among the most active in Central Eastern Europe. The fact that Czech TUs are not split in their representation at the EU level and in the position they represent plays an important role. Nevertheless, the European dimension does not have equal importance for all trade unions in the country. There is the strongest confederation, ČMKOS, which is the leading partner in international cooperation and there are strong branch trade unions active in the international and European arena, such as the Odborový svaz KOVO (OS KOVO)[25] or Odborový svaz Energeticko–chemického (OS ECHO, a trade union of energy and chemical workers).

Cooperation with European umbrella organisations represents the vertical level of cooperation. Other possibilities for exercising influence and seeking support were mentioned, including the European Foundation for the Improvement of Living and Working Conditions in Dublin (Eurofound), the European Agency for Safety and Health at Work in Bilbao, and the Luxembourg Advisory Committee on Safety, Hygiene and Health Protection at Work. There exist many opportunities for cooperation with different partners on the European level, which is positively evaluated; the problem and limit for the Czech trade unions is insufficient human capacity. The number of experts available and suitable for these tasks is limited.

At its congress in 2012, ETUC again supported the implementation of a social progress clause in the Treaty of the European Union. This clause is meant to underline the importance of social rights and social progress in the EU alongside the single market. Czech trade unions participate in the debate about a social progress clause and see this level of social protection as highly essential and important. One of the respondents has described the position with the following words:

> This is a fundamental question for the future of the European social model and the competitiveness of the European Union. If it is the purely economic stance that wins, then we would return to prehistoric times. It would be a return of the principle that strength prevails and that whoever can grab more will grab more. So we absolutely need this clause[26].

Trade unions do not believe that differences between labour costs in relation to the old EU member states are a legitimate way to protect workplaces in the Czech Republic. The argument that competitiveness increases if labour costs decrease is found to be untruthful.

ETUC has prepared 'A New Pact for Europe: European Trade Union Confederation Plan for Investment, Sustainable Growth and Quality Jobs'. It is a joint vision of European trade unions meant for political representations on the European and national levels.

25 For more about this trade union see the chapter by Mansfeldová in this volume, 'The Czech Metalworkers' Federation / Odborový svaz KOVO (OS KOVO) in Domestic and European Arenas'.

26 Interview with trade union representative, Czech Republic, Gn13, 15 May 2013.

The document was aimed at EU citizens, voters, political parties and their candidates before the elections for European Parliament in May 2014. ETUC mobilises for a social Europe, a Europe that provides its citizens with quality employment and a secure future. ČMKOS has expressed its support for this initiative and encouraged its member organisations and all employees to participate in European elections.

9.6. Connections between the EU and the National Level

Czech trade unions attempt to use the opportunity to influence European labour legislation during its preparation. On the other hand, they could also use EU directives and measures as arguments against their own representation. However, they are conscious of the complexity of this process, which is influenced by many factors. Whether the new EU directive will improve or worsen the domestic situation depends on good implementation of the EU directive into national legislation. A comparison of TU influence on the European and national levels demonstrates the change during the period from 2007 to 2013 (see Table 9-1).

Table 9-1: How Do You Assess Your Trade Union's Influence at the EU Level in Comparison to the National Level? (in %)

	Czech Republic	
	2013	**2007**
Larger	31.2	44.5
The same	56.2	22.2
Smaller	6.3	22.2
Do not know	6.3	11.1

In 2007, the influence at the EU level was evaluated as higher than at the national level; today, more than a half of respondents see the influence as being the same. Here, we must take into account the political context in which the trade unions operate. When the programmatic orientation of the government is closer to the trade unions' programme (as in typical social-democratic governments), national-level cooperation is smooth and TUs either evaluate their influence on the national level higher or their expectation toward EU level less highly. With a right-wing government, the situation is different; trade unions attempt to enforce through the EU claims their claims that they cannot enforce on the national level.

Our results showed that trade unions' operations at the European level sometimes or often affect their national activities. This may have the form of 'using Europe in argumentation'—setting an agenda or implementing European standards in the local environment (respondents often use the 'Europe argument'). It depends on the problem and the key tasks settled on at the European level. One of our respondents gave us an example:

> Three years ago, we made an agreement in industry that we will promote a common requirement in collective bargaining. It was against risky jobs, agency jobs or risky forms of employment. It was a gentlemen's agreement among members and all members have included these demands in their bargaining[27].

Another example is the further promotion of European-level agreements on the national level or support for the implementation of EU regulations on the national level. At the national level, trade unions refer to the EU in gaining support or justifying their positions. Under the Euroscepticism of former Czech governments and their narrowly liberal policy focus, support from the EU and argumentation 'with the EU' was necessary.

9.7. Bi- and Multilateral International Cooperation and Cooperation with Trade Unions from Old and New EU Member States

Czech trade unions have been involved in variety of international collaborations. Beneath the EU level, it is bilateral, in some cases trilateral, regional cooperation in border regions with Interregional Trade Union Councils (IRTUCs). There is one Czech-German IRTUC BoBa (Bohemia / Bavaria); one trilateral IRTUC,Elbe / Neisse (Germany, Poland and Czech Republic); and two Czech-Austrian IRTUCs, Danube / Vltava and South Moravia / Lower Austria. The aim of IRTUCs is the regulation of cross-border work while concentrating on specific sectors and problems of the cross-border region, perhaps in just a single sector, like the mining industry for IRTUC Elbe-Neisse. IRTUCs focus on themes of industrial relations, collective agreement issues and legal fundamentals in the countries involved. Mutual participation in demonstrations for wage and trade union demands—or in individual cases, cross-border support such as wage campaigns—is also a part of the cooperation. The activities are essentially coordinated on a regional level; methodical help from the centre is available when needed and requested.

Cross-border cooperation can have a different direction, intensity and character. As mentioned by Kahancova, there are two types of cross-border trade unionism: cooperative and competitive. Competition as a form of cross-border union interaction entails rivalry between different trade unions in the face of international competition for investment, threats of capital relocation, and the prospect of worsening working standards and pay levels.[28] According to our interviews, cross-border interaction has a predominantly cooperative character. Friendly contacts with unions in neighbour-

---

27 Interview with trade union representative, Czech Republic, Gn03, 25 February 2013.

28 Kahancova, Marta: Two Faces of Cross-Border Trade Unionism in Europe—Western and Eastern Unions between Cooperation and Competition. Paper presented at the Amsterdam Institute for Advanced Labour Studies seminar, Amsterdam, 11 June 2009.

ing countries were and are continuously nurtured. The ČMKOS delegation participated in the congresses of partner trade union centres in Slovakia, Germany, Austria and Poland. There is a long tradition of contacts with the Confederation of Trade Unions of the Slovak Republic (Konfederácia odborových zväzov Slovenskej republiky (KOZ SR)) with the exchange of official delegations, consultations concerning problems related to reforms undertaken in both countries and mutual support in protest actions. Such cooperation is also mentioned on the level of individual trade unions.

The Czech trade unions have wide cooperation and good contacts with trade unions from all old EU member states; Austria, Germany (specifically Bavaria), France, the Scandinavian countries, and Belgium were especially mentioned. The significant help that Czech TUs received during the 1990s from all European organisations was noted several times.

> They helped us create new post-communist trade unions[29].

Germany and Austria are seen as the most important partners among the old EU member states. One of the reasons might be the proportion of German investment in the Czech Republic.

With the old member countries, there is definitely long-lasting cooperation, so nothing has really changed here—and if so, only in the positive direction. Old member states can provide much more practical knowledge because they have more experience with the market economy and with the European approach to social dialogue. With the new member states, TUs instead exchange knowledge of how national governments attack social protection, labour law, etc. There are also different expectations towards international cooperation. Transfers of knowledge, inspiration and resources are expected from Western European trade unions; with Central Eastern European partners, the trade unions instead expect to align on common positions. As noted by one trade union representative, TUs attempt to take lessons from their partners:

> So we discuss when a new type of reform that has not been undertaken in our country is undertaken somewhere else—a good example of this is the pension reform and the experience with radical privatisation schemes undertaken in Poland, Hungary, Slovakia and other countries. When the Czech government came up with a similar plan, we managed to draw upon the experiences from these East European countries[30].

A specific form of regional cooperation is represented by the Vienna Memorandum Group, which is the cooperation network of branch trade unions in the metal industry from the closest neighbours among old and new EU member states, namely the Czech Republic, Slovakia and Hungary.[31]

29 Interview with trade union representative, Czech Republic, Gn01, 15 January 2013.
30 Interview with trade union representative, Czech Republic, Gn13, 15 May 2013.
31 See the chapter by Landgraf and Mansfeldová in this volume.

9.8. Summary

The integration into EU structures and its effects are generally evaluated positively, especially as regards consulting and the sharing of hard-to-access information. Trade unions appreciate the possibility of creating joint strategies in negotiating with employers, especially in industries dominated by supranational corporations (e.g., trading, heavy industry). Additionally, the possibility of commenting on European legislation applicable to individual industries is appreciated. The European level of interest representation is generally as important as the national level for trade unions, and they expect that the significance of the EU will continue growing. However, not all trade unions are active on the European level, pay equal attention to European issues and hold substantial internal debates on EU-related positions and strategies. There is a difference among confederations and unions; the most active in European matters are ČMKOS and the Czech Metalworkers' Federation. This enabled them to bring together different EU-related activities and act in a more systematic way.

Czech trade unions are not split in their representation at the EU level: they are able to unify their positions towards EU politics and measures and act as a collective actor. However, the debate on EU-related positions and strategies is held mainly on the national or confederation level and not all TU subjects are involved.

Of first importance for the trade unions are employment problems, social policy issues, and everything that concerns employees' position. They defend employees' interests, and so they coordinate on everything from labour law and social policy to free movement and wage conditions. The European level is an opportunity to exchange experiences and study what collective agreements—and anything that has to do with employees and collective bargaining—look like.

Czech trade unions still have not fully overcome the heritage of post-communism as membership, workshop authority, collective solidarity and political influence decline. There are some obstacles to union revival of an essentially ideological and organisational character. There are still ideological obstacles connected with coming to terms with the socialist past and the revival of capitalism without virtue. Organisational obstacles not only include declining membership but also declining opportunities for TU membership. The large unified enterprises of the past were replaced by a number of small firms in which it is difficult to organise trade unions. However, there are differences between branches and also within branches.

The crisis did not strengthen the position of trade unions—just the opposite. It has weakened their capacity to act and turned their interests more to domestic issues, such as government austerity measures and their efficiency and impact on the population, especially employees and low-income groups.

For representation on the supranational level, it is important to create sufficient capacity with necessary expertise and linguistic knowledge. It is not only funding and language skills that would help improve the representation of trade union interests at the EU level. A higher degree of self-reflection on unions' work is needed—a more flexible response to the changing domestic and international conditions and adjustments to some deeply settled work processes.

Christin Landgraf

10. Hungarian Trade Unions in EU Multilevel Governance. Interest Representation and Europeanisation

10.1. Introduction

In 2004, Hungary joined the EU together with other countries from Central Eastern Europe, namely Poland, the Czech Republic and Slovakia. Since then, trade unions from the new EU member states have had the opportunity to participate in decision-making processes at the EU level, e.g., by gaining access to EU institutions or by joining European umbrella organisations of trade unions. However, how interest groups from Central Eastern European countries respond to European integration and how they behave at the EU level are rarely examined by scholars of political science. Therefore, this article primarily aims to present major findings from interviews conducted with Hungarian trade unionists within this project by analysing the following questions: To what extent are Hungarian trade unions integrated into EU multilevel governance structures? How do they assess cooperation with unions from other EU member states? How do their activities at the EU level and beyond influence their work at the domestic level? All these questions are of importance for research on interest groups in EU governance. However, as studies show, the degree of Europeanization and interest representation at the EU level is also determined by national contexts of interest intermediation. As Beyers / Kerremans suggest, the Europeanization of domestic interest groups is determined by their integration into domestic structures, 'critical resource dependencies' as well as the policy field in which interest organisations are active.[1] Thus, if interest groups have good access to national institutions and their subsidies, their Europeanization is restricted:

> The dependence on domestic public institutions is a factor that affects the absence or presence of exit options and the potential Europeanization of an interest group. The more domestic interest groups depend on resources exclusively provided by government agencies such as subsidies, the more these groups restrict their actions to the domestic political system.[2]

Furthermore, as Greenwood suggests, domestic actors can also express their interests via domestic venues of interest representation and need not be exclusively active at the European level to influence EU policies.[3] The domestic context, therefore, also should be

---

1 Beyers, Jan / Kerremans, Bart: Critical Resource Dependencies and the Europeanization of Domestic Interest Groups, in: Journal of European Public Policy, 2007 (vol. 14), no. 3, pp. 460–481.

2 Ibid., here p. 465.

3 Greenwood, Justin: Interest Representation in the European Union, 3. ed., Basingstoke: Palgrave Macmillan, 2011.

considered, especially with regard to current political developments in Hungary, which have profoundly changed domestic patterns of interest representation for trade unions. These developments will also be considered, placing the results in a broader context.

This chapter is primarily based on 12 interviews with Hungarian trade unionists that were conducted between March and May 2013 with union representatives of two confederations and with branch unions in the fields of mining and energy, metal and trade / commerce. As the number of interviews indicates, the following data do not allow for statistical correlations. However, they might show tendencies within the examined branches and confederations. Concerning the representativeness of the data, one must also consider that the interviews were conducted only with unionists in the respective trade union headquarters. Trade unionists at the company level were not included in the study; such an inclusion might have resulted in a different dataset and picture.

To assess the integration in EU governance structures and Europeanization of trade unions from Hungary, this chapter will proceed as follows. The following two sections will focus on the Hungarian trade union landscape and the integration of Hungarian unions in the national context. The fourth and fifth parts will present major findings from our study regarding interest representation at the EU level, bilateral and multilateral cooperation and Europeanization. The last part will conclude by summarising major findings.

10.2. Hungarian Trade Unions

To be successful at the EU level, resources, such as financial capacities, expertise or a large membership that endow the organisation with legitimacy, are important for receiving access to EU decision-makers.[4] A closer examination of the trade unions' capacities therefore seems likely to be fruitful.

The Hungarian trade union landscape is very diverse and plural. Six trade union confederations were founded during the transition period. The majority of these confederations, namely the National Confederation of Hungarian Trade Unions (MSZOSZ), the Forum for the Cooperation of Trade Unions (SZEF), the Confederation of Unions of Professionals (ÉSZT) and the Autonomous Trade Unions Confederation (ASZSZ), were successor organisations of the socialist trade union SZOT (National Council of

4 Dür, Andreas: Interest Groups in the European Union. How Powerful are They?, in: West European Politics, 2008 (vol. 31), no. 6, pp. 1212–1230, here p. 1214. Eising, Rainer: Interest Groups in EU Policy-Making, in: Living Reviews in European Governance, 2008 (vol. 3), no. 4, http://europeangovernance.livingreviews.org/Articles/lreg-2008-4/, accessed 22 September 2011, here p. 15.

Trade Unions).[5] In May 2013, MSZOSZ, SZEF and ASZSZ published a declaration with the intention to merge confederations to represent employees' interests successfully:[6]

> The colourful and rivaling union structure brought results in the first years, but later separation and hostility became characteristic instead of cooperation. This has always been utilized by the political parties and used for their own goals, making successful workers' interest defence more difficult.
>
> Governments, in cooperation with the owners and entrepreneurs have pursued a divisive and unilateral policy against the trade unions occasionally. Particularly since 2010 it has been particularly characteristic that ones are given exclusive preference over others and ones are being ignored.
>
> We do have an answer: unification.[7]

In December 2013, these three unions founded the new organisation Hungarian Confederation of Trade Unions (MSZSZ).[8] According to Reutter / Träger, SZEF was the largest trade union organisation, with approximately 275.000 members. However, the members included many pensioners. MSZOSZ was the second-largest trade union confederation, with approximately 220.000 members. It represented 29 branch unions. ASZSZ had approximately 130.000 members, but it also included many pensioners. Additionally, among the former successor organisations, ÉSZT has approximately 90.000 members.[9]

In addition to these four organisations, the Democratic League of Independent Trade Unions (LIGA) and the National Federation of Workers' Council (Munkástanácsok) were founded as independent trade union confederations. Among these two confederations, LIGA is the largest trade union, with approximately 110.000 members.[10]

According to Deppe / Schroeder, the relationship between the successor organisations of SZOT and the new and independent confederations was characterised by fights over legitimacy and financial means in the first years after the system change. However, in the following years, the relationship between the confederations became

5 Krén, Ildikó: Thesen zur Standortbestimmung der Gewerkschaften in Ungarn [Theses positioning of the trade unions in Hungary], in: Friedrich-Ebert-Stiftung Budapest, 2011, http://library.fes.de/pdf-files/id/07790.pdf, accessed 14 November 2014, here p. 2.

6 ASZSZ, MSZOSZ, SZEF: Unification Statement, in: fesbp.hu, 1 May 2013, http://www.fesbp.hu/common/pdf/unification_statement20130501.pdf, accessed 14 November 2014.

7 Ibid.

8 Krén, Ildikó / Rindt, Zsuzsa: Hungary. Industrial Relations Profile, in: EurWORK European Observatory of Working Life, 22 October 2014, http://eurofound.europa.eu/observatories/eurwork/comparative-information/national-contributions/hungary/hungary-industrial-relations-profile, accessed 12 November 2014.

9 Reutter, Werner / Träger, Hendrik: Ungarn. NGOs, Verbände und Politik. viel Schein, wenig Sein? [Hungary. NGOs, Associations and Politics. Much Illusion, little Reality], in: Reutter, Werner (eds): Verbände und Interessengruppen in den Ländern der Europäischen Union, 2. ed., Wiesbaden: VS Verlag für Sozialwissenschaften, 2012, pp. 783–808, here p. 796.

10 Reutter, Werner / Träger, Hendrik: Ungarn. NGOs, Verbände und Politik. viel Schein, wenig Sein? [Hungary. NGOs, Associations and Politics. Much Illusion, little Reality], in: Reutter, Werner (eds): Verbände und Interessengruppen in den Ländern der Europäischen Union, 2. ed., Wiesbaden: VS Verlag für Sozialwissenschaften, 2012, pp. 783–808, here p. 796 f.

more stable.[11] Nonetheless, trust in the unions decreased. According to Eurobarometer surveys, in 2004, only 26% of the population indicated that they 'tend to trust' trade unions, whereas 53% 'tend not to trust' trade unions. Three years after the Eastern Enlargement, the new survey results were quite similar, with 23% of the population mentioning they 'tend to trust' unions, whereas 54% 'tend not to trust' unions.[12]

Additionally, during the transformation process, union density dramatically decreased in Hungary. In 2014, union density stood only at 11% (company level).[13]

As Bouwen suggests, the extent of decision processes influences the efficiency of interest groups in providing and offering information to EU institutions in exchange for access.[14] Foreign language competences of the staff also may play an important role here because the lack of foreign language competences is often mentioned by respondents to the project.[15] This might cause difficulties, as policy documents coming from the EU level must be translated into Hungarian and vice versa. Such documents are used to make decisions, participate at meetings, provide assessments and maintain contact with EU institutions. Internal working and decision processes within unions regarding EU-level activities might therefore be less flexible.

Furthermore, the proportion of employed union representatives in Hungarian unions is low (12%) compared with the EU average of 23%.[16] Thus, the staff size of Hungarian confederations ranges on average from approximately 2–20 employees,[17] whereas LIGA largely hired additional staff (approximately 100 employed unionists for work at the regional level and 30 for the headquarters).[18]

---

11 Deppe, Rainer / Schroeder, Wolfgang: Doppelte Transformation und Gewerkschaften in Polen, Ungarn und Ostdeutschland [Double transformation and trade unions in Poland, Hungary and East Germany], in: WSI Mitteilungen, 2002 (vol. 55), no. 11, http://www.boeckler.de/wsimit_2002_11_deppe.pdf, accessed 21 November 2014, pp. 663–669, here p. 665.

12 European Commission: Public Opinion. Eurobarometer surveys, in: europa.eu, http://ec.europa.eu/public_opinion/cf/showchart_column.cfm?keyID=2188&nationID=22,&startdate=2004.10&enddate=2007.10, accessed 12 November 2014.

13 Krén, Ildikó / Rindt, Zsuzsa: Hungary. Industrial Relations Profile, in: EurWORK European Observatory of Working Life, 22 October 2014, http://eurofound.europa.eu/observatories/eurwork/comparative-information/national-contributions/hungary/hungary-industrial-relations-profile, accessed 12 November 2014.

14 Bouwen, Pieter: Corporate Lobbying in the European Union. The Logic of Access, in: Journal of European Public Policy, 2002 (vol. 9), no. 3, pp. 365–390, here p. 375.

15 See country reports in this volume as well as the chapter on the interest representation and EU-level activities of the trade unions studied.

16 ETUI / Fulton, L.: Worker Representation in Europe. Labour Research Department and ETUI. Produced with the Assistance of the SEEurope Network, in worker-participation.eu, 2013, http://www.worker-participation.eu/National-Industrial-Relations/Across-Europe/Trade-Unions2, accessed 19 November 2014.

17 Krén, Ildikó: Hungary-Labour Relations and Social Dialogue, in: Annual Review 2013, Friedrich-Ebert-Stiftung, http://library.fes.de/pdf-files/bueros/warschau/10436-20140107.pdf, p. 16–19, accessed 14 November 2014.

18 Krén, Ildikó / Rindt, Zsuzsa: Hungary. Industrial Relations Profile, in: EurWORK European Observatory of Working Life, 22 October 2014, http://eurofound.europa.eu/observatories/

10.3. Hungarian Trade Unions and the National Context

According to Greenwood, interest groups can use different venues of interest representation to influence decision-making at the EU level. Via the 'national route', interest groups can represent their interests via national contacts. Via the 'Brussels route', interest organisations can represent interests directly at the EU level, e.g., by gaining access to the Commission.[19] Furthermore, as Beyers / Kerremans argue, the Europeanization of national interest organisations is determined by their integration into national structures, 'critical resource dependencies' as well as the policy field where they are active.[20] Therefore, to assess the Europeanization and interest representation of Hungarian unions, examination of the integration of the unions into the domestic intermediation system seems necessary.

After the system change of 1989, the new political system in Hungary quickly seemed to consolidate.

However, in 2010, the political constellation in Hungary completely changed due to the overwhelming victory of Fidesz in the parliamentary elections. Shortly after the elections, Fidesz used its majority to rebuild the political system of Hungary. Thus, the Fidesz-led government adopted a new constitution. This new constitution is dominated by the philosophy of Fidesz: views and ideas of other political actors are not considered.[21] Far-reaching laws have also been adopted in other fields of public life. Related changes within the economic sphere include, e.g., the reduction of the income tax rate to 16%, extraordinary taxes on certain types of branches and the socialisation of companies.[22]

Far-reaching changes were also made in the field of industrial relations. According to Tóth, by re-organising the system of industrial relations, the Fidesz government intended 'to remove a potential veto-point, a checking power on government actions, in the drive to re-organise the country.'[23] Thus, a new labour code has been introduced. According to Tóth, the new labour code limits the rights of trade unions to a large degree. For instance, the number of legally protected union representatives

eurwork/comparative-information/national-contributions/hungary/hungary-industrial-relations-profile, accessed 12 November 2014.

19 Greenwood, Justin: Interest Representation in the European Union, 3. ed., Basingstoke: Palgrave Macmillan, 2011, pp. 23–52.

20 Beyers, Jan / Kerremans, Bart: Critical Resource Dependencies and the Europeanization of Domestic Interest Groups, in: Journal of European Public Policy, 2007 (vol. 14), no. 3, pp. 460–481.

21 Küpper, Herbert: Mit Mängeln. Ungarns neues Grundgesetz [With defects. Hungary's new constitution], in: Osteuropa, 2011 (vol. 61), no. 12, pp. 135–144, here p. 138.

22 Farkas, Zoltán: Die Orbán-Regierung und ihre »unorthodoxe« Wirtschaftspolitik [The Orbán government and its 'unorthodox' economic policies], in: Friedrich-Ebert-Stiftung Budapest, 2013, http://fesbp.hu/common/pdf/Nachrichten_aus_Ungarn_mai_2013.pdf, accessed 14 November 2014.

23 Tóth, András: The Collapse of the post-Socialist Industrial Relations System in Hungary, in: Journal for Labour and Social Affairs in Eastern Europe, 2013 (vol. 16), no. 1, pp. 5–19, here p. 5.

has been reduced. Moreover, employers' duties to inform and to consult trade unions have been repealed. The unions must represent 10% of the company's employees to conclude collective agreements.[24] The Fidesz government also limited the opportunities for unions to represent interests in the political arena. The Hungarian social dialogue, the National Interest Reconciliation Council (OÉT), was eliminated and replaced by the National Economic and Social Council (NGTT).

Since October 2011, this new body has been functioning. The NGTT consists of 32 members from various fields such as the economy, employees, churches, NGOs and sciences. The new council has a consultative and advisory function.[25]

In addition, as Tóth summarises, the government also established a new body for interests in the economy that has a consultative function. For the confederations, only LIGA, MSZOSZ and the National Federation of Workers' Council and three employer's organisations are represented. The represented unions are also confronted with limited state subsidies.[26] Furthermore, as Krén / Rindt describe the competencies of this Consultative Forum of the Industry and the Government (VKF):

> If they come to a consensus, their proposal is submitted to the government, which consults the NGTT, announces and codifies the agreement. However, there is no legal obligation for the government to consult the VKF and the social partners' consultation power depends on the willingness of the government to consult.[27]

In summary, the Fidesz government transformed the political and juridical system of Hungary to a large degree and limited the rights of unions. Due to the domestic developments, it seems to become increasingly difficult for Hungarian unions to use domestic venues of interest representation to influence EU-level decision-making.

10.4. Interest Representation at the EU Level and Beyond

10.4.1. Interest Representation at the EU Level

We assume that interest groups are active at the EU level when EU regulation widely affects their work and activities. Therefore, our study asked respondents to assess the

24 Tóth, András: The New Hungarian Labour Code—Background, Conflicts, Compromises, in: Friedrich Ebert Foundation Budapest, 2012, http://www.fesbp.hu/common/pdf/Nachrichten_aus_Ungarn_june_2012.pdf, pp. 7–8, accessed 14 November 2014.

25 NGTT: The National Economic and Social Council of Hungary, in: ngtt.hu, 2012, http://www.ngtt.hu/index_eng.html, accessed 14 November 2014.

26 Tóth, András: The Collapse of the post-Socialist Industrial Relations System in Hungary, in: Journal for Labour and Social Affairs in Eastern Europe, 2013 (vol. 16), no. 1, pp. 5–19, here p. 13.

27 Krén, Ildikó / Rindt, Zsuzsa: Hungary. Industrial Relations Profile, in: EurWORK European Observatory of Working Life, 22 October 2014, http://eurofound.europa.eu/observatories/eurwork/comparative-information/national-contributions/hungary/hungary-industrial-relations-profile, accessed 12 November 2014.

importance of the EU for their work and activities of their trade unions and with regard to interest representation. The data show that the respondents we interviewed perceive the EU and EU regulation as very important for their work and the activities of their trade unions. The majority of the Hungarian respondents stated that the importance of the EU is equal to that of national politics. Only a minority believed that the EU is less important than national politics.[28] The majority of the respondents stated that the influence of the EU on national politics should grow, whereas no respondent stated that the influence of the EU on national politics should decrease.[29] Asked about the impact of the EU on trade union activities, the majority stated that the EU has a positive impact on the work of the trade unions, whereas no respondent mentioned that the EU has a negative impact on the work of the unions.[30]

When asked about positive or negative examples of the EU's impact, respondents stressed that there are many opportunities to represent interests and to take part in decision-making processes, e.g., via the European Social Dialogue, European Works Councils and Interregional Trade Union Councils. Furthermore, it has been argued that the EU represents a higher level, with more competences and specific norms and values one can address when interest representation at the national level is more difficult, e.g., with regard to the new Hungarian labour code. Respondents also mentioned more concrete positive examples such as the man-hour directive. However, the large variety of languages that are spoken within the EU was mentioned as a challenge to the work of the unions. Negative examples that were mentioned concerned more specific policy fields such as the liberalisation of the market.[31]

Respondents mentioned a broad palette of reasons for being active at the EU level including protection of employees and employees' rights and the work within the European Social Dialogue. Cooperation with European umbrella organisations of trade unions was seen as very important. However, activities regarding concrete policy fields that are of importance for single branches or for general trade union activities were also mentioned, such as employment policy and youth unemployment, energy policy, and environmental policy. Respondents also referred to European norms and values as a reason for being active at the EU level, e.g., regarding questions about the reduction of democratic rights at the national level, and the uniformity and stability of laws.[32]

---

28 Results of the questionnaire national trade unions, Q1 2013. The results are from the research project 'Europeanization of Trade Unions in the Countries of the Eastern Enlargement'.

29 Results of the questionnaire national trade unions, Q2 2013.

30 Results of the questionnaire national trade unions, Q3 2013. Please note the number of respondents: n = 11.

31 Results of the questionnaire national trade unions, Q4 2013.

32 Results of the questionnaire national trade unions, Q7 2013.

The data show that the EU is perceived to affect widely the work of the unions not only with regard to specific policy decisions but also with regard to general opportunities of interest representation in EU governance structures.

According to Pleines, trade unions can use different venues of interest representation, e.g., the EU institutions as well as via other EU bodies such as the European Social Dialogue or the European Economic and Social Committee (EESC).[33] As the data show, the unions we interviewed make use of several venues of interest representation at the EU level, including direct consultations with the Commission, the European Parliament and the Council as well as membership in the Social Dialogue, the EESC and, alternatively, membership in European umbrella organisations. However, the Hungarian respondents had in general less access to the Commission, the European Parliament and the Council.[34] This reflects general tendencies that correspond with the answers of respondents from the other countries under study.[35] However, access via the EESC is lower when compared with the results of the other unions, as only three Hungarian respondents mentioned using the EESC as a venue of interest representation at the EU level.[36]

To receive a more detailed picture of the chosen venues of interest representation at the EU level, we asked respondents to assess their satisfaction with the work of their trade union at the European level. Only a minority of the respondents were unsatisfied with the role of their trade union at the EU level. However, many respondents were neither satisfied nor dissatisfied with the work of their union at the EU level.[37] When elaborating on their answers, respondents stated, for instance, that the high number of Hungarian trade union confederations would reduce the possibility representing the interests of Hungarian employees successfully. Respondents also underlined the importance of liaison offices in Brussels that would contribute to interest representation at the EU level, e.g., to receive information about EU tenders. The respondents noted, however, that such offices do not currently exist. The lack of foreign language competence was also mentioned as a hindrance to trade unions representing their interests effectively.[38] In addition, respondents also underlined their good rela-

33 Pleines, Heiko (eds): Already Arrived in Brussels? Interest Representation of Trade Unions from the New EU Member States at the EU Level. Documentation of Interview Results, in: Working Paper of the Research Centre for East European Studies no. 91, 2008, http://www.forschungsstelle.uni-bremen.de/UserFiles/file/06-Publikationen/Arbeitspapiere/fsoAP91.pdf, accessed 19 November 2014, here p. 11.

34 Results of the questionnaire national trade unions, Q8 2013. Please note the number of respondents: n = 8.

35 See chapter on interest representation and EU-level activities of the trade unions studied.

36 Results of the questionnaire national trade unions, Q8 2013. Please note the number of respondents: n = 8.

37 Results of the questionnaire national trade unions, Q16 2013. Please note the number of respondents: n = 8.

38 Results of the questionnaire national trade unions, Q17 2013.

tions with the umbrella organisations, indicated that they could express interests via them and mentioned that they would support their members at the national level, e.g., with regard to the new labour code.[39] Thus, the answers show that satisfaction with interest representation at the EU level is varied.

However, European umbrella organisations were used extensively to gain access to the decision-making process of the EU.[40] All trade unions we contacted are members of their respective European umbrella organisations, e.g., European Trade Union Confederation (ETUC), IndustriAll Europe or Union Network International Europe (UNI Europa).[41] Collaboration with the European umbrella organisations of trade unions was assessed positively by the majority of respondents.[42] A majority of trade unionists mentioned they were satisfied with the work of their trade union within European umbrella organisations.[43]

According to the respondents, contact with the European umbrella organisations is very intensive. Respondents emphasised that they regularly contacted umbrella organisations, most frequently via email but also via telephone or in some cases by using modern media such as Facebook. Personal contact is regarded as very important.[44] The majority of the respondents mentioned attending quarterly or monthly meetings of European umbrella organisations.[45]

Asked about advantages of being members of European umbrella organisations, respondents emphasised the exchange of information and experiences as well as interest representation. Thus, respondents emphasised the exchange of experience regarding different modes of interest representation and information exchange with regard to general information on ongoing developments within the EU but also with regard to technical information and expertise relevant to their work. Regarding interest representation, respondents emphasised that, via European umbrella organisations, trade unions could more successfully maintain direct contact with EU institutions and that the umbrella organisations would support their members at the national level.[46]

Challenges for the membership in European umbrella organisations that were mentioned included the large variety of interests that can complicate decision-mak-

39 Results of the questionnaire national trade unions, Q17 2013.

40 Results of the questionnaire national trade unions, Q8 2013. Please note the number of respondents: n = 8.

41 Results of the questionnaire national trade unions, Q11 2013.

42 Results of the questionnaire national trade unions, Q21 2013. Please note the number of respondents: n = 8.

43 Results of the questionnaire national trade unions, Q22 2013. Please note the number of respondents: n = 8.

44 Results of the questionnaire national trade unions, Q24 2013.

45 Results of the questionnaire national trade unions, Q23 2013. Please note the number of respondents: n = 8.

46 Results of the questionnaire national trade unions, Q28 2013.

ing, a lack of language competences, high membership fees and the high cost of attending meetings.[47]

10.4.2. Bilateral and Multilateral Cooperation beyond the EU Level

To represent interests, trade unions may not exclusively use venues of interest representation at the EU level or the domestic level. Because political authority is shared among different levels within the EU, trade unions are able to use other forms of interest representation as well, namely bilateral and multilateral cooperation. This seems to be increasingly important especially with regard to the outsourcing of production and labour. Therefore, cross-border cooperation and cooperation between unions of different EU member states can play an important role in organising activities transnationally.[48]

As our study shows, Hungarian unions have contacts with a large number of unions from other EU member states. Respondents mentioned cooperating with trade unions from Central and Western European member states, such as Germany, Austria and France, but also from other regions within the EU, e.g., Scandinavia, Southern Europe and the Benelux countries. However, respondents also emphasised their good relations with trade unions from the Czech Republic and Slovakia within the scope of the Visegrad Group.[49]

Cooperation with trade unions from the old EU member states is usually long-term cooperation[50] consisting of an exchange of information, concrete projects and activities as well as a broader coordination of activities.[51] However, respondents also mentioned that cooperation included mutual visits, seminars, an exchange of experience, and participation at the congresses of partner unions.[52]

According to the respondents, cooperation takes mainly place in those policy fields relevant to the single branches. In addition, they mentioned a large variety of other policy fields of more general importance such as employment policy, youth unemployment, fiscal policy, atypical forms of employment, functioning of the social dialogue, European Works Councils, employment law, and labour leasing.[53] Respondents mentioned that cooperation between the unions could be intensified with regard to education and training as well as youth unemployment.[54]

Cooperation with trade unions from the old EU member states is assessed positively. Information exchange and exchange of experience are seen as major advantages.

47 Results of the questionnaire national trade unions, Q29 2013.
48 See also the chapter on the activities of the Vienna Memorandum Group.
49 Results of the questionnaire national trade unions, Q41 2013.
50 Results of the questionnaire national trade unions, Q42 2013.
51 Results of the questionnaire national trade unions, Q43 2013.
52 Results of the questionnaire national trade unions, Q 42, 43, 43+ 2013
53 Results of the questionnaire national trade unions, Q45 2013.
54 Results of the questionnaire national trade unions, Q46 2013.

An exchange of information takes place, for instance, with regard to the internal organisation and functioning of partner unions, the functioning of the social dialogue in partner countries and support, e.g., with regard to the foundation of European Works Councils or the support of trade unions from the old EU member states during wage and salary negotiations with multinational companies. In addition, it was also mentioned that contact with trade unionists from the old member states would enrich the possibilities of interest representation by gaining new contacts with other representatives and institutions.[55]

Bilateral and multilateral cooperation between unions within the EU also includes cooperation within Interregional Trade Union Councils. Respondents assessed this cooperation as important for the representation of workers' interests in Hungary.[56] One well-working example between unions from Hungary and neighbouring countries is the cooperation within the frame of the Interregional Trade Union Council (IRTUC) Burgenland–Western Hungary between the Austrian Trade Union Federation (ÖGB) and the Hungarian MSZOSZ. This IRTUC was set up in 2008 and worked until 2014 to support the labour market in the region.[57] Cooperation with European trade unions with regard to European Workers Councils (EWC) was also assessed as helpful for the representation of workers' interests in Hungary under certain circumstances.[58]

10.5. Europeanization of Hungarian Trade Unions

Interest groups' activities at the EU level may influence their national activities; that is why European interest group research also focuses on the effects that EU-level activities have on domestic interest groups. Therefore, we wanted to know whether trade unions' activities at the EU level influence their work and activities at the domestic level. The majority of the respondents mentioned that the activities of their unions at the EU level often or occasionally influenced work at the national level.[59] This occurs, for instance, with regard to the organisation of trade unions, e.g., by organising working groups corresponding to the working groups of European umbrella organisations or by taking the fusion of umbrella organisations at the European level as an example for merging unions at the national level to bundle forces and energy. However, respondents underlined that EU-level activities mainly affect the work of their trade union at

55 Results of the questionnaire national trade unions, Q47 2013.

56 Results of the questionnaire national trade unions, Q54 2013. Please note the number of respondents: n = 4.

57 For more information see the website of »IGR – Zukunft im Grenzraum«, http://www.igr.at/1001,,,2.html, accessed 20 September 2014.

58 Results of the questionnaire national trade unions, Q61 2013. Please note the number of respondents: n = 6.

59 Results of the questionnaire national trade unions, Q34 2013. Please note the number of respondents: n = 11.

a more technical level. Thus, it has been argued that issues discussed at the European level in umbrella organisations influence discussions at the national level, e.g., concerning issues such as social dialogue, health protection of workers, social issues, collective bargaining and wages.[60]

Additionally, the majority of the respondents stated that their trade unions always or often use the EU as an argument at the national level to justify or support their own positions or activities.[61] This occurs, for example, with regard to the conditions of the domestic social dialogue, social partnership or EWCs, the rights of trade unions at the national level or the modification of the labour law. Respondents also mentioned the strike law, equal payment of men and women and health protection of workers.[62]

We also wanted to know more about the internal decision-making process of trade unions regarding decisions to be represented at the EU level. The majority of the respondents stated that debates about the EU usually involve the broader leadership and those unionists responsible for EU-related issues. Only one respondent mentioned that debates about the EU also include many interested members of the union.[63] Respondents mentioned that debates about the EU focus on specific and rather narrow issues as well as on broader topics and general principles.[64]

The data show that the activities of unions at the EU level primarily affect internal discussions but also affect strategies used by the unions to represent interests in the domestic arena by referring to EU norms and values. The data on the internal decision-making processes, however, show that only representatives of the unions' headquarters are in most cases involved in discussions and decision-making regarding EU-level activities. In addition, as seen in the previous section, there are also channels of Europeanization beyond the EU level on a horizontal level via bilateral and multilateral cooperation. According to our respondents, bilateral and multilateral cooperation between trade unions is characterised by an exchange of experience, and knowledge that might be incorporated when proved of value in the work and activities of the unions. Thus, Europeanization might not only be a downloading or uploading process of policy ideas or practices but also a process with a horizontal dimension beyond the EU level.

10.6. Conclusion

This chapter aimed to analyse and assess the Europeanization and integration of Hungarian trade unions into EU governance structures. Therefore, it raised three major

60 Results of the questionnaire national trade unions, Q35 2013.

61 Results of the questionnaire national trade unions, Q37 2013.

62 Results of the questionnaire national trade unions, Q38 2013.

63 Results of the questionnaire national trade unions, Q12 2013. Please note the number of respondents: n = 8.

64 Results of the questionnaire national trade unions, Q13 2013. Please note the number of respondents: n = 8.

questions that are of importance for European interest group research: To what extent are Hungarian trade unions integrated into EU multilevel governance structures? How do they assess cooperation with unions from other EU member states? How do their activities at the EU level and beyond influence their work at the domestic level?

As the study shows, the majority of the interviewed trade unionists have a positive view of the EU. The EU is seen by the majority of respondents as an important level for interest representation. The influence of the EU on the work of the trade unions is perceived by the majority as positive. Interest representation, including the protection of employees' rights and workplaces as well as the work in policy fields that are of importance for the unions, are major reasons for being active at the EU level.

European umbrella organisations and the European Social Dialogue including its branch dialogues were the major venues of interest representation used by respondents responsible for the representation of their unions to exert influence at the EU level. Respondents had less access to central bodies within the decision-making process of the EU, namely the Commission, the European Parliament and the Council. These results correspond with those of the other countries under study. A lack of sufficient resources, including a lack of financial means and a broad staff but also missing language competences might be reasons for that reduced access.[65] In addition, European umbrella organisations of trade unions seem to be an integral part of interest representation at the EU level for Hungarian trade unions. Collaboration is assessed positively. The intensive exchange of information and experience is emphasised.

Bilateral and multilateral cooperation with trade unions from the old and the new EU member states, e.g., in the form of Interregional Trade Union Councils or European Works Councils, is likewise assessed positively. Here again, exchange of information and exchange of experience seem to be major advantages and incentives for cooperation.

Regarding Europeanization, the majority of the respondents stated that the activities of their unions at the EU level often influence work at the national level. Respondents mentioned that activities at the EU level affect the organisation of trade unions as well as internal discussions.

However, it may be that not only the European level counts when we speak of Europeanization. Our study suggests that there are also channels of Europeanization beyond the EU level on a horizontal level via bilateral and multilateral cooperation. According to our respondents, bilateral and multilateral cooperation between trade unions is characterised by an exchange of experience and knowledge that is incorporated when proved of value in the work and activities of the unions. Therefore, Europeanization might be not only a downloading or uploading process of policy ideas or specific practices but also a process with a dimension beyond the EU level in EU multilevel governance.

65 See country reports in this volume as well as the chapter on the interest representation and EU-level activities of the trade unions studied.

Part III: Case Studies

Vassil Kirov

11. The Integration of the Bulgarian Trade Union Confederation of Independent Trade Unions of Bulgaria (CITUB) into European Union (EU) Governance Structures

11.1. Introduction

The European Social Model was an attractive goal for trade unions in Central Eastern European countries after the fall of communism. At the beginning of the transition, Bulgarian trade unions had already established good relations with many trade union organisations in Europe, which supported them throughout said transition. The process of European integration, which formally started in Bulgaria in 1995, offered an opportunity for the unions to participate in consultations on the transposition of the social acquis communautaire to the country. After 2007, the largest trade union confederation in Bulgaria, the Confederation of Independent Trade Unions in Bulgaria, continued with its efforts to better integrate to the EU and the European trade-union structures.

This chapter examines the integration of CITUB into EU governance structures. The main question is the following: How is the trade union's degree of Europeanization affected by

- the internal organisation of the trade union;
- its resources;
- the preferences of its leaders and members within internal debates and decision-making processes?

The chapter is structured into several parts, presenting the sources used:

- the profile of the union;
- its resources and internal organisation;
- the integration of the trade union into international, national and subnational decision-making processes;
- the internal decision-making and internal debates concerning EU-related issues, respective decisions and their implementation;
- the preferences of leaders and members;
- the dynamics within the internal organisation;
- and other internal debates.

11.2. Methodology and Sources Used for the Case Study

The case study on which this chapter is based was prepared by analysing existing documents,[1] academic literature, and interviews carried out within the framework of the European comparative study 'Europeanisation of Trade Unions in the Countries of the Eastern Enlargement'.[2]

The eight interviews were conducted from April to September in 2013. They reflect the opinions of trade union leaders, both at confederational and at federational level, as well as experts of the trade union movement.

11.3. Brief Profile of CITUB. History, Activities, Strengths

11.3.1. History

The Confederation of Independent Trade Unions of Bulgaria[3] is the largest trade union in Bulgaria. CITUB was established in 1990 on the basis of the old single trade union during the communist period (Balgarski Profesionalni Sauzi (BPS)). It inherited important resources in terms of members, structures, experts, and other resources from the former communist trade union, although it was confronted with the challenge of internal reform and the need to prove its 'independence' from the Communist Party, which was itself under reform. In these new conditions, CITUB opted for painful internal reorganisation, while trying to participate actively in both establishing a new industrial relations system and designing reforms. Though established in February 1990, CITUB is one of the best reformed former trade unions (see the chapter on Bulgaria in this book) in the new member states,[4] and has been the largest national trade union centre since 1990. In the early 1990s, when the trade union membership was quasi-compulsory, CITUB had more than 3 million members. In the middle of the 2000s, it affiliated 35 federations, and had approximately 380,000 members. The membership con-

1 Konfederatsiyata na nezavisimite sindikati v Balgariya (KNSB): Official website of KNSB, in: knsb-bg.org, www.knsb-bg.org, accessed 31 August 2014. CITUB: Report for the VII Congress of CITUB, in: knsb-bg.org, http://www.knsb-bg.org/docs/Otcheten_doklad.pdf, accessed 31 August 2014. KNSB: Statii [Articles], in: knsb-bg.org, http://www.knsb-bg.org/index.php?option=com_content&view=category&id=14&Itemid=31&lang=en, accessed 31 August 2014.

2 I would like to express my gratitude to all my respondents for their availability and for the rich information provided in the course of the interviews and discussions.

3 KNSB: Official website of KNSB, in: knsb-bg.org, http://www.knsb-bg.org, accessed 31 August 2014.

4 Dimitrova, D. / Vilrokx, J. (eds): Trade union strategies in Central and Eastern Europe. Towards decent work. Budapest: ILO, 2005. Kirov, V.: Facing EU accession. Bulgarian trade unions at the crossroads, in: Dimitrova, D. / Vilrokx, J. (eds): Trade union strategies in Central and Eastern Europe. Towards decent work. Budapest: ILO, 2005, pp. 111–151.

tinued to decline and at present it is approximately 275,000[5] (or even 250,000, according to CITUB sources)[6].

CITUB has well-developed industry / sectoral trade union structures. During the transition, the number of CITUB federations has fluctuated considerably due to fragmentation and subsequent mergers between federations. Between December 1989 and February 1990, the number of federations had already increased from 14 to approximately 50.[7] In the following decade, the number of federations increased to approximately 78.[8] By 2003, the number of federations was 35, following a wave of mergers among member organisations. Still, in some sectors there is more than one federation. The impressive organisational performance in early transition resulted from a strategy of covering all 'niches' and also democratising the trade union movement, according to CITUB leaders[9]. Many federation leaders opposed change during the first years of transition, and thus a principle of direct membership of primary organisations was adopted in the Confederation. If this strategy seemed to be appropriate for the initial period, the proliferation of federations and unions increasingly became a barrier to rapid reaction by the confederation later. At the same time, a decrease in membership meant it was more difficult for some of these federations and unions to survive. Since 1996–1997, the policy of the confederation has been oriented towards the promotion of consolidation.

11.3.2. Present Situation

According to the 2012 census of employer and trade union organisations, only two trade union confederations still meet the representation criteria:[10] the CITUB with

5 Tomev, Lyuben / Mihailova, Tatyana / Daskalova, Nadezhda: Bulgaria. Industrial relations profile, in: EurWORK European Observatory of Working Life, 23 October 2014, http://eurofound.europa.eu/lt/observatories/eurwork/comparative-information/national-contributions/bulgaria/bulgaria-industrial-relations-profile, accessed 14 December 2014.

6 KNSB: Otcheten doklad [Report], in: knsb-bg.org, http://www.knsb-bg.org/docs/Otcheten_doklad.pdf, accessed 31 August 2014, here p. 179.

7 CITUB: Balgaskto sindikalno dvijenie. Minalo i nastoiashte [Bulgarian trade union movement. Past and present], Sofia, 2000, here p. 11.

8 Gradev, G.: Bulgarian trade unions in transition. The taming of the hedgehog, in: Crowly, S. / Ost, D. (eds): Workers after workers' states. Labor and politics in postcommunist Eastern Europe, Lanham: Rowman & Littlefield Publishers, 2001, pp. 121–140, here p. 127.

9 Kirov, V.: Facing EU Accession. Bulgarian Trade Unions at the Crossroads, in: Dimitrova, D. / Vilokx, J. (eds): Trade Unions Strategies in Central and Easter Europe. Towards Decent Work, Budapest: ILO, 2005, pp. 111–152.

10 According to the Bulgarian labour legislation (last amended in 2012), organisations recognized as representative of employees on a national level shall be the organisations which have at least 75,000 members; are active in more than a quarter of Nomenclature statistique des activités économiques dans la Communauté européenne (NACE) code-defined economic activities, with at least five members in each, or have at least 50 member organisations with at least five members from different NACE code economic activities; represent staff in local authorities in more than a quarter of Bulgaria's municipalities; and have both a national managing body and the

275,762 members and the second confederation, Confederation of Labour Podkrepa (CL Podkrepa) has 91,738[11] members. Trade union membership declined significantly in the years of transition following the Eastern Enlargement because of high unemployment, privatisation, anti-union behaviour of employers, especially private enterprise employers, lower trust in trade unions, etc. In 2013, the Confederation still affiliated 35 members (federations, unions), which were involved in collective bargaining processes at the sectoral / branch level. At the enterprise level, the Confederation has established 6,381 trade union organisations. Additionally, CITUB has 243 municipal structures (in most of the Bulgarian municipalities).[12]

According to the Bulgarian Industrial Relations (IR) profile prepared by Eurofound, the process of consolidating affiliated federations through mergers continues to be unpopular despite outstanding issues. In some sectors, several parallel structures are affiliated to CITUB (e.g., education, transport, energy, and metalworking).[13]

11.3.3. Activities

CITUB is engaged in number of activities—defence of rights, collective bargaining, training, etc.:

> The Confederation represents and defends the rights and interests of Bulgarian workers, both in respect of their rights and by providing individual counselling. In the field of training and qualification, the Confederation organises training courses to assist employees in improving their professional qualifications and adaptability to both the Bulgarian and the European labour market. As a trade union, the Confederation attaches great importance to collective bargaining as an essential tool for effective protection of the rights and interests of employees. Since 1995, the Confederation is a member of the European Trade Union Confederation, which is an institutional partner of the European Commission. Representatives of the Confederation participate actively in the work of the European Economic and Social Council[14].

11.4. Strengths and Weaknesses

CITUB could still be qualified as a strong union, but with decreasing resources. More than 20 years after the political changes, unions in Bulgaria have preserved and maintained influence and strength. The union movement succeeded in warding off

---

status of a legal entity, obtained by registration as a non-profit association at least three years before the census.

11 Tomev, Lyuben / Mihailova, Tatyana / Daskalova, Nadezhda: Bulgaria. Industrial relations profile, in: EurWORK European Observatory of Working Life, 23 October 2014, http://eurofound.europa.eu/lt/observatories/eurwork/comparative-information/national-contributions/bulgaria/bulgaria-industrial-relations-profile, accessed 14 December 2014.

12 Ibid.

13 Ibid.

14 CITUB: Official website of CITUB, in: knsb-bg.org, http://knsb-bg.org/, accessed 02 September 2013.

fragmentation. The 'old' trade union, CITUB, successfully reformed itself and participated in the establishment of the new industrial relations system, remaining the largest organisation throughout transition. Trade union presence has diminished in terms of membership, but there are still sectors where coverage is relatively high—however, the majority of these sectors belong to the public sector. The resources of trade unions in terms of expertise and financial resources are diminishing but are partly 'compensated' by access to EU funds.[15]

11.5. Internal Decision-Making and Internal Debates Concerning EU-Related Issues, Respective Decisions and Their Implementation

In order to present the decision-making mechanisms, we need to describe the governance structure of the union and the decision-making process for the EU-related issues. According to the interview respondents, the decisions related to EU are taken within the decision-making bodies envisaged in its statute.

The supreme body of CITUB is the Congress. According to the statute of the trade union, regular congresses[16] are held every five years (the seventh and most recent Congress was held in early May, 2012). The decision to hold a congress is made by the Coordination Council of CITUB. The acting members of the Coordination Council, the chairperson and deputy chairpersons of the Central Control Commission participate in the work of the Congress by right, as delegates. The Congress can start its work if more than half of the elected delegates attend it. The powers of the Congress are multiple and they include the ability to discuss and adopt the reports on the activity of the Coordination Council and the Central Control Commission of the Confederation; discuss and adopt the programme documents of the Confederation; adopt, supplement and amend the Statute; elect and dismiss the president and vice-presidents of CITUB, as well as the chairperson of the Central Control Commission and his deputies, for the mandate period; adopt the budget frame on the income and expenditures of CITUB for the mandate period, allocated by years; and make decisions on other issues concerning CITUB activities.

15 Kirov, V.: Facing EU accession. Bulgarian trade unions at the crossroads, in: Dimitrova, D. / Vilrokx, J. (eds): Trade union strategies in Central and Eastern Europe. Towards decent work. Budapest: ILO, 2005, pp. 111–151. Kirov, V.: Trade Unions in CEEs and the Challenges after the EU Accession. The Case of Bulgaria, in: Economia & Lavoro, 2008 (vol. 42), no. 3, pp. 83–94.

16 When necessary, extraordinary congresses can be convoked, which have all the legal rights and powers of the regular congress. The decision to hold an extraordinary congress is made by the Coordination Council through written request of one-third of the basic members, by the Executive Committee or by the CITUB President.

As can be seen from the listed activities, the Congress adopts the core documents of the organisation, namely the Programme and the resolutions and priorities (see more in the following paragraphs), which include special sections for European integration.

The Coordination Council (CC) of CITUB is a collective management body, which organises and carries out the overall activity of the confederation between two congresses. As it is stated on the site of the organisation, the CC is set up and functions in accordance to CITUB's statute.[17] It consists of the following members: the president, the vice-presidents, the executive secretaries, the presidents of the main trade union sections of CITUB (with more than 2,000 members) and the presidents of all Regional Coordination Councils. The number of the main members' representatives in CC is determined and changed according to the number of members. The Coordination Council's activities include some directly related to EU issues: making decisions for CITUB's membership in international trade union organisations and determining CITUB's representation policy in international forums.

The CC convenes not less than four times per year. Its decisions are made by open vote and a simple majority of the present members with the right to vote. The decisions of the CC are binding for all main members, as well as for the bodies and units of CITUB. As indicated by the list of activities, the CC is the main body that makes decisions about the concrete engagements of the trade union confederation in EU-related issues and international cooperation.

The Executive Committee (EC) is a constantly active collective body for the operational management of CITUB's activities. The EC is formed and implements its activities according to CITUB's statute.[18] The EC is composed of the president, the vice-presidents, the executive secretaries of CITUB and the representatives of the main members of the confederation, elected by the Coordination Council. On its own initiative, the EC can draw in external experts for consultative services and set up different working groups on various issues. The Executive Committee is in charge of multiple activities, some of them related to EU issues, such as organising the execution of the decisions of the CC and maintaining operational follow-up; submitting proposals to the CC for acceptance or exclusion of main members; budgeting and staffing of the confederation; changing the territorial borders of the regional structures, as well as their statutes; declaring, terminating and cancelling general strike, protest and solidarity activities; affiliating with international organisations; managing the financial / economic activity of the confederation; setting up expert, research and other working groups and units for the elaboration of documents connected to the confedera-

17 CITUB: Statue. Articles 18, 23, 24, 25, 26 and 27, in: knsb-bg.org, http://www.knsb-bg.org, accessed 02 September 2013.

18 CITUB: Statue. Articles 18, 28, 29 and 30, in: knsb-bg.org, http://www.knsb-bg.org, accessed 02 September 2013.

tion's activity; and, with the help of experts, developing projects for the realisation of concrete ideas based on CITUB's main goals, as set by the Congress.

The EC has sessions not less than once a month. Its decisions are made by open vote and a simple majority of the members present. Decisions for proposals to the CC are made by a qualified majority of two-thirds of its members. According to the website of CITUB, such decisions could be acceptance or exclusion of members of the confederation; termination or cancellation of general strike, protest and solidarity actions; and affiliation to international trade union formations and organisations. The rights of the EC are terminated when a congress of CITUB begins.[19]

It becomes clear from the interviews that the decisions related to EU issues and international cooperation are made by statutory bodies of the unions, namely the Coordination Council and the EC of CITUB, but in the framework of the programmes these decisions are made at the organisation's congresses.

Different bodies could be in charge of the realisation of previously made decisions. Different trade union documents could provide detailed information about the decisions made, the priorities set and the activities held. The reports for the Congresses[20] contain comprehensive sections about international cooperation and European integration. One of the decisions made at the sixth congress (held in 2007) of the organisation concerned the active international and European integration policy, and effective inclusion in the structures of the European Social Dialogue.[21] In this domain, the Congress assigned the confederation to draw clear priorities, coordinate activities, and increase the administrative capacity of its members, including their financing activities. The need for better action within the European Trade Union Confederation (ETUC) and the sectoral federations at the EU level is also outlined in the programme for the 2007–2012 period, as are priorities for bilateral relations (with trade unions from old and new member states: unions from the Western Balkans, Moldova and Turkey, and trade unions from Ukraine, Georgia, Armenia and Mediterranean countries).

The overview prepared for the Congress of the activities in the 2007–2012 period gives an idea about the progress made on all these priorities. Special attention is paid to the activities within ETUC, bilateral cooperation, and other specific projects.[22] However, it is important to notice that in these key documents, CITUB is not advancing specific objectives in order to better address its interests at the EU level; the impres-

19 KNSB: Official website of KNSB, in: knsb-bg.org, http://www.knsb-bg.org, accessed 02 September 2013.

20 See here for example the report for the sixth congress of CITUB available on http://www.knsb-bg.org/docs/Otcheten_doklad.pdf, accessed 02 September 2013.

21 CITUB: Otcheten doklad [Report]. 2007. Resolution 12, in: knsb-bg.org, http://www.knsb-bg.org, accessed 02 September 2013, here pp. 80–82.

22 Ibid, here pp. 248–252.

sion is that they follow EU-level trade union structures without attempting to further participate in the formulation of EU-level priorities.

11.6. Resources and Internal Organisation of CITUB

11.6.1. Internal Organisation

As mentioned above, the internal organisation of CITUB consists of managing bodies (described in the previous paragraph), regional bodies and sectoral federations (that have relations with European social partners and other organisations themselves). The headquarters of CITUB consists of the elected management,[23] and the functional directions and departments (as described in the previous paragraph).

The highest level of CITUB management is seriously involved in European integration issues. The president and one of the vice-presidents are members of the European Economic and Social Council (EESC).[24] This tradition started in the beginning of 2007, after Bulgaria joined the EU. This fact illustrates the importance of the EU dimension for CITUB.

In the administration of the trade union confederation there are bodies directly involved with the EU-related issues. There is a 'Training, projects and international cooperation' unit. In this body, there are Training and Projects[25] and International Cooperation departments (employing 8 and 4 experts, respectively). This body is directly involved in the international cooperation issues. However, many other bodies are also involved in direct contact with other unions, the ETUC, etc.

An important tool for European integration of CITUB is participation in projects funded by the European Commission through the European Social Fund or other programmes.[26] According to the projects described, CITUB is very active and is developing partnerships with a large circle of trade unions, employers' organisations, research bodies, NGOs, and other similar organisations from different European countries.

CITUB has a research unit, Institute for Social and Trade Union Research (ISTUR)[27], involved in expert and research activities related to EU issues.

---

23 KNSB: Statii. Kongresno rykovodstvo [Articles. Congress management], in: knsb-bg.org, http://www.knsb-bg.org/index.php?option=com_content&view=article&id=9&Itemid=76&lang=en, accessed 02 September 2013.

24 EESC: Members Search, in: eesc.europa.eu, http://memberspage.eesc.europa.eu/Result.aspx?f=2&s=0&o1=0&o2=0&o3 =0&co=BG, accessed 02 September 2014.

25 A short overview of various projects can be find in KNSB: Statii [Articles], in: knsb-bg.org, http://www.knsb-bg.org/index.php?option=com_content&view=category&id=14&Itemid=31&lang=en, accessed 14 December 2014.

26 Ibid.

27 You will find more information about ISTUR on KNSB's website at http://www.knsb-bg.org/index.php?option=com_content&view=article&id=4&Itemid=85&lang=en, accessed 02 September 2013 or http://knsb-flexicurity.org/, accessed 02 September 2013.

The cross-border cooperation is maintained both by the headquarters of the union and by the federations (some of them are more active than others, because of their sector of activity, the presence of foreign companies, the personnel involvement of their leaders, etc.).

The coordination of the European Workers Council (EWC) policy is achieved in several ways: through the informal network of the presidents of trade union sections in the multinational companies (MNC)[28]; [29] directly, by the respective trade union sections in the EWC together with their branch federations; and centrally, for example, through the different trainings and participation in projects centring on this topic.

11.6.2. Resources

The resources of the union's expertise are its staff, the involvement of its representatives in EU-level dialogue, the financial resources to participate in the EU-level activities, the language skills of its representatives, etc.

According to the interviewed respondents the participation of their representatives in the different trade union structures at the EU level is very important. From this perspective, it is interesting to investigate cases where trade union leaders from the region were elected to leadership positions in the European structures, ETUC or sectoral federations in order to analyse their roles and contributions. In this situation, the feeling of the Bulgarian (and NMS in general) union's importance in decision-making seems to be much greater. However, it is difficult to assume that only the presence of Bulgarian representatives in the governing bodies of European structures is sufficient to ensure proactive behaviour.

The question of expertise is also of considerable importance. Many EU-related projects and international exchanges require good preparation, experts, etc., which could be given for the confederation CITUB, but not for all the branch federations. Some federations (e.g., Metalici, the metallurgy federation of CITUB) have significant number of employees while other count only on their president and maximum one employee.

The question of the availability of experts is related to the financial resources unions possess. The Confederation is able to mobilise resources and to engage variety

28 In October 2001, shortly before the fifth congress of the confederation began, the initiative was launched to create a club of union presidents of organisations from multinational companies and other enterprises with foreign participation. The club was founded by 16 union presidents from different branches of multinational companies as a permanent forum through which trade unionists from these companies in different sectors and regions could communicate, exchange information and experience to provide mutual assistance in solving specific problems and conflicts. By the mid-2000s, It already has more than 40 people.

29 Daskalova, Nadejda / Tomev, Lyuben: Multinational companies in Bulgaria. Impact on labour and socialdevelopment, in: Schmidt, V. (eds): Trade union responses to globalization. A review by the Global Union Research Network, Geneva: International Labour Office, 2007, pp. 73–84.

of experts, as well as some of the branch federations. However, some of the other federations have rather limited budgets (as interviews show) and they are not able to involve sufficient expertise. However, of course, there should not be a direct correlation between available resources and active involvement—sometimes, smaller organisations could be active and motivated to create projects and develop initiatives.

The financial and language capacity of the Bulgarian unions are limited and this is addressed critically. According to one of our interviewees, the language problem is very serious. Often the well informed and competent experts / leaders do not know foreign languages sufficiently enough to participate in international meetings without interpretation:

> In order to be able to participate at the European level you need to have financial capacity. You need to have expert potential, which we have; we have the necessary experts. However, then, there is also linguistic...[capacity]. For example, when the Committee for Social Dialogue meets and I need to send the expert who is most qualified for that, it turns out he doesn't know a second [EU] language. So I must personally participate and I must translate the information, so that I can give it to him. He needs to understand it, respond to me and then I must translate it again and present it. That is a huge difficulty, which originates from the lack of financial capacity. It's a hindrance for us and our active participation. And I'd like to be more active. You know how it is with the big unions, which have representatives in Brussels. They have several representatives; each specialised in a specific topic and having detailed knowledge. The language barrier is a huge problem. You don't feel it and I don't, but...[30].

The issue of the financial resources is also important. Travel is expensive and some of the CITUB federations could rarely afford to participate in EU-level meetings on their own budgets.

11.7. Integration of the Trade Union into International, National and Subnational Decision-Making Processes

According to its founder and first president, the international integration of CITUB at the beginning of the transition was extremely difficult. Petkov argues:

> The tactics of CL Podkrepa in its race with CITUB was to isolate us in the international field, in order to win competitive advantages inside the country and monopolise the participation in bilateral and multilateral projects. For three years, our competitors hindered CITUB's admission to the European Trade Union Confederation and the International Confederation of Free Trade Unions in every possible way. It was the competing trade union that initiated the confiscation of CITUB's property, carried out by the government of Filip Dimitrov, aimed at paralysing CITUB[31].

30 Interview with CITUB representative, Bulgaria, BG-Gn04, 26 March 2013.

31 Petkov, Krastyo: How we created CITUB? A historical and sociological study. Prof. Krastyo Petkov, Founder and first president (1990–1997), in: Prof. Krastyo Petkov's Blog, 31 October 2011, http://www.kpetkov.eu/en/node/253, accessed 02 September 2013.

In order to integrate with the European trade union structures, CITUB initiated first a number of alliances with trade unions from Western Europe.[32]

The European integration was and still is a very important objective in the trade unions' actions, especially before the country joined the EU. As the current president of CITUB, Plamen Dimitrov, says in an article:

> For the trade unions in Bulgaria, the largest organisations in civil society seeking the protection of the workers' rights and interests, the values of Social Europe have been mobilising milestones, defining activities since the beginning of the transition[33].

In its programme from the sixth congress, the confederation declares:

> We have realised only part of this European vision and we have to work every day with the maximum of our abilities to be able to one day say—'European Dream' for millions of Bulgarians come true, not only because we are part of the most dynamic growing community, but because we are actively contributing to its prosperity. The European dream, based on sustainable growth, social welfare and humanism is not just an alternative to individualism, it draws a new vision for the future of humanity[34].

In its programme, CITUB has a section focused on the trade union and the European perspective.[35] After analysing the situation, CITUB lists a number of priorities, such as active participation in the absorption of Structural and Cohesion Funds and the implementation of the policy of ETUC in Bulgaria, Europeanization of the trade union action.

This document states that it is crucial for the Confederation to create the optimal conditions and environment for maximum absorption of EU funds, which is a reliable guarantee for accelerated development in the EU-27 and significantly raising the standard of living in Bulgaria. It is believed that the Confederation can support this process by promoting opportunities for financing projects financed by EU funds among union members, their regional and branch structures. CITUB is aware that they could benefit from these funds and for this reason they should train their members / experts to increase capacity in the project applications. In its programme, CITUB also set a goal

32 Ibid.

33 Dimitrov, Plamen: A Social Dimension For A Changing European Union. The Bulgarian Perspective, in: Social Europe Journal, 29 July 2013, http://www.social-europe.eu/2013/07/a-social-dimension-for-a-changing-european-union-the-bulgarian-perspective/, accessed 02 September 2013.

34 KNSB: Vyprosi i otgovori. Rezolyutsiya no. 13. Za ravnite byzmozhnosti, predotvartyavane na diskriminatsiyata i rabotata sys spetsifichni grupi [Questions and answers. Resolution no. 13. Equal opportunities, prevention of discrimination and work with specific groups], in: knsb-bg.org, http://www.knsb-bg.org/index.php?option=com_content&view=category&id=167&Itemid=205&lang=en, accessed 02 September 2013.

35 KNSB: Vyprosi i otgovori. Rezolyutsiya no. 12. Za aktivna mezhdunarodna i evrointegratsionna politika na KNSB i efektivno vklyuchvane v strukturite na evropeyski yasotsialen dialog [Questions and answers. Resolution no. 12. For active international and European integration policy of the confederation and effective involvement in the structures of the European Social Dialogue], in: knsb-bg.org, http://www.knsb-bg.org/index.php?option=com_content&view=article&id=1181%3A--12-----------------&catid=167%3A2010-06-24-07-29-59&Itemid=205&lang=en, accessed 02 September 2013.

of having an active role in the committees monitoring the implementation of operational programmes under the National Strategic Reference Framework 2007–2013[36] through its representatives.

The implementation of ETUC policy in the Bulgarian context is another important goal for CITUB. The Confederation considers it its duty to work for the improvement and implementation of the European Social Model and the ETUC programme in Bulgaria, as well as develop their ideas, mechanisms and instruments—as opposed to neo-liberal and radical market ideology, which is consistently instilled 'as being the only possible alternative for young democracies'[37]. From the union point of view, the European Social Model defines a framework of several supporting points (i.e. solidary social security systems, regulated by law and collective bargaining at the workplace; representation of interests and the right to participate in government, systems of industrial relations and social dialogue to achieve a balance of interests; and provision of public services of general interest) to be coordinated at EU level, but implemented through specific tools and according to the specific conditions of each country. CITUB declares its support for the 'open method of coordination' as an important tool to enhance the exchange of experience at the European level in the field of strategies for reforming the national security system and the formation of shared goals, but they believe that they must overcome attempts in various countries, including Bulgaria, where the reforms' financial implication stake precedence over the social ones. The Confederation relies on the active involvement of its key members in the work of European sectoral trade unions, through which the agreed-upon positions and measures to be carried forward as concrete policies reach the relevant sectors and enterprises in the country, and thus reach each union member.

The Confederations' guiding principle of 'Europeanization' is the adoption of ETUC as a major actor on the Brussels scene, which is 'able to effectively develop the interests of European workers and work even harder to represent them'[38]. In this context, CITUB aims at revealing its capacity, providing expert presence and effective involvement of their representatives in all committees, working groups, research networks, training teams as a confederation, at sectoral and European level.

In this context, the decisions made at the sixth congress of the Confederation provide a framework for an 'active international and European integration policy and effective inclusion in the structures of the European Social Dialogue'[39]. In this domain, the

---

36 Republic of Bulgaria: National Strategic References Framework. Programming Period 2007–2013, in: EU Structural Funds, http://www.eufunds.bg/en/page/66, accessed 02 September 2013.

37 KNSB: Official website of KNSB, in: knsb-bg.org, http://www.knsb-bg.org, accessed 02 September 2013

38 Ibid.

39 CITUB: Otcheten doklad [Report]. 2007. Resolution 12, in: knsb-bg.org, http://www.knsb-bg.org, accessed 02 September 2013, here pp. 80–82.

Congress assigns the Confederation the task of drawing clear priorities, coordinating activities, and increasing the administrative capacity of its members, including their financing activities. The need for better action within ETUC and the sectoral federations at the EU level is also outlined, as are priorities for bilateral relations (with trade unions from old and new member states: unions from the Western Balkans, Moldova and Turkey and trade unions from Ukraine, Georgia, Armenia and Mediterranean countries).

Before examining the different dimensions of Europeanization, it is important to understand CITUB leaders' perceptions of the European Union's effects on Bulgaria.

The respondents reflect this European conviction and speak about the positive effects of the EU in the country:

> Well, positive, in relation to the legislation, which creates stability. There are good laws, which are synchronised with the European [laws]. Also positive in respect to the good practices in applying the social dialogue. First, the legislation applies those practices and then the application process itself. The influence is positive as a whole...about the requirements for compliance with the law, compliance to solve problems such as corruption and other problems. These are all positive influences of the EU. There are also others, of course.[40]

There is a shared belief that the effects are positive in the domains of social dialogue, labour market policy, establishment of clear rules, etc.

However, at the same time, the respondents consider that there are negative effects of EU policies, or of the way in which EU norms are implemented in Bulgaria, in the sphere of economics among different sectors, with the introduction of quotas, environmental standards, etc.

> In the economic areas. Maybe it's not from the EU only, maybe it's what our politicians managed to negotiate. Here is a specific example. In the programs for European financing for increasing energy efficiency, the melting houses, which are one of the big energy consumers, are not in the priorities of the programs.
>
> Second, the tax requirements, ecological requirements, working conditions requirements, etc. They are not bad, but the level of development and the capabilities of the government do not allow for them to be implemented in the required time-frame. You know very well that if we do not compromise about the working conditions in some plants, they must stop working. Yes, but with those high unemployment rates, we should also help... we must conform to that.[41]

For others there are no negative effects, but

> the social standards development lags [behind] the integration of the single market[42].

The integration has many dimensions examined below, including bilateral relations, EWC, and transborder cooperation.

40 Interview with CITUB representative, Bulgaria, federation leader 2, 02 April 2013.

41 Ibid.

42 Interview with CITUB representative, Bulgaria, confederation expert 4, 26 March 2013.

11.7.1. Bilateral Relations

First of all, there has been bilateral cooperation between CITUB and other European trade unions since the beginning of the transition. As the founder of CITUB explains, at the beginning of the transition those relations were very important, in order to legitimise the newly reformed union and to ensure its integration in the ETUC.[43] Since this period, CITUB has developed a number of bilateral relations with many European unions. All interviewees, at confederation and federation levels, shared their experience about the various forms of bilateral cooperation, both long term and short term, with trade union federations from old and new member states and from the region of South Eastern Europe.

This cooperation could take the form of exchanges of information, organisation of trainings and seminars, participation at conferences, joint projects and other similar approaches, and could evolve in time, as the following illustrates:

> For example, with the Italians, it happened because the owners of an Italian company came here. That is how we got connected and we started inquiring whether we can establish European Workers Councils. It turned out that we couldn't, but we participated in two European projects with them[44].

The respondents consider that the existing partnership with trade unions from the old member states should be further developed and cover topics such as:

> sharing experiences, so that we can apply those practices in our countries. Gradually, the levels must be evened out[45];
>
> The partnership is mainly in the social area[46];
>
> Personally, I would like to be better in the area of collective bargaining. And also have joint actions, even demonstrations[47];
>
> European Social Dialogue, free movement of people, transnationalisation of the industrial relations[48].

The respondents see many advantages of the partnership with unions from the old member states; they are considered to have 'experience[,] information [and] traditions[49] and the following quote illustrates it well:

> Yes. The problems of the new member states are almost the same as ours. As to the old member states, we use the information and experience which they have, and how they have dealt with some problems. They have much better legislation and much better

43 Petkov, Krastyo: How we created CITUB? A historical and sociological study. Prof. Krastyo Petkov, Founder and first president (1990–1997), in: Prof. Krastyo Petkov's Blog, 31 October 2011, http://www.kpetkov.eu/en/node/253, accessed 02 September 2013.

44 Interview with CITUB representative, Bulgaria, federation leader 1, 02 April 2013.

45 Interview with CITUB representative, Bulgaria, federation leader 2, 02 April 2013.

46 Interview with CITUB representative, Bulgaria, federation leader 3, 04 June 2013.

47 Interview with CITUB representative, Bulgaria, confederation expert 4, 26 March 2013.

48 Interview with CITUB representative, Bulgaria, confederation expert 5, 26 March 2013.

49 Interview with CITUB representative, Bulgaria, confederation expert 5, 26 March 2013.

> experience…[with] good practices in the social partnerships, collective agreements, defending the interests[50].

However, these advantages are also accompanied by some inconveniences. While some of the respondents are more diplomatic, others are direct:

> The disadvantages arise from the fact that the representatives of the rich countries are looking down on us[51].

For other respondents there were disadvantages, mainly because some of the unions from the old member states were trying to impose 'models':

> Things have changed a lot. If you look in the past, there were advantages and disadvantages. The advantage was gaining experience. It was important for a country which used another model for 45 years. And the disadvantage was that sometimes there was a tendency to impose models on us which cannot be applied here. Because they are applied successfully in Sweden or elsewhere, it does not mean they will work here. However, this was in the past. Now, when we exclude the financial issue, we have a partnership, a more real one. We have grown up and now we play…[52].

11.7.2. The Participation in European Projects

The work on joint projects is very important for CITUB. It allows for improving expertise, benefitting from the expertise of the partners, advancing in specific policy domains and attracting external financing for education, training, networking and other activities:

> Projects with unions from Italy and Ireland on the topics of information and consulting; projects with unions from Greece, UK and Spain regarding the free movement of people; projects with Belgium regarding social security systems, regional development, rights of minorities; projects with Austria—for accession to the EU[53].

The projects are important tools to gain expertise, address problems, attract resources and be present in the European area. Some of these projects (like the one financed by the European Social Fund in Bulgaria) also allowed the union to employ new experts and to increase its resources. However, these trends of pursuing the development of projects have contradictory consequences. The trade union could become too focused on project development and neglect other activities.

11.7.3. The European Workers Councils

There are few Bulgarian companies that have representatives in the EWCs.[54] Until 2007, the Bulgarian representatives had the status of observers. The information and

50 Interview with CITUB representative, Bulgaria, federation leader 2, 02 April 2013.
51 Interview with CITUB representative, Bulgaria, federation leader 3, 04 June 2013.
52 Interview with CITUB representative, Bulgaria, confederation expert 4, 26 March 2013
53 Interview with CITUB representative, Bulgaria, confederation expert 5, 26 March 2013.
54 Daskalova, Nadejda / Tomev, Lyuben: Multinational companies in Bulgaria. Impact on labour and socialdevelopment, in: Schmidt, V. (eds): Trade union responses to globalization. A review

consultation process has made better progress in the subsidiaries of the multinational companies. In spite of that, not more than one-third of the existing subsidiaries with EWC shave elected Bulgarian representatives.[55] The information and consultation processes in companies with no trade union structures are progressing slowly. Still, in separate cases this is initiated by the employers, including subsidiaries of MNC.

CITUB was always very active in the domain of EWCs. It initiated a network of the presidents of trade unions in MNC and various projects, in order to better prepare and integrate the Bulgarian representatives in EWCs. In addition the confederation or its federations have developed international projects related to the preparation of these representatives and the facilitation of their networking with other members of EWCs from Europe.

In some of the examined trade union federations their members are involved in existing EWC:

> Yes. There is an EWC. The representatives are elected at a general assembly and are usually from our union. In all three cases they are from our union—Aurubis, SKF[56] and EnerSys. At Aurubis and SKF, our representatives are also the chairmen of our trade union sections.[57]

Here the decisions are in the hands of the federations (which could propose ideas and coordinate the EWC members' activity) and the respective trade union sections.[58]

> There is a common policy, but the sector federation and labour unions make the decisions[59].

11.7.4. Transborder Relations and Interregional Trade Union Councils

Transborder trade union cooperation was not a central topic for the Bulgarian unions for a long time. One of the most likely reasons for this was that the only border with an old EU member state was the one with Greece, while other neighbouring countries were lagging behind in European integration or were in a similar position to Bulgaria, as in the case of Romania. The transborder mobility of labour was relatively limited (except the case of undocumented workers in Greece) and the investors from Bulgaria's southern neighbour were mainly small and medium-sized enterprises (SMEs). However, after 2007, CITUB started to initiate talks for the establishment of an interregional trade union council with Greek—and more recently also Romanian—unions.

---

by the Global Union Research Network, Geneva: International Labour Office, 2007, pp. 73–84. Informia: National Report Bulgaria, in: informiaproject.org, 2010, http://www.informiaproject.org, accessed 02 September 2013.

55 Informia: National Report Bulgaria, in: informiaproject.org, 2010, http://www.informiaproject.org, accessed 02 September 2013, here p. 9.

56 SKF—Svenska Kullagerfabriken

57 Interview with CITUB representative, Bulgaria, federation leader 2, 02 April 2013.

58 My personal experience with the framework of such projects shows that the role of the federation could be very important.

59 Interview with CITUB representative, Bulgaria, confederation expert 4, 26 March 2013.

Because of the Greek crisis, this project was delayed, but as one of the respondents suggests, it will be activated again in 2014.[60] In the spring of 2013, the advancement of the project with the Romanian unions was already a fact, as an interview with one of the leaders of CITUB confirms; a number of meetings was scheduled in order to establish rules for future action.[61]

11.8. Preferences of Leaders and Members

According to the interviews held, the debates related to EU issues in CITUB involve many interested members of the organisation. These debates concern both general principles and specific topics. As mentioned, part of these debates is on the occasion of concrete projects implemented by the trade union confederation or in relation to specific legal initiatives.

The preferences of leaders and members of particular federations of CITUB for particular topics and issues are impacted by specifics of the sector (e.g., energy policy in case of the Miners Federation), the restructuring processes (e.g., the closure of big companies such as Kremikovtzi in the Bulgarian metallurgy), the need to know better European trade unions practices from specific countries (the example of Italy, etc.) because of the investments coming from these countries and the presence of the subsidiaries of MNC in the respective sectors.

11.9. Dynamics within the Internal Organisation and Internal Debates of the Trade Union

The advantages of the trade union cooperation with the European-level structures are manifold. As one of our respondents says:

> The advantages are that we use the expert potential of ETUC and we are informed about European issues. We know what is going on in Europe and what will happen. That gives us the chance to react quickly before some laws are adopted and to correct national policies. We have the opportunity to act on the adoption of some directives and corrections in some areas. Sometimes we use their experts by having consultations and asking them for information.[62]

The internal debates about Europeanization within the trade union confederation are shaped by the specific experiences and interests, etc. of the different groups within the union. However, most of the interviewees developed arguments for the importance and the effects, both negative and positive, of the European Union's impact:

60 Interview with CITUB representative, Bulgaria, confederation leader 6, 31.08.2013.
61 Interview with CITUB representative, Bulgaria, confederation leader 6, 31 August 2013.
62 Interview with CITUB representative, Bulgaria, confederation expert 4, 26 March 2013.

> Now, in general it is two-sided, you know; on one hand they pressure us, but on the other, you can refer [to a directive], so that you can accomplish better results. This directive requires something specific and you have to take it into consideration. So, from that perspective, it is positive. However, in some particular situations it may have the opposite effect. However, overall, positive, because you can use them…after all, there are better practices[63].

Examples of the positive effects are numerous—the fact that the respondents became part of the decision-making process at the EU level, that they are well informed, and that they could count on solidarity with and, especially, the rich experience and expertise of their colleagues from the European-level unions (or union organisations from old member states).

At the confederation level, some more general principles and processes are outlined by respondents:

> If you mean the trade union, one can say that it made an impact even before the accession. And after that—to restructure our programmes and to choose policies which are important in the context of European integration. As a union, we have also studied and promoted the common European law, policies and the Charter of Fundamental Rights of the EU. We have printed materials. At our last conference, we printed material and disseminated it. We also have seminars in studying the fundamental rights. What else? So, fundamentally, we present all our policies at the national level in front of the social partners and the employers, in the context of the European influence and European policies. In effect, we always require that the social dialogue is in unison with the European requirements. Also we have policies towards multinational companies, although they are from 2001. Moreover, the coordination network that we have, named The Club of the Chairmen, and other policies, are also consistent with it…the activities, the work with the labour councils, information systems and consulting[64].

However, some of the interviewees are critical about the importance of the EU level:

> So, if I understand correctly, there are no areas in which it is more important…However, the idea of the European Confederation is to have [such areas]. You know that for a long time there have been talks of collective agreements at the European level, [and a] minimum level of wages at the EU level. However, for now, at least from what I know, there is no such area.[65]

For some of the respondents the problems of the region or the country are not afforded the necessary attention:

> The cons are that there is not enough attention paid to the problems of the South Eastern region [of Europe], and ours in particular. And we have many big problems. There are mostly efforts to support the Third World countries. However, that is more valid for the international confederation. As to the European [unions from the old member states], it seems like it's looking more into the problems of the Central European countries and we are left behind, to deal on our own if we can. And our problems are much bigger than everyone else's—from low wages to high unemployment, etc. And we also have prob-

63 Interview with CITUB representative, Bulgaria, federation leader 1, 02 April 2013.
64 Interview with the former executive secretary of EU integration, Bulgaria 7, 31 August 2013.
65 Interview with CITUB representative, Bulgaria, confederation expert 4, 26 March 2013.

> lems with the division in the labour unions (at national level). So, there are no priorities being set forth. We should be a priority, but we are not[66].

The Bulgarian union representatives increasingly realise that coordination of interests could be very difficult:

> Different interests, tough coordination sometimes[67].

According to the respondents, the most important issue that should be presented to the union at the EU level is participation in the EU Social Dialogue and the possibility of impacting national policy as well. There are different policies which should be presented to the trade union:

> There are many important issues…because of all of the policies, which are proposed and defended by the European Trade Union Confederation at the EU level. In fact, all economic and social issues, which concern the employees, for which the EU prepares policies, are important. Additionally, they must be presented to the unions first—the ETUC and also in the European Social Dialogue—intersectoral and sectoral, different federations, and also in the European social committee. It cannot be determined which is the most important here. Many policies, all policies at the European level, which concern the employees are important and must be presented[68].

11.10. Conclusion

This conclusion summarises the main findings of the research about the impact of Europeanization on CITUB. CITUB is the largest trade union confederation in Bulgaria. Successfully reformed, the old single trade union kept its place as the primary trade union player in the country. The trade union still has important resources, including with regard to EU issues.

The decision-making process follows the decision-making structures of the trade union confederation. The Coordination Council is the body where the most important decisions about EU issues are normally made and where their implementation is monitored. Some of the decisions are made at the highest level (e.g., EESC participation—president and vice-president); the development of interregional trade union councils (vice-president) already shows the serious attention and focus on EU issues.

The central headquarters have a number of experts fully or partially involved in EU-related activities. Some of the federations of CITUB also have experts in EU issues. CITUB has its own research centre that brings additional experience in the domains of MNC, EWC, European integration, etc.

The internal structure of this union allows for several channels of action related to EU issues: central management, specific departments / units, the research unit and

66 Interview with CITUB representative, Bulgaria, federation leader 2, 02 April 2013.
67 Interview with CITUB representative, Bulgaria, confederation expert 5, 26 March 2013.
68 Ibid.

various informal structures, such as the club of trade union section presidents within MNC. Additionally, the main political documents of the union note the European engagements and concrete challenges for CITUB in this area.

The preferences of the leaders of CITUB at the confederational level (and in the federations) are clearly for the development of European integration. In their concrete activities—e.g., bilateral and other projects—they are driven by pragmatical reasons related to sectoral specifics, particular challenges, etc.

In conclusion, we could say that the impact of Europeanization on CITUB is important. The trade union confederation has developed structures and decision-making mechanisms in order to better integrate into EU structures and to advance the different issues related to Europe (EWC, transborder cooperation, bilateral cooperation) on both confederative and federation levels. The confederation is aware of the EU challenges for union action and implementation of the ETUC policy. However, its participation could be qualified as passive because there are few initiatives at the EU level that are formulated by CITUB.

Zdenka Mansfeldová

12. The Czech Metalworkers' Federation / Odborový svaz KOVO (OS KOVO) in Domestic and European Arenas

12.1. Introduction

The trade union (TU) OS KOVO (Czech Metalworkers' Federation) is one of the 29 trade unions affiliated in the Českomoravská konfederace odborových svazů (ČMKOS). With approximately 125,000 members (as of June 2014), OS KOVO is the largest union in the ČMKOS and the country. Several questions guide this case study: How does OS KOVO debate European Union (EU) related issues? How are decisions 'concerning EU related issues' being reached? How are these decisions being implemented?

The case study is based on six expert interviews; four interviews were conducted with members of OS KOVO and two with experts. Among the four members were a representative in the European Work Council and a representative of the Commission of Young OS KOVO members. These representatives provide a more diverse view regarding the activity and positions of OS KOVO. In addition to expert interviews, primary and secondary document sources were used. The primary sources were the homepage of OS KOVO[1] and documents collected during the interviews. Secondary sources were literature involving Czech trade unions, periodicals published by OS KOVO and other large company trade union organisations, and European Industrial Relations Observatory (EIRO) studies.

12.2. Brief Profile of OS KOVO

12.2.1. Organisational Structure and Activities

The supreme authority of OS KOVO is the Congress, which meets every four years. The highest authority in the period between congresses is the OS KOVO Council. The OS KOVO Council is the decision-making authority that implements the resolutions of the OS KOVO Congress. The OS KOVO Council is responsible to the Congress OS KOVO for its activities. The OS KOVO Council meets at least twice a year. The executive body of OS KOVO is the Bureau OS KOVO, which controls activities between Council meetings. The Bureau OS KOVO's major decisions are subsequently approved by the Council. The Bureau OS KOVO usually meets once every two months.

1 OS KOVO: Odborový svaz KOVO's official website, in: oskovo.cz, www.oskovo.cz, accessed 20 June 2014.

With the intention of being closer to the base, regional associations of OS KOVO exist (krajská sdružení (KS) OS KOVO). These regional associations are created to develop and implement regional policies consistent with the program objectives and principles of OS KOVO. According to the needs and requirements of the basic organisations, KS OS KOVO coordinates trade union activities in the areas of organisation, methodology, employment, health and safety, education, wage policies and collective bargaining. Regional offices (krajská sdružení) are located in 11 regions in the Czech Republic (out of 14 administrative regions in the country). The regional offices are situated in industrial regions and regions with economic difficulties. The tasks of the regional offices are consultations, education, distribution of information, and legal consultation.

OS KOVO members exercise their rights and fulfil their membership duties through basic organisations (základní organizace (ZO) OS KOVO). The minimum number of registered members in the basic organisation is five. The main duties of the basic organisation concerning its members are as follows:

- to negotiate rates, bonuses and other elements of wages in collective bargaining with the employer;
- to demand safe working conditions according to the law and collective agreement;
- to ensure free legal aid in legally justified labour disputes between a OS KOVO member and the employer according to Legal Aid Rules; and
- to protect the legal rights of a member and his or her rights under the collective agreement.

According to paragraph 24 of the statute[2], individual members and member groups, through OS KOVO ZO, defend their interests and enjoy the work of sections. The seven OS KOVO Branch sections are the following:[3]

- Automotive Industry Workers Section;
- External Assembly Section;
- Electrical Industry Workers Section;
- Apprentice Facilities Section;
- Smelting Branch Section;
- Aircraft Industry Workers Section; and
- Metallurgy Section.

The sections are structured exclusively on the industry, trade, and manufacturing principle. Their mission is to work primarily with the collective bargaining of Higher Level

2 OS KOVO: Stanovy Odborového svazu KOVO. Schválené na VI. sjezdu OS KOVO Hradec Králové, 20.–22. 6. 2013 [Statutes of OS KOVO. Approved at the VI. Congress OS KOVO Hradec Králové, 20 to 22 June 2013], in: oskovo.cz, http://www.oskovo.cz/sites/default/files/oskovo/Dokum/Stanovy/stanovy_2013_A5.pdf, here p. 22, accessed 1 December 2014.

3 OS KOVO: 1993–2014. 21 let jistoty. Současnost. Přelom přinesl rok 1989 [1993–2014. 21 years of history. Present times. The turn brought the year of 1989], in: oskovo.cz, http://www.oskovo.cz/os-kovo/soucasnost, accessed 1 December 2014.

Collective Agreements (HLCA) and communication employers' unions and employers' associations. The sections exchange experience regarding sector-specific features, including assisting OS KOVO ZO in areas concerning the industry. The sections propose their representatives to the commission for collective bargaining. The relevant sections also prepare opinions on the draft HLCA.

Concerning the HLCA, Czech law distinguishes between two types. Company-level collective agreements (CLCA) are concluded between the trade union body and an employer. HLCA are concluded for a greater number of employees by the higher-level trade union body and an organisation or organisations of employers. The most prevalent level of collective bargaining in the Czech Republic is the company-level collective agreement. According to the European Industrial Relations Report, online[4] coverage rates calculated for the largest confederation, ČMKOS, were the following:

CLCAs, approximately 33.2% (2013), a 0.8% drop compared with the previous year; HLCAs covered about 15.2% of all employees (2013 / 2012) decrease by about 0.6%. Extensions of HLCAs to another employer are possible under the conditions established by law. The Ministry of Labour and Social Affairs of the Czech Republic possesses the relevant power. Agreement extensions are based on a proposal made by both parties to the agreement, provided that the conditions established by law are met. In 2013, OS KOVO signed four HLCAs.[5]

The importance of collective bargaining and collective agreements is evident from analysis conducted by M. Myant.[6] Some unions have calculated the improvements in pay and the money-value of additional benefits. These calculations consistently confirm substantial gains. An analysis by OS KOVO showed additional benefits from collective bargaining, such as shorter working hours, worth the equivalent of 19% of the value of wages. This analysis also showed that pay in 2005 was 5% above the industry average when basic organisations negotiated a collective agreement and 10% below the average when they did not. This research suggests that the presence of a union organisation conferred little benefit but that there were clear gains when the union signed a collective agreement.[7]

Collective agreements, especially at the company level, address a variety of issues regarding labour law, such as the reduction of working hours without reducing wages and entitlement to time off. The agreements also cover employment conditions, for example, fixed-term work, part-time work, and temporary agency work. Furthermore,

4 Pojer, Petr: Czech Republic. Industrial relations profile, in: EurWORK European Observatory of Working Life, 24 October 2014, http://www.eurofound.europa.eu/observatories/eurwork/comparative-information/national-contributions/czech-republic/czech-republic-industrial-relations-profile, accessed 1 December 2014.

5 OS KOVO: Kolektivní vyjednávání [Collective bargaining], in: oskovo.cz, http://www.oskovo.cz/specializace/kolektivni-vyjednavani, accessed 20 June 2014.

6 Myant, Martin: Trade Unions in the Czech Republic, report 115, Brussels: ETUI aisbl, 2010.

7 Ibid., here pp. 19 f.

the agreements consider social policy, such as employee recreation and transport, as well as continuous vocational training (CVT), health and safety, and other matters. Usually, collective agreements also establish principles for the cooperation of contractual partners. The content of collective agreements has remained unchanged for years and is seldom subject to change. Topics such as stress at work or harassment in the workplace are rarely reflected in collective agreements. In contrast, arrangements relating to work-life balance tend to be relatively frequent.

These objectives for collective bargaining were also mentioned in the medium-term Strategy of OS KOVO from 2013–2017, adopted by the VI. Congress of OS KOVO in June 2013.

The objectives could be summarised by the following five groups:

- protection of employees: assistance in disputes with employers, health and safety matters, legal consultation, natural disasters;
- services and education: continuous vocational training, professional development;
- collective bargaining: bargaining concerning wages and working conditions, alternative agreements;
- publicity and PR: use of all methods of publicity targeted to specific groups; and
- membership: gaining new members.

There is a concern that membership will continue to decline because the number of employees in companies where OS KOVO is active is declining. For this reason, according to the Strategy, better coordination is important among trade unionists in companies with foreign owners and through European Work Councils (EWC) and contacts with the IndustriAll Global Union and Industrial Trade. Better connections with international networks created and coordinated by IndustriAll are necessary. Trade unions will need more assistance and must be able to offer assistance.

With declining membership, attracting the younger generation to trade union (TU) membership is very important. To better coordinate the work with young TU members, the executives of OS KOVO created the Commission of Young Metalworkers at OS KOVO. The Commission coordinates and designs activities for young trade union members in OS KOVO, organises special events, and educates young members. Members of the Commission of Young Metalworkers at OS KOVO participate in ČMKOS meetings and the international arena such as IndustriAll. The Commission also concentrates on specific problems of the younger generation, especially youth unemployment and trainees. The Commission tries to develop projects and impose changes in the apprentice training system. Support and know-how can be expected from IndustriAll and other organisations regarding training and education. For example, the conference organised by the Hans Böckler and Otto Brenner Foundations, 'Creating a better future for the young generation in Europe' in April 2014 brought young trade unionists from Austria, the Czech Republic, Germany, Hungary, Poland, Slovakia, and Spain.

The conference raised awareness of the dire situation young workers face and participants demanded immediate policy changes that focus on youth issues.[8]

Education is one activity of OS KOVO to which TU generally pays attention. The contribution by OS KOVO to the education of TU members represents, e.g., a project: Adaptability of OS KOVO members. The project started in 2008, and its main goal is to help those who are looking for a new occupation or would like to change occupations. The project offers information to TU members and helps them adapt to new conditions and demands. The project is supported by the state budget and the European Social Fund and is connected with European employment strategy. The project is a follow-up to the National Action Plan for Employment, first, by supporting an educated and flexible labour force, and second, to increase the employability of the long-term unemployed. Lifetime education and the role and use of new technologies in education (interactive web pages, E-learning, etc.) is also considered.

12.3. Visibility of OS KOVO and its Organisations

OS KOVO publishes its weekly magazine Kovak (since 2014 published every two weeks), which is also available online. The content is focused on the internal life and concerns of the branch. Sometimes the magazine offers short information from international TU life, such as meetings of the European Economic and Social Council, new regulations adopted by the European Commission that impact employee lives, etc. In addition to Kovak, other ways of communication are used, such as Bulletin or Facebook.

Trade union umbrella organisations in large international companies also have periodicals. These periodicals are also available online and offer not only 'local' information but also statements of particular EWCs or best practices samples. For example, Porkovák[9] published by TU Council OS KOVO ArcelorMittal Corporate Responsibility reports regarding the joint declaration of the EWC from December 2012 and joint demands concerning the company and European Commission. The trade unionists' weekly publication, Škodovácký odborář, published by TU Council OS KOVO ŠKODA AUTO a.s., Mladá Boleslav,[10] regularly publishes information from the EWC and international arena.

As the steel industry is declining, employees in several branches covered by OS KOVO are threatened by mass lay-offs, and this is a key subject for OS KOVO and for local and basic TU organisations. Good cooperation with legislative bodies and government representatives enables the TU to discuss and advance the demands of the

8 IndustriALL European Trade Union: Together for a better future. No to austerity! Yes to jobs for young people!, in industriall-europe.eu, 14 March 2013, http://www.industriall-europe.eu/news/news-archive2.asp?arc=arc, accessed 4 July 2014.

9 Editors information, in: Porkovák, 2013 (vol. 7), no. 1, from 20 January 2013.

10 ŠKODA-Auto a.s. is a member of the Volkswagen Group.

employees it represents. The chairman of OS KOVO is also member of the TU delegation in the Rada pro hospodářské a sociální dohody (RHSD).

12.4. Internal Tensions

The sections united by OS KOVO have different circumstances. Despite economic crisis, the automotive industry is in a better situation than the steel and similar industries. The different economic situation causes tension among the sections. These different circumstances also mean that some company organisations are more radical than others, and some require independence from political parties. During the VI. Congress of OS KOVO (2013), for example, there was a noticeable tension between OS KOVO and the company organisation OS KOVO ŠKODA AUTO a.s.

Reading the companies' periodicals and responses regarding the VI. Congress of OS KOVO, it seems that large company organisations (successful in bargaining) tend to have greater autonomy under OS KOVO. Several considerations make it better to be an independent or associated partner than a part of the hierarchical structure. As mentioned in an interview with a representative of OS KOVO ŠKODA AUTO a.s.:

> Another problem is that the structure of TUs is not modern, it is rigid, and without demonstrable results. We pointed out that the reorganisation and higher flexibility of processes is necessary, but it was not taken into account. The leadership of OS KOVO didn't hear our arguments, so the solution was to become independent. We are evolutionarily a step forward[11].

OS KOVO ŠKODA AUTO a.s. demands higher radicalisation concerning the government and employers, modernisation of OS KOVO, and presentation of a vision for trade unions in the changing world and in a time of globalisation. At the end of 2013, this tension resulted in a 'divorce'; OS KOVO ŠKODA AUTO left OS KOVO and became an independent registered TU organisation.[12] ŠKODA Auto is successful in collective bargaining.[13] Although the membership in OS KOVO as a whole is declining, ŠKODA Auto membership is increasing. In particular, the increase in the number of young members and apprentices of the vocational school is noteworthy.[14]

11 Interview with trade union representative, Czech Republic, Gn19, 12 February 2014.

12 Sjezd OS KOVO potvrdil zkostnatělost a nezájem na modernizaci svazu [Congress OS KOVO confirmed rigidity and lack of interest in modernizing the Union], in: Škodovácký odborář, 27 June 2013 (vol. 20), no. 24, here p. 1. Registred TU organisation means that the organisation is registred by the Ministry of Interior of the Czech Republic.

13 For example, the threat of a strike by workers at the car manufacturer ŠKODA AUTO a.s. in the Czech Republic was lifted when the company and unions agreed on a 4% wage increase on 31 March 2011. The ŠKODA Auto trade union organisation (OS KOVO) and independent unions at ŠKODA asked for a 7% rise, with the company originally offering 0.5%. The workers were also given a one-time performance bonus, plus other bonuses.

14 Členská základna odborů KOVO ve Škodovce nadále roste [Membership in KOVO trade union in Skoda continues to grow], Škodovácký odborář, 27 June2013 (vol. 20), no. 24, here p. 2.

This development demonstrates that economic crisis sharpened the focus of trade unions regarding the interests and immediate needs of their membership base. Solidarity in times of economic growth is a different issue compared with solidarity in times of economic hardship.

12.5. Opportunities for Participation in EU Governance

Evaluating the conditions of OS KOVO for international cooperation, we must mention first the support from the confederation ČMKOS, which has the human resources and expertise for international cooperation. The ČMKOS provides all TUs united in the confederation with a service in this area. The preparation activities for EU membership started early; in 1996, the European Integration Team (EIT) by the ČMKOS was founded as a joint initiative of the ČMKOS and the ETUC. The EIT comprised representatives from the ČMKOS and member trade unions. During the accession period, the European Integration Team prepared every year a summary report entitled 'ČMKOS and the European integration'. A successful project regarding the European Works Councils submitted by the ČMKOS and based on EU funding operated from 2006–2007. Among its outcomes were a handbook on European Works Councils and a module regarding training members and candidates of these councils.

Until 2004 (accession to EU), the European Integration Team predominantly addressed preparations for accession; after 1 May 2004, the scope of its activities was transformed.

To the most important tasks belongs:

- to contribute to the acknowledgement of TU as a social partner that is consulted by preparation of important documents and actions concerning activities of the Czech Republic in the EU;
- to prepare drafts of TU positions to questions connected with the EU for the ČMKOS leadership and to help give the ČMKOS activities a European dimension;
- to collect and distribute information regarding the EU and its policies among the ČMKOS TU members and regional TU councils and concerning positions of the ČMKOS and European trade unions regarding drafts of policies.

Distribution of information was first fulfilled starting in 1997 by publishing a bulletin, Information from EIT ČMKOS. OS KOVO closely cooperated with the EIT team. Members of EIT ČMKOS were also active as lecturers in education regarding European integration. The current OS KOVO website includes a section containing EU information with special emphasis on IndustriAll and IndustriAll Europe. As the largest TU in the Czech Republic, OS KOVO has human resources specialising in international cooperation and cooperation with the EU. A specialist in the International Department of OS KOVO has been a member of the European Economic and Social Committee (Group II) since 21 September 2010.

12.5.1. Contacts with Trade Unions in Neighbouring Countries

Friendly contacts with unions in neighbouring countries were and are continuously nurtured. Not only the confederation but also OS KOVO participates in the central congresses of partner trade unions in Slovakia, Germany, Austria, and Poland. OS KOVO belongs to the most active in the ČMKOS in international cooperation. The Union has a number of bilateral contacts with different traditions and intensities. First, we must mention Slovakia (Odborový zväz kováckých odborov (OZ KOVO)). Despite the division of Czechoslovakia and the subsequent division of the Czechoslovak OS KOVO Union, an intensive co-operation and exchange of information exists between the two succeeding unions on the levels of departments, sections and other levels. Delegates also attend meetings of the individual union bodies on a reciprocal basis, and the executives and boards of the Czech OS KOVO and the Slovak OZ KOVO meet regularly.

There is a long cooperation with Industriegewerkschaft Metall (IG Metall) in Germany; a range of activities has been organised jointly since 1993. In 1995, IG Metall appointed a special coordinator for the Czech Republic, Slovakia, and Slovenia, which has considerably accelerated mutual contacts and further intensified regional co-operation. The most important joint activities were as follows:

- OS KOVO delegates attend IG Metall collective bargaining as observers;
- OS KOVO supports the strike in Bavaria, and the delegates attend the preparations for the strike as observers and also the strike itself;
- delegates attend the IG Metall conference regarding a 35-hour week; and
- co-operation in the region addressing the specific issues and also co-operation of the companies where the German multinational capital is represented.

The cooperation with Austria (Produktionsgewerkschaft (PRO-GE)) is similar to the co-operation with IG Metall, with the specific co-operation in the border regions. There are two Interregional Trade Union Councils (IRTUC) on the border with Austria: Danube / Moldova (2004), South Moravia / Lower Austria (2006), and two on the border with Germany: Elbe / Neisse (Germany, Poland, Czech Republic, 1993), Bohemia / Bavaria (Germany, Czech Republic, 1997). The cooperation between the Czech Republic and Austria was supported by the project Zukunftsraum Wien-Niederösterreich-Südmähren (ZUWINS+). The project was supported by European Regional Development Fund (EFRR), The Federal Ministry of Labour, Social Affairs and Consumer Protection (BMASK), and Czech Ministry for Regional Development, and lasted four years (2009–2012). The project was oriented not only on regional cooperation between the Czech and Austrian trade unions but also on the education of active employee representatives in the Central European Trade Union Academy (Mitteleuropäische Gewerkschaftsakademie

(MEGAk). Another topic is legal consulting for Czech employees in Austria or for potential commuters.[15]

Despite 20 years of experience, IRTUC is something which is left to the regional organisations or decided at the leadership level without broader discussion. As mentioned by one of the respondents,

> These are usually one-page documents that rarely need further development of the problems, rather they are just recommendations. Usually, the decision is made by the leadership, which, of course, informs the wider membership base[16].

The implementation of IRTUC's decisions should be performed by leadership or by the regional level-representatives. Despite rather limited interest or information regarding IRTUC activities, we observe that participation in IRTUC activities sometimes influences internal discussions in the TU.

One respondent mentioned that

> It had to do with employment policy of some of these border regions. Cooperation was started, even on the level of individual companies. This means that it got transferred to the European Workers Councils. Somewhere, these two institutions worked together. This had to do with specific intra-company problems, regardless of whether it was the German, Czech, or Austrian branch. This is where these contacts are used to coordinate, mediate and transfer the problems[17].

Another respondent noted that important topics for IRTUC's agenda are regional unemployment, the movement of the labour force, and investment.[18]

The Visegrad countries, originally the Czech Republic, Slovakia, Hungary, Poland, and later Slovenia, have been cooperation partners for a long time. There has been a mutual exchange of information regarding specific issues and the situations in the individual countries. After an OS KOVO delegate was elected European Metalworkers' Federation (EMF) vice-chairman and after a Vasas Szakszervezeti Szövetsé (VASAS) delegate (Hungary) was elected an observer on the International Metalworkers' Federation (IMF) executive committee for Central Eastern Europe, an exchange of information occurred concerning the work of these committees and the situations in the particular countries.

A number of other close bilateral contacts were also established in the same time period, both because of OS KOVO's membership in the organisations mentioned and also individually. OS KOVO delegates have attended the congresses of the individual unions (IG Metall Germany, Centrale der Metaalbewerkers van België (CMB) and Christelijke Centrale der Metaalbewerkers van België (CCMB) Belgium, Iron and Steel

15 ZUWINS+: ZUWINS+ official website, in: www.zuwinsplus.eu, http://www.zuwinsplus.eu/cs/Satellite?pagename=S06/Index&n=S06_83.0, accessed 20 June 2014.
16 Interview with trade union representative, Czech Republic, Gn06, 25 March 2013.
17 Ibid.
18 Interview with trade union expert, Czech Republic, Gn11, 6 May 2013.

Trades Confederation (ISTC) Great Britain, and others) and other discussions or conferences regarding specific topics. There is a mutual exchange of information and contacts, such as when specific problems occur. OS KOVO cooperates closely with Belgian and Scandinavian unions. There is very close cooperation with Bavaria; especially on the Bavarian side, one can see the influence of many of the Czech people, particularly from different parts of the Plzen region. These individuals and organisations can use their existing connections well.

12.5.2. Cooperation with Old and New EU Member States

Cooperation plays a role notwithstanding whether the states are direct neighbours. Despite the common communist past, cooperation among the new EU member states is not easy. Cooperation is not according to old / new EU member states. If there was long-term cooperation, nothing changed after EU accession and if so, only in a positive direction. Cooperation is helped by common projects. As mentioned by one of the respondents,

> ...with the new ones, say Poland or Slovakia, we have a certain sympathetic cooperation but there are no direct projects. With the Slovak side, we certainly have the best mutual understanding because we used to be united. Even the 'KOVO' trade union, we visit each other quite often, but this still happens rather on an informal level. We simply cooperate more with the Germans and Austrians[19].

The most important areas of cooperation with trade unions from old member states are employment and social policy issues, and cooperation with the European Work Councils. A special and urgent topic is the unemployment of youth; cooperation between young Czech and German metalworkers might be helpful. What must be intensified is the coordination of positions and approaches concerning EU politics and proposals.

Collaboration with trade unions from the old EU member states has its advantages and disadvantages. Advantages are the reliability of partners in old member states, their experience, and the feeling that we are part of the club and are accepted by the partners. Of course, there are differences among the old member states. There is a slight reservation toward cooperation with the French and British trade unions.

The economic crisis was an endurance test for international cooperation. On the European level, we can discuss how we must solve some problem on the European level, but actually, everyone considers primarily how any solution will affect his or her homeland. Therefore, there is a certain discrepancy between what is said and what is done. As mentioned by one respondent, ideally, we should be able to accompany the migration of workplaces with a corresponding migration of demands for conditions and guarantees. This movement does not necessarily mean money but rather

19 Interview with trade union representative, Czech Republic, Gn06, 25 March 2013.

the migration of social rights.[20] Sensitivity exists regarding inequalities in wages and redistributive justice (profit surplus allocation).

Not only a long tradition of cooperation with close neighbours but also the development and stability of the organisational structure make neighbours more suitable and attractive. As mentioned by one interviewee,

> TUs in old member states have fixed structures, we know who to approach. We have the same good cooperation with our Eastern neighbours—Slovakia, Slovenia, Hungary and Poland. There exists a very close cooperation on a daily basis. The cooperation is more difficult with other Eastern partners—Bulgaria, Romania and Croatia. There exist many TU organisations and a non-transparent situation; the representatives change quickly[21].

This view was also shared by another respondent:

> With the new member states that are not our direct neighbours, it is often difficult to find a reliable partner. The structures there are very unstable and unreliable. The chance to identify a partner...It simply works differently, for instance, in Bulgaria or Romania.

12.5.3. Integration of the Trade Union in European Umbrella Organisations

The chairman of OS KOVO, Josef Středula, mentioned in his 2012 Christmas message, that

> The position of OS KOVO is both in European and global measure, very strong and it is not a self-appreciation. It was visible during the constituent congress of the biggest European trade union federation. Also in the world federation, we are represented in all important bodies. OS KOVO is perceived as a strong trade union, we are taken seriously, and in many cases we are asked for an opinion. We are considered one of the best functioning TUs. Within the European federation, a group for Eastern Europe was established with Poland, Slovenia, Hungary, Slovakia, and the Czech Republic. At the last executive meeting of the European federation, it was mentioned that concerning management, this group could be a role model for other regions within the EU[22].

Since 1991, OS KOVO has been a member of two large international trade union organisations: the IMF and the EMF. OS KOVO joined both organisations before the division of the Czechoslovak federation, when it was still the Czechoslovak federation metalworkers' union (Odborový svaz KOVO v ČSFR). After the division of the country, two succeeding organisations were formed: the OS KOVO for the Czech Republic and the OZ KOVO for the Slovak Republic.

The first contacts with IMF were established in 1993. Seminars regarding collective bargaining, restructuring the steel industry, apprentice training, and trade union

20 Interview with trade union representative, Czech Republic, Gn03, 4 February 2013.

21 Interview with trade union representative, Czech Republic, Gn18, 30 January 2013.

22 Středula, Josef: V roce 2012 se dále zvýšil význam odborů [In 2012 further increased the importance of trade unions], Interview with OS KOVO chairman Josef Středula, in: KOVÁK, 14 December 2012, no. 41, here p. 1 and Appendix pp. 2–3.

assets have been organised. A special seminar has been held for lecturers. OS KOVO is a member of the IMF central committee, which meets twice a year. OS KOVO representatives also participate in other meetings with specialised interests. The OS KOVO delegate has directly participated in the preparation of the IMF action programme for the IMF congress (USA, May 1997), in particular the section addressing the globalisation of the economy.

Every year, a KOVO delegate also attends the IMF / Organisation for Economic Co-operation and Development (OECD) meeting concerning the steel industry. The delegate attends the meeting as a member of the Czech government delegation. OS KOVO representatives also participate as IMF lecturers at seminars organised by the IMF at the trade union headquarters, e.g., in Bulgaria or Romania.

The European Metalworkers' Federation, since May 2012 'IndustriAll European trade union' associates European metalworkers' unions and has approximately 8 million members. OS KOVO is a member of the EMF executive and several of its working groups. OS KOVO, for example, in the past, actively participated in the preparation of the EMF congress, which was held in Vienna in June 1995. In addition, the OS KOVO delegate and chairman, Jan Uhlíř, has been one of the EMF's vice-chairmen representing Visegrad countries. OS KOVO also had its delegates in several specific EMF working groups.

12.6. European Work Councils

Thanks to a strong inflow of foreign investment in the Czech Republic since the 1990s, there were enough companies with trade unions eligible for membership in the EWC. It depends on the sector and whether the companies came primarily because of the less expensive labour force or whether they looked for a qualified (although less expensive) labour force.

If there was an EWC, trade unions were in contact with them, and OS KOVO was most likely the most active. The mother company determined whether there was interest in these contacts before the accession of the Czech Republic to the EU. Before accession to the EU, approximately one-fifth of eligible companies had their observer in the relevant EWC. This involvement created an expectation that the membership will improve social dialogue in the companies. In one interview given by the former OS KOVO chairman in August 2003, this expectation was characterised in the following way:

a. trade officials will gain access to information regarding the intentions and plans of the company, and
b. this information will make it possible to correct management, especially the new Czech management that was in many cases more predatory than foreign manage-

ment. Through the EWC, the Czech TU could establish contact with supranational management, which corrects Czechs when necessary.[23]

The importance of the EWC is noted by an EWC Newsletter.

> As the other countries joining the EU, the EWC directive came into effect on the day of Czech Republic's admission to the EU, that is, on 1st May 2004. Of 2,204 Europe-wide enterprises, which could potentially set up a European works council, 636 are represented by a branch office in the Czech Republic (according to the calculations of the European Trade Union Institute in June 2005). This number is more or less comparable with Denmark or Ireland. Amongst the new EU member countries, the Czech Republic ranks third after Poland and Hungary. The problem is that only eight of these 636 enterprises have their headquarters on Czech soil. So the national economy is in the hands of foreign groups, which frequently use the country as an 'extended workbench' of the European single market. As many as 231 of the 636 enterprises are German. Almost half of all enterprises with locations in the Czech Republic had already founded an EWC by June 2005. These 333 councils are now to be enlarged to include delegates from the Czech Republic. A study in 2003 shows that over 50 delegates from the Czech Republic were already involved in various EWC bodies, half of them in the metal industry.[24]

This emphasises the importance of the EWC and cooperation with IG Metall for OS KOVO.

Despite some preliminary experiences, it was necessary to be prepared for the standard work and practices in the EWCs. Where an EWC already exists, new representatives must prepare for their membership at the European level. In the event that an EWC had not been established, it is necessary to take steps to find agreement regarding the establishment of an EWC. This formation was the subject of the first project, which was conducted in the autumn of 2004 and the spring of 2005 and in which OS KOVO took part. The first project was a success and achieved its objectives. During the first half of 2006, the second project concerning the EWCs was initiated. This project's objectives were twofold. First, the project intended to provide OS KOVO representatives with all the relevant information available regarding EWCs in Timken, Mittal Steel, Tecumseh, Gorenje, Ronal and Hayes Lemmerz. Second, the project aspired to strengthen relations with partner organisations in Romania (Federaţia Naţională Sindicală Solidaritatea Metal and Federaţia Sindicală a Siderurgiştilor (METAROM)), Bulgaria (Natsionalna federatsiya „tekhnicheska industriya, nauka, informatika" (NFTINI), Confederation of Labour Podkrepa (CL Podkrepa)), Slovenia (Sindikata kovinske in elektro industrije Slovenije

23 Mansfeldová, Zdenka: Foreign Direct Investment in the Czech Republic from the perspective of representatives of trade unions, employer associations and the executive. Report WP3 for the project The Impact of Foreign Direct Investments of EU based Companies on the Labour Relations in EU Candidate Countries—Taking the Examples of Germany, Poland, the Czech Republic and Slovakia, sponsored by Hans Böckler Foundation and Otto-Brenner-Stiftung. Unpublished manuscript, 2004.

24 Euro-workscouncil.net: EWC News, in: ewc-news.com, no. 1 2007, here p. 11, http://www.ewc-news.com/en012007.htm#8, accessed 4 July 2014.

(SKEI)) and the EMF in Brussels. Specifically, the project intended to strengthen relations with potential EWC members in these trade unions.[25]

The importance of obtaining information was mentioned several times during our interviews. One of our respondents stated:

> The institution of the European Works Council is one of the possible, and most frequently used in practice, forms and information system—the consultation on a transnational company operating in the European Community. In the context of understanding what the EWCs are and what their role is, we have to mention that we have 100 representatives in EWCs and 427 representatives on the supervisory board of companies[26].

Decisions that must be represented in the EWC are made mostly by the relevant basic TU organisation rather than at headquarters.

> This is done by the relevant base organisations rather than the trade union, i.e. directly at the given firm. We do not coordinate anything; at the maximum, we provide consultations, but that is it[27].

Consultations with the union's specialist are also mentioned, and personal communication within the relevant organisation is emphasised. The responsibility for implementation of the EWC decisions rests on the given enterprise. With more important issues, the executive leadership might be involved.

12.7. Internal Decision-Making and Internal Debates Concerning EU-Related Issues, Respective Decisions and their Implementation

To present the decision-making mechanisms, we must examine the governance structure of OS KOVO in general and regarding the EU related issues. According to the interviewed respondents, the decisions related to the EU are made within the decision-making bodies envisaged in its statute.

The activities of OS KOVO at the EU-level influence its work at the national level. For example:

> Three years ago, we made an agreement in IndustriAll that we will promote a common requirement in collective bargaining. It was against risky jobs, agency jobs, or risky forms of employment. It was a gentleman's agreement among members, and all members included these demands in their bargaining[28].

The respondent continues:

---

25 Hála, Jaroslav: Metalworkers' federation completes project on European Works Councils, in: EurWORK European Observatory of Working Life, 2006, http://eurofound.europa.eu/eiro/2006/11/articles/cz0611079i.htm, accessed 4 July 2014.

26 Interview with trade union representative, Czech Republic, Gn06, 25 March 2013.

27 Interview with trade union representative, Czech Republic, Gn12, 9 May 2013.

28 Interview with trade union representative, Czech Republic, Gn03, 4 February 2013.

> We have, for example, agreed in the European federation in IndustriAll on supporting collective bargaining. So three years ago, we agreed on activities against precarious work, agency work, and precarious forms of employment. There is a gentleman's agreement nevertheless approved by the authorities. So all the unions that negotiated have had some form of this requirement linked to it, for instance, to reduce the number of agency employees or to reduce professions. So there is clear influence[29].

OS KOVO generally supports the implementation of specific EU regulations and tries to implement them. However, implementation is not always easy because particular interests might be affected. One example might be CO_2 emissions or the noisiness of cars. The automotive industry is part of OS KOVO, and they are not happy regarding these regulations because it might affect production in the country.

12.8. Dynamics in the Internal Organisation and Debates of the Trade Union

OS KOVO has a democratic decision-making structure that is anchored in its documents. Our respondent from the organisational department of OS KOVO described the structure in the following way:

> Our union is headed by its executive leadership, i.e. the president and three vice-presidents. This is the statutory body that carries responsibility for decisions. Below this, there is the presidency, which consists of representatives of individual regional associations. There are sixteen of these plus there are also members of the executive leadership—but what is important, all the regions have their voice. Then, there is the so-called council of the 'KOVO' trade union, which meets three times a year and consists of 67 members and includes also, e.g., representatives of the narrower voting districts. And then there is the wider membership base consisting of 672 base organisations.
>
> Here, we discuss the long-term plans, i.e. annual planning of what is to be done each month, what is to be approved and what we should focus on. This year, it will be even more important because we have our general assembly, which takes place every four years and where key executives are elected. Then, there are decisions within the council about key documents, the budget, etc. Then, a bit of decision-making is done within the presidency, and then there are some quick discussions to be held. All major and political decisions are, however, made by the executive leadership[30].

The supreme body of the union is the general assembly, which meets once every four years. Between the general assemblies, decisions are made by the union council, which meets four times a year. The decision-making process could be described in the following way:[31]

1. information or a proposal comes from the commission;
2. there is a division of agendas in the trade union, for example, one vice-chairman has in his portfolio collective bargaining, wages, and he must prepare the position;

29 Ibid.
30 Interview with trade union representative, Czech Republic, Gn06, 25 March 2013.
31 Interview with trade union representative, Czech Republic, Gn03, 4 February 2013.

3. consultation occurs with the international department; and
4. the leadership of the trade union must approve the position—but in reality, this fourth step is often missing.

12.9. Resources and Internal Organisation of the Trade Union Regarding Cooperation at the EU Level

Access to the EU represented for the Czech trade unions not only new opportunities but also higher costs, because it was necessary to pay fees to the European federations. Activities of the trade union at the EU level are financed by OS KOVO. The sources of income did not increase; the opposite occurred. The decreasing income applies to the TU generally and also for OS KOVO. OS KOVO is first funded from membership contributions. There are also other sources (projects or profit from property), but they are minor. The situation is roughly consistent; however, the share of membership contributions in the overall budget is beginning to decrease.

Several times the role of external support and specifically the role of Friedrich Ebert Stiftung (FES) was mentioned. FES and OS KOVO have had mutual contacts since 1993. FES has helped to conduct a number of Czech-German activities, such as holding seminars, arranging contacts, and providing interpreters and organisational assistance.

12.10. Conclusion

OS KOVO is the largest and strongest trade union in the country and covers the industries crucial for the economy, export, and employment. OS KOVO is an active and respected partner in the international and domestic arenas. The union strongly defends the rights of metalworkers and related industries. The TU is generally successful in collective bargaining; however, there is a difference among basic organisations and company organisations.

OS KOVO has a number of bilateral international contacts with different traditions and intensities. Cooperation plays a role notwithstanding whether the states are direct neighbours. Despite the common communist past, cooperation among new EU member states is not easy. Cooperation is not according to old / new EU member states but rather according to past cooperation and geographical closeness. If there was long-term cooperation, nothing changed after EU accession and if so, only in a positive direction. Cooperation is helped when there are common projects and several past projects.

Thanks to a strong inflow of foreign investment in the Czech Republic since the 1990s, there are enough companies with trade unions eligible for membership in the EWC. It depends on the sector and on whether the companies came primarily because of the less expensive labour force or whether they looked for a qualified (although less expensive) labour force. Membership in the EWC is perceived as an important factor for getting information and sharing best practices.

Evaluating the activity of OS KOVO, we must mention its strengths and weaknesses. There is a well-functioning multilevel international cooperation, and OS KOVO is an active and respected partner. In contrast, the economic crisis indicates that solidarity in times of economic growth is a different issue from solidarity in times of economic hardship. In the latter case, we observe the return to a primary focus on the national level and to performance based on a cost-benefit analysis.

Aleksandra Lis

13. Different Faces of Europeanization. The Case of Niezależny Samorządny Związek Zawodowy Solidarność (NSZZ Solidarność)

13.1. Introduction

NSZZ Solidarność is one of the most famous and well-researched trade union organisations in Central Eastern Europe. Currently, NSZZ Solidarność is undergoing changes by becoming active in national, European and international arenas. This chapter examines NSZZ Solidarność as a European organisation and attempts to understand what European integration meant to the organisation. What type of organisational changes has the European Union (EU) brought to the trade union? What has NSZZ Solidarność learnt from the EU? How has the EU influenced its identity and how NSZZ Solidarność is impacting contemporary labour politics in the EU?

In the following sections, I examine the internal structural re-organisation of NSZZ Solidarność concerning European issues and European integration. I also present how NSZZ Solidarność was integrated in the EU's organisation. Finally, I examine the internal decision-making process and debates concerning EU-related issues. A separate section is devoted to the negotiations concerning the EU climate change and energy package. During these negotiations, NSZZ Solidarność opposed a decision of the European Trade Union Confederation to support the package of directives proposed by the European Commission. This opposition was the beginning of an important debate that did not end with the adoption of the climate change and energy package in 2009. EU climate policies are still problematic for the Polish mining and energy unions, and NSZZ Solidarność is actively trying to influence this policy area.

In the conclusion, I observe the concept of Europeanization more broadly. I also consider how NSZZ Solidarność because of its historical engagement with European ideas and actors, may be opposed to the concept of Europeanization if this was too narrowly defined as learning to do things in the European way.[1] I consider Europeanization as a process of policy and political learning. Poland's EU accession has certainly brought new knowledge to NSZZ Solidarność regarding social and employment policies, and it has given NSZZ Solidarność a new political identity. The European Trade Union Confederation has been a strong example for NSZZ Solidarność until the climate

1 Radaelli, C.: Whither Europeanization? Concept Stretching and Substantive Change, in: European Integration online Papers (EIoP), 2000 (vol. 4), no. 8, http://eiop.or.at/eiop/pdf/2000-008.pdf, accessed 28 January 2014.

change and energy package debate. During this debate, the Mining and Energy Secretariat of NSZZ Solidarność distanced the organisation from the European Trade Union Confederation's (ETUC) politics.

13.2. Sources Used for the Case Study

The case study is based on 21 interviews conducted in 2008, 2009 and 2012.

In 2008 and 2009, eight interviews were conducted in NSZZ Solidarność in Gdańsk. An interview with the head of the International Department of NSZZ Solidarność and the European Economic and Social Committee (EESC) member was conducted in Gdansk on 7 November 2008. Three interviews with representatives from the Expert in Health and Safety were conducted in Gdańsk on 17 November 2008, 12 February 2009 and 1 October 2009. Two interviews were completed with the president of the Mining and Energy Secretariat (Sekretariat Górnictwa i Energetyki (SGiE)) of NSZZ Solidarność in Warsaw on 22 October 2008 and by phone on 17 January 2009. One interview was conducted with the president of the National Section of Hard Coal Mining (Sekcji Krajowej Górnictwa Węgla Kamiennego (SKGWK)) of NSZZ Solidarność by phone on 24 October 2008. One interview with the president of the National Section of Brown Coal Mining (Sekcji Krajowej Górnictwa Węgla Brunatnego (SKGWB)) of NSZZ Solidarność was conducted by phone on 26 January 2008.

In 2009, seven interviews were conducted in Brussels and by phone. Two interviews were completed in the ETUC. An interview with the leader of the ETUC Working Group on Sustainable Development was conducted in Brussels on 2 July 2009. Two interviews were conducted in the European Mine, Chemical and Energy Workers' Federation (EMCEF). An interview with a senior advisor was conducted in Brussels on 24 June 2009. An interview with the president of the EMCEF was conducted by phone on 12 August 2009. One interview with a senior advisor of the Industriegewerkschaft Bergbau, Chemie, Energie (IGBCE) was conducted by phone on 4 August 2009.

In 2012, four interviews were completed with members of NSZZ Solidarność. An interview with the head of the International Department and three officials from the International Department (official 1, official 2 and official 3) were held in Gdańsk on 12 December 2012. Additionally, in 2013, two interviews were completed with experts—Dr. Magdalena Bernaciak (phone, 12 June 2013) and Dr. Adam Mrozowicki (phone, 23 June 2013). Both, Mrozowicki and Bernaciak, wrote their Ph.D. dissertations on trade unions. Mrozowicki works at the University of Wrocław, and Bernaciak works at the European Trade Union Institute (ETUI) in Brussels.

Additionally, the following documents were collected regarding NSZZ Solidarność:

- the NSZZ Solidarność membership list in international organisations;
- position papers;
- e-mails;

- press releases; and
- media articles (in particular, regarding the EU climate change and energy package).

In addition, other types of documents were used, such as the recommendations of the tripartite commission in Poland and the report of the Green Effort Group (2008)—the lobbying group established to represent the interests of the Polish energy and industry sectors.

13.3. Profile of the Selected Trade Union

The history of NSZZ Solidarność dates back to 1980 when NSZZ Solidarność emerged as an anti-communist social movement at the Lenin Shipyard in Gdańsk. By the end of 1981, NSZZ Solidarność had up to 10 million members, which constituted one-third of the whole working age population in Poland. In November 1980, NSZZ Solidarność was formally registered as a nationwide organisation. By non-bureaucratic and non-violent means of social resistance, NSZZ Solidarność fought for workers' rights. In September 1981, Lech Wałęsa was elected president at the first national congress of NSZZ Solidarność. The round table talks between the opposition, led by NSZZ Solidarność, and the government resulted in semi-free elections that occurred in 1989. By the end of August, a new government was formed with the NSZZ Solidarność member, Tadeusz Mazowiecki, elected prime minister. During the transition period, NSZZ Solidarność functioned as a traditional trade union organisation. The political ambitions of NSZZ Solidarność were revived in the second half of the 1990s when a political party, the Akcja Wyborcza Solidarność (AWS), was founded in 1996. The party won the 1997 parliamentary elections but lost political support during the following elections in 2001.

The supreme powers of the union are vested in a legislative body, the National Convention of Delegates (Narodowy Zjazd Delegatów), and the executive power is vested in the National Commission (Komisja Krajowa). The union is divided into 37 regions that reflect, to a large degree, Poland's territorial structure since 1975. NSZZ Solidarność comprises 8,292 trade unions, 37 regional federations and 16 branch unions. NSZZ Solidarność has 649,000 members of which 39% are unskilled and semi-skilled workers, 34% are skilled workers and 27% are highly skilled workers.[2] As Gardawski et al. note, 'despite this significant decline, Solidarność is still the largest union "confederation" in Poland and within all the CEE countries that are members of the EU'[3] (CEE—Central Eastern Europe). In general, the Polish unions are ageing. The same applies

2 Trappmann, Vera: Trade Unions in Poland. Current Situation, Organisation and Challenges, Berlin, Bonn: Friedrich Ebert Foundation, 2012.

3 Gardawski, Juliusz / Mrozowicki, Adam / Czarzasty, Jan: Trade Unions in Poland. Report 123, Brussels: ETUI, 2012, here p. 8.

to NSZZ Solidarność where the average age of its members is forty seven years. The union established a special department to recruit new young members.[4]

Delegates are elected at the regional conventions. The number of spaces in a region is proportional to the number of union members in that region.

Table 13-1: The Largest Regions in Terms of the Number of Delegates

Region	Number of delegates
Śląsko-Dąbrowski	45
Małopolska	29
Mazowsze	28
Gdańsk	20
Dolny Śląsk	20
Wielkopolska	17
Ziemia Łódzka	13
Środkowo-Wschodni	12
Pomorze Zachodnie	10

NSZZ Solidarność Komisja Krajowa: Liczba delegatów w poszczególnych regionach [Number of delegates in each region], in: solidarnosc.org.pl, http://www.solidarnosc.org.pl/wladze/krajowy-zjazd-delegatow/liczba-delegatow-w-poszczegolnych-regionach, accessed 20 July 2014.

Other regions have less than ten delegates each. The National Convention of Delegates also includes the presidents of the regions and the national councils of the industry secretariats as well as the leader of the National Secretariat of Pensioners. Currently, the National Convention of Delegates has 325 members. The power of the secretariat includes the following: adoption of amendments to the statutes, adoption of the action program of the union, determining the membership fee, adoption of resolutions that are binding for all union structures; and powers that have not been reserved in the statute for other governing bodies of the union.[5]

The National Commission is a supreme power to the regional directorates, secretariat councils and industry sections.[6] The responsibilities and rights of the National Commission include the following:

- representation of the union before the government, other institutions and organisations;
- coordination of union activities;

4 Trappmann, Vera: Trade Unions in Poland. Current Situation, Organisation and Challenges, Berlin, Bonn: Friedrich Ebert Foundation, 2012.

5 The National Convention of Delegates also implements union positions, elects the president of the National Commission, elects members of the National Commission and the National Audit Commission, reviews reports of the National Commission and the National Audit Commission, grants a discharge to the National Commission and honorary membership of the union.

6 The National Commission consists of the president of the National Commission, presidents of the regional directorates, presidents of the national councils of the industry secretariats, president of the Council of the National Secretariat of Pensioners, and other members of the National Commission elected by the National Convention of Delegates.

- adoption of binding rules for all organisational structures of the union;
- adoption of the budget; and
- registration of the national industry structures.

The National Commission also conducts and concludes collective bargaining with the possibility to transfer this authority to other union structures or representative bodies. The National Commission also makes decisions regarding entering a labour dispute or launching a protest action with a supra-regional reach; in addition, the National Commission elects members of the presidium. The leaders of NSZZ Solidarność have been the following:

- Lech Wałęsa (1980–1990);
- Marian Krzaklewski (1991–2002);
- Janusz Śniadek (2002–2010); and
- Piotr Duda (since 2010).

NSZZ Solidarność has its own weekly newspaper, Tygodnik Solidarność, which was first published in April 1981. The weekly is a good source of information regarding NSZZ Solidarność and labour related issues for union members. Currently, Tygodnik Solidarność has a circulation of 20,000 copies. The National Commission also issues a monthly bulletin, the Unionists' Notebook and the Solidarność Information Service. Currently, the main objective of the union, according to a statement on its official website, is to fight for better labour standards in Poland.[7]

13.4. Re-Organisation of NSZZ Solidarność to Represent European Issues

International activities of NSZZ Solidarność date back to its beginnings. In the fall of 1981, leaders of NSZZ Solidarność invited the International Confederation of Free Trade Unions (ICFTU) and the World Confederation of Labour (WCL) to the first Congress of NSZZ Solidarność. Early on, between 1885 and 1886, NSZZ Solidarność started to consider joining the ETUC. At that time, as Mrozowicki noted in an interview,[8] NSZZ Solidarność hesitated between two affiliations—the European and the global. The leadership of NSZZ Solidarność wanted to join the ETUC. Because the ETUC was affiliated with the WCL; the leaders of NSZZ Solidarność thought that through ETUC membership they could strengthen contacts with both organisations at the same time. However, in the end, as a trade union organisation from a non-member state of the European Community, NSZZ Solidarność could not join the ETUC. Consequently, in 1886, NSZZ Solidarność joined the WCL, which proved important and formative to the

7 NSZZ Solidarność: O NSZZ „Solidarność" [About NSZZ 'Solidarność'], in: solidarnosc.org.pl, http://www.solidarnosc.org.pl/o-nszz-solidarnosc/o-nszz-solidarnosc , accessed 20 July 2014.

8 Interview with the trade union expert Adam Mrozowicki, Poland, A. M. 23 June 2013.

organisational structure of NSZZ Solidarność. For example, the number and names of the secretariats of NSZZ Solidarność reflect the WCL's organisational structure.

Currently, NSZZ Solidarność does not have an organisational unit that exclusively addresses the European Union. The International Department of NSZZ Solidarność is responsible for the following:

- working out directions of the international policy of the union;
- representing the union in international and European structures;
- coordinating, directing and assisting other departments in the National Commission to address international issues; and
- supporting the regional and industry structures of the union in their international activities.

The International Department was established in 1981 to address foreign affairs. This involved cooperation with the International Labour Organisation (ILO), WCL, ETUC and United States donors. Gradually, prior to EU accession, the work of the International Department increased in importance in the union. The department engaged in explaining EU-related issues to union members and in establishing relations between NSZZ Solidarność and EU structures.

In 1996, NSZZ Solidarność created a one-person Office of the Coordinator for European Integration. In 1997, a two-person unit, the Commission for the EU Accession, was created. This unit comprised a coordinator (Józef Niemiec) and an assistant (Katarzyna Bartkiewicz). When Niemiec became the secretary of the National Commission, Bartkiewicz became the coordinator of the EU Commission for the EU Accession. This unit worked for several years with economists and lawyers from NSZZ Solidarność to prepare the union for EU accession 'to function well in the EU structures and to know what the EU is about'[9]. This unit organised training for union members to prepare them for the pre-accession referendum. This unit also prepared statements and positions on accession issues. Bartkiewicz from the International Department currently admits that, at that time, people who worked in NSZZ Solidarność did not have a very thorough practical knowledge regarding the EU. 'We did not know what a directive was. We would only get titles of directives in English and we had to take a position on them.'[10] With time, this unit was incorporated in the International Department of NSZZ Solidarność.

Other units in the National Commission of NSZZ Solidarność and other sections of the union began to incorporate a European perspective in their activities. According to my interviewees, currently, the European Union is present in the work of all members and officials of NSZZ Solidarność who are affected by it.[11] Problems emerging at

9 Interview with trade union representative, Poland, official 2, M. D., 12 December 2012.
10 Ibid.
11 Ibid.

and in relation to the EU level are always consulted in the appropriate departments and secretariats. These consultations are coordinated by the International Department. The International Department is also responsible for communication with EU level organisational bodies. However, the International Department does not coordinate European projects. There is a separate department that is responsible for the participation of NSZZ Solidarność in EU-funded projects. According to the interviewed officials from the International Department, the EU accession did not change the general organisational structure of NSZZ Solidarność.[12]

> The International Department coordinates the EU-related issues but it does not deal with all the European issues. We have people working in other departments. We have the expert department that includes the Political Economy Office, the Legal Unit and the Industry Unit. The last one coordinates collective bargaining at the international level, cooperation with the European Industry Federations and with the global union federations. We have a Legal Department that gives opinions on directives, e.g., on the Working Time Directive.

The International Department employs seven people. According to the expert, Bernaciak, for the amount of work that it must address, the International Department is too small.[13] Apart from the head of the International Department, there are people responsible for particular countries—each person has several countries under his or her supervision. The International Department runs the archive of agreements between NSZZ Solidarność and other international organisations and monitors their compliance. Since the EU accession in 2004, the International Department has been divided into a European Team and a Team for International Affairs and Globalisation. The European Team is responsible for cooperation with the European Trade Union Confederation and with the Pan-European Regional Council (the European trade union arm of the International Trade Union Confederation). This collaboration is responsible for:

- participating in European negotiations;
- overseeing the work of the European Works Councils; and
- cooperation with EU institutions and the European Council.

Moreover, the European Team works on migration and the integration of the European labour market. The Team for International Affairs and Globalisation is responsible for the cooperation with Global Unions, the International Trade Union Confederation (ITUC) and Trade Union Advisory Committee to the Organisation for Economic Co-operation and Development (TUAC), International Labour Organization (ILO), international financial institutions (the International Monetary Fund, World Bank, World Trade Organisation) and works on migration beyond the EU borders.[14]

---

12 Interview with the trade union representative, Poland, official 1, R. S., 12 December 2012.

13 Interview with trade union expert Magdalena Bernaciak, Poland, M. B., 12 June 2013.

14 A short description can be found online on http://www.solidarnosc.org.pl/dzialalnosc-miedzy narodowa/zagraniczne-o-dziale, accessed 12 December 2014.

NSZZ Solidarność identifies strongly with the ETUC and perceives itself as an integral part of it. According to the interviewed expert, Mrozowicki, the narrative concerns 'Solidarność introducing the world to Europe rather than about the ETUC introducing the world and Europe to Solidarność'[15]. NSZZ Solidarność became a member of the ETUC in 1995. In comparison, Ogolnopolskie Porozumienie Zwiazkow Zawodowych (OPZZ) joined the ETUC in 2006 and Forum Związków Zawodowych (FZZ) in 2012. Although officials from the International Department do not consider that the EU accession caused organisational changes to NSZZ Solidarność, they are aware that the ETUC became an important example to and identification for them. During interviews, these officials noted that the ETUC brought to NSZZ Solidarność new topics for debates, new ways of framing labour issues, and new ideological standpoints. The ETUC also brought to NSZZ Solidarność new knowledge, learning processes and development of expertise.[16]

People with language skills are an important asset for the International Department in NSZZ Solidarność. Everyone who works in the International Department speaks English and some employees speak English and an additional language (Swedish, Danish, Norwegian, Russian or German). At the National Commission of NSZZ Solidarność in Gdańsk, at least one person in each department speaks English. This ensures easy communication regarding EU-related issues among the departments. However, language skills are much poorer in the regional and industrial secretariats of NSZZ Solidarność. Therefore, there often is a need for a written translation of various documents because some documents, such as those prepared by the ETUC, are available only in the EU's official languages. Usually, this job is performed internally in the Foreign Department. The most important excerpts are selected and translated.[17] In case of larger texts, such as books, NSZZ Solidarność orders translation services outside of the organisation. According to my interviewees, translation of every document would be too costly, and there is not always enough time for the people working in NSZZ Solidarność to translate.

Activities of the International Department are financed from the general budget of the National Commission. Often, the costs of some activities are reimbursed by EU institutions or by the ETUC. Reimbursements, in particular, concern trips to Brussels and Strasburg. Another costly activity is the participation of NSZZ Solidarność in European protest actions.

> We are in general fully supportive of the direction presented by the ETUC when it comes to crises, but we are not always of the opinion that it is necessary to mobilise great masses of members, for example, to get thousands of people to Warsaw.[18]

15 Interview with trade union expert Adam Mrozowicki, Poland, A. M., 23 June 2013.
16 Interview with trade union representatives, Poland, official 1, R. S., 12 December 2012.
17 Ibid.
18 Interview with the head of the International Department, Poland, A. A., 12 December 2012.

At the level of the NSZZ Solidarność secretariats, involvement in EU affairs is often financed from EU project money. As Bernaciak notes, projects come to the secretariats from the outside and thus restrict the EU-related activities of secretariats to particular issues. Leaders of secretariats do not have much freedom in selecting issues that are most important to them and their organisation. Secretariats with low membership are particularly dependent on project funding. They receive a small portion of membership fees and have very limited budgets. Because of the lack of funding, these secretariats rarely employ staff for EU relations.[19]

Decisions regarding EU issues are made in NSZZ Solidarność with two different methods. First, the European approach is applied when an EU-related issue requires negotiations with the commission and the employers, such as the Working Time Directive. In this and similar situations, NSZZ Solidarność usually sends a representative to participate in the negotiations as a part of the ETUC team. Prior to the negotiations, the NSZZ Solidarność experts meet to provide their representative with knowledge and recommendations. However, the position of NSZZ Solidarność often gets subsumed in a more general position of the ETUC, which is then represented before the commission or the employers' organisations.

The second method of EU decision-making is the national approach. For example, prior to making a decision concerning European legislation regarding social policy, the government consults NSZZ Solidarność for an opinion. This method is usually not very efficient for NSZZ Solidarność because the government does not allow much time for comments. NSZZ Solidarność must usually reply in one day. With these time constraints, it is impossible to have a thorough debate concerning a given issue, although officials at NSZZ Solidarność prepare opinions when asked. Moreover, the national approach attracts more attention among union members.

> This path, no matter how its efficiency is doubtful, attracts more attention here in the organisation because these matters are symptoms of national affairs, which naturally seem more important. It will still take some time before people in our organisation understand that European issues concern us very directly, and that it is difficult to separate them from national affairs. Often, things discussed in the ETUC come to us through the government, and it turns out that we are well informed by the ETUC. However, since we hadn't had a discussion here in the union we cannot prepare a position anyway.[20]

Making decisions and taking positions in NSZZ Solidarność, which, unlike OPZZ, is not a federation but one organisation, also depends on the shifting influences between the two main centres of the union. As Mrozowicki notes, there have always been two dominant centres of NSZZ Solidarność—one in Gdańsk and the other in Katowice—both of which have large membership bases. The current President of NSZZ Solidarność, Piotr Duda, comes from the Śląsko-Dąbrowski region. He gained support of the younger

19 Interview with trade union expert Magdalena Bernaciak, Poland, M. B., 12 June 2013.
20 Interview with the head of the International Department, Poland, A. A., 12 December 2012.

generation of members who did not participate in creating NSZZ Solidarność. Janusz Śniadek was much more an 'old type of leader' who represented the old ethos of NSZZ Solidarność with its historical legacy as an opposition movement. Duda represents a pragmatic approach. According to Mrozowicki, Duda seems to be more of a modern leader focused on the efficiency of his political actions.[21]

13.5. Integration of NSZZ Solidarność in the EU's Organisational Arena

The history of the integration of NSZZ Solidarność in the European Community cannot be told without several important people such as Jan Kułakowski[22] and Józef Niemiec[23]. These individuals had a significant impact on the pre-accession negotiations with the EU. Since 2003, Niemiec has been the secretary of the ETUC in Brussels where he is responsible for matters regarding social security, socio-economic coherence, regional policy, internal markets and public services. Currently, Józef Niemiec, who often guides his colleagues through the ETUC's and EU's politics, is possibly the most important contact of NSZZ Solidarność in the ETUC. The third important figure is Jerzy Buzek, the prime minister of Poland from 1997–2001, who has also been an active member of NSZZ Solidarność since 1980. In 2004, he became a member of the European Parliament, and from 2009–2012, he was the president of the European Parliament. While prime minister, Buzek worked closely with Józef Niemiec and Jan Kułakowski on European issues. For several years Buzek has been another 'man in

21 Interview with trade union expert Adam Mrozowicki, Poland, A. M., 23 June 2013.

22 During World War II, Kułakowski fought in the Warsaw uprising, and in 1946 he emigrated to Belgium. In 1953, he graduated from law at Catholic University in Leuven where he also obtained his Ph.D. In 1954, he became a member of the General Secretariat of the International Confederation of Christian Trade Unions for which he participated in negotiations with authoritarian regimes to free people repressed for trade union activity. In 1958, Kulakowski was the secretary and in 1962, the general secretary of the European organisation of the International Confederation of the Christian Trade Unions. Later, he was the general secretary of the European Organisation of the World Confederation of Labor. From 1974 to 1988, he was the secretary general of the World Confederation of Labor. From 1990 to 1996, he was the ambassador extraordinary and plenipotentiary of the Republic of Poland and head of the Polish mission to the European Community. In 1998, in the government of Jerzy Buzek, he was the secretary of state in the chancellery of the prime minister and government plenipotentiary for Poland's accession negotiations to the European Union. In 2004, he was elected a member of the European Parliament as a non-partisan candidate from the election list of the Freedom's Union (Unia Wolności). He was also a friend of NSZZ Solidarność and he played a crucial role in facilitating the accession of NSZZ Solidarność to the World Confederation of Labor. Later, he also helped NSZZ Solidarność in communications with the ETUC.

23 Between 1982 and 1989, Niemiec was active in the NSZZ Solidarność opposition. In the early pre-accession phase, from 1997 to 1998, he coordinated the Commission for European Integration at NSZZ Solidarność. Between 1998 and 2001, he was a member of the negotiation committee in the government of Jerzy Buzek.

Brussels' for NSZZ Solidarność, serving with advice and opening many doors. NSZZ Solidarność, as an organisation of Polish opposition elites, currently benefits from having its members in various political structures, such as the European political structure.

NSZZ Solidarność is a member of many labour organisations. The most important association is the European Trade Union Confederation. Józef Niemiec is the ETUC Confederal Secretary, Piotr Duda is a member of the Steering and Executive Committees with Andrzej Adamczyk as his deputy. Other members of NSZZ Solidarność are active in the ETUC.[24] Another important European institution for trade unions is the European Economic and Social Committee. In total, Polish trade unions have seven seats in the EESC[25]—two seats are allocated to NSZZ Solidarność, two seats to OPZZ and three seats to FZZ. Currently, the EESC has two members from NSZZ Solidarność: Andrzej Adamczyk and Marian Krzaklewski. NSZZ Solidarność also has a representative on the Committee of the European Social Fund[26]. Marian Krzaklewski is also the vice-president of the Eurocadres, and Robert Szewczyk participates in the plenary sessions of the TUAC. Joanna Szymonek is the vice-president of the Pan-European Regional Council

24 Danuta Wodat is a member of the Women's Committee, Sławomir Adamczyk is a member of the Coordination Committee for Collective Bargaining, and Ewa Kędzior is a member of the Committee for Economy and Employment. The ETUC also comprises working groups. Andrzej Matla is a member of the Working Group on Workers' Participation, Katarzyna Zimmer-Drabczyk is a member of the Working Group on Trade, Globalization, Development, and Decent Work, Agata Baranowska-Grycuk is a member of the Working Group on Social Security, and Andrzej Matla is a member of the Working Group on Campaigns. Moreover, Sławomir Adamczyk is a member of the task force of the Coordination Committee for Collective Bargaining, Krzyosztof Woźniwski is a member of the ETUC Network of Trade Union Legal Experts (NETLEX), and Joanna Unterschuetzis a member of the Network for Judicial Disputes.

25 Andrzej Adamczyk has been in the EESC since 2004 sitting on various sections—External Relations section (REX) and Section for the Single Market, Production and Consumption (INT). Katarzyna Bartkiewicz has been in the EESC from 2004 to 2010. Prior to that time, from 1997 to 1998, she was on the Joint Committee for Cooperation with the EESC, which became the Joint Consultative Committee in 2000. Many members of this committee became members of the EESC. Bartkiewicz sat on the Employment, Social Affairs and Citizenship (SOC), and Agriculture, Rural Development and Environment (NAT) sections. Marian Krzaklewski joined the EESC when Bartkiewicz left. He sat on the Transport, Energy, Infrastructure and Information Society (TEN), SOC, Economic and Monetary Union, and Economic and Social Cohesion (ECO), and Consultative Commission on Industrial Change (CCMI) sections. Krzaklewski is also an observer of the Labor Market and Sustainable Development. In the EESC, there are plenary sessions, which take place every month; there are eight sessions a year, and sections usually meet eight times a year. Opinions are prepared in analytical groups or in permanent committees, and later, they are reviewed in the sections and discussed in the plenary sessions.

26 That member is Agata Baranowska-Grycuk. Bogdan Olszewski is the member deputy on the advisory committee on Freedom of Movement for Workers of which Iwona Pawlaczyk is a member, and Andrzej Szczepaniak is the member deputy on the advisory committee on Safety and Health at Work. Bogdan Olszewski is a member on the Administrative Council of the European Foundation for the Improvement of Living and Working Conditions and Iwona Pawlaczyk is a deputy member on the administrative council of the European Agency for Safety and Health at Work.

(PERC). Andrzej Adamczyk is a member, and Jaonna Szymonek is a deputy member of the Executive Committee of PERC.

The leaders of NSZZ Solidarność and the regional sections as well as the secretariats often communicate with members of the European Parliament. This communication is their main source of information regarding EU affairs after Józef Niemiec and members of the EESC.[27] Not much communication and information flows between the European Works Councils and the National Commission of NSZZ Solidarność. Many union organisations in the EU have particular persons assigned to monitor particular organisations. This is not the case with NSZZ Solidarność. Some coordination occurs at the level of secretariats, but secretariats do not have many resources, and often, only one person (the leader) does all the work on his own. In the first accession years, Andrzej Matla from the International Department put together a database of all members of NSZZ Solidarność who sit on the European Works Councils. However, currently, this database is already outdated, and Andrzej Marla admits that it is not possible for him to track all the new members.[28]

13.6. Together with the ETUC for Social Europe

The Europeanization of NSZZ Solidarność cannot be analysed without a historical look at changes taking place in the European Union. At the time NSZZ Solidarność joined the ETUC, the social Europe was still strong. My interviewees, who have worked in NSZZ Solidarność since its beginning, like to recall the 1988 speech of Jacques Delors at the British Trade Union Congress. Delors promised that the European Commission would be a force to require governments to introduce pro-labour legislation.[29] NSZZ Solidarność was 'brought up' in the spirit of the social Europe of the late 1980s and early 1990s through its various exchanges with the ETUC and the WLC. There were common fears that the Central Eastern European unions would undermine what the western European unions had achieved in social and labour policies.[30] The background in the spirit of the social Europe may be one of the reasons why NSZZ Solidarność tended to ally with the ETUC when those achievements were threatened, sometimes against the Polish government. On many occasions, for example, in the form of a common protest action, NSZZ Solidarność joined the ETUC in its battle against the expansion of the neo-liberal order in the EU. The pro-business sympathies of the European

27 Lis, A.: Strategies of Interest Representation. Polish Trade Unions in EU Governance, in: Europe-Asia Studies, 2014 (vol. 66), no. 3, pp. 444–466.

28 Interview with trade union representative, Poland, official 3, A. M., 12 December 2012.

29 Ibid.

30 Crowley, S.: Explaining Labor Weakness in Post-Communist Europe. Historical Legacies and Comparative Perspective, in: East European Politics and Society, 2004 (vol. 10), no. 3, pp. 394–429. Meardi, G.: The Trojan Horse for the Americanization of Europe? Polish Industrial Relations towards the EU, in: European Journal of Industrial Relations, 2002 (vol. 8), no. 1, pp. 77–99.

Commission under President Barroso generally weakened the position of the unions in Brussels. My interviewees from NSZZ Solidarność understand this change and the importance of labour movement solidarity in the EU currently.[31]

The first occasion to express this solidarity arrived in the accession year, 2004, during the negotiations of the Services Directive on the Internal Market (the Bolkestein Directive). The most controversial proposition included in the Commission's proposal was the country of origin principle. The country of origin principle stated that, where an action or service is performed in one country but received in another, the applicable law is the law of the country where the action or service is performed. Many western governments, leftist NGOs and the ETUC opposed this principle and warned against strengthening the neo-liberal order of the EU. Western governments feared that cheap service providers from Central Eastern Europe would out-compete western companies and unions and perceived the proposal as encouraging social dumping in Europe. The Polish government and employers' organisations supported the country of origin principle as an opportunity for the domestic service sector to expand in the EU.

The debate on the Directive on Services is most likely one of the best examined cases of NSZZ Solidarność participating in the common European cause.[32] In this debate, NSZZ Solidarność actively supported the ETUC against Polish employers' organisations and the government. As a response to the ETUC's call to sign under the citizens' project, NSZZ Solidarność collected a huge number of signatures in Poland. Andrzej Adamczyk and Andrzej Matla from the International Department travelled all over Poland to persuade people to sign the petition. It was a huge campaign. It did not only regard public services but, as my interviewees explained, 'It was also a matter of preventing a great chaos in the labour market in Europe'[33]. NSZZ Solidarność feared that although working at the same construction site in the EU, Polish, Lithuanian and Spanish workers might work in different conditions. My interviewees stated firmly that NSZZ Solidarność opposed social dumping and entrenching inequalities among employees in the EU.[34]

The debate regarding the Charter of Fundamental Rights of the European Union is another example of a situation when NSZZ Solidarność stood with the ETUC but against the then-ruling government of Poland of the Law and Justice, and Self-Defence (Prawo i Sprawiedliwość (PiS) and Samoobrona). The Charter of Fundamental Rights was signed by the prime ministers during the summit in Nice in December 2000 and

31 Interview with trade union representative, Poland, official 3, A. M., 12 December 2012.

32 Gajewska, K.: Polish Trade Unions for the European Cause. The Case of the EU Directive on Services in the Internal Market, in: Kusznir, J. / Pleines, H. (eds): Trade Unions from Post-Socialist Member States in EU Governance Changing Europe. Book Series 5, Stuttgart: Ibidem, 2008, pp. 89–104. Gajewska, K.: The Emergence of a European Protest Movement?, in: European Journal of Industrial Relations, 2008 (vol. 14), no. 1, pp. 104–121.

33 Interview with trade union representative, Poland, official 3, A. M., 12 December 2012.

34 Ibid.

later, with some amendments, it was signed again during the Lisbon summit in 2007. The disagreement between NSZZ Solidarność and the government was not easy to predict because the two cooperated well representing a conservative option of the Polish political scene. To support the charter, the ETUC organised a large information campaign, which also involved NSZZ Solidarność. Although it did not manage to persuade the government to sign the charter, NSZZ Solidarność supported it with the ETUC.

> We consider it our failure that logical arguments did not manage to persuade the government, especially given that the union cooperated tightly with the government at that time and it seemed to us that they should have understood such basic things like labour rights[35].

I have selected these two cases because they represent well how NSZZ Solidarność oriented their political choices regarding the general problems of European labour after the accession. NSZZ Solidarność usually supported the position of the ETUC, with general goals to preserve high labour standards and against social dumping. This support has not always been the case regarding sectorial interests. In the next section, I present the debate regarding the climate change and energy package where the Mining and Energy Secretariat from NSZZ Solidarność had a different position than the ETUC regarding the proposed directives. The Mining Secretariat managed to influence the position of NSZZ Solidarność as a whole, which led to internal debates within the ETUC where the Polish unions opposed the leaders and experts from the ETUC. Because the European Union is still pushing its climate action agenda, a fracture between NSZZ Solidarność and the ETUC concerning EU climate policies has not yet been healed.

13.7. The EU Climate Policies

During the debate regarding the EU climate change and energy package, the initial support given by NSZZ Solidarność for the ETUC's favourable position regarding the European Commission's proposals became oppositional. The opposition did not originate from the National Commission in Gdańsk but from the Secretariat for the Energy and Mine Workers, SGiE, in Katowice. The president of the SGiE supported the position of the Polish government and industries. However, it is difficult to say that the disagreement was the Polish unions' opposition concerning the ETUC's general position. In interactions with colleagues from the European Industry Federations, the initial fight for 'Polish jobs' gradually changed to a fight for 'European jobs'. Interest representation in the EU, as well as the need for coalition building and expertise, made

35 Ibid.

it necessary for Polish unions to cooperate with the EMCEF and redefine the 'Polish economic interest' as a 'European economic interest'.[36]

In March 2008, ETUC supported the European Commission's proposal regarding the climate change and energy package with its 20-20-20 target by 2020.[37] The ETUC published an official position paper, 'The ETUC's position on the Climate change and energy package',[38] which was adopted by the Executive Committee of the ETUC at its meeting on 4 March 2008 in Brussels. The text of the ETUC's position was debated in the course of several meetings of the ETUC's Working Group on Sustainable Development. As the leader of the Working Group said, there has always been only a small group of representatives—approximately 15 people at each meeting.[39] Poland was represented by one person from NSZZ Solidarność.

'The ETUC's position on the Climate change and energy package' was adopted by the Executive Committee of the ETUC at its meeting on 4 March 2008 in Brussels. The position paper was accepted and signed by all national affiliates of the ETUC, including three Polish national union organisations: FZZ, OPZZ and NSZZ Solidarność. At this meeting, NSZZ Solidarność was represented by the head of the International Department from the National Commission in Gdańsk who said that the ETUC's position paper 'had all it needed'[40] and agreed with the ETUC's strong support for European climate policies.

Meanwhile, the head of the International Department said he was not optimistic regarding the social consequences of the Commission's 2008 legislative proposals. Achieving long-term low carbon growth could come at a high cost to the short-term competitiveness of European economies. The staggering European economy could be easily overtaken by China and India, which did not burden their industries with costly emission reductions. 'Carbon leakage', a massive flow of industrial production, from Europe to Asia would result in more industrial production in places where labour rights were not respected. Even if some industries stayed in Europe, they could be forced to cut salaries to compensate for the cost of emission reductions to stay globally competitive. Threats of higher electricity prices and energy poverty in Europe

36 Lis, A.: Strategies of Interest Representation. Polish Trade Unions in EU Governance, in: Europe-Asia Studies, 2014 (vol. 66), no. 3, pp. 444–466.

37 20% of emission reductions compared with 1990, 20% of renewable energy production and 20% increase in energy efficiency by 2020.

38 European Trade Union Confederation (ETUC): ETUC's position on the Climate change and energy package. Position adopted by the Executive Committee of the ETUC at its meeting of 4 March in Brussels EC.179, in: etuc.org, http://www.etuc.org/IMG/pdf/Paquet_ETUCposition_EN4-5-03-08.pdf, accessed 12 January 2014.

39 Interview with trade union representative from ETUC, Belgium, S. D., 2 July 2009.

40 Interview with the head of the International Department, Poland, A. A., 7 November 2008.

were also discussed by my interviewee. As he noted, apart from social tariffs, a real and rapid transformation of European electricity production systems was necessary.[41]

However, not all members of the ETUC and not all members of NSZZ Solidarność shared the ETUC's position. Despite an early and unanimous (no veto vote) adoption of the ETUC by its Executive Committee, some unions did not approve of the way the ETUC supported the Commission's proposal. The main actors reinvigorating this debate were the European Metalworkers' Federation (EMF), the EMCEF, German unions representing mining, chemical and energy workers (e.g., Industriegewerkschaft Bergbau, Chemie, Energie (IG BCE)), and Polish unions representing miners and energy workers (SGiE NSZZ Solidarność and Związku Zawodowego Górników w Polsce (ZZG w Polsce)). Unions representing workers in European industries feared 'carbon leakage', which would also mean 'employment leakage' from 'cleaner' Europe to 'dirty' regions. Unions representing workers from power and mining sectors feared unemployment because of a gradual phase-out of coal from electricity generation in Europe and the closing of coal-fired power plants.[42]

Polish unions' actions regarding the proposed package of climate policies came only in the second half of 2008, at least four months after the ETUC's March vote on the position paper. When the SGiE identified potential threats to the Polish economy and Polish workers, it initiated actions on two levels—the European and national levels. Between June and July 2008, the SGiE turned to the ETUC to warn it regarding the potential damaging impact of the proposed legislative package on the Polish economy and asked for a revision of the ETUC's position concerning the package. The SGiE demanded that various levels of economic development and specificities of countries' energy mixes be considered. The SGiE argued that Poland, depending extensively on coal, would have to pay the highest price for a transition to a low carbon economy. Meanwhile, the SGiE issued a common position[43] regarding the climate change and energy package with representatives of the coal sector and the government within the Tripartite Commission for the Mine Workers Social Security in Poland.[44]

Because the ETUC refused to revise its position concerning the package according to SGiE's proposal, the president of SGiE sought support for his demands in the European industry federations. The president of SGiE turned to the EMCEF of which the SGiE and ZZG w Polsce are members.[45] The EMCEF had been working on the climate

41 Interview with the head of the International Department, Poland, A. A., 7 November 2008.

42 Interview with SGiE representative, Poland, K. G., 22 October 2008. Interview with EMCEF representative, Belgium, P. K., 24 June 2009. Interview with EMCEF representative, Belgium, R. R., 12 August 2009. Interview with IG BCE representative, Germany, M. W., 4 August 2009.

43 The Tripartite Commission for the Mine Workers Social Security: Position Regarding a Proposal of the European Commission known as the Climate and Energy Package, Katowice, 30 July 2008. Documents were provided to the author by Solidarity representatives.

44 Interview with SGiE representative, Poland, K. G., 22 October 2008.

45 Ibid.

change and energy package and also had asked the ETUC to revise its position.[46] In the course of mobilising allies and expanding alternative positions to the ETUC, what was primarily perceived as a 'national interest' had to be reframed into a European matter and placed in a wider European context of economic and workers' concerns.

On 2 September a meeting was held in Katowice where the secretary general of the EMCEF, Reinhard Reibsch, participated in the Coordination Council of the EMCEF Poland. The coordination council proposed a motion to summon the Executive Committee of the EMCEF regarding the climate change and energy package. On 6 and 7 September, Kazimierz Grajcarek participated in three meetings in Brussels. Two of these meetings were attended by representatives of a lobbying project, the Green Effort Group, created in July 2008 to represent interests of the Polish power and industrial sectors in negotiations regarding the climate change and energy package.[47]

On 8 and 9 September, Grajcarek participated in a conference on the Polish position in negotiations concerning the climate change and energy package organised by Buzek. Grajcarek also met with Jan Tombiński, the ambassador of Poland, the permanent representative of the European Union, Mieczysław Janowski, Polish member of European Parliament, Marian Krzaklewski, EESC, and Maciej Nowicki, Ministry of Environment, and Krzysztof Żmijewski, the initiator and the main lobbyists of the Green Effort Group. In this way, Grajcarek and NSZZ Solidarność became a part of a larger Polish lobbying project in 2008. On 16 September, with Buzek's assistance, Grajcarek also met with Vladimir Spidla, the commissioner for Employment, Social Affairs and Equal Chances, to discuss the impact on employment of the proposed legislation.[48]

A crucial visit to Brussels occurred at the end of September. This visit was preceded by letters sent to Polish members of European Parliament with a request for support of the workers' protest against the European Commission's proposal. Letters were also sent to the commissioners, Stavros Dimas, the commissioner for Environment, and Andris Pielbalgs, the commissioner for Energy, with a request to support amendments to the climate change and energy package proposed by the Polish government. A protest of Polish mine and chemical workers occurred before the European Commission on 25 September (260 participants). The same day, a meeting occurred with Stavros Dimas, the commissioner for the Environment, and Günter Verheugen, the commissioner for Industry and Enterprise. This meeting was also attended by Buzek. During this meeting, Günter Verheugen expressed his satisfaction with the conversation and

46 Interview with EMCEF representative, Belgium, P. K., 24 June 2009. Interview with EMCEF representative, Belgium, R. R. 12 August 2009. Interview with IG BCE representative, Germany, M. W., 4 August 2009.

47 Green Effort Group: Green Effort Group Report 2008, in: proinwestycje.pl, http://www.proinwestycje.pl/index.php?option.com_content&view.article&id.181&Itemid.100152&lang.pl, accessed 10 January 2014.

48 Ibid.

shared a similar uneasiness regarding the potential threats to the European economy posed by the proposed package. He hoped that workers' protests would strengthen his position with the Commission in this debate.[49]

In early October, two positions regarding the climate change and energy package were issued. The first position was written in Katowice by the Coordination Council EMCEF attended by Erik Macak, the secretary of the EMCEF and Józef Niemiec, the confederal secretary of the ETUC as well as the following representatives of the EMCEF Coordination Council Poland: Kazimierz Grajcarek (SGiE), Krzysztof Stefanek (Porozumienie Zwiazków Zawodowych KADRA), Andrzej Chwiluk (ZZG w Polsce), and Józef Woźny (FZZ Przemysłu Chemicznego). Three days later, the National Congress of Solidarność occurred in Wadowice. A decision was made to assign Grajcarek as a representative of NSZZ Solidarność in the climate package debate. Another position concerning the climate change and energy package was adopted.[50]

The two positions, one adopted at the Coordination Council of the EMCEF in Katowice and the other adopted three days later at the National Congress of NSZZ Solidarność in Wadowice, reveal a shift in the framing of workers' concerns regarding the proposed climate change and energy package.[51] Workers' arguments are structured as national or European interests depending on which arena they address—the European or the national arena. Similar to Polish industries and government officials, the definition of the situation and union interests, and the development of potential solutions to future challenges have been formed within heterogeneous networks of communication. The president of SGiE, the most active unionist participating in the debate on the Emission Trading System (ETS) in 2008, admitted that he was better able to articulate potential problems stemming from the Commission's proposal after a conversation with the leader of the Green Effort Group. Talking to Buzek also helped. With time, a closer cooperation with the EMCEF and a common coordination of positions and protest actions made it possible for the president of SGiE to better understand various consequences of the ETS for Polish and European employees in the mining, industrial and power sectors.[52]

On 13 November, SGiE with the EMCEF Coordination Office Poland, organised an international conference in Katowice to prepare the unions for a bigger protest at the beginning of December 2008 before the final vote in the European Parliament on the ETS Directive. This conference was attended by 30 people, most of whom were from the

49 SGiE: Informacje. „Pikieta w Brukseli" [Information. Picket in Brussels], in: sgie.pl, 26 September 2008, http://www.sgie.pl/aktualnosci,5, 99.html, accessed 28 September 2008.

50 Coordination Council EMCEF: Position of the Coordination Office of EMCEF-Poland about the Climate and Energy Package. 7 October 2008, Katowice (document provided to the author by SGiE), 2008.

51 The National Congress of NSZZ Solidarność: Position 10 of the XXII National Congress of Solidarność concerning the Climate Change and Energy Package, Wadowice, October 2008 (document provided to the author by NSZZ Solidarność), 2008.

52 Interview with SGiE representative, Poland, K. G., 22 October 2008.

Polish mine and energy sector unions.[53] In addition to these 12 representatives of the Polish unions, the following ten representatives from other national and European unions arrived: Anabella Rosemberg from the international trade union federation, the ITUC / TUAC; Reiner Koch from the German union Vereinte Dienstleistungsgewerkschaft (Ver.di); Peter Kerckhofs from the sectoral umbrella organisation, the EMCEF; Sophie Dupressoir from the European union federation, the ETUC; Michael Wolters from the German IG BCE; Matteo Auriemma from the Italian Confederazione Italiana Sindacati Lavoratori (CISL), Ioan Feurdean and Emil Gheorghe from the Romaniam Federatia Nationala Mine Energie (FNME); and Pencho Tokmakchiev and Alexandra Kanev from the Bulgarian Federatsiyata na nezavisimite sindikati na minyorite (FNSM). The meeting was also attended by Bernard Błaszczyk, an official in the Polish Ministry for Environment, Marina Coey, the administrator of the lobbying project the Green Effort Group and Sanjeev Kumar from the World Wide Fund For Nature European Policy Office (WWF EPO).[54]

The meeting in Katowice was the largest event organised by the SGiE and the EMCEF Coordination Office in Poland during negotiations of the EU climate change and energy package. Because the final vote in the European Parliament was postponed till mid-December after the European Council, the protest action lost its purpose and was cancelled. However, 13 November showed the SGiE's capacity to mobilise actors and bring them together. Tensions and heated debates, especially between Polish unions, with the EMCEF on one side, and the ETUC, the ITUC / TUAC and the World Wide Fund For Nature (WWF) on the other side, showed to the Polish unions that they were not fighting their own battle but a European battle. My interviewee from the EMCEF commented that:

> For us, it is not a matter of this country or another one. For us, it was more a European thing where we should work together with employers and with government actors and work together on a European basis.[55]

Despite the tensions, the meeting in Katowice concluded in a common statement signed by all participants. Again, an appeal was made to the European Commission to launch negotiations with social partners regarding the climate change and energy package. Participants of the meeting in Katowice stated that:

> The climate change and energy package should be introduced. However, introducing the package in its current state may result in a shutdown of hundreds of thousands of workplaces in the EU, and at the same time, the CO2 emitting industry and investments connected to it might move outside of the EU. These possible consequences will shatter the goals of the climate change and energy package.[56]

53 Green Effort Group: Green Effort Group Report 2008, in: proinwestycje.pl, http://www.proinwestycje.pl/index.php?option.com_content&view.article&id.181&Itemid.100152&lang.pl, accessed 10 January 2014.

54 Ibid.

55 Interview with trade union representative, Belgium, P. K., 24 June 2009.

56 Coordination Office of EMCEF Poland: Appeal to the European Commission to Launch Negotiations with the Social Partners about the Climate and Energy Package, 13 November 2008.

The meeting participants also drew attention to the 'threat of making the EU dependent on the carriers of energy coming from outside of the EU.'[57] This dependency would substantially reduce the EU's energy security. The meeting participants asked the European Commission for another round of negotiations with social partners. Meanwhile, the attendees participated in these negotiations and presented their own proposals. The problem identified by the SGiE in the middle of 2008 was framed as not only a national but also a European problem. Although Poland's heavy dependence on coal for power generation provided the first opportunity to calculate costs and benefits of the proposed ETS Directive, the competitiveness of industrial sectors were similarly important. An argument referring to future losses in the mining sector could mobilise support from a limited number of countries, which also relied on coal to a large extent (such as the Czech Republic or Germany). However, an argument concerning the loss of competitiveness in industrial sectors because of their internationalisation and dependence on global competition, had a strong mobilising effect.

13.8. Conclusion

As the analysis has shown, the presence of NSZZ Solidarność in Europe involves a much longer and more diverse experience than its activities after Poland's EU accession. According to the collected material, the internal organisation of NSZZ Solidarność reflects its early experience as a member of the WCL in the 1980s rather than its later experience as a member of the ETUC in the 1990s. Influenced by the WCL, NSZZ Solidarność organised its structure in secretariats. At the end of the 1990s, the EU accession caused some organisational changes, such as the establishment of the Office for the Coordinator for the European Integration and the Commission for the EU Accession. Currently, the International Department does not solely address EU affairs, but it coordinates international relations of the union in general.

Europeanization, according to Mrozowicki, is controversial for NSZZ Solidarność, which perceives it as stigmatising. NSZZ Solidarność is currently convinced that it was born as a part of a European cultural and political legacy, and that it never ceased to be part of Europe.[58] However, two aspects of Europeanization may be related to the European accession, which can be distinguished based on the conducted case study. The first aspect is the policy learning produced in NSZZ Solidarność through its participation in various EU bodies, structures and debates. Learning is a 'technical [process that we could call] knowledge acquisition.'[59] However, learning is also a political process when NSZZ Solidarność is trying to understand the politics of policy-making and to take the correct position on particular issues. According to my interviewees,

57 Ibid.
58 Interview with trade union expert Adam Mrozowicki, Poland, A. M., 23 June 2013.
59 Interview with trade union experts Magdalena Bernaciak, Belgium, M. B., 12 June 2013.

the NSZZ Solidarność officials and experts, NSZZ Solidarność is often not capable of digesting all policy issues on its own.[60] In these situations, it tends to resort to the positions established by the ETUC, sometimes by discussing controversial issues with their men in Brussels, Józef Niemiec and Jerzy Buzek.

The other aspect of Europeanization, which might be called a soft one, refers to the new identity gained by NSZZ Solidarność with its accession to the ETUC.[61] All my interviewees stated that membership in the ETUC is of great importance to NSZZ Solidarność. My interviewees feel that NSZZ Solidarność is a part of the ETUC. According to Bernaciak, participation in the European Works Councils also taught Polish unionists to negotiate problems instead of generating conflicts and sharp confrontations.[62] In bilateral relations and European Works Councils, Polish unionists became more professional, which is an important cultural change within NSZZ Solidarność.

However, this identification with the ETUC is not even across the NSZZ Solidarność organisational structure. The climate change and energy package debate demonstrated that industry secretariats, such as the Secretariat for Energy and Mine Workers, may have less enthusiasm for the position of the ETUC and may be more willing to align with the European Industry Federations. This disparity is not an argument against Europeanization of the industry secretariats of NSZZ Solidarność. However, this inconsistency indicates a diversity of Europeanization processes that may follow sectorial interests. The ETUC, with its mission to represent European labour, may not always be able to unite all the unions under its umbrella.

Domestically, the EU accession had another consequence. According to Mrozowicki, one of the major consequences of the Polish EU accession for NSZZ Solidarność, as well as for the other two unions' federations, has been a growing realisation of the need for cooperation among Polish unions.[63] Representation of the Polish labour interests at the EU level is impossible without an agreement and cooperation among the three unions—NSZZ Solidarność, OPZZ and FZZ. The Polish unions realised that they are stronger in the EU together. This cooperation does not only concern common policy and ideological positions but also affects organisational issues. The three national union organisations communicate and cooperate to share the posts available to Polish unions in the European organisations, e.g., the allocation of functions in the negotiation committees to members of particular unions. One of these agreements occurred in fall 2012.

60 Interview with trade union representative, Poland, official 2, K. B., 12 December 2012. Interview with trade union expert Magdalena Bernaciak, Belgium, M. B., 12 June 2013. Interview with trade union expert Adam Mrozowicki, Poland, A. M., 23 June 2013.

61 Interview with trade union expert Magdalena Bernaciak, Belgium, M. B., 12 June 2013.

62 Ibid.

63 Interview with trade union expert Adam Mrozowicki, Poland, A. M., 23 June 2013.

Leyla Safta-Zecheria

14. European Governance and the Romanian Cartel Alfa Trade Union Confederation

14.1. Introduction

The present case study analyses the integration of the Romanian Trade Union Confederation Cartel Alfa into European governance structures by examining the way in which this cooperation occurs and is perceived by trade union leaders on the confederation level as well as by representatives of the member federations. The chapter examines which representatives participate in European Union affairs, as well as the reasons why others do not participate, and it also examines the way in which European integration has affected different levels of workers' representation brought together by the Cartel Alfa confederation. The case of energy policy is explored at length, as it gives a good example of how European policy can enter the national political discourse and give rise to a consistent position that cuts through different levels of representation within the trade union confederation (TUC) explored here. The paper puts forward evidence that while the structures of the confederation seem to have adapted to the new institutional context, the same cannot be said about most federations. Nevertheless, certain issues, such as energy policy issues, have acquired salience in the national political discourse and have become part of the agendas of both branch federations and the confederation. This is due to the very high perceived negative effects that the way in which energy policy was implemented in Romania had on workers' interests.

14.2. Description of Sources

The present case study draws on structured interviews with leaders of the trade union confederation and trade union federation (TUF) (ten interviews) as well as a member of the professional staff of the confederation (one further interview). A further semi-structured interview with one of the confederation's vice presidents, as well as a significant number of informal conversations with federation leaders, were also conducted.[1] This part of the research was conducted in Bucharest, at the headquarters of the federations and Cartel Alfa confederation in the period between March and June 2013.

1 The Information obtained during the informal conversations only served as background information for the study and was used as a starting point for desktop research. A small amount of very relevant information from these conversations was also included without mentioning the respondents' identity.

Furthermore, desktop research regarding the professional backgrounds of the confederations' leadership, the historical development of the confederation and federations and the involvement on a European level was carried out. Expert reports and academic literature were included in this analysis, as was information available on the websites of the confederation, the federations, and the European and international level federations. Finally, media reports covering Cartel Alfa's advocacy within the field of energy policy were also analysed.

14.3. Collective Bargaining in Romania

The Romanian trade union landscape is fragmented by five major confederations active on the national level. Of these, Cartel Alfa and Confederaţia Naţională a Sindicatelor Libere din Romania—Frăţia (CNSLR Frăţia) are the two largest. Confederations act as umbrella organisations for federations, which in turn act as umbrella organisations for unit / basis trade unions.

Previous to the recent legislative modifications collective bargaining in Romania took place on three-levels: national, branch and company levels. The unique national agreement set minimal standards in terms of minimal rights and obligations applicable to all employees in Romania, which set a framework for branch and company-level negotiations. Moreover, this agreement was applicable to all employees, irrespective of whether branch or company-level agreements had been concluded.[2]

The unique national agreement was abolished in 2010 as a result of the legislative modifications. Furthermore, the branch level was replaced by sector-level agreements, with sectors being redefined in the process, leading to a significant relapse in collective negotiations at this level.[3] At the same time, stricter criteria for obtaining representativeness at company, sector and national level were also introduced in 2010.[4]

These changes imposed significant difficulties on the fragmented Romanian trade union (TU) movement and on the federations affiliated with Cartel Alfa, as the bodies had to reorganise themselves to maintain or re-obtain representativeness and needed to allocate further resources to this process.

2 Clauwert, S. / Schönman, I: The crisis and national labour law reforms. A mapping exercise. Country report. Romania, in: ETUI, January 2013, http://www.etui.org/Publications2/Working-Papers/The-crisis-and-national-labour-law-reforms-a-mapping-exercise, accessed 18 September 2014.

3 Chivu, Luminita / Ciutacu, Constantin / Dumitriu, Raluca / Ţiclea, Tiberiu: The impact of Legislative Reforms on Industrial Relations in Romania, Decent Work Technical Support Team and Country Office for Central and Eastern Europe, International Labour Organisation, 2013.

4 Stoiciu, Victoria: Austerity and structural reforms in Romania. Severe measures, questionable economic results and negative social consequences, in: Friedrich-Ebert-Stiftung, International Policy Analysis, 2012, August, http://library.fes.de/pdf-files/id-moe/09310.pdf, accessed 2 February 2014.

14.4. Cartel Alfa. An Overview

Cartel Alfa is one of the five national-level TU confederations in Romania. According to the Ministry of Labour Cartel Alfa has 301,785 members[5] and is one of the two largest organisations. As opposed to CNSLR Frăţia, Cartel Alfa is not seen as a structure that was built on the infrastructure of the previous trade union confederation, as the Uniunea Generală a Sindicatelor din România (UGSR) and its leadership entered the realm of high-level trade union politics only after 1989. It constituted itself to represent workers in heavy industry (such as mining, steel, heavy and electrical equipment manufacturing, etc.) and had a strong anti-communist and anti-Frontul Salvarii Nationale (FSN)[6] attitude at the time that it emerged.[7]

Presently, the confederation represents members from both the private and public sectors and includes forty-five professional federations, including the raw materials industry, agriculture, consumer goods production, culture and education, as well as the transportation and service industries.[8]

Cartel Alfa was established in 1990, and Bogdan Hossu, the current president, has been the head of the TUC without any interruptions since 1992.[9] Most of the five members in the political leadership body of Cartel Alfa[10] have a background in the metals industry and were part of the leadership structure of branch federations before being elected into the trade union leadership.[11]

Cartel Alfa was the first Romanian TUC to become affiliated with the European Trade Union Confederation (ETUC) in 1995. It has also been affiliated with the World

5 Bărbuceanu, Ştefania: Annual Review 2012 on Labour Relations and Social Dialogue in South East Europe. Romania, in: Friedrich-Ebert-Stiftung, Labour Relations and Social Dialogue in South East Europe, 2013, January, http://library.fes.de/pdf-files/bueros/belgrad/09646.pdf, accessed 31 January 2014. The number of 1 million members, had been declared by Cartel Alfa (see the same report). The difference in numbers has also been interpreted as a result of the decrease in membership after the recent legislative modifications, see Chivu, Luminita / Ciutacu, Constantin / Dumitriu, Raluca / Ţiclea, Tiberiu: The impact of Legislative Reforms on Industrial Relations in Romania, Decent Work Technical Support Team and Country Office for Central and Eastern Europe, International Labour Organisation, 2013, here p. 13.

6 Frontul Salvarii Nationale, National Salvation Front, the front constituted directly after the events of December 1989 to 'manage' the transition to democracy. Later, it became a party under the leadership of Ion Iliescu.

7 Keil, Thomas J. / Keil, Jacqueline M.: The State and Labor Conflict in Post-revolutionary Romania, in: Radical History Review, 2002 (vol. 82), winter, pp. 9–36, here p. 16.

8 Cartel Alfa: Members. Information regarding members on Cartel Alfa, in: cartel-alfa.ro, http://www.cartel-alfa.ro/default.asp?nod=2, accessed 23 December 2013.

9 Cartel Alfa: Curriculum Vitae Bogdan Hossu, in: cartel-alfa.ro, http://www.cartel-alfa.ro/default.asp?nod=2, accessed 23 December 2013.

10 The staff of Cartel Alfa is composed of the political leadership (5 members) as well as regular employees organised according to resorts of responsibility, such as the department of international relations, etc.

11 The Curriculum Vitae of most of the trade union leadership are available here: http://www.cartel-alfa.ro/default.asp?nod=8, accessed 01 February 2014.

Confederation of Labour (WCL) since 1991, and it became part of International Trade Union Confederation (ITUC) in 2006. Its orientation is geared towards the promotion of Christian and Democratic values,[12] as is apparent from the initial international affiliation.

As an umbrella organisation of federations, Cartel Alfa's political leadership is elected by the Confederation's Congress, which meets every four years and consists of trade union members. The Congress sets out the general lines of policy. The second most important institutional body is the General Council, which consists of representatives of the member federations and those of the regional branch organisations.[13] This body meets twice per year and formulates the concrete targets for action. The executive bureau and the general secretariat operate on a daily basis by applying the decisions made by the two representative bodies,[14] the Congress and the Council. For punctual decisions that do not suffer delay, the Confederative Committee, made up of the presidents of federations, can make important decisions that do not exceed the competences of the Council.[15]

14.4.1. Trade Union Federations in the Metals Industry

Two TU federations from the metals industry have been included in this case study, Federația Națională Sindicală Solidaritatea Metal (FNS Solidaritatea Metal) and Federația Sindicală a Siderurgiștilor METAROM (FSS METAROM). According to a Friedrich-Ebert-Stiftung (FES) report from 2012, FNS Solidaritatea Metal had 7,693 members, and FSS METAROM was the larger of the two Cartel Alfa metals federations with 13,108 members.[16] FSS METAROM was constituted in 2006 through the merger of two previous

---

12 Romanian confederations: Presentation of Cartel Alfa, in: confederatii.ro, http://www.confederatii.ro/article/251/C-N-S-C-A-Confederatia-Nationala-Sindicala-Cartel-Alfa, accessed 28 February 2014. Trif, Aurora: Overview of Industrial relations in Romania, in: SEER South East Europe Review for Labour and Social Affairs, 2004, no. 2, pp 43–64, here p. 54.

13 Regional branch organisations are regional inter-professional trade unions. The total number of which is 42. See http://www.cartel-alfa.ro/default.asp?nod=2, accessed 18 September 2014.

14 The interviews carried out within the present project were conducted with people that operate on a daily basis as professional staff or as political representatives in the permanent bureau of the confederation.

15 Interviews with trade union representatives, Romania, Gn01, 29 March 2013 and Gn33, 18 June 2013.

16 Bărbuceanu, Ştefania: Annual Review 2012 on Labour Relations and Social Dialogue in South East Europe. Romanian, in: Friedrich Ebert Stiftung, Labour Relations and Social Dialogue in South East Europe, January 2013, http://library.fes.de/pdf-files/bueros/belgrad/09646.pdf, accessed 31 January 2014.

metal federations Federaţia Natională Sindicală METAROM and Federaţia Sindicală a Siderurgiştilor,[17] and it is the largest metals federation in Romania.[18]

FNS Solidaritatea Metal was constituted in 1990 under the name Federaţia Sindicatelor Libere din Electrotehnică, Electronică si Informatică and was founded under the leadership of Bogdan Hossu. The federation remained under the leadership of Bogdan Hossu until 2002; in the meantime, it changed its name to Federatia Naţională Sindicală din Electrotehnică, Electronică, Mecanică, Maşini Unelte şi Apărare SOLIDARITATEA 90. In 2002, Gheorghe Sora and Doru Puiu, the current president and vice-president, respectively, were first elected to these positions. In 2004, the federation merged with the U Metal federation, and the present name, FSN Solidaritatea Metal, was first used.[19]

Both trade union federations are members of IndustriALL.

14.4.2. Trade Union Federations in the Mining Industry

The only active federation that exclusively specialises in mining is a member federation of Cartel Alfa, Federaţia Naţională Mine Energie. With 19,613 members,[20] it is a relatively strong federation in terms of numbers. It was established in Petroşani, Valea Jiului in 1990.[21] According to the current secretary general of the TUF, it constituted itself to counter the pro-Russian politics of then-president Ion Iliescu and his supporters,[22] envisioning an orientation towards Europe. It is also a member of IndustriALL.

14.4.3. The Trade Union Federation in the Banking Sector

The only TUF in the banking sector affiliated on an international level to (Union Network International Europa (UNI Europa)), Federaţia Sindicatelor din Bănci şi Asigurări (FSAB),

17 FSS Metarom: Official website of FSS Metarom, in: fss-metarom.ro, http://www.fss-metarom.ro/index.php?meniu=14&value=0, accessed 31 January 2014.

18 Ibid., as well as Bărbuceanu, Ştefania: Annual Review 2012 on Labour Relations and Social Dialogue in South East Europe. Romanian, in: Friedrich Ebert Stiftung, Labour Relations and Social Dialogue in South East Europe, January 2013, http://library.fes.de/pdf-files/bueros/bel grad/09646.pdf, accessed 31 January 2014 (the report does not include the membership numbers for FSLI Metal).

19 FSN Solidaritatea Metal: History of the federation, in: fnssm.ro, http://www.fnssm.ro/istoric, accessed 31 January 2014.

20 Bărbuceanu, Ştefania: Annual Review 2012 on Labour Relations and Social Dialogue in South East Europe. Romanian, in: Friedrich Ebert Stiftung, Labour Relations and Social Dialogue in South East Europe, January 2013, http://library.fes.de/pdf-files/bueros/belgrad/09646.pdf, accessed 31 January 2014.

21 FNME: FNME official website, in: fnme.ro, http://www.fnme.ro/, accessed 31 January 2014.

22 Another mining trade union in Valea Jiului chose to remain independent of any confederative structures, see for example Keil, Thomas J. / Keil, Jacqueline M.: The State and Labor Conflict in Post-revolutionary Romania, in: Radical History Review, 2002 (vol. 82), winter, pp. 9–36, here p. 16.

is a member of Cartel Alfa.[23] FSAB was established in 2002 by trade unions from three banks to represent the interests of this sector on the national level. According to data provided on the FSAB website, the TUF represents 16,000 members of 14 trade unions.[24]

14.4.4. The Trade Union Federation in the Commerce Sector

Federaţia Sindicatelor din Comerţ (FSC) is the most significant commerce federation in Romania.[25] It was established in 1990 and presently has 12,000 members in 18 trade unions.[26] Recently, it terminated its affiliation with CNSLR Frăţia and became affiliated with Cartel Alfa. On a European level, FSC is also a member of UNI Europa.

14.5. Channels of Influence on European Governance Processes

Influence on European, national or company decision-making is delegated to one of the levels that exist in the Romanian trade union organisation structure. Whereas bodies at the highest level, that is, confederations, can nominate representatives in the European Economic and Social Committee (EESC) and attend ETUC meetings, federation-level bodies do not engage with European representation except under exceptional circumstances. The federation level elects the confederation representatives, so the influence is exercised indirectly; at the same time, the federation level is affiliated directly to sectorial representative bodies, UNI Europa and IndustriALL. The lowest level of interest aggregation, that of basis trade unions, is also involved in European processes in the broader sense through participation in European Works Councils. Despite this division of tasks, there are salient policy issues that cut across all of these levels and bodies and unite different 'levels' of representation and governance. One example of such a case is EU energy policy, which will be presented towards the end of this chapter.

23 When the research for this case study was conducted, two federations that were included in this research were planning a merger, as their leadership envisioned a later affiliation with European structures. These TUFs are based in individual banks; one of them is based in Casa de Economii şi Consemnaţiuni (CEC) Bank and the other in Banca Comercială Română (BCR). The first is affiliated with the TUC Blocul Naţional Sindical (BNS), and the second is affiliated with Confederaţia Sindicatelor Democratice din România (CSDR).

24 Federatia Sindicatelor din Asigurari si Banci (FSAB): FSAB official website, in: fsab.ro, http://www.fsab.ro/prezentare, accessed 31 January 2014.

25 Confederdaraţia Naţională a Sindicatelor din Cooperaţia de Consum (CONSINCOP) a federation specialized in the field of commerce cooperation also exists, but it is significantly less active.

26 Federatia Sindicatelor din Comert (FSC): FSC official website, in: fscomert.ro, http://www.fscomert.ro/pages/despre-noi-43, accessed 31 January 2014.

14.6. Resources and European Participation on the Confederation Level

Cartel Alfa is a member of ETUC, which it joined in 1995[27] as the first Romanian TUC. According to a Cartel Alfa leader, this was because only Cartel Alfa was considered prepared for membership at that point in time, and the other Romanian confederations joined two to three years later.[28]

According to the leadership of Cartel Alfa, there was little if any preparation for Romania's accession on the side of the confederation. One leader mentioned an information caravan organised by all Romanian TUCs that was aimed at disseminating information about European accession to trade union members. According to a vice president, the process of European integration was constructed of a process of learning by doing, as Cartel Alfa was involved in ETUC activities long before EU accession occurred. The major problem faced by the confederation at the time prior to EU accession was that of the changing pattern of collective negotiations through the advent of multinationals.[29] This problem persists, and it has determined an organisational transformation based on the creation of regional TU structures that are independent of the employers.[30]

The presence and influence of the confederation on the European level are mainly exercised through ETUC, another channel of tripartite consultative committees at the European Commission level[31] and the European Economic and Social Committee[32].

The possibility of opening a Brussels-based office with one or two employees who cater to the activity regarding ETUC, as well as further lobbying activities within the contact structures established by ETUC with the European Socialist Group, was abandoned due to a lack of (financial) resources.[33]

27 Cartel Alfa: Cartel Alfa official website, in: cartel-alfa.ro, http://www.cartel-alfa.ro/default.asp?nod=11, accessed 31 January 2014.

28 Confederatia Sindicala Nationala (CSN) Meridian is the only Romanian TUC that is not currently a member of ETUC.

29 These replaced the state as central employer and central negotiation partner for the trade unions; for information on the role of the state in collective negotiations during the 1990s in Romania, see Trif, Aurora: Overview of Industrial relations in Romania, in: SEER South-East Europe Review for Labour and Social Affairs, 2004, No 2, pp. 43–64, here p. 46.

30 Interview with one of Cartel Alfa's vice presidents, Romania, Gn01, June 2013.

31 However in these bodies, only a representative of the Romanian TU movement (including the other three confederations) is named to participate on a specific issue (Interview with Cartel Alfa's vice president, Romania, Ro Gn 01, June 2013.). Therefore this channel can be considered less relevant for the representation of the interests of the confederation and will not be treated in the present chapter. For an example of a tripartite committee: Advisory Committee on Health and Safety at Work: Health and safety at work, http://ec.europa.eu/social/main.jsp?catId–148&langId=en&intPageId=683, in: Europa.eu, accessed 28 February 2014.

32 Access to these institutions does not directly translate into policy influence, as these are only 'soft' channels of influence.

33 Interview with Cartel Alfa's vice president, Romania, Gn 01, June 2013.

Another essential resource for participation in European-level decision-making processes is the knowledge of foreign languages. Here, as a confederation, Cartel Alfa fares well, as several of the five members of the leadership speak English, one speaks German, and another speaks French. Cartel Alfa has an international relations department with further professional staff that is skilled in at least one foreign language.[34]

This is apparent, for example, in the activity within the EESC, where Cartel Alfa is represented by Sorin Petru Dandea, a vice president with knowledge of both English and French. In this position, Dandea acted as rapporteur on several occasions on issues pertaining to taxation and pensions,[35] a function that was exercised by only one other Romanian confederation representative within the Workers' Group.[36]

Another less material resource that is essential to participation on the European level, namely, a network of reliable contacts that includes a path-dependent element, was established through its membership in the international confederation WCL since 1991 until its incorporation into ITUC.[37] This led to closer relations with members of this confederation within European structures and to transnational cooperation outside of European Union institutions. When asked about the cooperation with trade unions from Western Europe, one of the vice presidents of Cartel Alfa answered:

> With all, we are all in ETUC. But we have good bilateral relations with those confederations with which we were colleagues in the former WCL. ...As a consequence, we still have better relations with those trade unions from the old member states that were part of this confederation. Namely, the Confederation of Christian TUs from Belgium, Holland, France, Luxemburg, but also the confederations from more occidental Europe that have a section for Christian workers. This is the case for OGB[38], which, although it was not affiliated to WCL, it had a section, which frequently participated in our activities there.[39]

14.7. Resources and European Participation on the Federation Level

Resources are more limited at the federation level than at the confederation level. In addition, direct participation in the EESC is not accessible to most federation leaders because their participation is not funded. Participation in ETUC meetings is possible

34 Cartel Alfa: Members of the political leadership of Cartel Alfa. Curriculum Vitae, in: cartel-alfa.ro, http://www.cartel-alfa.ro/default.asp?nod=10, accessed 31 January 2014.

35 EESC: Profiles. Dandea, in: memberspage.eesc.europa.eu, http://memberspage.eesc.europa.eu/Detail.aspx?id=2021510&f=11&s= 0&o1=0&o2=0&o3=0&gr=2101, accessed 02 March 2014.

36 CSN Meridian: Profiles. Dumitru Fornea (other representative), in: memberspage.eesc.europa.eu http://memberspage.eesc.europa.eu/Detail.aspx?id =2021511&f=2&s=0&o1=0&o2=0&o3=0&co=RO, accessed 02 March 2014.

37 Cartel Alfa: Official website, in: cartel-alfa.ro, http://www.cartel-alfa.ro/default.asp?nod=11, accessed 31 January 2014.

38 ÖGB—Österreichischer Gewerkschaftsbund

39 Interview with trade union representative, Romania, Gn01, 29 March 2013.

and encouraged for leaders of TUFs, but because costs are not covered, these leaders cannot attend the meetings.

The resource barrier is also visible in the organisation at the national level and how the connection is managed to the European umbrella organisations of which the respective TUFs are members. The first challenge posed to the attempts by trade union federations to participate in the aggregation of interests on a European level is posed by the understanding of how this process works. A federation leader from the mining industry explained:

> We are not that well-structured, and this is why we do not know what to ask of them and do not know how to act. When I look down at my member trade unions I say, well, they really don't know what to ask of me. And I look up to the European organisations and I say, well, I don't know what to ask of them. Because we are not really fully aware of the mechanism and not aware of the power a trade union has as a member of the European federations. They are more powerful than the national trade unions.[40]

This problem leads in certain cases to apathy towards the European level of decision-making, as seen by the answer given by a commerce trade union leader who stated that the TUF does not represent interests on the European level.[41] Similarly, the problem of European-level representation and how it remains an issue that is addressed mainly by the confederation is explained by another commerce trade union leader:

> I think the problem with EU relations is that they do not reach the federation level. It is a closed relationship with a double-closed system between the confederative structures and [EU] organs; it does not even reach the federative level, let alone simple trade unions or the perception among trade union members. This does not exist. This is solved as follows: A few people from confederations frequently attend some meetings; sometimes, they send some materials with no explanations about certain things that for our trade union members look like utopias. But there are no instruments, no mechanisms that they would know of, about with whom or how they could cooperate. There is no culture for that.[42]

Financial resources are also an impediment that affects TU organisations in different ways. Primarily, it allows trade union representatives from the federation level to only attend meetings when the costs of attendance are covered by the organiser. However, there are other more subtle barriers to European-level participation, as a TU representative from the commerce sector explained:

> The membership contribution is the same for the Danish, where the minimum wage is 2000 euro, and for a Romanian, who earns 200 euros. I cannot afford to pay the contribution for the entire number of members I have because I would be left with no money at the federation level. At the same time, the distribution of votes goes accordingly to the number of members paying contribution, and this is why our vote always remains insignificant.[43]

40 Interview with trade union representative, Romania, Gn05, 03 April 2013.
41 Interview with trade union representative, Romania, Gn21, 24 May 2013.
42 Interview with trade union representative, Romania, Gn03, 05 April 2013.
43 Ibid.

The lack of financial resources therefore translates directly into the incapacity to influence the aggregation of interests on the European level. The amount of the contribution has been mentioned by other TU leaders as well, and a leader in the metal federation even mentioned that his federation could barely afford to pay the minimum contribution as a result of its shrinking size. The fact that a lack of resources translates into the incapacity to participate in collective debates and be taken seriously is also well illustrated by this quote from the same metals TUF leader:

> The participation is very low because of the lack of financial means to support our participation, but in the seldom case that we do participate at organised meetings—apart from being heard—our position is not really even balanced against that of other federations from Europe for the simple fact that we are not taken seriously with the problems we have here. This is also due to the fact that we cannot make our position clear by attending these debates, there are many [meetings] which we miss out on mainly because of [lacking] financial means, and at the same time, there would be the possibility to inform our position and the situation in Romania via the electronic channel, but here as well, it doesn't work because we have a very backward informatics system, and we are not very well equipped. It is difficult to work [because of] the lack of thorough knowledge of a foreign language of European circulation, no one in our federation has this knowledge, so we are suffering because of the lack of adaptation to the new requirements of European Social Dialogue, of European participation and information. Through three points: lack of financial means, of informatics training, of linguistic training. We have many problems which we would like to make known, but we are not succeeding.[44]

A TUF leader from the commerce branch gave one more example of the way the difference in incomes reflects the ability to influence outcomes and find supporters for initiatives:

> I will give you an example,...there is the pretty phase, where the speeches are held and the decisions made. But there are also the informal meetings, where people go out for a beer, where you put the basis of interpersonal relations, look for support, primarily for the organisation. But for me, it's difficult to participate in such a meal, where everyone pays for himself, because a meal at a restaurant in Brussels equals my income for two weeks. I can't do it.[45]

Other federation leaders also mentioned financial difficulties and how these affect their ability to participate through hiring qualified staff that could access information from the European level:

> I wanted us to have an IR[46] department that could be involved in all these things, and you need someone who is trained for this and has knowledge of foreign languages, and this means financial expenses that we cannot afford. When a federation constitutes itself, you constitute it in order to represent immediate interests. At the time when we constituted ourselves, we were eyeing Europe and Iliescu, and his people were eyeing Russia. Of course, we hoped to become part of Europe, and now we are, but we did not manage to bring two or three people, we barely managed to hire one person who is specialised in Law, who has some expertise in working in projects and will work for us. I am unsatisfied

44 Interview with trade union representative, Romania, Gn07, 23 April 2013.
45 Interview with trade union representative, Romania, Gn03, 05 April 2013.
46 IR—industrial relations

> with the fact that we were not able to develop in this direction through an IR department, and we wouldn't need so much consulting to see what to do for it to be ours but independent at the same time.[47]

Language is another central barrier to participation in European-level decision-making processes on the federation level. Whereas on the confederation level, both experts and political representatives have a thorough knowledge of foreign languages, this is only true of two representatives interviewed on the federation level (from a total of over ten respondents). As demonstrated in some of the quotes above, this strongly inhibits participation. This also diminishes information flows, and some federation leaders conceded informally that they have used Google translate to translate information from European-level organisations and even emails.

Information, funding and language competences that act as barriers to participation are strongly interconnected. Due to the lack of financial opportunities, the hiring of qualified staff that could increase information flows through their literacy in a European circulation language and awareness of the functioning of European decision-making processes becomes highly difficult.

14.8. The Basis Trade Union Level and the Participation in European Works Councils

The European Works Councils (EWCs) constitute a form of participation that is directly accessible to basis trade union members. The responsibility for EWC-related decision-making when the EWC member of a company is also a trade union member lies completely with the basis trade union. The confederation only intervenes when it becomes apparent that a problem cannot be solved by the basis trade union and would be better solved at a national or European level, although there is a political leader within the confederation leadership that is responsible for coordinating activity within the EWCs.[48] The federation level generally advises the EWC member upon his or her request for information. The functioning of the relationship between the trade union federation and the representatives in the EWC is best illustrated by a representative of a commerce branch federation:

> In Romania, in accordance to the legislation, trade unions are organised on company level and not on branch level; this is why a federation does not have representatives in a EWC, the trade union delegates from Metro; in order for someone to attend EWC meetings, s/he has to be an employee of Metro and we do not have this quality; this is why we prepare the delegates, the representatives in EWCs, we receive information from them and counsel them on decisions that should be made and positions to be adopted, but we do not have any direct involvement. Our member trade unions do; Real, Metro and Carrefour have representatives in EWCs, and those from Selgros do not have a EWC as a company.

47 Interview with trade union representative, Romania, Gn05, 03 April 2013.

48 Interview with trade union representative, Romania, Gn01, 29 March 2013.

> We have these three, and we coordinate their activities, but we as a federation do not participate.[49]

EWCs can be seen as parallel, obstructive structures by regular trade unions or as a potential beneficial structure. A more negative view of EWCs was given by a metal federation representative:

> For some, it was important; for some, obstructive. It has been noticed that there, where there is a EWC in four countries and we are the newest, the others [already] had a position that did not take ours into consideration. We have this major issue, which is the most important—creating most discussions in EWCs—the difference in salaries, independent of the firm, the salary of one working in Romania and one working in France, Germany, etc.—the difference is big and they will never cede, they will support it [an increase in salaries for Romanian workers] as a general policy that we should receive more [a higher salary], but the discussions I hear are these. So, discussions are still being carried out in this way, and no matter what we try to say, the TU movement also acts in relation to financial power.[50]

This case proves that the path-dependency of aggregated positions can act as an impediment to the cooperation within a EWC. However, generally, the cooperation in EWCs is seen positively, as this example from a banking trade union federation and EWC representatives supports:

> In the trade union, access to information is the crucial point; we escape cascade information flows and can avoid information not reaching us; we are informed about top management decisions and rarely also consulted. We have access to the group's economic and financial records, and this helps us in negotiating collective agreements; we can see whether the trend is rising or going down, and we can see whether the salary policy, bonus policy, and payment [are] in line with the principles they advocate. [This happens I]f social dialogue is okay.[51]

14.9. Organisational Effects of European Affiliation and International Cooperation on Trade Union Federations

Mainly, affiliations with European-level bodies were brought about with the support of the confederation. These processes have had interesting organisational effects on the trade union federations that will be outlined below. One such effect can be observed when tackling the fragmentation of the Romanian TU movement in the metals industry, which has traditionally been very fragmented:

> The TUC always gave a hand to federations when it came to affiliations to EU branch federations. The most difficult was with the federations in the branch of metallurgy-machine construction; at a European level, there is only one federation in the metal branch as they call it, and Romania had quite a difficult problem. Those in the European metals federation blocked the affiliation of the Romanian structures not just in Cartel Alfa but also in CNSLR Frăţia, where these TUFs were to be found. They were actually trying to put pressure on

49 Interview with trade union representative, Romania, Gn03, 05 April 2013.
50 Interview with trade union representative, Romania, Gn28, 05 June 2013.
51 Interview with trade union representative, Romania, Gn34, 21 June 2013.

> national federations to unite because the TU movement in this field was very fragmented. They said we cannot affiliate you, twenty federations from Romania, we have national federations that have three times more members than all twenty of you together. They were not saying this very directly, but in the discussion with us, when we discussed this seriously, which we did many times, they advised us to coagulate the movement, at least what big fields are concerned. So, try to have a federation in metallurgy, one in machine construction, one in electro-technologies, defence or whatever else. But not this way. At the beginning of 2000s, we had two federations dealing with machine construction in Cartel Alfa, but in BNS[52], there were 15. This was it, but generally, when we as Cartel Alfa supported the affiliation of a TUF at a European level, it wasn't a problem. Things went easy, naturally and we managed to do it in a reasonable time. However, in this sector, we really had a problem because of the division of these sectors between three confederations.[53]

The balance between federations on a national level also shifted due to their European federation, as we found out from one federation president:

> The federation itself grew as well due to its position on a European level because a number of trade unions, especially from multinational companies, seeing the international recognition and the solidary cooperation between Western trade unions and our federation, decided to affiliate to our federation because we are a recognised federation with merits, activities and results.[54]

Not only does the balance between federations seem to be shifting due to European-level cooperation, but as another federation leader described it, European affiliation also has certain branding effects that affect the position of trade union federations in collective negotiation processes:

> Being represented on a European level is also a matter of posing a threat; there were cases where all we did was show the emblem of the organisation to which we are affiliated, saying that we will inform them about how a certain employer in Romania is acting and the positions of the employer become radically more refined. European representation is also an armour against attacks that would have surely been more ferocious than they are now. This is a means of protection, and it influences our activity to the extent that we know how to benefit from it.[55]

A similar effect of the modification of the position of trade union federations within the negotiation process that is not directly related to prevalent legislation or the direct participation in European institutions was given by a federation leader from the commerce branch:

> In Romania, all the commercial agents have reached a quiet understanding that three holidays should be respected every year: the first day of Christmas, the first day of Easter and the first day of the year. It is tacit respect, since the law actually guarantees around twelve holidays a year during which commercial agents should not be open. One company thought that three days were still too much and that they should open their gates on these three days as well. It was not EU legislation that does not exist in this field, but the support that we received from NGOs, trade unions, the church—the Catholic one

52 BNS—Blocul National Sindical
53 Interview with Cartel Alfa vice president, Romania, Gn 01, June 2013.
54 Interview with trade union representative, Romania, Gn20, 21 May 2013.
55 Interview with trade union representative, Romania, Gn07, 23 April 2013.

> and other ones—from all around the world but mainly from the EU that helped to stop the attempt of the Real company at that time to put an end to even these three holidays. Because if they would have succeeded in doing this the year after, all others would also open their doors, saying they don't want to disappoint or lose clients in favour of the other company. So, we can say that the messages that came from organisations within the EU, including the European Commission, all those that sent emails, blocked the mailboxes of the company, including the personal ones of the company leaders, who then said: Okay, we won't open anymore but please stop the avalanche. So, there was a then-incredible reaction a couple of years ago, support from all the factors that could support us.[56]

As seen in this example, European solidarity and participation has many organisational effects, including the shift of power relations within the confederation, and they contribute to a certain branding effect of trade union federations in the collective negotiation process on subnational levels.

14.10. Position on European Legislation[57]

Generally, participation in European-level legislative processes has been seen as a viable alternative to the lack of responsiveness on the national level. In describing how the traditional tendencies to influence national legislation changed after the possibility for European participation opened, a federation TU leader said:

> The EU activity influences the national level—we try to explain to our colleagues what our interest on the national level would be if on the European level, such or such a decision would be taken: this big European directive that will affect all of us would be a lot more useful if this would be put like this. In the beginning, my colleagues would ask: Isn't it easier to try and solve it on a national level? Yes, if we had had logical partners both on the government and the employers' side, it would have been very easy. But we don't have this possibility; this is why we prefer to go to you, who understand the phenomenon to negotiate this, and it should come as an obligation to the national level; we only follow it, and when the directive has arrived, we go to the minister, saying, here is the directive you have to implement, and he has to implement it or we tell on him to his bosses at the European Commission.[58]

This example refers directly to the participation in European decision-making processes and their influence on European legislation. Another example proves the enthusiasm for the (already-made) provisions of European social legislation and comes from a federation leader of the commerce sector federation:

> We are also very lucky that the EU legislation is prevalent to national legislation. Where national legislation is not yet in accord with EU legislation, we can solve our problems like this. An example is the recreational holiday, which, according to the current labour code, is quite interpretably legislated. Some companies started proportionally reducing the number of holiday days settled through collective labour agreements when an employee had been on medical leave, saying, you have had one, two or three months' holiday. Whereas European legislation comes and clarifies this: that even more so when

56 Interview with trade union representative, Romania, Gn03, 05 April 2013.

57 For a better understanding of which changes the European legislation brought to Labour Law and implicitly to trade union activity, please see the chapter on Romania in this book.

58 Interview with trade union representative, Romania, Gn20, 24 May 2013.

> a person has been ill that s/he should benefit from recreational holiday. On the ground of this, we were able to interdict this practice among companies.[59]

This generally very positive view of the influence of European social legislation is true for many TU representatives in Romania, including some of those within Cartel Alfa. This view is not to be confused with the stance of the Cartel Alfa leadership regarding the impact of austerity measures mentioned at the beginning of this chapter, which is unequivocally negative.[60]

14.11. Position towards EU Energy Policy

Given the limitations of developing a position regarding European policy issues within member federations, the question arises of which policy issues are relevant and pressing enough to determine the aggregation of a political position that transcends the confederation level. European energy policy offers a good example of a field in which an issue unites more member federations as well as the confederation level of Cartel Alfa in taking a stance against a specific European policy. It also provides an illustrative example of how a policy issue can cut across both governance bodies and traditional employer-employee representation cleavages because employers' associations as well as Cartel Alfa and its member federations advocated the same stance.

The metals industry representatives of both federations, as well as the mining federation and confederation representatives, were dissatisfied with the implementation of European energy policy, as it led to an increase in energy prices for both industrial producers and citizens and caused a priority shift away from extractive industries. Nevertheless, the environmental underpinning of supporting green energy is not questioned per se, just the impact on workers, as they may lose their employment as a consequence of potential industry closure due to increases in costs or the downsizing of extractive industries. This is illustrated by the following quote from a leader from the FSS METAROM federation:

> Renewable energies and the support of those who produce it, it is a policy and a field that come from a very generous idea, that of not polluting anymore by producing and consuming classic hydrocarbon-based energy, oil and coals, and the transition to an ecological green way. It is a generous idea, as I said, and the EU translates this into far-reaching concrete legislation. But in Romania, it has a negative impact because it forces the high consumers, like those in the metallurgical branch, into higher costs because they use classic energy and automatically, they have to pay for each megawatt of classic energy they consume. This is done so that it can be invested in this field promoted by the EU of developing green energies. These generous ideas only burden our metal producers, who cannot remain competitive given these supplementary costs of green energy, which has to develop in Romania. There is the danger of closing down. Right now, this is an acute problem of how to turn European legislation into something less aggressive for the big

59 Interview with trade union representative, Romania, Gn03, 05 April 2013.
60 Interview with trade union representative, Romania, Gn01, 29 March 2013.

> consumers but also for the small ones because the megawatts which have to be paid have to be redistributed to the bills of all the consumers like you and me who use light bulbs, etc. at home. Practically, Romanians like Europeans, but they can afford this, pay twice: once at home through consumed energy and a second time through the risk of losing one's job where he is paid, and they can lose competitiveness. A good idea that does not catch root in Romania, because of different conditions.[61]

Similarly, representatives from the mining federation also described EU energy policy as having a negative impact, as the targeted increase of the percentage of green energy production occurs to the detriment of using and thus also extracting energy from coal.[62]

The confederation leadership has voiced a critique of the implementation of EU energy policy[63] on several occasions. Most recently, in March 2014, Cartel Alfa and the industrial member federations as well as a number of employers' associations addressed relevant national political representatives, voicing a critique of the Romanian implementation of energy policy. The open letter[64] criticised the consequences of rising energy prices for the entire industrial sector and mentioned the deindustrialisation of Romania as the consequence of the continuation of the Romanian implementation process.[65] This, according to the authors of the letter, would lead in a very short time to the unemployment of hundreds of thousands of people from Romania as well as a decrease in the country's investment attractiveness.[66]

Bogdan Hossu, the president of Cartel Alfa, also voiced an explicit criticism of the Romanian implementation process of European energy policy, stating that European

61 Interview with trade union representative, Romania, Gn07, 23 April 2013.

62 Interview with trade union representative, Romania, Gn08, 03 April 2013.

63 I refer to EU energy policy concerning the 2020 Climate and Energy package; European Commission: Climate Action, The 2020 climate and energy package, http://ec.europa.eu/clima/policies/package/, accessed 13 May 2014. This was the term most used by the TU representatives interviewed to describe this policy field.

64 Asociația Marilor Consumatori Industriali de Energie (ABIEC), Confederația Patronală din Industrie, Agricultură, Construcții și Servicii din România (CONPIROM), Federația patronală a ramurii metalurgie feroasă și neferoasă și produse refractare (METALURGIA), Federația patronală a producătorilor din chimie (METACHIM), Organizația patronală din industria sticlei și ceramicii fine (STICEF), Federația patronală din industria materialelor de construcții din România (PATROMAT), Confederația Națională Sindicala Cartel Alfa, METAROM, Federația Sindicatelor din Metalurgia Neferoasa, Federația Solidaritatea Metal, Federația Sindicatelor Libere din Chimie și Petrochimie, and Federația Generală a Sindicatelor „Familia": Dacă nu își reface politicile de energie, România se va confrunta cu dezindustrializarea [If you do not replenish their energy policies, Romania will face deindustrialization. Open letter], in: cartel-alfa.ro, 17 February 2014, http://www.cartel-alfa.ro/default.asp?nod=20&info=48069, accessed 12 May 2014. The letter was addressed to a wide number of Romanian national political representatives as well as the head of the International Monetary Fund mission and of the representation of the European Commission in Romania.

65 The liberalization process of the natural gas market is also a central point of the critique voiced in the letter but does not form the object of the present analysis.

66 ABIEC et al.: Dacă nu își reface politicile de energie, România se va confrunta cu dezindustrializarea [If you do not replenish their energy policies, Romania will face deindustrialization, open letter], in: cartel-alfa.ro, 17 February 2014, http://www.cartel-alfa.ro/default.asp?nod=20&info=48069, accessed 12 May 2014.

countries can offer exceptions of up to 80–85% from green energy certificates and that both Germany and Spain have already followed paths leading in this direction. According to Hossu, Romania should therefore follow these trends from within the EU and offer the local industry fair treatment that would contribute to its competiveness.[67]

After the open letter, as well as the protests organised by Cartel Alfa in Bucharest and Slatina, the president agreed to sign law no. 23/2014,[68] which was aimed at changing the implementation process of EU energy policy in Romania. The justification provided by Traian Băsescu mentioned that he signed the law[69] despite the fact that an approval from the European Commission had not yet been given 'to eliminate trade union disputes' and that he was looking forward to the 'energy price going down'[70]. This statement speaks for the role of trade union advocacy in shaping the national implementation process of European legislation.

The case of energy policy shows that while certain policy fields travel from the European level to the national institutional levels, so do the loci of advocacy, where Cartel Alfa, its member federations and regular TU members[71] voice their concerns and try to influence policy and decision-making. This example points to the weaknesses of conceptualising policy influence as occurring either on a national level or a European level. Rather than this, certain issues are followed up on the European level and then further on by different workers' representatives.

---

67 Bogdan Hossu quoted in Severin, Magda: UPDATE! Protest la Guvern împotriva suprataxării energiei electrice. Ceartă Ponta-Băsescupe pe OUG 57/2013 [UPDATE! Government protest against electricity overtaxation. Quarrel Ponta-Băsescu on OUG 57/2013], in: ziuacargo.ro, 13 March 2014, http://www.ziuacargo.ro/stiri/focus-stiri/protest-la-guvern-impotriva-suprataxarii-energiei-electrice-cearta-ponta-basescu-pe-oug-572013, accessed 12 May 2014, as well as Ziare.com: Băsescu a promulgat legea certificatelor verzi. Aștept ieftinirea energiei [Băsescu passed the green certificate law. I am waiting for the energy price to go down], in: Ziare.com, 13 March 2014, http://www.ziare.com/basescu/presedinte/traian-basescu-declaratii-de-la-palatul-cotroceni-live-1287676, accessed 26 August 2014.

68 The emergency order by the government OUG 57/2013, in: Monitorul Oficial, Partea I nr. 335, 7 June 2013, http://www.dreptonline.ro/legislatie/oug_57_2013_modificare_lege_220_2008_sistemul_promovare_producere_energie_surse_regenerabile_energie.php, accessed 12 May 2014. It was enacted as a law (no. 23/2014) with certain modifications on the 13 March 2014 and published in: Monitorul Oficial, Partea I, Nr. 184, 14 March 2013, http://www.anre.ro/documente.php?id=393, accessed [through one supplementary link] 12 May 2014;

69 A procedure necessary for this type of normative act.

70 Băsescu, Traian quoted in Severin, Magda: UPDATE! Protest la Guvern împotriva suprataxării energiei electrice. Ceartă Ponta-Băsescupe pe OUG 57/2013 [UPDATE! Government protest against electricity overtaxation. Quarrel Ponta-Băsescu on OUG 57/2013], in: ziuacargo.ro, 13 March 2014, http://www.ziuacargo.ro/stiri/focus-stiri/protest-la-guvern-impotriva-suprataxarii-energiei-electrice-cearta-ponta-basescu-pe-oug-572013, accessed 12 May 2014.

71 Costel Mirea: Protest împotriva certificatelor verzi la Slatina [Protest against green certificates in Slatina], in: Olt-Alert.ro, 12 March 2014, http://olt-alert.ro/local/protest-impotriva-certificatelor-verzi-la-slatina/, accessed 12 May 2014. The article describes the protest of 500 workers mainly from the trade union that represented the workers of SC Alro SA·(an aluminium production company) that protested against energy policy in Slatina at the same time as the protest in Bucharest organised by Cartel Alfa in March 2014.

The case of energy policy also shows that issues that are perceived as central to the overall development of an entire sector can transcend the confederation level, reaching that of regular trade union members. At the same time, it contributed to the establishment of alliances between Cartel Alfa and employers' organisations in taking a stance against the implementation of previously developed provisions of European legislation into national policies.

14.12. Conclusions

Participation in the European decision-making process is mostly confined to the confederation level. Participation on the federation level is possible within the given institutional framework. Nevertheless, the lack of necessary financial resources, language competences and of adequate knowledge of European level decision-making processes act as barriers to the European-level participation of the member federations of Cartel Alfa. On the basic trade union level, when information reaches the members, it is difficult to assimilate due to the lack of contextual knowledge. At the same time, EWCs act as institutions that assist basis trade union representatives with information regarding companies, which can then be used in the collective negotiation process. Integration into European representation structures also had un-intended and mostly organisational effects on the balance of power between federations and that between federations and employers. Through membership, certain trade union federations from the metals and commerce industries could profit from the branding effect that European representation had in intimidating employers. Additionally, this process caused those trade union federations that knew how to interact with European structures to develop more rapidly, to the detriment of those that did not. European legislation is perceived by federation leaders within Cartel Alfa to have had a mixed effect on their activity. Some regulations, such as those regarding working hours, work security and health, are seen as improvements to former Romanian provisions. On the other hand, the introduction of green energy incentives had clear negative effects on the workers and on the entire industrial sector. This is seen as both a European problem and a national problem and led to a coalescence of a clear stance within Cartel Alfa regarding European energy policy and its implementation on the national level. This position not only seems to be aggregated on a confederation level, but it also includes lower-level trade unions and federations and contributed to the forging of alliances with employers' associations. To a certain extent, the case of energy policy contradicts the previously elaborated findings of this case study, as it shows both the involvement of basis trade unions and federations in a policy issue that is perceived as both European and national. Nevertheless, energy policy provides a good example of what the politics of a 'multilevel' governance system can resemble when the stakes are high.

Monika Čambáliková

15. Slovak Trade Unions between the European Union and the Enterprise Level. A Case Study of Odborový zväz KOVO (OZ KOVO)

15.1. Introduction

Trade unions are specific actors in the processes of interest intermediation and multi-level management. Just like other political and non-political actors who formulate, represent and intermediate interests, trade unions undergo continuous process of change. The first change, which occurs in new EU member states, primarily relates to the processes of political and economic transformation. The second change, which occurs in all EU member states, primarily relates to processes of economic globalisation and the challenges of European integration.

Both external and internal changes in member states' economies and policies, which are primarily connected to economic globalisation and the internationalisation of capital, lead to the weakening of trade unions at the national level. This fact is also reflected in the decline of their ability to act as strong social partners in the processes of collective bargaining and in the structures of social dialogue from the plant level to EU level. Additionally, due to the above-mentioned fact, it is important for trade unions at the national level in the EU member states to integrate into the processes of negotiation, bargaining and decision-making at the EU level, to come together inter-regionally and to co-ordinate their activities.

Integration does not refer only to formal integration of national trade unions into European structures in the form of formal membership in their respective EU institutions, nor does it refer to the mere existence of formal contacts with relevant EU partners. It is not exhausted by the effect of EU institutions and the influence of EU policy on trade union activities at the national level; instead, it also demands their active participation and co-operation and anticipates backwards movement by national trade unions towards EU policy and their participation in the decision-making and resolution adoption processes along with policy-making and strategy-creation at the EU level.

The overall trend of weakening trade unions as social partners was fully manifested in Slovakia during the period of the post-socialist transformation, and it continues to the present.[1] Because the liberal character of national policies has been forced

1 Čambáliková, Monika: Slovak Trade Union in EU Governance, in: Kusznir, Julia / Heiko, Pleines (eds): Trade Union from Post-Socialist Member States in EU Governance, Stuttgart: ibidem Verlag, 2008, pp. 141–153.

and there is an increase of legitimisation and apologetisation of that type of policy, not only the trade unions but also the principles and interests advocated by them are in a difficult position. The structures of the trade unions were often—either directly or indirectly—viewed as 'old structures' that retard the inevitable transformation and reforms in the new Slovakia.

We can say that the process of integration into the EU structures had positive effects on the Slovak trade unions, but it has been difficult. The requirements and criteria of the EU have created pressure and had a positive influence on trade unions' position. The pressure of these criteria encouraged Slovakia as a candidate country—and later as an EU member state—to strengthen its democratic institutions, i.e. to institute the social partnership and to support a stance that prefers agreement and consensus achieving, both of which are enabled via institutions of social partnership.[2]

Put simply, in Slovakia, the EU has strengthened not only the legitimacy of the trade unions as an actor of a social partnership but also the trade union policy connected to the core of the European social model.

The values of the 'European model' and policies rooted in those values have been continuously viewed as an essential reason that Slovak trade-union representatives wish for increased EU-level influence on national policy.

The type of policy rooted in the 'European social model' is not only similar to the Slovak trade unions' programme strategy and vision in its basic principles and ideas but also eases the legitimisation, enforcement and protection of employees'—including trade unions'—rights. It was proven that particularly during periods of realising the policy of liberalism and reforms, the policy rooted in the European social model might constitute—at least in the form of vision—a legitimate socio-democratic alternative to the policy of strongly liberal national government; additionally, it may increase the protection of employees related to employers.

Social dialogue is an integral part of EU decision-making processes. New European rules, particularly in the field of employment and intermediating in the field of social policy, are also created via social dialogue. The Maastricht and Amsterdam Treaties provided a broader radius for European social partners' activities because they not only enable mutual bargaining, negotiations and agreement conclusion between the social partners but also insist on implementing the resulting agreements according to EU law.

Slovak trade-union representatives assess their inclusion into European structures positively—they appreciate the ability to share difficult-to-obtain information, to engage in mutual communication and in particular, they welcome the possibility of forming joint strategies towards employers, especially in cases involving supranational plants. They also appreciate having the ability to comment on EU law while it

2 Čambáliková, Monika: Slovenskí sociálni partneri doma a v Bruseli [Slovenian social partner, a home in Brussels], in: AUSPICIA, České Budějovice, 2010 (vol. 7), no. 2, pp. 90–94.

is being prepared: the European Commission (EC) is obliged to consult with them on law relating to social partners.

Participation of the representatives of Slovak trade unions in the processes of decision-making and policy-creation at the EU level is not direct one (save for those institutions and commissions in which they are members, namely, the European Social Dialogue and the European Economic and Social Council); instead, it is intermediated. Both individual direct consultations and direct contacts with the European Commission or European Parliament (EP) are exceptional. Slovak trade unions communicate with the EC primarily through European trade-union umbrella associations and with the EP only randomly primarily via Slovak members of the EP.

The strongest and most active Slovak national trade union is OZ KOVO, which is also a strong and active actor at the EU level. OZ KOVO representatives indicate that their best co-operation is with the European Economic and Social Committee (EESC), while OZ KOVO's chairman is a member. They also greatly appreciate their co-operation with the EP and with Slovakia's representatives in the Council of Europe.

15.2. OZ KOVO and EU Multilevel Governance

In our interviews, representatives of OZ KOVO declared that EU politics are as important to them as national politics and expressed their congruent opinion that the impact of the EU on the member states' national policies should increase. They also believe that in general, the EU has a positive effect and impact on their work. As an example of this positive effect and impact of the EU, OZ KOVO chairman Emil Machyna highlights EU law and key EU documents, primarily the European Social Charter and the concept of the European Works Council (EWC). OZ KOVO's international secretary similarly sees positive effects and impacts of the EU: 'All EU directives in the labour law sphere and recommendations of the EU in the labour and social law sphere are positives because they help us to push through the standards and interests of employees'[3]. In addition, it is the 'implementation of the above-mentioned standards, negotiated and agreed at the EU level, primarily with respect to the social rights of employees'[4] that is viewed by M. Hrušecká as a policy area in which the EU is more important than the nation state. However, in this respect, she also asserts that 'we are still not witnessing the growth of harmonisation in this area'[5] and therefore, she perceives that this task and challenge is also an actual policy priority at the national level.[6] The chairman of OZ KOVO deems representation of interests at the EU level as more important than the national level in the area of 'global policy—Europe surely retains its position

3 Interview with OZ KOVO's international secretary M. Hrušecká, Slovakia, MH, 8 May 2013.
4 Ibid.
5 Ibid.
6 Ibid.

as a global economic player while social standards are maintained'[7]. In the opinion of OZ KOVO chairman, the priority area of the interest in national-level representation is related to industry policy at the plant level.[8]

According to the OZ KOVO chairman, the major reason that the trade union should be present at the EU level is to be involved in joint proceedings, solidarity, EWC and informative systems on collective bargaining at the globalised companies.[9]

The international secretary of OZ KOVO assumes that

> [n]ot the trade union, but employees should be represented at the EU level. [The major purpose of this representation should be] to enable employees to participate, at the EU level, social standards and standards for working and wage conditions, and to have an opportunity to influence EU policies.[10]

OZ KOVO communicates with the EC primarily via IndustriAll as its member, and it communicates with the European Parliament primarily via Slovak members. However, OZ KOVO is most active at the European Economic and Social Committee (OZ KOVO's chairman is a member) and via membership in IndustriAll. When Slovak trade unions exert their influence at the EU level, they do so mainly via their European branch federation: 'They are more important and more significant players and they are our partners'[11], stresses the chairman of OZ KOVO. He also notes another important way to exert influence at the EU level, namely, through the Vienna Memorandum, its interconnected activities and the co-operation of countries that signed it.[12]

Policy positions to be represented at EU-level organisations and institutions are created and put into their final form in co-operation with relevant foreign trade unions:

> OZ KOVO co-operates with colleagues from Hungary, the Czech Republic, Poland and Slovenia—the so-called V-5 i.e. the Vysegrad 4 plus Slovenia. We have regional meetings twice per year where we formulate joint positions that are subsequently advanced.[13]

With respect to the 'first rounds' of these debates within OZ KOVO, the process depends on the issue: 'we have working groups specialising in particular issues that study those issues, evaluate them and prepare informative papers,'[14] is how OZ KOVO's describes the process of creating policy positions.

OZ KOVO engages in long-term co-operation with partner trade-union associations from older EU member states, primarily in Germany, Austria, France, Sweden,

7 Machyna, Emil: 10 rokov spolupráce v priebehu meniacej sa doby [10 years of cooperation during changing times], in: 10 rokov Viedenského memoranda [10 years of the Vienna Memorandum], Bratislava, 2009, pp. 14–17.
8 Ibid.
9 Ibid.
10 Interview with OZ KOVO's international secretary M. Hrušecká, Slovakia, MH, 8 May 2013.
11 Interview with OZ KOVO's chairman E. Machyna, Slovakia, EM, 16 April 2013.
12 Ibid.
13 Ibid.
14 Ibid.

Finland and Belgium. This co-operation and its continuity also relates to the fact that the mother companies of plants located in Slovakia are from those countries, a fact that intensifies co-operation. 'Every time that we contact any, for example, an Austrian company, we inform the Austrian metallurgy union'[15], according to the international secretary. She also explains how that co-operation is co-ordinated: '[R]epresentatives of the trade unions from the respective region always inform OZ KOVO's headquarters and headquarters in each co-operating member state.'[16]

Co-operation with trade unions from older member states is focused on the areas of industry policy, collective bargaining policy, and the relationship between politics and trade unions. OZ KOVO's chairman would welcome extending that co-operation to the plant level and personal contacts. Slovak trade-union representatives deem this co-operation important and wish to continue it. They primarily appreciate information exchange and co-ordination of joint procedures. They anticipate that these will have a positive impact on the process of closer integration within Europe. According to OZ KOVO's international secretary, the biggest challenges to this co-operation are connected to 'continuous relocation of production from old to new EU member states, which is the area where we should co-operate and look for solutions. Employees of the closed-down plant need a good social plan and the prevention of social dumping.'[17]

OZ KOVO representatives today do not see—and do not cause—any significant differences between co-operation with trade unions from old versus new EU member states: 'There are no differences now. There were approximately ten years ago when we were receiving their help, but now we are partners—it is equalised'[18]. Additionally, the advantages of co-operation with older EU member states are viewed the same as and equal to the advantages of co-operation with newer EU member states. 'The difference between old and new member states is afield, it has been overcome'[19], the international secretary of OZ KOVO says. She believes in that purpose and that another challenge of mutual trade-union co-operation is

> to avoid having employees exclude one another from the working process and depriving one another of good working conditions. That can be achieved—thanks to the exchange of information and the co-ordination of procedures. Employees are not forced to give up their demand in the fear that unless they give them up, they will lose their jobs because others will give up their own demands.[20]

15 Interview with OZ KOVO's international secretary M. Hrušecká, Slovakia, MH 8, May 2013.
16 Ibid.
17 Ibid.
18 Ibid.
19 Ibid.
20 Ibid.

Implementation of the decisions is within the competence and responsibility of OZ KOVO's office holders. The chairman of OZ KOVO acknowledges his own personal liability and responsibility in this respect.

Representatives of the Slovak trade union are satisfied with the position of their trade union at the EU level, primarily because of their joint proceedings and their membership in strong federations: 'We belong to the strongest trade unions: IndustriALL, of which we are a member, has the biggest influence within ETUC.'[21] (European Trade Union Confederation). They are more moderate in their evaluation of their own influence and position and in this respect they are satisfied with only 'taking into account our resources and possibilities,'[22] while stressing 'there are totally different players such as Germany and the like.'[23] Thus, representatives of OZ KOVO do not see their trade union as a key player or as solitary, and they assess it necessary to be a member of the joint European team to be successful in Europe. At the same time one can say that they perceive the current team, of which they are members, as strong, influential and amicable with respect to the EU.

The chairman of OZ KOVO elaborates as follows:

> The exchange of information and knowledge has been very important for us on the preparation of collective bargaining and its strategy. Common meetings in training activities, along with exchanges of experience by negotiators and persons who organise collective bargaining have given us much knowledge useful in our work with supranational companies, in EWC and in the implementation of European Metalworkers' Federation (EMF) rules.[24]

He also sees improvements over time: 'At first, we only received information and learned about new forms of our work. Now we are becoming partners and we are able to provide information and knowledge to our colleagues from other countries'[25].

On the pages of priority, OZ KOVO's new monthly journal, the union's vice-chairman, M. Bendeková, writes about the 'Negotiation of our future' conference organised by the Vienna headquarters of IndustriAll Europe, which took place on July 12 and 13, 2014.

> In spite of the fact that the financial crises strongly hit primarily industry employees, this conference confirmed that the strong system of collective bargaining provides mechanisms that enable trade unionists to protect jobs and to contribute to the activation and renewal of industry in Europe[26],

---

21 Interview with OZ KOVO's chairman E. Machyna, Slovakia, EM, 16 April 2013.
22 Ibid.
23 Ibid.
24 Ibid.
25 Ibid.
26 Bendeková, Monika: Konferencia s názvom „Vyjednávanie našej budúcnosti" [Conference with the name 'Negotiating our Future'], in: priority, monthly journal of OZ KOVO, 2014 (vol. XXII), no. 6, p. 3.

she wrote. At the end of her article, she speaks about unanimously adopted main message and resolution of the conference:

> In these hard times, European trade unions must firmly stand together. Solidarity is not a fair-weather concept. We will act jointly in these economically difficult times and we will not allow anyone to set us against each other at the national, branch or plant levels.[27]

Co-operation with European trade union associations is assessed very positively by OZ KOVO representatives. Representatives of the Slovak trade unions regularly participate at meetings of European organisations and institutions, whether monthly, quarterly or semi-annually.

Slovak trade unions' activities at the EU level are paid from their own funds. However, when the unions are representing their interests, they are proceeding in co-operation with others. They co-operate both bilaterally and multilaterally with other trade unions (primarily from Austria, the Czech Republic, Germany, Hungary, Poland and Slovenia) and exert their interests primarily through European trade-union umbrella organisations (primarily IndustriAll Europe, ETUC, and Economic and Social Council (ECOSOC)).

The most common method of communication is the internet (i.e. e-mail). 'We have created a whole-European network, EUCOB@N[28], where all trade unions regularly report recent information about collective bargaining, primarily from the automotive industry'[29], the international secretary of OZ KOVO says. Important communication channels also continue to include joint meetings of committees, ad hoc groups, direct consultation and personal contacts. OZ KOVO's chairman primarily highlights personal contacts and mutual co-operation in this time of crises and growing competition:

> Direct consultations and personal contacts, which I prefer and EUCOB@N. However, it is mainly personal contacts, via electronic means or telephone, because we have great co-operation and we advise each other. However, during the crisis, the national approach becomes more important[30].

OZ KOVO actively supported all significant protests and actions organised by the European headquarters. Slovak trade unionists fully identify themselves and agree with the message and requirements of these actions. Actions such as the World Day for Decent Work and the European Action Day were intensively advertised and supported by OZ KOVO, and over the long term, OZ KOVO attempts to implement the requirements of those events into its priorities and activities.

Joint policy and procedure, co-ordination of activities and exchanges of experience and knowledge with the aim of protecting and strengthening its members'

27 Ibid.
28 EUCOB@N—European Collective Bargaining Network
29 Interview with OZ KOVO's international secretary M. Hrušecká, Slovakia, MH, 8 May 2013.
30 Interview with OZ KOVO's chairman E. Machyna, Slovakia, EM, 16 April 2013.

interests are the primary advantages of co-operation with the European trade union associations, as perceived by Slovak trade unions.

> Additionally, becoming known and being in touch with other colleagues is positive. For instance, there may be a situation in which the management of a particular company argues that unless employees and trade unions will accept their conditions, they will move out and give work to people in, for example, Romania. However, thanks to co-operation, we know that our Romanian colleagues also require certain standards and will not go below them,[31]

comments OZ KOVO's international secretary.

The union's representatives do not perceive any significant disadvantage to EU-level co-operation. However, if they must critically note any weak points of co-operation, OZ KOVO's chairman remembers time-consuming processes and procedures used to come to a joint position and notes 'cultural differences—but it is an obstacle to co-operation, not a disadvantage'[32].

OZ KOVO representatives assume that their trade-union activities provide an important contribution to the overall interest in trade-union representation at the EU level. On the one hand, the chairman of OZ KOVO says that 'the bigger countries have a stronger influence than we have'[33], but on the other hand, the role of Slovak trade union is deemed adequate to Slovakia's size and importance within Europe.[34]

In addition to their clear support of protest actions at the EU level, Slovak trade unionists also clearly supporting ETUC's requirement for implementation of the social progress clause. The chairman of OZ KOVO reasons as follows:

> Europe has today two important areas in which it is not unified: the social area and taxes. If we wish for social unification, the respective model should be chosen—whether German or Scandinavian or which one. This clause provides a minimal framework for these standards[35].

Slovak trade unionists believe and hope that social progress clause implementation will lead to the harmonisation of at least minimal social standards within EU and the convergence of the EU member states in this area. The interpretation of the interviews indicates that the gradual unification of social standards is perceived by Slovak trade-union representatives as an example of the EU's positive political impact on Slovakia.[36]

Representatives of Slovak trade unions assume that current differences between labour costs in relation to the older EU member states are not justified, even if they are not advocated as a method of protecting workers in Slovakia. They highlight the fact that 'today we have much higher productivity of work but the labour costs are

31 Interview with OZ KOVO's international secretary M. Hrušecká, Slovakia, MH, 8 May 2013.
32 Interview with OZ KOVO's chairman E. Machyna, Slovakia, EM 16, April 2013.
33 Ibid.
34 Ibid.
35 Ibid.
36 Ibid.

still very low'[37] and critically assess that wage dumping, inter alia, 'damages the social status of our people'[38].

Activities in which OZ KOVO participates at the EU level often influence its work at the national level. Examples of this influence that were highlighted include the following: (1) joint strategy in relation to and during the work of the EWC; (2) the process of collective bargaining in supra-national companies; and (3) with respect to the European Commission, joint legal positions to adopt, primarily through the implementation of some EU directives into Slovak law.

OZ KOVO occasionally uses the EU as an argument to justify or support its position or activities at the national level. As an example, the representatives of OZ KOVO mentioned the issue of agency workers' request for equal pay (e.g., a Volkswagen (VW) plant in Martin, a town located in the middle of Slovakia, paid its workers lower wages than VW workers doing the same job at a VW plant in Bratislava).

Among Slovak trade union representatives, a highly positive evaluation of the impact of EU policy on Slovakia prevails with respect to almost all policy areas. One negative noted by the chairman of OZ KOVO is 'crisis and financing of the banks and the member states in bankruptcy.'[39]

OZ KOVO's member unions are represented in EWC, and representatives of OZ KOVO co-operate with them and view them as influential and important institutions, even from the perspective of representing employees' interests' in Slovakia.

OZ KOVO co-operates with EWC primarily through IndustriAll Europe, namely, via that organisation's committee of area co-ordinators. The international secretary of OZ KOVO is a member of that committee: 'there I co-operate with particular EWC not as their member but as a co-ordinator'[40]. From that platform, the union's position is formulated 'jointly at the level of IndustriALL Europe. That standpoint is further consulted at the national levels and flows to the plant level. One (unified) conclusion is agreed upon and is further advanced at the EWC.'[41]

The practical meaning of the EWC concept is perceived as the exchange of information and the effort to harmonise 'different working conditions in particular plants that lead to negative stances that must be solved.'[42]

The centre and focus of EWC work is at the plant level and there—at the plant level—are also formed standpoints to be represented in the EWC. Usually, this is done within the competence of and directed by chairmen of the plant-level trade union organisations. The work in EWC significantly affects not only internal discussion at OZ

37 Ibid.
38 Ibid.
39 Ibid.
40 Interview with OZ KOVO's international secretary M. Hrušecká, Slovakia, MH, 8 May 2013.
41 Ibid.
42 Ibid.

KOVO but also 'joint strategies, investments, employment—to be brief, everything that makes an industrial relation'[43], concludes OZ KOVO chairman Emil Machyna.

15.3. Case Study: Kromberg & Schubert in Slovakia

> Only co-ordinated co-operation provided the possibility not to fall into the competition for the lowest wage and the worst working conditions.[44]

Emil Machyna, chairman of OZ KOVO, identifies the Vienna Memorandum Group as an important tool and platform for European trade union policy and co-operation. He perceives the European social dialogue and co-ordination of collective bargaining at the international level as a possible way to create the social dimension of European integration and a potential tool to prevent of wage and social dumping.[45]

When assessing 10 years of activity in the Vienna Memorandum Group, one of its signatories and General Secretary remembered,

> When we established our Vienna Memorandum Group in March 1999, it consisted of metalwork trade unions from two EU Member States (Austria and Germany (Bavaria)) and four then-candidate countries (Slovakia, Hungary, Slovenia and the Czech Republic). We wished to initiate the process of introducing the social dimension into the European extension process.[46]

The goal was to support amicable trade unions in the creation of networks of collective agreements at the branch level (if possible) and thus to attempt to achieve wage and living-standard harmonisation via a joint, long-term collective bargaining policy.

However, when assessing the real situation, he was forced to note,

> as a trade union, we are confronted by employers who barely defend against implementation of employee representatives and EWC in their plants in Middle and Eastern Europe in situations in which such groups are active in their mother-companies in Austria or Germany. We needed to make a great effort in the case of Austrian automotive subdelivery firm Kromber & Schubert in the case of its Slovakian daughter company, which employs approximately 3,000. First, representatives of the Austrian company refused to accept the plant-level trade union as their partner. Later, they did not adhere to the collective agreement and they put their employees under psychological pressure, thus sparking protests and actions by OZ KOVO, our partner trade union in Slovakia, in April 2008. After the employer received information about the strike, every member of the strike committee received a notice of employment termination and a court petition was filed by the employer. Slovak colleagues asked us for help and we successfully intervened at the

43 Interview with OZ KOVO's chairman E. Machyna, Slovakia, EM, 16 April 2013.

44 Manfred, Anderle: Od začiatkov po dnešok [From the beginnings to the present day], in: 10 rokov Viedenského memoranda [10 years of Vienna Memorandum], Bratislava, 2009, pp. 8–10, here p. 8.

45 Interview with OZ KOVO's chairman E. Machyna, Slovakia, EM, 16 April 2013.

46 Manfred, Anderle: Od začiatkov po dnešok [From the beginnings to the present day], in: 10 rokov Viedenského memoranda [10 years of Vienna Memorandum], Bratislava, 2009, pp. 8–10, here p. 8.

> Austrian mother company: we have managed to divert the court's petition and improve working conditions for workers producing cables in Kolárovo.[47]

The above example inspired us to closely explore the 2008 and (July) 2014 situation at that plant.[48]

15.3.1. Kromberg & Schubert in Slovakia in 2008. An Example of a Successful Collective Protest

The Kromberg & Schubert plant in Slovakia produces components for the automotive industry has been active in Slovakia since 1997. Its seat is in Kolárovo, in the District of Komárno. The owner (shareholder) is the Austrian company that is a member of the German concern. In 2006, the plant provided jobs for 2,385 employees in the Slovak town of Kolárovo, which has approximately 10,000 inhabitants. In the pre-strike period, approximately 200 employees worked there, one-fourth of whom were from abroad. The reason for the foreign employees was the lack of a qualified workforce in the regional labour market.

The dispute arose over allegedly improper behaviour of supervisors and a wage issue. Improper behaviour of management and supervisors was a long-term issue at the plant, which worsened after most of the Austrian managers, who had worked at the undertaking's start-up in Slovakia, left. Vladimír Kopčaj, based on interviews with the workers, identified two major forms of improper behaviour by superiors related to the workers:

- repeated breaches of labour law, including forced 12-hour days and obligatory work on Saturdays, Sundays and holidays; and
- discrimination, insults and disparagement of employees—i.e. communication with and handling of workers by superiors inconsistent with human dignity.[49]

Some workers labelled the undertaking (company) as a 'concentration camp' or 'slavery'.[50]

The stance of the (foreign) company's management towards the above findings was (is) not clear. It seems that lower (Slovak) management was forced to maximise profits and to achieve goals. Some supervisors improperly forced workers to work to

47 Ibid., here p. 9.

48 The information provided herein was primarily obtained from the following sources: interviews with the chairman of the plant-level trade union at Kromberg & Schubert in Kolárovo (July 2014); internal trade-union documents and materials; and a paper by Kopčaj, Vladimír: Kolektívny protest na pracovisku. Prípadová štúdia vybraného sociálneho konfliktu. [Collective protest at the workplace. A case study of selected social conflicts], diploma thesis, Bratislava, 2010, p. 118.

49 Kopčaj, Vladimír: Kolektívny protest na pracovisku. Prípadová štúdia vybraného sociálneho konfliktu. [Collective protest at the workplace. A case study of selected social conflicts], diploma thesis, Bratislava, 2010, p. 118.

50 Ibid, here p. 73.

their maximum or even more. The available information confirms that upper management made no effort to change this approach or to engage in any personal exchanges.

The plant-level trade union began its activity in the company in January 2004. At that time, there was also an active work council consisting primarily of employees who were close to management. This was reflected in the council's reluctance to solve workers' problems. 'In that situation, we saw two options: either to revoke the council or to nominate (infiltrate) it with trade unionists as worker representatives. Because the second option was impossible, the council was shut down,'[51] the current chairman of the plant trade union explains.

OZ KOVO representatives assisted plant workers in establishing a plant-level trade union. OZ KOVO provided its experience, knowledge and methodology for establishing a plant-level trade union; it provided organisational support and legal help for free.

OZ KOVO ensured the participation of new trade unionists in educational and training activities. Members of the trade union (TU) committee had no experience with the work of the trade unionists at the plant or with the employer communication. They earned this experience step by step via their own activities and with the assistance of OZ KOVO.

> We were beginners in trade union activities. We have obtained and appreciated the advice of OZ KOVO, and we trusted them. In addition, the trainings helped us; not just by providing knowledge but by creating a feeling of community and collegiality[52]

says the (current and former) chairman of the plant-level TU.

The TU's primary effort was devoted to collective bargaining, with the aim of concluding the collective agreement. However, the undertaking's management questioned the legitimacy and competence of the plant-level trade union to collectively bargain, and it denied the competence of the Ministry of Labour, Social Affairs and Family to appoint a mediator or arbiter to resolve the issue, deeming it an improper intervention into the undertaking's internal affairs. The conclusion of the plant-level collective agreement took more than two years and required unusual supervision of the conciliator.

The relationship between the TU and management did not change significantly even after the conclusion of the plant-level collective agreement, and in 2008, the conciliator was again asked to assist in solving the disputes because the collective agreement had not been fulfilled (the biggest issue was remuneration). During the pre-strike period, management continued to be reluctant to engage the TU and the collective-bargaining process.

---

51 Interview with trade union chairwoman in the plant Kromberg & Schubert Mária Kobidová, Slovakia, MK, 22 July 2014.

52 Ibid.

The chairman of the plant-level TU wrote letters to the German owner (shareholder) and to the Austrian company's executive and informed them about the situation in the undertaking in Slovakia (translation into German was provided by OZ KOVO). This initiative led to a meeting of the TU and Slovak and German plant management, but solutions were not achieved and tensions were not reduced.

After four years of existence, the plant-level trade union had more than 300 members in the pre-strike period and more than 550 members in the short period after the strike. Most of the members were production workers.

The conciliator did not help to conclude the plant-level collective agreement in 2004. Therefore, the next step should have been either appointment of an arbiter to decide on the collective agreement or to strike. For almost 2.5 years, the dispute was before the conciliator. OZ KOVO was afraid that the strike would be unsuccessful because people would not join it. However, in 2008 the situation was different—workers' dissatisfaction had risen.

On January 26, 2008, the TU decided to enter the strike if necessary. The employer was informed that the strike was not ruled out unless the collective agreement was respected, management changed its position and the company's behaviour towards workers and working conditions improved. On February 28, 2008, the TU and OZ KOVO organised a protest in front of the plant.

On April 11, 2008, the TU agreed to strike. The date of the strike was determined only after another round of unsuccessful negotiations with management. On April 17, management was served with notice of a two-hour strike to take place on April 21, 2008. In the case of unsuccessful negotiations and bargaining, the strike was to be extended for an indefinite period of time.

'It was important, but at the same time difficult, to persuade employees that they were entitled to strike and to advocate the legality of striking'[53], remembers the TU chairman. OZ KOVO played an important role in this respect. OZ KOVO drafted, printed, and distributed a short paper that was delivered to workers in front of the undertaking's building. The paper explained that the employer had been intimidating them with no legal basis to do so. Additionally, the legitimacy of striking was recognised by the law, and OZ KOVO underlined that only the court (not the employer) can decide whether a strike is legal.

The activities of the TU caused management to react. Kopčaj identified three ways to mobilise against a strike: (1) petition—the employer required workers to sign a paper disapproving of the strike; (2) distributing a paper describing negative aspects

53 Ibid.

of a strike, particularly its negative impact on employees; and (3) limiting the activities of TU committee members.[54]

'Indirect discouragement was conducted by making the argument that when the German owner (shareholder) finds out what the Slovak workers are doing, the company will leave Slovakia and people will lose their jobs'[55], the TU chairman remembers. 'However, the employees had information about the high quality of their products compared to other plants in Europe,'[56] she says of the workers' courage to continue strike activities.

Management's next step was later discovered to be very bad: immediately terminating all of the TU committee members and having security personnel escort them from the plant.

The key day of the pre-strike period was April 17, when OZ KOVO representatives visited the plant and chairman of the OZ KOVO, E. Machyna, repeated to management that the strike was avoidable if workers' demands were met.

After four years of problematic collective bargaining with management, and in a situation in which it was obvious that an agreement would not be achieved, OZ KOVO's chairman advised plant-level TU committee to ask for a 5% wage increase. This request, like the workers' other requests, were refused. Bargaining ended with delivery of a strike notice for April 21, 2008.

On April 18, 2008, OZ KOVO organised a briefing in Bratislava and informed the public about the strike and the demands of the TU. On the same day, OZ KOVO members delivered to company workers informative papers on the planned strike, which included the following information: the reasons for the strike, its date, a description of what would happen if no agreement was concluded, information about constitutional rights (primarily the right to strike) and advice on how to proceed in the event of problems. Organisation of the strike was prepared and realised according to OZ KOVO's manual.[57]

At 12:30 the first round of debates with the highest German management took place, and the TU again stating that in the event of agreement, no strike would occur. However, an agreement was refused and therefore, at 12:50, the TU committee members left the undertaking, announced a strike and asked other employees to join them.

The management hired lawyers who used megaphones to inform employees of the unlawfulness and illegality of the strike and of the negative impact of the strike on

54 Kopčaj, Vladimír: Kolektívny protest na pracovisku. Prípadová štúdia vybraného sociálneho konfliktu. [Collective protest at the workplace. A case study of selected social conflicts], diploma thesis, Bratislava, 2010, here p. 57.

55 Interview with trade union chairwoman in the plant Kromberg & Schubert Mária Kobidová, Slovakia, MK, 22 July 2014.

56 Ibid.

57 Ibid.

employees. However, OZ KOVO representatives also used megaphones and informed employees that their strike was legal and that they were merely exercising their constitutional rights.

Collective bargaining also took place during the strike. The plant was represented by part of the Slovak management, supported by management from Austria and Germany. 'Management had strong support from professional negotiators from Germany who had extensive experience with strikes and similar situations'[58], the chairman of the TU remembers, concluding that 'the outcome of the bargaining was compromise and set-backs on both sides.'[59]

Management filed a court petition to determine the illegality (unlawfulness) of the strike but continued to bargain and accepted some of the TU's requirements. The strike and resulting inability to continue production, blocking of product movement, caused losses.

At the end, an agreement was concluded. The management agreed to increase the basic wage by 5% starting on June 1, 2008, to pay lump sum bonus of Slovenská Koruna (SKK) 1,000 (33.20 Euro) in May 2008, to increase bonuses for Saturday work from 25% to 35% and for Sunday work from 50% to 100%, to provide an equipped office for the TU committee and to meet with the TU representatives every two weeks. It also agreed to provide the TU with the ability to inform and directly contact the highest level of German management.

The TU was at the apex of its power after the strike. It had a relatively high level of membership along with non-formal respect and authority among non-organised employees. However since that time, unity has been deteriorating and the TU's influence and power have been weakening.

The first rupture was created soon after the strike, when management provided special bonuses[60] to employees who did not join the strike and publicly thanked those employees for their approach in saving the undertaking, thus implying that employees who joined the strike had harmed the firm.

Two weeks after the strike, production was launched on a new machine, occupying all of the TU committee members and activists and thus isolating them from other employees. Previously, these had not worked together, but in different places at different machines, what enabled their smoother communication with other employees. Other workers quickly nicknamed the machine the trade-unionists machine. Management declared it they had chosen the cleverest workers; before the strike,

58 Ibid.

59 Ibid.

60 Due to their participation in the strike, all striking employees lost their right to wages (for the strike days) and their right to the presence bonuses. OZ KOVO repaid them 60% of their average wages and a portion of their lost bonuses. Employees who did not join the strike were provided with special bonus of SKK 750 (29.90 Euro) per strike day.

however, new machines had been occupied by new workers. This act by management therefore can be viewed as another effort to break up the collective, to isolate trade unionists and TU activists from other workers, to decrease the union's influence on other workers and to complicate the exchange of information and communication between workers and TU activists.

The position of the TU chairman was professionalised. Management provided the chairman with the promised office, but not in the undertaking. That decision not only complicates daily and non-formal communication but also, over the long term, it leads to alienating workers from the TU.

15.3.2. Kromberg & Schubert in Slovakia in 2014. (Non-)Repetitiveness of the Protest Action or What Has Changed

By 2006, following the idea that on the globalised labour market 'only co-ordinated co-operation provides the possibility of not falling into the competition for the lowest wage and worst working conditions'[61] and with the need for 'better co-ordination of the aims and tools of active collective bargaining'[62] in the mind of the chairman of the plant-level TU at Kromberg & Schubert in Kolárovo, Slovakia asked the management of the German mother-company to establish the European Works Council.

In reaction to this petition, the firm's central management (headquarters) organised a meeting in Regensberg on May 22, 2006, which the minutes show was a '[m]eeting with the aim of creating the EWC Kromberg & Schubert (Automotive) in Abensberg'[63]. The meeting was only attended by representatives from plants in Abensberg, Austria and Slovakia, and they only agreed that 'local employee representatives will send a petition to establish the EWC to their local management, asking local management to resend the petition to the headquarters in Germany.'[64] The EWC still has not been established at Kromberg & Schubert. In addition, no form of interregional collective bargaining or similar co-operation has been realised in practice.

The plant-level collective agreement is concluded by the undertaking and is always bargained two years in advance; each year, it is actualised using the social fund and wages. However, the collective agreement usually contains only minimal obligations and guarantees to employees—the minimum required by law. Under Slovak law, collective bargaining and collective agreements cover all company employees, whether they are union members or not. However, the benefits and the employer's obligations under the collective agreement relate only to production workers, and represent a roof

61 Interview with trade union chairwoman in the plant Kromberg & Schubert Mária Kobidová, Slovakia, MK, 22 July 2014.

62 Ibid.

63 Ibid.

64 Ibid.

for them. Higher employee benefits, including higher wages, are provided to management and development workers in their individual employment contracts. However, those individuals are usually not members of the trade union. The dualisation of the world of work and employment that is observable in this undertaking makes it more difficult for trade unions to protect the interests of those who are the most endangered and disadvantaged (and who are simultaneously members of the trade unions). Their interests remain more difficult to assert, and their (legitimate) requirements remain less acceptable to employers. The wages of this undertaking's production workers over the long term are well under the average wage in Slovakia. The current plant-level collective agreement provides only a minimal increase: on average, 7 Euros per month.

> However, even in this situation, the employer says that we are too expensive for him. And now I see that we are, when I see where there are moving. They are relocating to Romania, Ukraine, China.... They almost left Hungary, and they still took some production from us[65],

explains the chairman of the plant-level trade union.

The situation in the regional labour market was relatively positive at the time of strike in April 2008. The unemployment rate in the district of Komárno was approximately 7.1%.[66] In 2014, it is 18.5%, and it is even higher in the town of Kolárovo, where it is 17.5%.[67] Kromberg & Schubert employed 2,385 employees in 2006, but by summer 2014 this figure had been reduced to 622.[68] At the time of the strike, another large regional employer had approximately 1,200 workers, whereas today it employs barely 80.[69]

As a result, real fears of job loss and the lack of opportunities for new jobs have weakened the will to be active in the TU and have completely dampened any demonstration of dissatisfaction. 'Today, a strike is not the solution: it would not be supported by employees'[70], according to the assessment of the chairman of the TU.

At the Kromberg & Schubert plant, the employee structure has changed: today there are only 337 industrial production workers, 102 non-production employees and 183 administration staff. Of the industrial workers, the large majority (227) are employed through a service agency. This is not the case for the other groups of employees; only 31 of the non-production employees and only one member of the administrative staff are agency workers.[71]

65 Ibid.
66 Slovak Statistical Office: http://px-web.statistics.sk/PXWebSlovak/, accessed 14. July 2014
67 Ibid.
68 Interview with trade union chairwoman in the plant Kromberg & Schubert Mária Kobidová, Slovakia, MK, 22 July 2014.
69 Ibid.
70 Ibid.
71 Ibid.

The significant drop in employees, especially core industrial workers, in combination with the increase in agency workers, has led to a significant drop in the plant-level TU membership base. 'Today, we are hardly 70, which strongly limits us at the collective bargaining and in everything'[72], the chairman of the plant-level TU says.

The bad labour-market situation and job insecurity are primarily problematic for those who form the core of the trade union membership base in the undertaking, and who created the core of the TU influence and mobilisation potential in the 2008 strike.

> We are witnessing the trend of reducing the end-products' physical production and an increase in the number of developers, engineers and other non-production employees. But they are not interested in becoming members of the TU; they even avoid TUs[73],

the chairman of the TU says.

15.4. Conclusion

It is difficult for the Slovak trade-union associations to take advantage of the opportunities provided by their formal inclusion in European trade-union structures. The respondents identified the main reason for this fact as a lack of funding and a lack of personnel. The lack of funding makes it impossible to travel abroad regularly, which is a precondition for active participation in European structures. Some Slovak trade-union associations at the national level are even unable to pay membership fees in European and international organisations and associations. The issue also arises in the domestic field. As trade unions' membership base shrinks, some associations have so few staff that they can barely address their domestic agenda (which to them is more important than the EU agenda) and have left the European arena to the Konfederácia odborových zväzov Slovenskej republiky (KOZ SR) and to large trade-union associations, namely, to OZ KOVO.

However, funding sources and staff capacities are not the only issues. The motivation of trade-union representatives and their actionability in EU governance also play an important role. Moreover, as the case study of Kromberg & Schubert has clearly demonstrated, economic factors in a global context can set very strict constraints on trade-union activities.

72 Ibid.
73 Ibid.

Conclusion

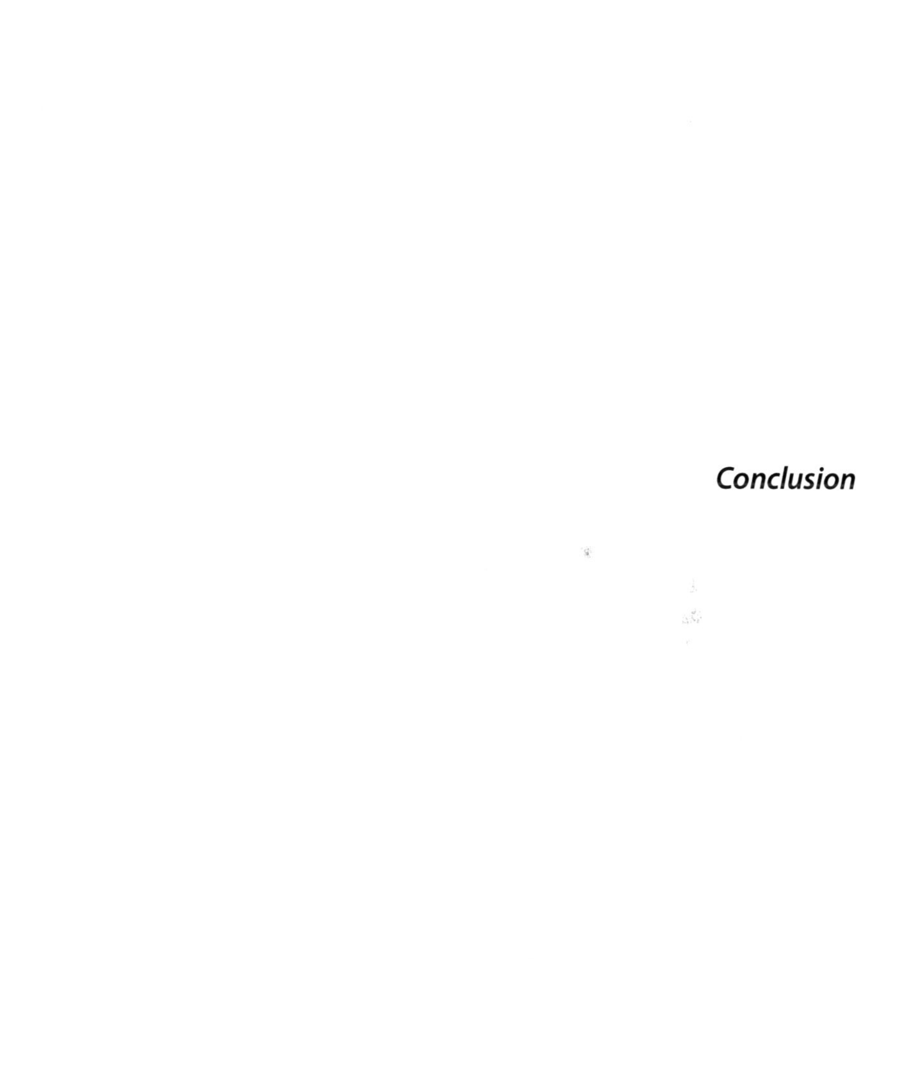

Christin Landgraf and Heiko Pleines

16. Conclusion

The contributions in this book have examined the challenges the integration into EU governance has posed for trade unions from the member countries of the Eastern Enlargement. In doing so, the major objective has been to assess how far the trade unions have been integrated into European Union (EU) governance structures, which strategies they follow when participating in EU governance and how satisfied they are with the state of affairs.

The fifty trade unions covered in the analysis have been selected following a most similar cases approach – including only the strongest trade unions from the biggest countries and thus focusing on trade unions from six countries that are either general umbrella organisations (confederations) or branch unions (federations) from metal / mining or trade / finance with a country-wide reach. Nevertheless, the focused comparison between these unions demonstrates as much diversity as similarity.

One similarity that is actually shared by all trade unions included in our study and is especially striking through its contrast with West European unions is the rather positive assessment of the EU. Another similarity is the relatively weak role all the trade unions from the EU member states of the Eastern Enlargement play at the EU level, although our focus has been on the strongest unions in these countries. Diversity concerns the unions themselves, with different historical trajectories and varying capacities to participate in EU governance. Diversity is also visible when looking at the role trade unions play in the national politics of their respective countries.

This conclusion is, therefore, not meant to summarise all the results of our research project or all the chapters in this book. The aim is, instead, to highlight some of our findings that we consider to be of special relevance for the broader literature on interest groups and Europeanization.

The examination of EU-level venues of interest representation employed by trade unions from the member states of the Eastern Enlargement demonstrates diversity in the access to decision-making bodies at the EU level but, overall, clearly confirms the established view of a weaker integration, as Christin Landgraf has shown in her respective chapter in this book. A lack of sufficient resources, including a lack of financial means and staff but also missing language competences, appears to be the major reason for that limited access. As a result, participation in EU governance is strongly focused on EU bodies that are not at the centre of decision-making, such as the European Economic and Social Committee (EESC) or the Social Dialogue, and is often delegated to the trade unions' European umbrella organisations.

Within the European umbrella organisations, the trade unions from the member states of the Eastern Enlargement are again rather weak, as the case studies by Klaus

Henning in his respective chapter confirm. As a result, these trade unions do not so much participate in decision-making processes at the EU level but rather use their activities and presence at the EU level to collect information that they can use at the domestic level.

It has already been discussed elsewhere[1] that the weak integration of such interest groups challenges the view introduced by the European Commission, that the participation of interest groups in political consultations at the EU level can work as a remedy to the EU's perceived 'democratic deficit'.

However, interest group research has so far largely failed to consider the perception of interest groups themselves. The implicit assumption of most studies appears to be that all interest groups aim at the highest possible influence on political decision-making. That is why surveys of interest groups concentrate on channels and resources and also on tactics and strategies. In addition, we have included explicit questions about satisfaction with different aspects of EU politics and with representation in EU governance in our survey. The results indicate that some interest groups can be quite satisfied despite their limited access to and influence on decision-making processes at the EU level, if they consider the state of affairs to be ok, rendering efforts to change the situation redundant.

Moreover, the assessment of the state of affairs can differ from what is generally assumed. While a representative of an influential German trade union claimed that 'everything bad comes from Brussels', the trade unions from the Central Eastern European countries in their majority hold a positive view of the role of the EU and do not see the need for major changes. At the same time, many appear to assume that the European umbrella organisations, where the German unions play a major role, are a sufficient safeguard for the role of trade unions at the EU level. That is why they also react positively to calls from the umbrella organisations for EU-wide solidarity.

This positive assessment of international cooperation aimed mainly at information and experience exchange also holds true for cooperation below the EU level, as the case study of the Vienna Memorandum, i.e. of interregional cooperation among trade unions from six countries, in this book has shown.

The situation is somewhat different at the lowest level of EU governance, which in the case of trade unions is the company level, where the European umbrella organisations are not directly involved and where the impact of each individual trade union is much more important, as the overall number of unions involved is much smaller. That is why the case study of Polish representatives in European Works Councils, presented by Karoline Mis, reported very sceptical views on this aspect of EU governance. Here,

1 See, e.g., Pleines for the case of trade unions: Pleines, Heiko: Representing workers or presenting EU prescriptions? Trade unions from post-socialist Member States in EU multi-level governance, in: Kröger, Sandra / Friedrich, Dawid (eds): The challenge of democratic representation in the European Union, Basingstoke: Palgrave Macmillan, 2012, pp. 241–257.

too, trade unions can profit from international information flows, but at the lower governance level, expectations appear to go beyond that.

The case study from Slovakia, authored by Monika Čambáliková, also demonstrates that trade unions first of all aim to be able to act at the company level. In this specific case, engagement at the EU level is viewed as less vital and has therefore been sacrificed to concentrate resources on local activities. In a similar vein, the Romanian case study, written by Leyla Safta-Zecheria, states that participation in the EU-level decision-making processes is mostly confined to the confederations, and Zdenka Mansfeldová confirms in her case study of the Czech trade union OS KOVO that in times of economic crisis, a shift of attention from the EU level to the national level can be observed.

At the same time, the engagement and non-engagement of trade unions at the different levels of EU governance has multi-fold effects across the levels. For the trade unions themselves, the role they play at the EU level impacts on their role in the national arena. The case study on Poland, for example, reports that joint membership in EU-level organisations has largely contributed to a more pragmatic cooperation between the three Polish trade unions, which earlier would boycott each other. The case study on Romania notes that access to information gained at or received from the EU level is an important resource that puts some Romanian trade unions at an advantage *vis-à-vis* their peers. These trade unions can also profit from the branding effect that the European representation had in intimidating employers in Romania. Involvement in EU governance can also lead to a professionalisation of trade union representatives, which then impacts on their capacity to act at the national or company level.

Our case studies thus provide evidence for multiple links between the different levels of EU governance, as they have been summarised by Coen and Richardson:

> As a result, we no longer see EU interest politics in terms of 'bottom–up' national interests feeding into the EU, or 'top–down' coordination of EU lobbying, rather we see a managed multilevel process with numerous feedback loops and entry points constrained by the size of the interest group, lobbying budget, origin, and the policy area.[2]

On the contrary, research on Europeanization is still very much stuck in the top–down versus bottom–up debate, as we have demonstrated in our introductory chapter on the research questions and research context. However, for Europeanization, too, our case studies provide numerous examples of more complex links between the different levels of EU governance. Even if Europeanization is a priori defined as a top–down process, as in Radaelli's often-quoted definition,[3] the transmission process is not

2 Coen, David / Richardson, Jeremy: Learning to Lobby the European Union. 20 Years of Change, in: Coen, David / Richardson, Jeremy (eds): Lobbying the European Union. Institutions, Actors, and Issues, Oxford: Oxford Univ. Press, 2009, pp. 3–15, here p. 7.

3 'Europeanisation consists of processes of a) construction, b) diffusion and c) institutionalisation of formal and informal rules, procedures, policy paradigms, styles, "ways of doing things" and shared beliefs and norms which are first defined and consolidated in the EU policy process and

necessarily a direct and linear one. As our case studies demonstrate, institutions at different levels, such as the Vienna Memorandum at the regional level or European Works Council at the company level, can function as intermediaries for Europeanization processes. For example, the top–down Europeanization impact on well-integrated trade unions is transferred to representatives of other trade unions by way of the European Works Councils, i.e. through a horizontal link at the company level. The representatives of these trade unions then bring the respective Europeanization effects back to their own trade union, potentially uploading them to the national level. Indications of such processes have been documented in the two chapters addressing Polish trade unions and also in the Romanian case study.

Moreover, our analysis demonstrates that the agency of those intended to become Europeanized has to be considered. Although the trade unions we study are perceived to be relatively weak, they do not simply adjust to Europeanization pressure. On the one hand, they support European solidarity even in cases where their own core interests are not concerned. On the other hand, they reject policies and positions they consider to be contrary to their interests and convictions. The conflicts between European umbrella organisations of trade unions and national trade unions from Poland and Romania over energy policy clearly demonstrate that Tanja Börzel's concept of misfit cannot only be applied to domestic state actors and national legislation but is also relevant for the impact of Europeanization on interest groups. First, interest groups that are confronted with a huge misfit can become critical of Europeanization. Second, as in our case studies, strongly varying degrees of misfit between members of the same EU-level umbrella organisation can cause severe tensions within the umbrella organisation and can thus potentially hamper collective action at the EU level.

The question of agency points to a further problem, namely, the level of analysis. Research on interest groups and on Europeanization focuses on organisations as units of analysis, while our case studies provide ample evidence of the fragmentation and personalisation of trade union activities in EU governance.

For trade unions as interest groups, it can still be argued that even in the case of trade unionists acting on their own without real links to their organisation, they are representing their trade union based on authorisation. That means as long as the trade union does not contradict its own representative, this person can be analysed as representing the full trade union in political decision-making processes.

However, in the case of Europeanization, it cannot be assumed that the trade union has been Europeanized only because a single representative of this trade union has been. Our survey of trade union representatives with responsibility for activities

then incorporated in the logic of domestic (national and subnational) discourse, political structures and public policies.' Radaelli, Claudio: Europeanisation. Solution or Problem?, in: European Integration online Papers, 2004 (vol. 8), no. 16, http://eiop.or.at/eiop/texte/2004-016a.htm, here p. 3.

related to EU governance demonstrates that members of the same trade union often do not really share a common assessment or vision of EU governance or their own trade union's role in it. That means that a proper understanding of Europeanization processes of interest groups requires an analysis of the internal workings of these groups. One questionnaire per organisation may be enough to identify the utilised venues of interest representation and access at the EU level, but it is definitely not enough to assess their reaction to Europeanization. The case study on Poland's NSZZ Solidarność by Aleksandra Lis, for example, elaborates that in relation to the EU's energy policy, there are conflicting interests within the trade union along sectoral lines, which indicate a diversity of Europeanization processes that may follow sectoral interests.

About the Authors

Dr. **Monika Čambáliková** is a senior research fellow at the Institute of Sociology, Slovak Academy of Sciences. In addition, she is editor-in-chief of the Slovak sociological journal Sociologia. Her fields of work include the labour market, social policy, industrial relations, the social dialogue, social partnership and regional development.

Dr. **Klaus Henning**, a political scientist, is lecturer at the University of Potsdam and teaches politics of trade unions, labor market policy and social policy. He is an associate researcher at the Department of Trade Union Policy at Freie Universität Berlin and participates in the network 'Strategic unionism' of the Department of Sociology, University of Jena. His doctoral dissertation 'European Integration and Trade Union Policy' examines the development of the European Metalworkers Federation (EMF) to a transnational trade union organization.

Vassil Kirov Phd (Sciences Po) is a Senior Reseacher at the Centre Pierre Naville, University of Evry, Associate Professor in the Institute for the Study of Societies and Knowledge, Bulgarian Academy of Sciences (ISSK-BAS) and associate researcher of the ETUI. His research interests are in the sociology of enterprise, work and organisation, industrial relations and Europeanisation. Vassil Kirov has been a researcher in large EU-funded research projects (SMALL, WORKS, WALQING) and has worked as an external expert for the European Commission, the International Labour Organisation, the European Foundation for Working and Living Conditions, etc. He has published several books and articles in international scientific journals.

Christin Landgraf is a research fellow at the Chair of Political Communication at Zeppelin University, Germany. Her research focuses on the strategic communication of interest groups from Western and Eastern EU member states and on interest representation in EU multilevel governance.

Dr. **Aleksandra Lis** is Lecturer at Adam Mickiewicz University Poznan. She holds her PhD from the Central European University in Budapest. In her PhD dissertation she examined the politics of the EU carbon market organization, mainly focusing on the 2008–2009 negotiations of the Climate change and energy package. She also worked extensively on the role of Polish trade unions in national politics and EU governance.

Dr. **Zdenka Mansfeldová** is a senior researcher, head of the Department of the Sociology of Politics and chairman of the Institute Board at the Institute of Sociology, Academy of Sciences of the Czech Republic. Her research focuses on political institutionalization and representation of interests in both political terms (parties and parliament) and the non-political meso-structures of social interests as well as on emerging security treats and dilemma between security and civil liberties. Zdenka Mansfeldová has been researcher in large EU-funded research projects (NEWGOV, Intune, RECON, SECONOMICS).

Dr. **Karoline Mis** works as expert for the European Works Council of an automotive supplier from Stuttgart. From 2010 to 2014 she was a PhD student at the University of Kassel with a thesis about the Europeanisation of Polish industrial relations using the example of EWCs. Before that she worked as researcher and consultant in Poland, Germany and Belgium.

Prof. Dr. **Heiko Pleines** is head of the Department of Politics and Economics at the Research Centre for East European Studies and Professor of Comparative Politics and Integrated European Studies at the University of Bremen. His research focuses on the role of non-state actors in political decision-making. He has worked extensively on the integration of interest groups from the member states of Eastern Enlargement into EU governance.

Leyla Safta-Zecheria is a PhD candidate at the Doctoral School of Political Science, Public Policy and International Relations at the Central European University in Budapest. Her research focuses on Romanian social policy issues and on interpretive approaches to policy studies.

CHANGING EUROPE

Edited by Dr. Sabine Fischer, Dr. Heiko Pleines and Prof. Dr. Hans-Henning Schröder

ISSN 1863-8716

1 *Sabine Fischer, Heiko Pleines, Hans-Henning Schröder (eds.)*
Movements, Migrants, Marginalisation
Challenges of societal and political participation in Eastern Europe and the enlarged EU
ISBN 978-3-89821-733-0

2 *David Lane, György Lengyel, Jochen Tholen (eds.)*
Restructuring of the Economic Elites after State Socialism
Recruitment, Institutions and Attitudes
ISBN 978-3-89821-754-5

3 *Daniela Obradovic, Heiko Pleines (eds.)*
The Capacity of Central and East European Interest Groups to Participate in EU Governance
ISBN 978-3-89821-750-7

4 *Sabine Fischer, Heiko Pleines (eds.)*
Crises and Conflicts in Post-Socialist Societies
The Role of Ethnic, Political and Social Identities
ISBN 978-3-89821-855-9

5 *Julia Kusznir, Heiko Pleines (eds.)*
Trade Unions from Post-Socialist Member States in EU Governance
ISBN 978-3-89821-857-3

6 *Sabine Fischer, Heiko Pleines (eds.)*
The EU and Central & Eastern Europe
Successes and Failures of Europeanization in Politics and Society
ISBN 978-3-89821-948-8

7 *Sabine Fischer, Heiko Pleines (eds.)*
Civil Society in Central and Eastern Europe
ISBN 978-3-8382-0041-5

8 *Zdenka Mansfeldová, Heiko Pleines (eds.)*
Informal Relations from Democratic Representation to Corruption
Case Studies from Central and Eastern Europe
ISBN 978-3-8382-0173-3

9 *Leonid Kosals, Heiko Pleines (eds.)*
Governance Failure and Reform Attempts after the Global Economic Crisis of 2008/09
Case Studies from Central and Eastern Europe
ISBN 978-3-8382-0336-2

10 *Andreas Heinrich, Heiko Pleines (eds.)*
Export Pipelines from the CIS Region
Geopolitics, Securitization, and Political Decision-Making
ISBN 978-3-8382-0539-7

11 *Christin Landgraf, Heiko Pleines (eds.)*
Interest Representation and Europeanization of Trade Unions from EU Member States of the Eastern Enlargement
ISBN 978-3-8382-0744-5

ibidem-Verlag / *ibidem* Press
Melchiorstr. 15
70439 Stuttgart
Germany

ibidem@ibidem.eu
ibidem.eu